SERIOUS STRAW BALE

THE REAL GOODS SOLAR LIVING BOOKS

Real Goods Trading Company in Ukiah, California, was founded in 1978 to make available new tools to help people live self-sufficiently and sustainably. Through seasonal catalogs, a periodical (*The Real Goods News*), a bi-annual *Solar Living Sourcebook*, as well as retail outlets and a Web site (www.realgoods.com), Real Goods provides a broad range of tools for independent living.

"Knowledge is our most important product" is the Real Goods motto. To further its mission, Real Goods has joined with Chelsea Green Publishing Company to co-create and co-publish the Real Goods Solar Living Book series. The titles in this series are written by pioneering individuals who have firsthand experience in using innovative technology to live lightly on the planet. Chelsea Green books are both practical and inspirational, and they enlarge our view of what is possible as we enter the next millennium.

Stephen Morris
President, Chelsea Green

John Schaeffer
President, Real Goods

SERIOUS STRAW BALE

A Home Construction Guide for All Climates

Paul Lacinski and Michel Bergeron

CHELSEA GREEN PUBLISHING COMPANY
White River Junction, Vermont
Totnes, England

Designed by Andrea Gray.
Cover by Ann Aspell.

Printed in Canada.

First printing, October 2000.
03 02 01 00   1 2 3 4 5

Printed on acid-free, recycled paper.

Due to the variability of local conditions, materials, skills, site, and so forth, Chelsea
Green Publishing Company and the authors assume no liability for personal injury,
property damage, or loss from actions inspired by information in this book. Remember
that any construction process can be dangerous. Moreover, because building codes in most
areas do not yet address the practice of straw bale construction, and because each new
straw bale building may serve as an example and prototype for others, it is especially
important that builders approach their work with due caution, care, and a sense of
responsibility.

Library of Congress Cataloging-in-Publication Data
Lacinski, Paul, 1967-
    Serious straw bale : a home construction guide for all climates / Paul Lacinski and Michel
Bergeron.
        p. cm. (The Real Goods solar living books)
    Includes bibliographical references and index.
    ISBN 1-890132-64-0 (alk. paper)
    1. Straw bale houses—Design and construction. I. Bergeron, Michel, 1946- II. Title.
III. Real Goods solar living book.

TH4818.S77 L33 2000
693'.997—dc21   00-058943

Green Books Ltd
Foxhole, Dartington
Totnes, Devon TQ9 6EB, United Kingdom
44-1-803-863-843

Chelsea Green Publishing Company
Post Office Box 428
White River Junction, VT 05001
(800) 639-4099
www.chelseagreen.com

CONTENTS

PREFACE

THIS IS A BOOK ABOUT WALLS—about how to design and build beautiful (and hopefully durable) walls of bales and plaster. It is written with one intention, to provide you with the background necessary to *think* your way through a straw bale project even in an extremely cold and/or wet climate. It is emphatically not a book that aims to prescribe one best way of doing things; part of what is exciting about bale and plaster walls is that they are not yet (and perhaps never will be) streamlined into a "one-size-fits-all" system.

This is also not a book about the general topic of building design. Materials are only a small portion of good design; they are subservient to the many interlocking issues—the needs of the occupant, aesthetics, energy use, site, structure, and budget among them—that weave a design program. This book does not attempt to lead the reader through all the stages of this intricate process. Many good books already do that. Instead, it looks at design issues from the specific perspective of the straw bale builder, and at each turn, offers strategies for how to integrate these types of walls into the larger process of design.

The central text of this book revolves around design issues. We hope these will be of use to anyone—architect, builder, owner-builder, Renaissance woman—who is thinking about how best to detail a bale-walled building. Some issues that are primarily the concern of owner-builders are covered in sidebars, as are some construction issues. Part 1 of the book, and most notably chapter 3 ("Plans, Permits, and Project Management") is written with owner-builders particularly in mind.

Wherever possible, we have offered our opinion on the efficiency of a particular method or durability of a particular detail. You must understand that while we (and the many others who have contributed ideas to this book) have been at this work for some time, we don't have all the answers to all the questions about straw bale construction. Much experimentation, systematization, and testing remains to be done. The goal of this book is to supply you with the best of the tools now available, so that you may begin to participate in this process. We hope the material that follows is useful to you, and that your bale adventure is as fun and rewarding as ours has been.

All building sites produce waste. On a straw bale construction site, the waste straw can be used as mulch!

Keep those Bales Dry!

The basic principles of bale construction, especially crucial in cold and/or wet climates, can be broken down as follows. Each of these is explored in substantial detail in later chapters, but just to start off with the big picture, we've herded them all together, here. The overriding design goal in straw bale construction is: Keep those bales dry! The way to accomplish that goal is to consider these elements:

Siting

The site, which includes climate, local landforms, vegetation, and the character of the neighborhood, is the number one factor that determines whether bales are a good choice for a wall material, and how they should be finished.

Architectural Features

Precipitation is the greatest threat to bale walls; to a certain degree, site features can be ameliorated by roof overhangs, porches, connected sheds, and other features that help protect the walls from rain and snow.

Isolation from Ground Moisture

Bales should be held at least as far from finished grade as specified by the local code minimum for wood. They must also be protected from moisture that can make its way up through the foundation.

All building sites produce waste. On a straw bale construction site, the waste straw can be used as mulch!

Flashing Details

Flashing and dripsills are crucial to prevent concentrated volumes of water from leaking into and sheeting down the wall.

Choice of Finish

There is no standard finish for straw bale walls. Choice of finish is an act of balance between the structural strength of more rigid materials and the higher drying potential and reduced cracking of more flexible materials.

Vapor-Permeable Construction

Whenever possible, those materials that are more vapor-permeable are a safer choice than those which are less so. In cold climates, this is especially true on the exterior.

Airtight Construction and Mechanical Ventilation

Airtight construction and mechanical ventilation ensure good indoor air quality, reduce energy use, and control interior humidity levels, thereby greatly reducing interior moisture sources as a potential threat to bale walls.

Moisture Sensors

Without sensors, there is no way of knowing what is really going on inside the walls over the long term. All new bale houses should have at least a few, as insurance against moisture problems, and to allow residents to contribute to the body of knowledge about building with straw bales.

Acknowledgments

In the ever-growing field of information and experience from which this book has emerged, a special acknowledgment must go out to all those anonymous heroes of harsh climate construction who have, against the better judgment of their neighbors, built their own houses with this oddball material known as straw. Squaring off to uncertainties about its appropriateness, these faithful souls continue to pour out a stream of new details and techniques, forever refining bale construction to meet the demands of their local conditions. Without their invaluable contributions, the authors and the several other bale enthusiasts whose names appear in this book would have needed many lifetimes of experimentation in order to access such a pool of creative ideas.

If new cold-climate straw bale homes survive as long as their original Nebraska cousins have, these people should be remembered as the pioneers of what is slowly becoming a vernacular architecture of our modern era.

Paul's Personal Gratitudes

I must first thank the many warmhearted people across the northern U.S. and southern Canada who took time out from their own busy lives to share their work and their hospitality with me. Many of you are mentioned in this book, and many are not; I wish to thank each of you (especially those with whom I have not had the good manners to remain in touch!) for making my various research trips more fun and useful than I could ever have expected. Your generosity in sharing technical information has added tremendously to the vitality of this book. Your generosity in offering hospitality, stimulating conversation, and a glimpse into the ways in which you are trying to live decent lives has given me some real hope for the future of our species upon this fine planet.

I would also like to thank the many people who contributed photos, writing, or feedback to this project, and who were consistently willing to answer and re-answer my questions on topics about which they knew much more than I. Marc Rosenbaum and Rory Brennan deserve a special thanks for taking the time to read (and by your comments, improve) entire chapters of this book.

Then there is the matter of beginnings. I would like to thank John and Melissa Bissell for asking, eight years ago over excellent food and a friendly bottle of wine, "What would you do if you could do whatever you want?" And Matts Myhrmann and Judy Knox for taking me in and teaching me all I could handle, about subjects ranging far beyond straw bale construction.

Martha Twombly and Hannah Silverstein of Chelsea Green get an enormous thank-you for pulling this book together, and especially for the cheerfulness with which you both dealt with my somewhat erratic attention to submission details. I also thank Martha for getting me started on this book project, three long years ago.

Finally, three people deserve the deepest thanks: Michel, for the depth of experience you brought to the book, and for your openness and flexibility on issues small and large; Amy, for your continual encouragement and everlasting patience with the fact that I always worked later than I said I would; and Mom, for equipping me, early on, with the notion that I could do whatever I set my mind to.

Michel's Personal Gratitudes

I want to address a very special *merci* to my co-author and new friend Paul for his extreme generosity while dealing for almost two years with the unavoidable English discrepancies of an author whose native language is French.

Also to Jim Schley for his patience and friendship, and to Alan Berolzheimer for his special editing contribution.

And finally, to one very important person, my Master of Arts in life by his everlasting creative attitude, my eighty-seven-year-old father, Gérard, *merci beaucoup!*

PART 1

Straw Bale Buildings in Perspective

CHAPTER 1

WHY STRAW BALES?

W HAT IS A STRAW BALE HOUSE? Why are bales a good choice in a cold climate? Can bale walls be designed to withstand the vagaries of weather in the snow belt? These are questions we've been asking of ourselves for a good many years, and they have now become the guiding questions behind this book. To begin at the beginning, however, we must ponder this question of why. The idea of building a wall of bales seems to entice people's imaginations. Why bales? We have come to believe that people are searching for alternatives to the plywood palace, to the modular mentality that has come to dominate the mainstream construction industry. Most new houses today are made of the same materials: machined sticks and sheets of wood, plastic, metal, and gypsum. They are usually assembled according to the same set of principles, so that once you've built a few, they get pretty boring. Except for that small percentage in which a designer, owner, or builder puts some real thought into creating a form and finish that suits the owner and the site, these houses somehow feel the same.

There are three main reasons that straw bale construction is different. First of all, bale walls look very different from sheetrock walls. They look like the product of a human, rather than the product of a machine. Though bales are a new material (which makes design work challenging and fun), the feel of the finished wall harkens back to the preindustrial era. It seems that as our lives become increasingly technological, more and more people want to surround themselves with spaces that feel handmade and timeless.

Process is the second reason. Conventional construction is mathematical and precise, while bales and plaster are sloppy and intuitive. These characteristics are inviting to amateur builders, not only because they make bale construction easy to learn, but because they stand in contrast to the obsessive efficiency that most of us have had to accept as a part of the industrial economy. People see bale construction as a chance to cut loose.

Third, bale construction feels like an alternative to ecological waste. It's akin to recycling. Recycling enjoys broad support across the political spectrum, because it's obvious, it's easy, and it gives people a sense that they can at least do *something* that is not harmful to the planet. While our agriculture is far from perfect, it does produce a lot of straw, so using some of it for construction makes intuitive sense.

Bruce Millard, a thoughtful architect from Sandpoint, Idaho, has developed this idea about building with bales a bit further. "Once people try this type of construction, they absorb it and agree with it, and begin to recognize it as a concept, as a psychological departure from the idea that industry is somehow more sophisticated than nature. It brings the left and the right together; it functions as a stepping block into an ecological way of building and living. People begin to ask, 'How can I put this to work in the rest of my life?'"

Bruce sees the bale itself as a short-lived material. "We will soon realize that straw is very valuable—it will start going into particleboard and panelized materials, and it might be mixed with wood fiber for paper production." Bruce uses the bale as an introduction to a whole array of recycled-content panels and blocks.

Bales also tend to serve as an introduction to traditional natural building techniques from around the world, all of which have much longer track records than the bale itself. Loose straw has been used for millennia in combination with clay and sand, for everything from plasters to load-

Straw can provide thermal and sound insulation or even serve as a load-bearing wall, all in the form of a compact, portable, nontoxic, and recyclable bale.

bearing walls. Five-hundred-year-old examples of straw and clay infill are still in use in Germany, and this material has actually been rewetted and put back into wall cavities during restoration. Thatch makes a beautiful, durable, insulative roof. These and other techniques must be explored and developed if we are to continue to create decent housing for future generations on this planet. (See chapter 15, "Beyond the Bale.")

Why Build a House of Straw Bales?

"Didn't you learn anything from the first little pig?"

A mouthful of oatmeal and an earful of propaganda against building with straw; many of us were spoon-fed this breakfast throughout our childhoods. How is it, then, that perfectly sane people can consider living in a house whose walls are bales of straw? Maybe urbanization, suburbanization, and the decrease in the North American wolf population has lulled them into a sense of complacency about this domestic predator. Or maybe bales make such unusual walls that many of us are just willing to take the risk.

Beauty

The most compelling among many reasons to build with bales is the quiet beauty of bale walls. Unlike walls of panelized materials, which require layers of ornamentation to bring life to their unnaturally uniform surfaces, bale walls look and feel as if they were made by hand. Their deep windowsills and gentle undulations lend a comfortably safe, quiet feeling to the interior of a home, while the plaster finish softly gathers and reflects light, changing in subtle ways as the sun shifts through each day and season. The effect is a heightened connection between indoor and outdoor worlds, an especially important relationship in climates where people spend a good part of the year inside buildings.

"We fell in love with the deep windowsills and rounded corners."
"I like the massive feel, and the flexibility, of the bales; you can do anything with them, curvy or straight."
"The house has a solid, embracing feeling, like it has its arms wrapped around me."

Paul often describes bale walls as "plastered stone for the person of moderate means." This is not to imply that bale walls don't have a character of their own, which they certainly do; the point is that the massive, rounded feel of the bale wall is reminiscent of the old-world solidity of stone. (Bale walls also offer far more insulation value than stone walls, but we'll get to that later.) Part of the appeal of bale buildings is that they just feel safe. Storms can be howling outside, or cars roaring along a nearby highway at twice the reasonable rate, and after the (good-quality) door clicks shut on a straw bale house, you will find yourself in near total silence. This sort of quiet allows the home to act as a refuge for the psyche; a place where the senses can escape the busy din of the postindustrial world.

Insulation Value

Straw bale houses may look and feel like plastered stone or earth houses, but they are in a different thermal category, entirely. Old stone houses are cold. New stone houses are typically built with foam insulation, either sandwiched between two independent stone walls, or blown onto the inside face of the stone. Both of these methods are quite expensive. Plastered bales, on the other hand, provide a highly insulative wall at a price that is competitive with quality conventional construction.

Not all that long ago in Western societies, and in some societies still, most people spent most of their waking hours outside, in the unfiltered presence of fresh air, warm (and sometimes hot) sun, cooling (and sometimes downright cold) breezes, and the visual, aural, mental, and spiritual stimulation of the ever changing natural world. Now that most of our society seems to have moved indoors, exchanging fresh air and physical work for office partitions, stress, and air heated, cooled, and otherwise denatured by a central delivery system, it has become quite necessary for the home to serve not only as a refuge, but also as a vehicle of connection to the natural world, a world whose subtleties are easily overlooked when your senses have been trodden by the glaring images of the TV and computer screen.

A person building with bales can bring the outside in by playing subtly with light, texture, and form. This requires a certain sensitivity on the part of the bale layer and the plasterer. On the one hand, it is possible to allow the short sight of the trowel too much control over the plastering process; the result is a flat, rather dead surface that speaks only of the mechanical ability of the hand that applied the plaster. It is also possible to get so carried away with lumpy textures and wild paints that the subtlety of the space disappears into a gawky argument between elements. A quietly beautiful wall lies between these two extremes.

What do I mean by this? The relationship between windows and views serves as a parallel example. Let's say you come to a site. It's a nice spot for a house, and it has this incredible view of a range of mountains. You sit there, maybe eat a picnic lunch and drink a glass of wine, and you look at the view. The sun is warm, and maybe you're just a touch sleepy, but you're also excited and so you're talking with your partner about this great spot that you've found, about how beautiful it is, and about the future. You do this a few times, maybe a whole bunch of times, and you're designing a house in your mind, and of course this view must be the central feature of the living room, because it's been the central feature of your experience of this place. So you build the house, and you spend quite a sum of money on a big picture window, or maybe on a whole gable end of the house filled with glass, so that you can bring those mountains in.

For a while, maybe during the construction process and for a few months after you move in, you spend a few minutes after supper looking out at the mountains, and you feel good. One day, a year later, you're stopped in front of the window; maybe you're cleaning the glass, and you pause for a minute, realizing that you haven't actually looked at those mountains for some time. You've glanced at them in passing (how could you not, they're right there, staring you in the face), but you haven't really stopped to look in detail at the change in color with the change of seasons, or at the movement of the snowline, or at individual trees and boulders. For all of your effort and expense, you haven't succeeded in bringing the mountains in, at all. The wall of glass has come, as walls inevitably do, to simply define the perimeter of your living space. (Meanwhile you're cold whenever you sit near that wall in winter, and your heating bills are quite a bit higher than they ought to be.)

Why has this happened? There are two reasons. First, an unmoving scene is not really all that interesting when viewed through a pane of glass. Birds at feeders, trees blowing in the wind, fire trucks racing by, these things work because motion attracts the eye, causes you to look through and beyond the window. If you attempt to fix your attention upon an unmoving object, however, a pane becomes a lens, a psychological obstruction between you and the thing you are trying to see.

Second, anything becomes commonplace when it is constantly staring you in the face, precisely because you soon stop taking the time to look at it closely. Instant gratification is incompatible with visual richness—nothing in this world is truly interesting to look at more than once or twice, until you learn to pause, even for only a few seconds at a time, and look closely.

The most beautiful bale walls I have seen have a quiet feeling; they invite a person to slow down, look longer, look closer. They make utmost use of the light that strikes them, which is to say that they look different at different times of the day, and through the seasons. They also change as you look closer, or back away. My favorite bale walls tend to be light in color, with a flat, typically unpainted finish, so that light can reflect from them without creating an unpleasant glare. Their surfaces are less lumpy than what Matts Myhrman describes as "softly irregular." Flecks of mica or finely chopped straw, or subtle variations in color, keep the wall interesting right up to the point where you fairly well have your nose pressed against it. I prefer curved window wells to those that are flat or beveled, because they react with far greater variety to changes in angle and intensity of light.

All of this surface irregularity and general curvaceousness creates a wall whose outstanding features are the small pools of light and shadow that move across its surface as the sun makes its way up and down the sky. Not surprisingly, this effect is most pronounced in rooms with access to early-morning and late-afternoon light.

Buildings consume roughly one-third of the energy used annually in the United States. Super-insulated buildings (bales provide a super-insulated wall) keep their occupants more comfortable than their conventional counterparts, while pumping far less carbon dioxide and pollutants into the atmosphere. In other words, they cost less to heat and cool, to you and to the planet.

In 1998 tests at Oak Ridge National Laboratory in Tennessee found that the R-value of a bale wall laid flat measured at 1.45 per inch, while tests by the California Energy Commission found a bale wall laid on edge to measure at 2.06 per inch. (This translates to R-26 for a two-string bale laid flat; R-29 for a two-string bale on edge; R-33.5 for a three-string bale laid flat; and R-33 for a three-string bale on edge.)

The insulation in a bale wall is continuous; it is not interrupted by less insulative wooden members, as is the case with conventional construction. A 2-by-6 and fiberglass wall, rated at R-19, will really only achieve this value in the insulation cavities. In designs that do not specify advanced framing techniques to reduce wood

use in corners, around windows, and in other detailing, the decrease in overall wall R-value due to thermal bridging through the studs can be substantial. Imperfections in the installation of insulation materials can also reduce the performance of conventional walls, to the point where their effective R-value is not much more than half that of a bale wall.

The actual performance of a bale wall system is also influenced by the thermal mass of both the bales and the plaster. This factor has a significant effect on the wall's ability to store heat, and thus to maintain a constant temperature. It also appears to affect the rate at which heat flows through the wall. In the Oak Ridge tests, one side of the wall was heated to 70°F (21°C) and the other chilled to 0°F (–18°C). It took most of two weeks at this temperature difference before the wall began to lose heat at a steady rate. This means that as heat moved through the wall, some portion of it was being stored within the mass of the wall. Presumably, it was only after the wall temperature had stabilized that heat began to flow through at a consistent rate. David Eisenberg points out that in real world conditions in most cold climates, two straight weeks at a 70°F temperature difference would be quite an unusual event. Temperatures typically swing up in the daytime and down at night. The combination of mass and uninterrupted insulation in a plastered bale wall flattens these swings, providing even greater comfort and energy savings than the wall system's rated R-value would imply.

Veteran solar architect Ken Haggard, of San Luis Obispo, California, points out a further benefit of the bale and plaster combination: "The thermal mass is integral to the wall finish." Good passive solar design, of course, relies on a combination of southerly glazing, superinsulation,

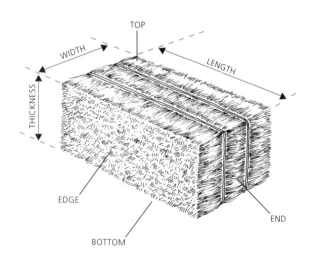

TOP

WIDTH

LENGTH

THICKNESS

EDGE

END

BOTTOM

Basic bale nomenclature.

Guest room. Wisbaum home, Charlotte, Vermont.

In a bale building, there is no practical way around the application of one inch or so of plaster on the interior of the walls. This adds up to quite a lot of thermal mass, which translates into opportunity (and room for error) in the passive solar components of the design. It also means that a well-designed solar bale house cannot be spoiled in the construction phase by a foolish decision to eliminate the mass, in order to save a few dollars.

Nontoxic

Bales are a natural material. Unlike many manufactured building products, they contain no toxic ingredients, and are chemically stable. They will release no unhealthy chemicals into your home, and will not emit poisonous fumes in case of a fire. A relatively small amount of fossil fuel energy is consumed in the production of straw bales, and no toxins are released during the production or installation processes. Straw can eventually be composted back into the soil.

Use of Resources

A great deal of straw is grown around the world every year, enough for millions of houses. Some percentage of this straw (depending on soil type and the fertility program of any given farm) should be going back into the soil, ideally mixed with animal manure, which provides the nitrogen necessary for its decomposition. (This scenario bears no relationship to current agricultural practices in the industrialized world, but it is a worthy ideal, nonetheless.) Much of this straw is now burned in the field. By incorporating straw into buildings, we reduce particulate pollution and lock up carbon in a solid state, rather

and internal mass. In conventional buildings (½-inch drywall, wood floors) the amount of glazing that can be added for solar gain is limited by the heat storage capacity of the building's interior. Since adding mass to the interior is often viewed as an extra expense, many houses with good solar orientation end up with a disappointingly small proportion of their heat provided by the sun. Or (and this might be more common), lots of windows are shoved into the south wall, with little thought given to where the heat will be stored. The result is excessive heat buildup on sunny afternoons, coupled with excessive heat loss at night.

than releasing it as carbon dioxide, the most important greenhouse gas. We might also reduce the pressure on forests (the most important carbon sinks and oxygen producers on the planet) and the demand for relatively energy- and pollution-intensive industrial insulation materials.

Pliny Fisk III, of the Center for Maximum Potential Building Systems in Austin, Texas, points out that a better idea than using the straw from annual grains is baling the stems of native perennial grasses (as the original bale builders did) and invasive exotic species. GreenSpace (Paul's company) has begun to experiment with the mixed stems of old field succession plants: goldenrod, milkweed, mixed native grasses, various woody perennials, small saplings. These are the plants that move in when pastures or hay fields in our region are allowed to fall out of agricultural use. New England hill farmers are often happy to part with these bales for half the price of good straw or hay, as the inputs are less, and part of their payment comes in preventing their land from growing up to brush.

A further development, suggested by biologist and landscape architect Ruth Parnall, of Conway, Massachusetts, would be a baler that could wade into marshes, to harvest phragmites (*Phragmites communis*). This European reed (used for thatch) has overrun much of the wetlands of the Mid-Atlantic and Northeast regions of the United States Consistent, aggressive baling of phragmites could become a useful tool in containing its spread.

> Whether the labor is volunteer or professional, almost every project is a custom project, with details and techniques invented during the design and construction phases.

Economical

"Plastered stone for the person of reasonable means." Have you priced out a stone building lately? Or calculated the time to build one yourself? Most traditional earth and stone building systems have become quite expensive nowadays, because human labor has become expensive, compared with efficient assembly of machine-produced building components. The reason bales have risen to such prominence in Santa Fe is that the building code there requires that everything (including strip malls) look as if it is made of adobe. Bale houses are substantially less expensive than real adobes, and look and perform a whole lot better than stick frames masquerading as earth.

In the industrialized world, bale construction is getting to be cost-competitive with good-quality stick-framed construction, assuming a tight design that doesn't drive labor costs through the roof. Mechanical or volunteer application of plasters and hands-on experience with a few bale projects help substantially, here. Availability of bales is also important. It is not really fair, however, to compare bale walls with 2-by-6 walls. They look more like stone or earth, and they perform more like double-stud, 10-inch-deep walls, blown full of cellulose.

Because bale construction is still maturing, it is also reasonable to assume that the cost of walls will continue to drop. Whether the labor is vol-

A small pile of recyclable materials is often all that is left over after construction of a straw bale house.

unteer or professional, almost every project is still a custom project, with details and techniques invented during the design and construction phases. We are all constantly refining our methods, hunting down those details that make for an efficient construction process. This is part of the fun, of course.

In areas of the world where machined materials are expensive or unavailable, and straw and labor are cheap, bales will compare favorably with any other type of construction. Bale houses tend to be more durable and comfortable than either government houses (typified by the random and horribly expensive application of industrial techniques), or scabbed-together houses (usually built of whatever cast-off materials happen to be lying around). Bales offer a route back toward the

sensible, owner-built, locally adapted housing that could be found everywhere on this planet, before the Industrial and Green Revolutions swelled our population and our egos.

Owner-Builder Friendly

At the time of this writing, most of the bale buildings in the world have been owner-built. This ratio is sure to change over time, as bale buildings develop a longer track record, as more mainstream home buyers and financers begin to recognize the strengths of walls built with bales, and as more contractors develop expertise in and enthusiasm for this type of construction.

Bales will remain a choice material of owner-builders, however, because they are so well suited

With a good design, careful organization, and the guidance of a few skilled people, it is possible to keep dozens of volunteers engaged in various stages of bale and plaster work.

tractors seem not to mind hanging and taping wallboard.

Bale construction is fun for two reasons. The first is because its two main components—stacking bales and smearing plaster—lend themselves to work parties. With a good design, careful organization, and the guidance of a few skilled people, it is possible to keep dozens of volunteers engaged in various stages of bale and plaster work. Because the process can be broken down into many distinct tasks, people are free to try different jobs and learn various skills. There are niches to be filled by persons of all levels of physical ability and experience. The synergy of this group effort (not to mention the sheer volume of work possible in a day) is one of the greatest thrills of straw bale construction.

The second reason is that laying bales and applying plaster are essentially right-brain activities. Stacking bales is much more like playing with blocks than it is like any mainstream construction practice. This is especially true when the structure is framed in advance, because in this case plumb and level have already been determined by the framing crew. Clay plaster work is reminiscent of making mud pies. You can smear the stuff on the wall with the heel of your hand. You can throw it at the person working next to you. If you are so inclined, you can get yourself completely coated in earth.

to a "gang of friends" method of construction. (See below, under "Fun.") Novices are also attracted to the apparent simplicity of the wall system. Even people who have no experience with construction can wrap their minds around the idea of stacking bales. On many occasions, this initial sense that "I can do this!" leads an otherwise intimidated nonbuilder out of his or her shell, toward a willingness to take on framing, plaster, finish work, and so forth.

Fun

Many aspects of construction can be great fun. Framing is enjoyable unless you are stuck doing it every day, because it goes so quickly that structures seem to appear out of thin air. Some people love the attention to detail required by finish work. Hard as it is to believe, many drywall con-

Durable

The oldest bale structures in Nebraska date back nearly one hundred years, to the invention of the baler. The oldest bale house in New England has kept its occupants warm and dry through twenty-five wet, coastal winters, and is still in excellent condition. (See the profile of the Hay House, following this chapter.) Bale walls appear to last indefinitely, if kept dry.

Combinations of straw and clay have been used for millennia all around the world, and five hundred-year-old houses with straw-clay walls are still inhabited in Germany. (See chapter 15, Beyond the Bale.)

Fire Resistance

Plastered bale-wall systems have outperformed wood-framed walls in fire tests. In a trial performed by SHB Agra Engineering and Environmental Services Laboratory in Albuquerque, New Mexico, in 1993, walls built of two-string, wheat-straw bales were examined both bare and with plaster skins.

In the first case, on an uncoated wall, the fire took 34 minutes to work its way through, at a seam between two bales. The maximum applied temperature was 1,691°F (921°C).

The second test, on a wall finished with gypsum plaster on the heated side and cement stucco on the unheated side, was even more impressive. The heated side of the wall reached 1,942°F (1,060°C), while the highest rise in temperature on the unheated side, after two hours of exposure, was only 21°F. Behind cracks in the gypsum plaster on the heated side of the wall, charring in the straw was only 2 inches deep.

Unfortunately, the final report on this test has never been produced, because of a lack of funding. The U.S. and Canadian national code bodies, therefore, have yet to issue a fire rating for plastered bale construction. Nonetheless, the results of this test have been very influential in convincing local and state code officials that plastered bale walls pose no unusual threats to their occupants, in the case of fire. At the Sivananda Lodge (see profile following chapter 8) bales were easily accepted for a one-hour fire rating. The case has also been made that plastered bale walls, because of their density, are more fire resistant than the ubiquitous studs and drywall.

Rodents and Insects

When detailed correctly, bale walls are highly resistant to damage from insects or rodents. Tiny

Happy crew at work during a straw bale workshop.

bugs (springtails, most often) have sometimes been present on the interior surface of plaster while it is drying, or in houses that have experienced high moisture levels within the bales. Under normal circumstances, they seem to depart once the plaster has cured fully. The best defense against insects seems to be to keep your walls dry.

The same set of details that protect your bales from damage by moisture should also be sufficient to keep out rodents, for at least as long a period as in conventional construction. We will not claim that mice will never get in: Rare is the building that has stood for fifty years without these little monsters finding a way into the walls. Typical plaster finishes (or appropriate screening, in the case of a sided building) should provide reasonable protection against their entry.

> The best defense against insects is to keep your walls dry.

Even if mice do eventually sneak in, it is distinctly possible that they will matter less than in a conventional cavity wall. Rodents rarely bore into bales; they favor the slightly less dense horizontal runs between courses. Their movement throughout the wall is, therefore, limited. Also, without a large cavity to scratch around in, the occasional mouse should not be very much of a nuisance to the occupants of a bale building.

The first of Paul's two favorite stories about rodents and straw comes from the Hay House, in Connecticut, the oldest bale house in New England. Over the past twenty-five years, squirrels have, at times, taken up residence in the rafter cavities. David Brown, who owns the Hay House, explains that at one point the squirrels could even get into the living space; they apparently enjoyed standing on top of a bookshelf and watching him dress in the morning. Never, in all of this time, has there been any evidence of squirrels moving into the bale walls, even though the top of the north wall has never been plastered.

Marc Rosenbaum, P.E., of Energysmiths, in Plainfield, New Hampshire, relates another story: At one point he had some bales stacked under a porch roof, near his front door. They were to be incorporated into the walls of an entryway addition. In preparation for the work, he had an electrician disconnect an electrical box that was cut into the foam-core, stressed-skin panel wall of his house. Within weeks, he found evidence of mice chewing into the newly exposed foam, and tacked a board over the hole. Come spring, and upon removing the board, he found an entire family of dehydrated mice within the foam panel; when he then moved the straw bales, mouse signs were nowhere in evidence.

Such anecdotes do not necessarily add up to the assumption that rodents are not an issue in bale houses. The fact is, however, that we have yet to come across a well-detailed building that has had any problems with these unwelcome guests.

EARTHQUAKES

The solid, unshakable feeling of bale walls turns out to be based in physics. In 1998 tests by David Riley and his students at the University of Washington found that bale walls finished with gypsum plaster on one face and cement stucco on the other (both reinforced by wire) showed an unusual ability to absorb the sort of push-pull shear forces (no, that's not the official engineering term) that are typical of seismic events. "Only

The Pilgrim Holiness Church in Arthur, Nebraska, built by the congregation with donated rye-straw bales.

under substantial displacement (e.g., an earthquake) would bales in a wall be subjected to the movement applied in this test; however, the test results show that the bale walls were capable of absorbing a significant amount of energy on repeated cycles. For this reason, a bale structure should behave favorably under seismic loads."[1]

Another revealing test was performed in Berkeley, California, in the spring of 1998, on a straw

1. David Riley, Gregory MacRaw, and Juan Carlo Ramirez, "Strength Testing of Stucco and Plaster Veneered Straw Bale Walls," *The Last Straw,* 24 (winter 1998): 8–9.

bale arch. The arch and test were designed by Skillful Means and structural engineer David Mar, with input from other experienced members of the California straw bale community. The arch was built of three-string bales, finished with mesh-reinforced cement stucco, inside and out. The inner and outer curtains of mesh were fastened together by wire ties run through the bale core of the structure. A specially calibrated hydraulic jack simulated earthquake forces by simultaneously pushing in and pulling out on the arch.

The arch performed extremely well. Its elastic limit (the point at which the stucco began to crack) was not reached until the out-of-plane load totaled 55 percent of its weight—nearly double the seismic code requirement of 30 percent. The test rig was incapable of causing the arch to fail. The maximum load was 115 percent of the weight of the structure; this is the equivalent of turning it on its edge and applying a further 15 percent of its weight.

David Mar thinks that bales will turn out to be an unusually appropriate material for earthquake-prone regions. He believes that bale walls designed according to the seismic principles that govern masonry walls offer the advantages of lighter weight, greater ductility, and, most important of all, the ability to absorb significant quantities of energy without failing catastrophically.

Historical Background to Modern Bale Building

Straw bale construction began with the invention of the baler, at the tail end of the 19th century, in the Sand Hills region of Nebraska. The Sand Hills are a vast tract of grass-covered dunes, formerly the margin of a sea that filled up the

Mississippi Basin. As water receded, the shore-line sands drifted into the Sand Hills formation.

When homesteaders began to move into this country in the 1880s, they found that wood for construction was available only in the river bottoms. Since most farms had no access to this resource, lumber for building quickly became an expensive commodity. By this time, using wide strips of turf to build up the walls of a house was a common method of conserving wood in homestead construction. Because the primary work in the early years of a farm was breaking the dense plains sod to plant crops, it made good sense to incorporate this material into buildings. In areas where the soil was appropriate, these "soddies" were excellent houses. Many still stand today.

Unfortunately for some Sand Hills homesteaders (but fortunately, for the rest of us), the loose Sand Hills soil produced a turf of poor quality for construction. Nobody knows how many Sand Hills sod houses collapsed before some ingenious farmer came up with the idea of stacking bales of grass—a product of the newly invented baler—into the walls of a house. Stories about early bale houses inevitably involve imminent winter and a large group of neighbors gathering to move a roof, wholesale, off a crumbling sod house and onto a freshly stacked set of bale walls. Oral history also indicates that many of the early houses were originally plastered only on their interiors; the owners intended, before long, to build a "real house." Within five or so years, they typically came to realize that they possessed a house that was not only real, but comfortably warm in the winter and cool in the summer; at this point the exterior plaster would be applied.

While some of the details may be apocryphal, there is no question that this type of story captures the spirit of early bale construction. The original bale builders were eminently practical people doing what needed doing in order to carve a life out of a raw and difficult land. If creating shelter for winter meant carrying a roof through knee-deep snow, there is little doubt that they would have been up to the task. And if it took five years to accept the idea that bales and plaster could make the walls of a real house, that is a blip compared to the hundred years it has taken for this same idea to begin to reach a wider audience.

It seems no coincidence that bale construction was revived among another generation of homesteaders. The technique may have died out completely, were it not for an article by Roger Welsch in *Shelter,* a compendium of indigenous and off-beat building styles from around the world, written for a 1970s back-to-the-land audience. This article inspired a few practical and independent-minded people, including Jon Hammond in California, Jorg Ostrowski in Alberta, Louis Gagné, Francois Tanguay, Clément Doyer, and Michel Bergeron in Quebec, Ben Gleason in Connecticut, and a handful of others, to begin experimenting with this technique. An article on Hammond's straw bale studio, published in 1983 in *Fine Homebulding,* led others in the mid-1980s, Steve and Nena MacDonald among them, to give a try at stacking simple, inexpensive walls of bales. By the late 1980s, Matts Myhrman and Judy Knox, Athena and Bill Steen, David Bainbridge, and Pliny Fisk III began to have a close look at the wider implications of bale construction for grassland regions.

Like the Sand Hills homesteaders, the early rediscoverers of this technique usually had rather immediate reasons for choosing bales: they needed a place to live, and needed to make do with what they had lying around. Ben Gleason put it best: "We knew that we'd only be farming a few more years in Connecticut, then we were moving to Vermont. I built this place for $500 in materials, and figured if it lasted five years, that would be good enough." Ten years later and in a drier climate, the MacDonalds had greater hopes for the longevity of their building, but they, too, were primarily concerned with getting up a habitable shelter on a very tight budget. Luckily, the MacDonalds decided to share what they had learned. With the 1991 publication of Steve's *Straw Bale Primer* (illustrated by his son, Orien) straw bale construction became available to a much wider audience.

Straw bale construction has come a long way since these early pioneering efforts. Several excellent books, videos, and hundreds of articles have been produced on the subject. The indefatigable David Eisenberg has brought awareness of bale construction to the highest echelons of the international building code hierarchy, while thousands of people, by patiently working with their local officials, have received project approval in jurisdictions around the world. Bales have been incorporated into homes of many different styles, which cross a very wide range of expense. As our understanding of how a bale wall works has become more sophisticated, new options have emerged for meshing bales with other materials. What hasn't changed, however, is the simple beauty of these early bale houses.

The Past Meets the Present

Nebraska-style straw bale houses built in the early part of the 20th century can be compared to any other type of vernacular architecture. They were all built with the same set of materials and according to a common system by people

Stud frame house with straw-clay walls. Lauzon, Quebec.

who shared both cultural background and physical environment. Today's examples of straw bale houses, even those that were directly inspired by the Nebraska dwellings, have departed from the characteristics of vernacular houses; they are designed and built by individuals of all imaginable cultural backgrounds, with access to very different material and economic resources, responding to an endless variety of site and lifestyle conditions. As these buildings have spread around the world, they have been influenced by practitioners of many different trades, bearing a great diversity of local construction wisdom, many of whom got interested *because* of the creative challenge of working with an odd new material. The original system has traveled as far in new ideas and concepts as it has across continents. Intuitively or deliberately, modern bale pioneers have done their utmost to adapt the system to different environmental conditions.

What straw bale builders share around the world is access to the basic information and their

Straw bale house under construction, using a preplastered, load-bearing system. Saint-Faustin, Quebec.

attraction to a material that has been used in vernacular architecture since the beginning of humanity: straw.

Straw in its modern baled form seems to have reconnected many of us to our roots. The growing popularity of straw bale houses is likely akin to an increasing interest in other techniques that use straw in its loose form. Cob and straw-clay walls, plasters, and blocks are gaining repute as alternatives to modern industrialized materials and techniques. As designers look further back at the history of straw in construction, they have become increasingly likely to blend these methods into their straw bale houses.

As straw bale construction has bloomed in the 1990s, so has electronic communications. (If only the humble bale were to receive as much media attention as the Internet!) Bale building designers have made extensive use of these technologies to keep each other appraised of the latest experimentation, sometimes on a day-to-day level. This has been generally useful and occasionally hazardous: there is a natural temptation to copy at home what seems to work well at the other end of the planet. As straw bale houses pop up all over, many inexperienced builders have fortified their frenzy of excitement over the well-adapted simplicity of the early Nebraska buildings with incomplete contemporary information, without ever stopping to think critically about how to adjust these prototype designs to their own environment.

Much experimentation, field testing, and monitoring remains to be carried out, across many geographical regions, before local cultures establish their own standards for bale construction. But with time and with investment by local communities in this research, straw bales may yet become a key material in the definition of new vernacular architectures in parts of the world where the originals have been replaced by anonymous, industrialized dwellings.

A Straw Bale Reality Check

Though this might come as a surprise to some enthusiasts, we are quite sure that bales are not a perfect construction material. Their bulky and uneven size, their unwillingness to hold nails, and their need to be kept dry forever make for a substantial set of design limitations. Similarly, the fact that straw bale construction is still in an

The Owner–Builder: Eyes Wide Open

When we hear about extremely inexpensive bale houses, we have discovered the product of an equation: labor × money. It is possible, up to a point, to substitute labor for money in a building. For a patient and talented person, this is where the real savings can happen.

What does this mean? Trees, especially standing trees, are far less expensive than milled lumber. Cut and peel timbers, from your land or a neighbor's. Bring in a mill to saw dimensional lumber on-site. Better yet, salvage an old building. Salvage good-quality, double-paned windows. Salvage slate or metal roofing materials. Do your own site work, with rented equipment, or by hand. Minimize trim. Buy used appliances and plumbing fixtures (if you live in a jurisdiction where you are allowed to install them yourself). Build small. Build small. Build small. Expect to realize very little return, on a dollars saved per hour spent basis, for the time you spend in salvage and handwork. The reason why most people in the industrialized world don't do these things is because they can work for money and buy materials (and, to some degree, skilled labor time) more efficiently than they can throw their relatively unskilled hours at salvage and building projects.

There is no such thing as a cheap house of good quality, except maybe in depressed areas where the real-estate market has been deflated. Quality costs a combination of time and money. This combination can be varied somewhat, but the bottom line is the same: House construction boils down to a skillful reorganization of a massive quantity of raw materials into an absolutely necessary end product. This end product *should* be expensive, especially if the owner insists on its being unnecessarily large, as is the norm in North America. The idea that enduring, comfortable, and even elegant shelter can be had for a minimal amount of work is an illusion of our stock market and lottery-oriented society, and shows a complete disrespect for all of human history. If you only care about cheap, then you should save up $1,000 and buy an old trailer.

We are not advocating a huge mortgage and a turnkey house. We are firm believers in the pay-as-you-go, owner-built house. The point is that this method entails a lot of hard work, both physically and mentally. Using bales for your walls won't really change that fact, so you had better be prepared for it.

evolving state means that when labor is paid, straw can actually turn out to be more expensive than conventional alternatives.

At GreenSpace, we ritually explain to potential clients that we are 90 percent sure that straw bale construction is a good idea, in our cold and wet climate. This is based on the fact that, while we employ a set of details that *seem* as if they should work, straw (at least in baled form, and as a component in an overall strategy for super-insulation) does not have a long track record, in our climate. It is crucial that modern straw builders proceed with humility and an open mind, and with the assumption that many of the true strengths and weaknesses of this technique have yet to be defined. We are in the business of experimentation, and only a fool treats an experiment as a sure thing.

Cost, Labor, and the Strange Values of Western Society

The greatest myth about bale buildings is that they are cheap. Bale construction can be less expensive than its thin-walled cousins, if the raw materials are locally abundant and human hours spent fiddling with bales and applying plasters by hand do not count as costs. Walls typically account for between 10 and 15 percent of the price of a house in the industrialized world, however—so if someone tells you that you can build a very inexpensive house on account of using bales in your walls, you should probably look elsewhere for advice.

Good-quality, relatively inexpensive bale houses have been built in cold climates. At least in North America, they have not been built for the 10 or 20 U.S. dollars per square foot that is sometimes possible in climates that require a minimal investment in foundation, roof, windows, or heating system.

The fact remains that a large percentage of people first get interested in straw bale construction because they think a bale house is going to be less expensive than its conventional counterpart. Whether this turns out to be the case has less to do with the bales than with the character of the homeowner. Buildings are complicated enough that no one material choice can have all that great an effect on their total cost. We have seen simple bale-walled utility buildings constructed of salvaged materials and basically for free; we have also seen bale-walled houses that finished out at $200 plus per square foot. What really affects the cost of these buildings is how the bales and the many other components fit into the larger issues of budget and lifestyle choices.

Houses are built by one of three processes. The first, and by far the most common method in the industrialized world, is by contracted crews of professional tradespeople working with purchased materials. The second method is by the owner, probably with some paid help and subcontracted phases, and with mostly purchased materials. Most owner-built houses in the Western world fall into this category. The third method is by the owner, with the help of whatever free or cheap labor can be scrounged up, and with as few purchased materials as possible. This is the model that is typical in the developing world.

Bales will save no money in process number one. In fact, it is only with a careful design and efficient on-site organization that the bales can even compete with mainstream materials. Compared with dimensional lumber, plywood, drywall, concrete blocks, and the many other premachined components available today, bales are relatively imprecise and cumbersome to handle.

They soak up time, and time, in this scenario, is expensive. (And appropriately so. Wading to their elbows through a swamp of overpaid office workers, tradespeople, the providers of shelter, can still usually afford some simple privileges—such as owning the place where they live. Unlike other basic service providers, such as farmers and garment industry workers, they have not yet been mechanized into poverty.)

So, bales will not save any money if your house is built by professional tradespeople; at this early stage of their development they will often cost more to install than the conventional materials familar to contractors. All of the other reasons to use them still apply, of course. And here is a unique reason: The bales and plaster offer an ideal opportunity for the homeowner and his or her friends to become involved in the construction process. Owner labor during these phases can keep the cost of the building down to (or slightly below) conventional standards. More significantly, it helps the owner balance the stress of constant financial and aesthetic decisions with some good old-fashioned hard work. Most people (and especially those whose careers require nothing of their hands) get a real kick out of pitching in on their own house. They have fun, and they feel a sense of competence and ownership. Regardless of what the realtors may tell you, when it comes time for the final accounting of satisfaction gained per dollar spent, all of this is at least as valuable as the number of square feet under roof, and whether or not the countertops are made of Corian.

> The fact remains that a large percentage of people first get interested in straw bale construction because they think a bale house is going to be less expensive than its conventional counterpart.

In process number two, what we might call the conventionally organized owner-built house, bales and plaster can save some money. Plaster materials (especially if clay is used as the binder) are relatively inexpensive; bales can also be less expensive than conventional insulation materials, though this varies tremendously by region and season. The plaster component will add substantial labor time over the cost of drywall and cladding, so bales will only save money if the owner-builder is skilled at gathering and coordinating large work parties, or if the project progresses on a relaxed schedule. The danger with owner-built houses that are on a tight schedule (especially when the owner is not an experienced contractor) is that time will begin to press in on the process, and labor will have to be hired in to speed up the finish. Such unplanned outlays can quickly wipe out the economic benefits of inexpensive, labor-intensive materials choices.

All of the benefits of bales that apply in the first case apply in the second scenario, also. Additionally, we have met many owner-builders for whom bales (the idea of bales, really) made the self-build route psychologically possible. Most of these owner-builders also say they wish they knew in advance how much work would ultimately go into the bale and plaster walls. We have yet to come across one, however, who was not ultimately happy about their decision to use bales, or about the quality of the space they were able to create.

In the third scenario, the true low-income, self-help housing model, bales can be a godsend.

They might not cost any less than other salvageable options, but their use will almost always lead to a better building. The straw, in this case, will certainly be grown locally, and might be hauled directly from the field, by the builder. He might even do the baling himself, with a handpress. Plaster will be composed primarily of materials that are free for the taking. Interior finishes will be simple and integral to the structure. Foundation, roof, windows, and heating system will likely be the elements that consume what limited funds are available to the owner. If a large percentage of the materials are to be salvaged, the building will usually be a small one, because salvage is a lot of work. This type of house will almost always grow over time, in a pay-as-you-go fashion. Sometimes, it will possess more elegance and humanity than buildings that cost 100 times as much.

Grass Cellulose and Wood-Pulp Cellulose

If there is one point to this discourse, it is that straw bales are not a panacea. They are one of many excellent materials that, when used in intelligent combination, can provide a beautiful, durable, and unusually functional house. One obvious comparison is with a close cousin of straw—blown cellulose insulation. Cellulose is recycled newspaper. Skilled installers can pack it dense enough that it functions as an air barrier; it also has a tremendous ability to diffuse moisture out of wall and ceiling cavities. It blows around obstructions such as pipes, wires, and ducts. It is much lighter than baled straw.

Straw has a very low embodied energy; so does cellulose. ("Embodied" energy is the amount of energy used to produce, transport, and install a unit of material.) Extrapolating from Ann Ed-

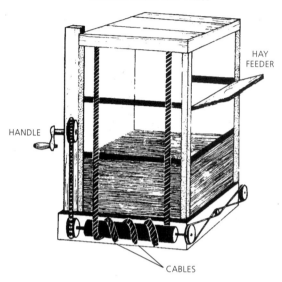

A handpress can make longer or shorter bales. From LaVie Paysanne, *1860–1900.*

minster's *Investigation of Environmental Impacts of Straw Bale Construction,* one can reasonably assume that a 45-pound, two-string straw bale will embody 250 Btus of energy per square foot of wall surface. Blown cellulose embodies 600 Btus per square foot, installed at a density appropriate to achieve R-20 in a 5½ inch wall.[2] The bales come in quite a bit lower than the cellulose (especially if you increase the cellulose numbers by 50 percent to create a more direct insulation comparison with a bale wall), but both the cellulose and the bales embody far less energy than fiberglass (4,550 Btus per square foot, R-20) or EPS foam (18,000 Btus per square foot, R-20).

In GreenSpace projects, we generally use blown cellulose in ceilings, in floors when necessary, and in any sections of wall where bales do not make sense. On more than one occasion we have sug-

2. Alex Wilson, "Insulation Materials: Environmental Comparisons," *Environmental Building News* (January/February 1995): 15.

gested to potential bale builders who wanted flat walls that they were probably better off with double-stud construction, drywall, and cellulose. That's basically how we see it, from the perspective of the eastern woodlands: if you want wavy walls, use bales and plaster. If you want flat walls, use cellulose and drywall.

The issues of land use, biodiversity, and soil conservation are also significant. Logging practices in old-growth forests have finally begun to receive the attention that they deserve, and just in time. But when did you last hear someone squawk about the demise of old-growth grasslands? Aldo Leopold had a thing or two to say about it, but fifty years ago; he was already too late.

It is economically feasible to manage a woodland for biodiversity, and soil conservation, and log production. Under our current agricultural system, the same can rarely be said for cropland. Putting sentimentality aside for a moment, we might recognize the "amber waves of grain" for what they are, in biological terms: a vast monoculture that exists for the sole purpose of maximizing production of food for humans. The high percentage of the North American continent that has been converted from prairie and woodland to grain production loses millions of tons of topsoil every year, while absorbing equally stupendous quantities of petroleum-derived fertilizers, herbicides, and (to a lesser degree) pesticides. Millions of gallons of fuel are consumed in driving over this land, several times per year, in order to plant, maintain, and harvest this monoculture. The great majority of straw used in construction, quite unfortunately, is a by-product of an industrial agriculture whose patterns are no less ecologically destructive than those of industry in general.

We could, as Pliny Fisk points out, be building with the baled stems of native perennial grasses; we might also practice baling as a technique to control the spread of invasive exotic species. We could harvest straw from smaller, more diverse farms that employ crop rotations and animals in an overall fertility program. Sadly, the new orthodoxy of The Economy seems not to preach an interest in such approaches. Until a new Luther arises to correct the gross overindulgences of this all-powerful cult, we must proceed with a humble recognition of how imperfect a material our lovely straw really is.

Moisture

Moisture, of course, is the major issue facing straw bale construction in cold climates. Bales need to be kept dry once they are in the building, but they also need to be kept dry during construction. No other non-ground-contact insulation material is installed until after the building is dried in—which is to say the roof and exterior walls (including sheathing and windows) are in place. Because bales are typically the substrate for the exterior skin, and are also, in the case of Nebraska-style methods, the support system for the roof, keeping them dry during construction becomes a major design issue.

Damage from moisture can be a problem throughout the life of the building, of course.

> The major issue in a bale building, as in a wood building, is control of rainwater; the secondary issue is control of condensed interior moisture.

A pay-as-you-go project. Bellow's Falls, Vermont.

Luckily, this is also the case with wood, and bale buildings can borrow many details from traditional wood buildings. The major issue in a bale building, as in a wood building, is control of rainwater; the secondary issue is control (or dissipation) of condensed interior moisture. The key to success in cold-climate straw bale design is to think obsessively about where and how water may enter the wall, by either of these processes, and to design a forgiving system with a high po-

tential to dry any moisture that gets past your initial defenses. Strategies for dealing with these issues will be detailed in the following chapters.

MOLD

Only under one circumstance are bales known to be dangerous: if a specific mold, *Stachybotrys atra,* is allowed to grow in very wet straw. This mold can also live in many other common building materials, including water-soaked wood, ceiling tiles, wall paneling, unpainted plasterboard surfaces, cotton items, cardboard boxes, and stacks of newspaper, though it prefers straw over almost anything else, according to Canadian mold and fungal specialist, Dr. David Miller.[3] *Stachybotrys* has recently received attention as a health risk in conventional buildings, as well. According to the November 1999 issue of *Environmental Building News,* "One Canadian study found evidence of the mold in 2 percent to 3 percent of the homes surveyed, and Dorr Dearborn of Case Western Reserve University . . . was quoted as saying that he has found evidence of the mold in more than half of inner-city homes surveyed." *Stachybotrys* seems primarily to be a danger to infants.

The point here is that bales need to be kept dry. If your walls get so wet that *Stachybotrys* begins to grow, then you have other problems beyond mold.

3. Don Fugler and Habib Gonzales, "Mold Warning: *Stachybotrys Atra,*" *The Last Straw* 22 (spring 1998): 11.

The Hay House

OLD SAYBROOK, CONNECTICUT

by Paul Lacinski

The most obvious fact about the Hay House is that it should no longer be. Any visitor who is accustomed to hanging around in old buildings cannot help but think that entropy, that great march of nature that eventually brings down all the work of human hands, should have had the place by now. When he was designing the house in the mid-1970s, Ben Gleason's concerns were more immediate; he needed a place to live for five years or so, and he needed to move in soon. Ben decided on a 12 x 20 rectangle, with some sleeping space in a loft, a simple form that would go up quickly. He then selected materials according to one unifying principle—that they be free or nearly so—and between farmwork, he set about stacking some hay bales (which were too poor to feed to animals) into the walls of what is now the oldest bale building in the northeastern quadrant of North America.

Ben knew a thing or two about New England weather, and was probably quite aware that once he moved on to his new farm in Vermont, each year his Hay House would sink closer to the earth. There is no reason why this should have troubled him, as even in full health the house is not far from the ground. Its foundation is a berm of soil stabilized with cement and a few sheets of plastic over the top; its roof and window framing, salvaged. Ben split the roof shakes out of cedar from the nearby swamp. The original plaster was also a gift from the nearby swamp; Ben calls it "dirt plaster," a mix of sand and orange muck. As much a gathering as a building, the Hay House, left to weather and gravity, would have slouched into a concentration of the neighborhood fertility. It would have made a few white oak trees very happy.

As it happened, regeneration came, in the form of David Brown. In the process of creating the world that now surrounds and includes the Hay House, David has been more than equal to entropy, and he has also challenged many of the assumptions that rule our modern world. From his perspective, the industrial definition of growth (the new religion of the modern world?) might also be considered a form of entropy. While industrial "progress" may continue to create quantifiable increases in the quantity of our possessions, it is also extremely effective at scattering our attention away from the home, away from family and friends, away from our individual talents and quiet pleasures, and aiming it at the many places in the world where we may conceivably make money or buy something.

David has stuck by a more traditional definition of growth. He has tended to his homestead, improving it in increments, year by year. The Hay House is still a house today because David Brown understands the value of respecting what you have, rather than constantly pushing for something new. David's consistent attention

In 1974, Ben Gleason built the Hay House, now the oldest bale building in the northeastern United States, "for $500 in materials, figuring if it lasted five years, that would be good enough."

changed since Ben first formed them in 1975. Depending on the time of year, the house may be clothed in a skirt of a thousand daffodils, or draped in a shawl of vines so thick that they completely shade the greenhouse from the hot summer sun.

I first arrived there on a cold, stormy day in March, accompanied by my wife, Amy Klippenstein, Ben Gleason, and David Eisenberg, the high priest of straw bale testing and code issues. We were accompanied by David E.'s Protimeter bale moisture probe, and we were concerned, because in that run-for-the-doorway weather, the Hay House, even under the shelter of Ben's ample eaves and extended gables, looked mighty vulnerable. Inside, the warmth of the little stove and cups of tea and David's hospitality bound us into an immediate love for the place. As David's Slovak grandparents looked down from the wall, one could easily believe that we had ducked into a plastered stone cottage somewhere in the peasant country of Eastern Europe, happy to escape the driving rain. The building felt far older than the man who had built it.

Voicing the general concern that this place was too good to be true, someone advanced the idea that it was a lousy day for drilling holes around the outside of a building. But there was no way around the call of science, so worried or not, we had no choice but to carry out our mis-

has kept this minimally endowed building dry and quite healthy. Moreover, what separates the Hay House from so many of our modern houses and the lives that are lived in them—is David Brown's unyielding devotion to growth as a biological and personal phenomenon. Out of himself and a sandy patch of ground in coastal Connecticut, he has built a vibrant economy of beauty.

David is an artist and a gardener, and the Hay House and its gardens bear the mark of his fertile imagination. The inside of the house feels like a well-painted still life. It is calm, but definitely not static. Tea is warming on the kitchen stove, and heat is radiating from the small central woodburner, the pitcher pump wheezing as David or one of the Tibetan refugees who are employed in the gardens draws water into the sink. Except for a tiny greenhouse added to the south wall, the facades of the building haven't sion. Exposing the backs of our necks to the roof's dripline, we prodded those walls relentlessly, nagging at their weak points—under windows, near the ground, inside the greenhouse—so they would divulge any dark secrets hidden behind the plaster. Everywhere, the hay was dry, and the bits we could see through the test holes appeared to be in excellent condition. That a building so primitive, in a difficult climate, could be in such good shape after twenty-five years was both a revelation and a great source of hope. Only David Brown was not surprised; having lived with the building for fifteen years, he knew the source of its quiet endurance.

David has described the Hay House as a work in progress, a living example of little a person really needs in order to live a fulfilling life. The schoolchildren, flower lovers, art lovers, and Tibetan independence supporters who have visited the Hay House can attest to the fact that if people are willing to turn their full attention and skills to creating their own version of the world out of what they have at hand, a little can go a long way.

CHAPTER 2

DESIGN CHALLENGES:

Heat Loss, Air Quality, and Moisture

MOISTURE, AIR QUALITY, AND THERMAL CONTROL are relevant straw bale design issues in all climates, but they are most crucial in cold and/or wet climates. Bales are a good choice for cold-climate walls, because they insulate well. They can only perform to their highest potential, however, when incorporated into an overall strategy for super-insulation. This chapter will define, for owner-builders and others not already familiar with them, the basic concepts and terms relevant to heat loss, air quality, and moisture control—the three technical criteria that form the foundation of cold climate design.[1] Don't be dismayed about encountering this technical discussion before we dive into the practical aspects of building with bales. Dealing effectively with these design challenges is without a doubt *the key* to building a successful, durable straw bale house.

Heat Loss and Indoor Air Quality

If we look only at conserving heat, the ideal house would have thick, well-insulated walls, floors, and ceilings. Because we want no cold air to enter or warm air to leave, there would be no fans or chimney stacks. Neither would there be any doors or windows, except maybe for some

1. Much of the information in this chapter is derived from *The Moisture Control Handbook* by Joe Lstiburek and John Carmody, republished several times; most recently by John Wiley & Sons, (1996). The best all-around book on moisture theory, but hard to come by.

insulating glass on the south side, for solar gain. On the other hand, a house designed only with air quality in mind might hardly be a house at all. A cave (with no campfire allowed) might serve well, or a roof and a couple of flimsy walls, for protection from wind and rain. If it were an actual house, people might not be allowed inside, on account of their CO_2 emissions. Clearly, cold-climate design strategies must involve a compromise between heating efficiency and ventilation.

We can see this need for compromise in real houses that people are struggling to live in. Some of the early attempts at airtight, superinsulated construction have poor air quality because they were designed only to conserve heat. On the other hand, many old houses allow an excessive amount of outdoor air to leak in. If you've ever lived in one, you know all about closing off rooms, keeping close to the stove to stay warm, and waking up with a sore throat on account of excessively dry indoor air. The key to comfort lies in striking a balance between heat loss and fresh air. To balance them wisely the designer must understand the relationship between them.

A building's ability to hold heat depends on the quality of its doors and windows, the insulating properties of its shell components, and the rate at which air passes in and out. To some degree it also depends on the mass inside the building, though this has more to do with the quantity of heat energy that can be stored than the rate at which it escapes. (See sidebar, "What Is R-Value Anyway?")

Door and window makers publish product guides for designers that provide the insulation and infiltration (air leakage) characteristics of their products. Compare them and buy (or build) the best ones you can afford.

Insulation is largely what this book is about—bales of straw as wall insulation. Bales provide an R-value of 1.45 per inch when laid flat (heat flow along the length of the straws, "with the grain") and somewhere upward of 2.06 per inch on their edge (heat flow perpendicular to the straws, "across the grain"). Regardless of how you use them, bales provide a superinsulated wall to retain heat inside a building.

Infiltration, which is responsible for 28 percent of the heat loss in a typical, new, code-built house in the United States, is a more complicated issue. Anyone who has spent a winter in an unplastered straw bale house can tell you that bales alone do not prevent massive quantities of cold air from leaking into a building. They need the inside and outside coats of plaster to provide a cavity of still air. This is true of most insulation materials. Even if insulation materials could block the flow of air, however, they would not stop the majority of infiltration into the typical house. The plaster and drywall planes of walls and ceilings are usually relatively airtight; most leakage occurs at seams between these surfaces, and around windows, doors, lights, electrical outlets, vents, and other openings; at framing intersections; and through holes drilled between conditioned and unconditioned spaces for pipes, wires, and heating ducts. An efficient building shell controls leakage at all of these points.

Many people say that a building needs to "breathe," so that its occupants might do likewise. This is obviously the case; the key to balancing heat loss with ventilation is to regulate the breathing. In the same way that a person breathes through a portal known as the mouth, by the action of a pump known as the lungs, and takes in more or less air depending on the body's need at the moment, an efficiently designed house breathes through windows and fans, and takes in more or less air, according to the activities going on inside. (This "breathing" is not, unfortunately, a very useful term, as it is also sometimes meant to indicate a wall's ability to slowly diffuse water vapor and other gases. Openness to vapor diffusion is a good idea in bale walls, but it has nothing to do with inhaling or exhaling air. This ambiguity has caused endless confusion among bale enthusiasts. If we had our way, we would purge this term from the construction lexicon. See "Vapor Permeability," and "Paul's Diatribe against 'Breathable,'" later in this chapter.)

Often, in mainstream construction, little effort is made to close the many small gaps in a typical building's shell, the idea being that these will provide fresh air to the occupants. This is only crudely true. The problem with this approach is that the amount of fresh air bears no relationship to the needs of the people inside. It might or might not be distributed where they need it, and its volume is determined by the weather. Thanks to the stack effect and to wind pressure (see sidebar, "The Driving Forces Behind Air Movement"), such a house will exchange more air with the outdoors as the temperature drops (as the difference between indoor and outdoor temperatures increases), or as the wind blows harder. It is highly unlikely that these would consistently be the times when a house requires extra ventilation. This fact does, however, create an extra incentive for owners of old houses to host parties on the coldest nights of the year. You are already paying for a copious supply of fresh air, so why not help your neighbors through the loneliness of winter?

When the temperature difference between indoors and outdoors is not all that great, such as in spring and fall, a house with many small gaps but no real controls may not provide enough ventilation for its occupants. Though it might seem obvious that people would simply open their windows at such times, this does not always happen. In Western societies, most people are now away at work during most days, trying to keep up with their next mortgage payment. In the spring and fall, it is typically only in the middle of the day when temperatures are warm enough to make people want to open a window. By the time they get home, and begin their evening rituals of breathing, cooking, and showering, the temperature will usually have dropped enough that they are less inclined to open the windows. It may not have dropped enough, however, for the stack effect to provide ample fresh air.

Let's look at a building whose air intake is controlled by the needs of the occupants. To begin with, such a building would be detailed to minimize air leakage. Openings between heated and unheated spaces would be avoided wherever possible, and the unavoidable seams in the building's framing would be sealed. Wind and weather, therefore, would have a much reduced effect on the environment inside the house. All combustion appliances would be of the "sealed" variety, drawing none of their combustion air from within the building. In these appliances, exhaust and intake are ducted directly to and from the outdoors, and all combustion takes place within a sealed chamber. Equipment of this sort has no effect on airflow patterns, and cannot pollute interior air.

In this building with minimal air leakage, fresh air is provided by quiet, efficient, timer-controlled fans, often the same fans that handle heavy moisture loads from showering and cooking. Two ventilation methods are suitable for cold climates: heat recovery and exhaust only.

This HRV controller features an electronic button, which kicks on an exhaust fan for a preset period when the bathroom is in use.

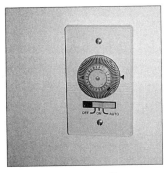

This simple controller runs an exhaust fan for a portion of each hour, converting a bath fan into an exhaust-only ventilation system.

A makeup air vent with a closable lid.

Heat-Recovery Ventilation

Heat-recovery ventilators, more commonly known as HRVs or air-to-air heat exchangers, transfer heat from the warm air leaving a house to the cool air that is entering. They are beautifully simple devices. The two streams of air (which are typically broken into many small streams, to maximize surface area) are separated only by a thin sheet of heat-conducting material. Heat energy moves across this membrane, flowing naturally from the warm air to the cool air. As much as 80 percent of the heat is recovered from the outgoing air.

HRVs can connect directly to the indoors, or they can be incorporated into the supply side of a forced-air heating system. They are typically designed to run continuously at a low level, providing a constant supply of fresh air. Override switches in bathrooms and kitchens allow the occupants to kick the fan to full volume during cooking, showers, or dance parties.

The most obvious strength of an HRV is the heat-recovery feature. You can have your warmth and breathe it too! But their merits don't end there. Because the in- and out-flows are balanced in an HRV, they have no effect on other air pressures within the building. This is important in very tightly constructed houses where backdrafting duels between various fans and chimneys can be a real problem.

Heat recovery ventilators are only worth installing on buildings that are quite airtight. At $600–$1,100 U.S., these units are not inexpensive. While they can offer good value in an airtight house, in both heat saved and indoor air quality, they will never pay for themselves in a leaky house in which their effects are diluted by lots of uncontrolled air changes.

Exhaust-Only Ventilation

Exhaust-only ventilation means that air is sucked out of the building, usually by fans. Makeup air enters where it can—typically through the multiple seams that remain unsealed in most houses, even in those that we attempt to build airtight. In some cases special makeup air vents with closeable lids are inserted in the walls, as intentional leaks through which air can enter.

Exhaust-only ventilation has the benefit of being substantially less expensive to install than heat-recovery ventilation. In a sophisticated system a basement-mounted fan is hitched to a timer or other controller and ducted to bathrooms and the kitchen (though not to the range hood, as these fans are not intended to handle grease). The timer typically runs the fan for a portion of each hour, or continuously, at low power. An override switch allows the occupants to kick the fan on, at full bore, at times of major moisture production.

A less expensive system converts the bathroom and kitchen fans (which will already be there anyway) into a ventilation system, by rigging them with timers. The trick to keeping such a system in operation over the years is to install high-quality, quiet fans. Manufacturers publish sone (noise) and power consumption ratings for their fans, and these are worth comparing: 1 to 1.5 sones at maximum speed is very quiet. This is no place to cut corners; spend the extra money and buy a good-quality fan. It will last longer and consume less electricity than a cheap one, and you will never be bothered by the sound of its running.

Fan controllers are available in a number of different styles and function combinations. The crucial matter is to install one that allows both consistent and on-demand use. Two units worth mentioning are the Airetrak and Humitrak, produced by Tamarack Technologies in Wareham, Massachusetts. These are available in both AC and DC models. The Airetrak is a nifty little gadget. It runs your fan at intervals that you set, and at a speed that you set. It also includes an override button (the only part of the unit that is visible through the cover plate) that kicks the fan on for twenty minutes at full speed. The Humitrak turns your fan on when the humidity inside the house reaches a set level, anywhere between 10 and 90 percent. Units are available with built-in

or remote sensing devices. The Humitrak also includes an override switch, which kicks the fan on for twelve minutes. Each of these units retails for less than a hundred U.S. dollars.

The Driving Forces Behind Air Movement

Air is pretty light stuff, easily pushed around. The three forces that do most of the pushing are the stack effect, wind pressure, and power-vented appliances.

THE STACK EFFECT

Warm air rises. This is known as the stack effect because it is the force that makes chimneys (smokestacks) work. Warm air finds the most direct route to the highest point; the role of the chimney is to provide a channel to the sky.

The stack effect isn't confined to chimneys, however. If you squint your eyes a bit, you can probably imagine your entire house as something of a chimney, built of lots of pieces, with small gaps where these pieces meet, and with an imperfectly fitting lid. Now imagine a heat source—let's say, for the sake of simplicity, an electric heater—in the center of the first floor of the house.

What happens in this chimneylike house? The air around the heater warms up, and because warm air is less dense, it begins to rise. The warm air fans out as it rises, giving up heat to everything it touches. At first it cools and sinks back down; before long, however, enough warm air has reached into the higher parts of the house that the air there has become warmer than the outside air. It pushes against the roof and upper walls of the house and leaks out through small openings between the building's parts. Some sneaks out around second-story windows, some

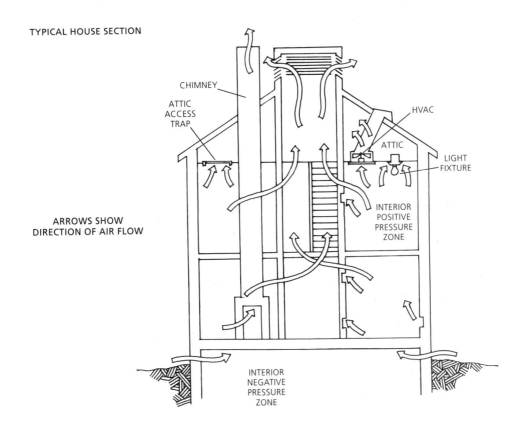

CHIMNEY

ATTIC
ACCESS
TRAP

HVAC

ATTIC

LIGHT
FIXTURE

ARROWS SHOW
DIRECTION OF AIR FLOW

INTERIOR
POSITIVE
PRESSURE
ZONE

INTERIOR
NEGATIVE
PRESSURE
ZONE

The stack effect: warm air rises to the highest point.

through ceiling-mounted light fixtures. Quite a lot finds the attic hatch, and exits around the perimeter of the door. Since nature abhors a vacuum, this escaping air must be replaced by cold air coming in at the lower parts of the house: around windows and electrical outlets, under doors, and from the basement, through small gaps between floorboards.

WIND PRESSURE

Wind pressure can be a very powerful force in determining how air moves in and out of buildings. During particularly windy periods it can overwhelm the stack effect. Wind increases the air pressure on the windward side of a building and reduces it on the leeward side, so that air

leaks in on the wind side and out on the lee. In leaky houses, this can result in very significant energy losses, and unpleasant cold drafts.

POWER-VENTED APPLIANCES

Power-vented appliances, typically boilers, furnaces, hot water heaters, dryers, range hoods, and central vacuum cleaners, draw air from inside the building. Occasionally, in a tight building, such an appliance can actually backdraft a conventional chimney, drawing flue gases back down. To avoid this, we recommend sealed combustion equipment, in which combustion air is drawn directly from the outdoors and combustion gases returned there. The burn chamber in such a unit is actually sealed off from the living space; there is no opportunity for waste gases to leak into the house and no chance that the appliance will affect house air pressures.

Envelope Efficiency vs. Thermal Mass

While this chapter is primarily concerned with the design of a building's envelope—those surfaces that divide the conditioned interior space from the vagaries of the outdoor world—it is worth taking a moment to note the role of thermal mass in the overall equation of building efficiency. The efficiency of the envelope is determined by two factors: the degree of insulation of walls, floors, ceilings, windows, and doors, and the rate of air leakage through these components. A simple way to understand this is to imagine one Btu of heat put into a building. How soon will it be able to get out? The answer depends upon lots of factors, especially the difference in temperature between inside and outside. However, the consistent truth is that the more insulated and airtight the building's shell is, the longer this Btu will be trapped inside.

> The efficiency of the envelope is determined by two factors: the degree of insulation of walls, floors, ceilings, windows, and doors, and the rate of air leakage through these components.

The quality of the building's envelope determines the *rate* at which it will lose heat.

Thermal mass, on the other hand, determines the *quantity* of heat energy that the building is capable of storing. Let's oversimplify again by imagining a house from which no heat escapes—the envelope is built infinitely well, so the rate of heat loss is zero. Let's also imagine, for a moment, that the building has no thermal mass. What happens as we begin to add heat energy, a few Btus at a time? The air inside begins to warm up. Pretty soon it feels like a sauna, and after a while we go outside and jump in a river. With our heads cleared, we begin to reason. We need to do something to store some of this heat; so we turn off the heat source and haul in a few rocks, and as the rocks absorb heat energy out of the air, the indoor temperature begins to drop down to a comfortable level. Because we are living in a simplified example, we also realize that if we keep hauling in rocks, we can keep the heat source cranked up without overheating the air inside the building, because the rocks are absorbing the energy—they're warming up. We have discovered the function of thermal mass: The quantity of mass in a building determines the quantity of heat that can be stored inside.

This storage capability is not very important in an example where the envelope is incapable of passing heat, but what about in an actual building? In the real world, some amount of heat would have been escaping all along. The role of the warmed-up rocks, then, would be to provide a reservoir of energy, so that the space would remain comfortable for a while, even if the heat source were turned off. This is the whole point of cold-climate design: to keep interior spaces comfortable while running the furnace or boiler or stove as little as possible.

Thermal mass is especially important in houses where some proportion of the heat is to be provided by the sun. The mass serves two functions here. It absorbs solar radiation during the day, (hopefully) keeping the air in the building from overheating on a sunny afternoon. It then releases the heat at night, thereby reducing the need to burn something in order to keep the place warm. The extent to which the mass can do this job is determined by the amount of insolation (solar input) received during the day, and by—you guessed it!—the quality of the envelope—the rate at which the house is losing heat to the outdoors. Thermal mass is most effective when spread out over a large area, so plastered bale walls are ideal, because they provide relatively thin mass everywhere!

A well-built thermal envelope is always a good idea in cold climates. Interior thermal mass is usually a good idea as well, because, regardless of the solar heating component, buildings that

<table>
<tr><td>

What Is
R–Value,
Anyway?[2]

</td><td>

R-value is a contrived (derived) number that the insulation industry came up with in the 1950s to sell its product. It is a measure of thermal *resistance,* and is the inverse of U-value, a measure of thermal *conductance* (R = 1/U). So, the smaller the U-value, the less heat is conducted and the better the thermal performance of the material. In a land where we tend to think "bigger is better," it is easy to understand why the insulation industry made up the "R-value." The larger the R-value the better the product is at resisting heat loss in the winter and some types of heat gain in the summer.

Just what is U-value? It's hard to simplify. U-value is: the number of British Thermal Units of energy (Btu) that will flow through 1 square foot of a material during one hour (at whatever thickness the material is) with a one degree Fahrenheit difference between the air temperatures at the two sides of the material. As a formula, U = Btu/([Temp In–Temp Out] X sq. ft. X hours).

Let's take an example. Say we have 1 square foot of "pink insulation" separating two spaces. The temperature on one side is 70°F, and the temperature on the other side is 0°F. We can find the U-value once we know how much heat energy it takes to keep the warm side at 70 degrees for one hour. Let's say it took exactly 3.68 Btus to maintain the 70-degree temperature difference: 3.68 Btu/(70 degrees X 1 hour X 1 sq. ft.) = 0.05263. That's the U-value of that insulation material. To get the R-value we divide the U-value into 1. And 1 divided by 0.05263 = 19. Therefore, the material has an R-value of 19. This happens to be the standard value for 6-inch-thick fiberglass batts.

</td></tr>
</table>

2. This is excerpted from an article by Nehemiah Stone, "Energy and Straw Bale Walls: Basic Heat Transfer," *The Last Straw* (winter 1999/2000).

coast along at a consistent temperature tend to be more comfortable than those whose temperatures rise and fall noticeably as the heat source kicks on and off. Mass is like momentum for a building: it can keep it cruising along in between inputs of fuel. Mass can be of disservice, however, when a building will be allowed to cool down for long periods between heating. A weekend house in the woods might be a good example. Because it receives no solar input, such a building would spend the whole week losing heat. When the owners arrive on Friday night they fire up the woodstove and furnace, they try to stay away from the cold walls and near the stove, and they spend the entire weekend heating up the mass of the house, just so it can cool down again. The building, in this case, is like a tractor-trailer stuck in a row of stoplights; it requires repeated large energy inputs in order to slowly climb up through its gears, only to be stopped before it reaches cruising speed. This is not very efficient.

Moisture

Water is the main enemy of straw. Straw that gets wet and stays wet will surely decompose; kept dry, it seems to last forever. In the straw bale construction world, as well as the wider building world, many people misunderstand how moisture gets into and out of walls, and such

Ventilating Off-the-Grid Houses

Stand-alone power systems often run so close to the bone that they cannot afford the small amount of electricity (less than 20 watts for some exhaust-only fans) required to operate a continuous or intermittent ventilation system. Until recently, even night-lights were taboo in many off-grid homes. The owners of such systems are necessarily willing to adjust their electrical usage to the charge of their batteries, and must remember where their furniture is to avoid wandering into it during nocturnal jaunts. It would seem that such independent souls would also be quite capable of moderating the air quality inside their homes by opening windows every day. Unfortunately, this often does not happen; people seem to have a basic aversion to opening a window when it's 0 degrees outside.

Traditionally, woodstoves have acted as defacto exhaust-only ventilation systems in off-the-grid houses. Older woodstoves draw a lot of air out of the living space and send it up the chimney. Replacement air must come from somewhere, so it comes in through small leaks in the building envelope, as it would in an exhaust-only ventilation system. (The same thing happens with a fireplace, at a volume that is orders of magnitude greater than with a woodstove. Thus the misunderstanding can lead to ineffective house design. Water enters straw bale walls from four major sources:

1. From the interior, in the form of condensation from leaking air or diffused vapor.
2. From the ground, in the form of groundwater or condensation, transported primarily by capillary action in the foundations, and also by vapor diffusion.
3. During construction, as liquid water from almost anywhere.
4. From the exterior, as rain or, to some degree, melting snow. This, obviously, is the most dangerous long-term source.

Interior Moisture Sources

We begin with interior sources of moisture, not because they are the most important, but because the definitions of terms that are required here will be useful through the remainder of this chapter.

Vapor and Relative Humidity

Most readers of this book have heard about water vapor, that mysterious stuff in the air that, when it gets into the fabric of a building, can cause moisture problems. What is this stuff? Air is a mixture of many gases, including water. In this gaseous state water is known as water vapor. How does it get into the air? Out of doors,

adage about a roaring fire warming the area directly in front of it, while making the rest of the house feel colder; it doesn't just feel colder by comparison, it actually gets colder, as winter air rushes in to slake the thirsty draft of the chimney.) The problem with this approach is that newer, airtight stoves, designed to waste less heat, also send less air up the chimney. Add in the fact that it is now common practice to duct combustion air directly to the stove, and it becomes entirely unreliable as an exhaust mechanism. (The reason for ducting air to the stove is to avoid the real danger that, if the house truly is built tightly, the chimney might not draw well, especially if other exhaust appliances are running. Then toxic gases and black, smelly smoke will back up into the room.)

Opening the windows for a portion of each day is not the most energy-efficient means of providing a house with ventilation. Neither is it the simplest, since the homeowner must consistently remember to do it. However, where heat energy is more readily available than electrical energy, and where the occupants enjoy attending to the details of operating their home (or enjoy opening windows), such a system can work quite adequately. The key is, before designing a house this way, you need to ask yourself whether you will, in fact, open the windows!

An off-the-grid house should still have ventilation fans to exhaust brief, intense moisture loads and smells from the kitchen and bath. These fans run for such short periods (typically twenty minutes or less) and at low enough wattages that they use a minimal amount of power. Excellent-quality, quiet fans are available in both AC and DC models.

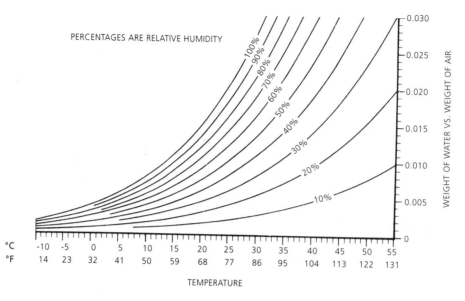

PERCENTAGES ARE RELATIVE HUMIDITY

Moisture content of air.

it is largely the product of evaporation or transpiration—from oceans, lakes, rivers, the ground, and plants. Indoors, it comes from obvious sources such as showers and cooking, and also from less obvious sources, including people breathing, transpiration from house plants, evaporation from washed dishes and clothing, and even from drying firewood. In addition, just like outside, evaporation from the ground into the living space is potentially a huge source. Unvented cooking and heating appliances that burn any fuel also create water vapor as a by-product of combustion.

The ability of a given volume of air to hold moisture varies with temperature. The warmer air gets, the more water vapor it can hold; the colder it gets, the less it can hold. This is why outdoor winter air is dry in cold climates—it is simply not capable of holding much moisture. "Relative humidity," then, is a term for expressing how "full" air is—how the amount of water in the air compares with the maximum amount

of water that the air could hold. In more mathematical terms, relative humidity is defined as the percentage of possible water vapor that is present in a given volume of air, at a particular temperature. For the sake of illustration, let's say that a volume of air is capable of holding 100 molecules of water vapor at 75 degrees. If those 100 molecules are present, the air is said to be at 100 percent relative humidity. The air is saturated; it is holding all the moisture that it possibly can at that temperature. Now let's remove 50 of those molecules. The air is still at 75 degrees, and can still hold 100 molecules, but now we only have 50 molecules of water vapor left; the air is now at 50 percent relative humidity. If we further reduced the number of vapor molecules to 25, the air would be at 25 percent relative humidity, and so on. So, it is possible to change the relative humidity of air by changing the amount of moisture in it.

It is also possible to change relative humidity by changing the temperature of the air. That

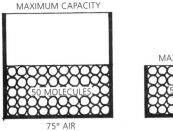
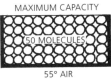

Air temperature vs. holding capacity of moisture.

same 75-degree air, at 50 percent relative humidity, is holding 50 molecules of water vapor while able to hold 100 molecules. If we cool the air, we reduce its maximum capacity. If we cool it enough that its capacity is dropped to 50 molecules, it will now be at 100 percent relative humidity; the 50 molecules present are 100 percent of the new maximum. Likewise, if we warm the air we decrease the relative humidity because warm air is capable of holding more vapor.

Condensation and Dewpoint

How do vapor and relative humidity relate to what goes on within the fabric of buildings? Warm, relatively moist interior air, traveling outward through holes in a wall in winter, will eventually hit a surface cold enough that the air is chilled below the point of 100 percent relative humidity. This is known as the dewpoint temperature—the temperature at which, for a given starting temperature and relative humidity, the air will come to contain more molecules of water than it is capable of holding. Some of this vapor drops out of the air, and is deposited on a surface, as liquid water. This is called "condensation" in a wall; it is "dew" when it happens outdoors, on grass.

The tricky thing about condensation in conventional walls is that, while the dewpoint tem-

perature might be reached at some point between the interior gypsum and the exterior sheathing, condensation will only actually happen on a surface, typically on the inside face of the sheathing. Water does not condense in substantial quantities on the fibers of cellulose or fiberglass insulation, because condensation gives up heat, which raises the temperature of these low-mass materials above the dewpoint. Because straw has much higher mass than these other materials, it would be healthy to assume that vapor can condense into water at whatever depth the dewpoint temperature may be reached, within a straw bale wall.

Air Leakage and Vapor Diffusion

Water vapor makes its way into walls from the inside by two mechanisms: air leakage and vapor diffusion. Of the two, air leakage is by far the most significant; it is typically responsible for over 90 percent of the total vapor that gets into walls.

This clever building in Minnesota had one problem: the steel baseplate of the Quonset hut is as wide as the bale wall, upon which it rested directly. Cold steel created a perfect surface for condensation, saturating the top course of bales. The resourceful owners have removed a layer of straw, and isolated the straw from the steel.

A Colloquial Condensation Conversation

Two changes in the condition of the air can cause condensation. The first is an increase in the amount of water vapor in the air, the second is a decrease in temperature. You have probably often experienced condensation as a result of adding too much moisture to the air. Let's say you get up in the morning and head for the shower. You don't know it, but the relative humidity of the air in your bathroom is hanging around at 30 or 40 or 50 percent. You turn on the shower, and as the water heats up, steam (water vapor) begins to waft into the room. The amount of water vapor in the bathroom air begins to climb; the relative humidity of the bathroom air begins to climb. At some point, the relative humidity of the bathroom air reaches 100 percent. The air is full. In order for the air in the bathroom to continue to receive the water vapor being produced by your shower (which it has no choice but to do) it must relieve itself of some—in the form of condensation on bathroom surfaces. Thus the fogged mirror.

You have probably also experienced condensation caused by lowered temperature, though you may not have recognized it as such. Take a particularly hot and humid day in summer, 90°F (32°C) and 90 percent relative humidity. You've been working all day, and decide it's time for one of those homebrews you've got stashed at the back of the fridge. You get out the beer, pop off the cap, and just as you're about to pour it into a glass, the phone rings. It's your good friend Art, with whom you have a lively running debate over whether the giant cabbages at Findhorn have to do with the gardeners' unusual sensitivity to particular earth energies, or whether they are a simple function of growing so far north, in the long light of the Scottish summer. After twenty minutes of international cabbage statistics you return to your beer to find the bottle so wet that the handwriting on the label has begun to run. Why has this happened? As the air moves around your kitchen, some of it passes around the cold bottle of beer on the counter. This air cools, quickly reaching the point of 100 percent relative humidity. As the air continues to cool, it must give up some of its moisture; this is deposited on the bottle. If the bottle were left on the counter long enough that its temperature could equalize with the rest of the room, and if the air were still at 90 percent relative humidity, the air would begin to take that moisture back in. Eventually, and if you don't mind drinking 90-degree homebrew, you could pour that beer without getting your hands wet. When people talk about condensation happening within a wall, this is the exact process that they are describing.

Ice Dams

Aside from wasting energy and providing an inconsistent supply of fresh air to a house's occupants, air leakage is also a major contributor to ice dam problems on roofs. In a typical code-built house no attention is paid to maintaining a continuous air barrier between the living space and the attic. The ceiling of each room is an individual unit, separated from others by the top plates of partition walls. As if this partition framing were not leaky enough to begin with, it is then drilled for wire runs and plumbing stacks. The wall surfaces, meanwhile, are punched full of holes for electrical outlets and switches. Interior partition walls thus become chimneys, drawing warm air into the attic. This air rises to the underside of the roof sheathing, where it begins to give off its heat, melting the snow above. The melt runs down the roof surface until it reaches the cold eave; it then refreezes into icicles and a dam, removing gutters and shingles in the process.

The simplest way to avoid this problem is to install a continuous membrane of plaster, drywall, or poly at the upper story ceiling *before* framing interior partitions, and then to carefully seal any holes drilled for the installation of services.

(Air leakage also accounts for 25 percent or more of the heat loss in a typical code-built home.)

Air leakage takes two forms, infiltration and exfiltration. Air is said to be infiltrating when (like a spy!) it is making its way from the exterior, through the building enclosure, and into the living space. Exfiltrating air is on exactly the opposite course, passing (like an exile or expatriate) through the fabric of the building on its way from inside to outside. Infiltration and exfiltration are always in balance, which is to say that for each cubic foot of air that leaves a building, a cubic foot comes in.

During the heating season, infiltrating air is usually cold. If it enters by too large a stream we call it a draft, and nobody likes to sit in a draft. Too much infiltration in a specific area can also lower the local surface temperature to the point where condensation occurs and mold begins to grow. Air that is infiltrating in many small streams can cause problems as well; too much infiltration can add up to a house that is difficult to heat. On the plus side, controlled infiltration can serve two very necessary functions. It is the most obvious source of fresh air for the home's occupants and, as it warms, this relatively dry air can reduce interior humidity levels.

Exfiltrating air is riskier stuff; it is the source of many moisture problems in cold-climate houses. As warm, moist air makes its way out through the fabric of a building it begins to cool. The temperature of this exfiltrating air can eventually drop to the dewpoint level, so that the condensation of water begins. In a conventional house this happens at the inner side of the sheathing; in a bale house we must assume that it can happen at any depth in the wall where the dewpoint is reached.

Some air must leave the building, of course, if fresh air is to make its way in. The secret to avoiding problems is to control the rate and points of departure. Exfiltration that is directed through windows and fans poses no threat to your home, your health, or your heating bill. In fact, we don't even call it exfiltration. We call it ventilation.

Diffusion through surface materials is another method by which water vapor can enter building assemblies, though this is a much less important factor than air leakage. Diffusion is not governed by air pressure, but by vapor pressure. In a practical sense, vapor pressure can be understood as the tendency of water vapor (any gas, really) to migrate from an area of higher concentration to an area of lower concentration. In the winter, the vapor pressure (concentration of water molecules) inside a cold-climate house is higher than the vapor pressure outside. Water vapor, therefore, will want to move from inside to outside, through your building assembly.

You have two choices about how to deal with this issue. The conventional approach, which

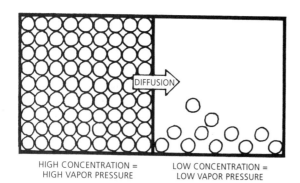

HIGH CONCENTRATION =
HIGH VAPOR PRESSURE

LOW CONCENTRATION =
LOW VAPOR PRESSURE

Diffusion is governed by vapor pressure.

came to the fore during the second half of the 20th century, is to stop vapor before it reaches the insulation layer, either by installing a polyethylene vapor barrier behind the sheetrock or by painting the sheetrock (or plaster) surface with a manufactured paint. The logic here is that if vapor is prevented from entering the wall cavity, then it cannot do any damage.

The traditional approach, employed for millennia in houses all around the world, is to construct the building envelope in such a way that any vapor that enters will be allowed to keep on moving toward the outside. When people talk about allowing a wall to "breathe," this is generally what they mean. In cold climates, the trick here is to *design the wall so that the exterior is at least as vapor permeable, and ideally more so, than the interior,* so that there is no danger of water vapor entering the assembly more quickly than it can escape.

Builders have had success with each of these approaches to bale walls. Typically, the choice of exterior finish determines which design makes the most sense. If the exterior will receive cement stucco, which is the least permeable of plasters, then the interior should probably be coated in a vapor-retardant paint. (This has been a common practice, and seems to have worked well to this point, though no long-term examples exist in cold and wet climates.) The main drawback to such a system is that the drying potential (ability of vapor to make its way out by diffusion) is lower than in almost any other configuration. So, if such a wall takes in an unusual amount of water, say from a poor flashing detail or a crack in the stucco at a particularly exposed location, or from a large quantity of condensation due to air leakage, it will be slower to dry than with just about any other combination of finishes.

VAPOR DIFFUSION CAPACITY OF CONVENTIONAL BUILDING MATERIALS[a]

	PERM	PERM PER INCH		PERM	PERM PER INCH
Materials used in construction			Asp.-saturated, not coated sheathing paper (22)[d]	20.2	—
Concrete (1:2:4 mix)	—	3.2	15-lb asphalt felt (70)[d]	5.6	—
Brick-masonry (4 in. thick)	0.8–1.1	—	15-lb tar felt (70)[d]	18.2	—
Concrete block (8 in. cored, limestone agg.)	2.4	—	Single-kraft, double infused (16)[d]	42.0	—
Asbestos-cement board (0.2 in. thick)	0.54	—			
Plaster on metal lath (¾ in.)	15.0	—	*Liquid-applied coating materials*		
Plaster on plain gypsum lath (with studs)	20.0	—	*PAINT 2 COATS*		
Gypsum wallboard (⅜ in. plain)	50.0	—	Aluminum varnish on wood	0.3–0.5	—
Struct. insulating bd. (sheathing qual.)	—	20–50	Enamels on smooth plaster	0.5–1.5	—
Struct. insulating bd. (int., uncoated., ½ in.)	50–90	—	Primers and sealers on interior insulation board	0.9–2.1	
Hardboard (⅛ in. standard)	11.0	—	Misc. primers plus 1 coat flat oil paint on plas.	1.6–3.0	—
Hardboard (⅛ in. tempered)	5.0	—	Flat paint on interior insulation bd.	30–85	—
Built-up roofing (hot-mopped)	0.0	—	Water emulsion on interior insulation bd.	4	—
Wood, fir sheathing, ¾ in.	2.9	—			
Plywood (douglas-fir, exterior glue, ¼ in.)	0.7	—	*PAINT 3 COATS*		
Plywood (douglas-fir, interior, glue, ¼ in.)	1.9	—	Ext. paint, white lead and oil on wood siding	0.3–1.0	—
Acrylic, glass fiber reinforced sheet, 56 mil	0.12	—	Ext. paint, white lead-zinc oxide and oil on wood	0.9	—
Polyester, glass fiber reinforced sheet, 48 mil	0.05	—	Sytrene-butadiene latex coating, 2 oz./sq.ft.	11.0	—
			Polyvinyl acetate latex coating, 4 oz./sq.ft.	5.5	—
Thermal insulations			Asphalt cut-back bastic,		
Cellular glass	—	0.0	1/16 in. dry	0.14	—
Mineral wool, unprotected	29.0	—	3/16 in. dry	0.0	—
Expanded polyurethane (R-11 blown)	—	0.4–1.6	Hot melt asphalt,		
Expanded polystyrene-extruded	—	1.2	2 oz./sq.ft.	0.5	—
Expanded polystrene-bead	—	2.0–5.8	3.5 oz./sq.ft.	0.1	—

	PERM	PERM PER INCH
Plastic and Metal Foils and Films[b]		
Aluminum foil (1 mil)	0.0	—
Polyethylene (4 mil)	0.08	—
Polyethylene (6 mil)	0.06	—
Polyethylene (8 mil)	0.04	—
Polyester (1 mil)	0.7	—
Polyvinylchloride, unplasticized (2 mil)	0.68	—
Polyvinylchloride, plasticized (4 mil)	0.8–1.4	—
Building papers, felts, roofing papers[c]		
DUPLEX SHEET, ASP. LAM., ALUM. FOIL ONE SIDE (43)[d] SATURATED AND COATED ROLL ROOFING (326)[d]		
Kraft paper and asp. lam., reinf. 30-120-30 (34)[d]	1.8	—
Asp.-saturated, coated vapor-barrier paper (43)[d]	0.6	—

a. Vapor transmission rates listed will permit comparisons of materials, but selection of vapor barrier materials should be based on rates obtained from the manufacturer or from laboratory tests. A range of values shown indicates variation among mean values for materials that are similar but of different density. Values are intended for design guidance only.

b. Usually installed as vapor barriers. If used as exterior finish and elsewhere near cold sid, special considerations are required.

c. Low permeance sheets used as vapor barriers. High permeance used elsewhere in construction.

d. Basis weight in lb. per 500 sq.ft.

Based on data from *ASHRAE Handbook of Fundamentals,* 1967, Chapter 19. Owen L. Delevantz, AIA, Glen Rock, New Jersey; and E.C. Shuman, P.E., Consulting Engineer, State College, Pennsylvania.

This disadvantage must be weighed against the structural advantages of cement.

If the exterior of the building will be finished in lime, clay, or wood, on the other hand, the drying potential to the outside will be much greater than in the cement scenario. A vapor-permeable exterior wall also opens up the option of a more vapor-permeable interior wall, one of unpainted lime or clay plaster. Such a system will allow the wall to dry to either side, rather than only to the outside.

It is worth mentioning that this system of relatively permeable interior and exterior walls is particularly well suited to the specific demands of mixed heating and cooling climates. This is the beautiful flexibility of a wall whose two sides

---

Paul's Diatribe Against "Breathable"

In the language of straw bale construction, no single word has caused greater confusion than "breathable." It has been impossible to form any sort of consensus on a definition because, though in normal life it clearly has something to do with air, its intended meaning in buildings usually (but not always) has to do with moisture.

I've heard this term used several ways. The most common is to indicate a wall that allows a high rate of vapor diffusion, as in, "you want a wall to breathe, so that it will not trap any moisture." See the ambiguity? Many people take this to mean that air leaking through or into a wall will help to keep it dry. Running with this idea, the ingenious straw bale crowd has concocted any number of "venting systems" for their walls, in an attempt to dry them by "breathing." One building industry professional even contacted me with the notion of leaving one side of the wall unplastered, so that it might "breathe." At their best, such schemes degrade the insulative value of the wall, by introducing cold (and windy) exterior air into what should be a still cavity; at their worst, they create the possibility of serious condensation-based moisture problems, by allowing large quantities of moist interior air to leak into the wall.

Not surprisingly, this notion of "breathing" also leads people to conclude that proper ventilation is not required in a straw bale house, because all of the air required for human respiration will somehow be inhaled through the fabric of the building. This is probably true until the plaster goes on, as bales themselves are hardly airtight. I can assure you that this is not the case in a finished house, however; I've been inside lots of straw bale houses, and some of them have terrible air quality. Almost without exception, the owner of such a house, when asked about the ventilation system, has explained that the walls "breathe." I'd breathe pretty hard too, running for the door.

So, please, when we want to talk about moisture moving through a wall, let's say "drying potential" or "vapor permeability." When we mean fresh air, "ventilation" ought to do. A little less throaty than "breathe," maybe, but at least we might get the right idea across.

When we speak of the permeance of various materials, we are talking about their ability to allow water vapor to pass through them. Perm ratings exist for many common building materials; the higher the number the greater the permeance. Materials with a perm rating below 1 are considered vapor diffusion retarders, the "vapor barriers" of common parlance (see the chart on page 43). Unfortunately, perm ratings for many of the materials common to straw bale construction (lime plaster, earth plaster) do not exist (Though perm ratings for lime mortars are available; see chapter 11, "Lime Plaster"). To determine which approach makes the most sense in a given situation, we need to proceed, to some degree, based on empirical evidence and common sense.

are open to the passage of vapor; regardless of where the major moisture source and possible condensation point may lie, the wall should be capable of drying by diffusion. Regardless of climatic region or which of these strategies you choose, it is wise to insert at least a few moisture probes in the walls, as long-term indicators of whether your system is working. (Sensors are discussed in chapter 14, "Moisture Studies and Sensors.")

Ground Sources of Moisture

In conventional construction, the concrete foundation wall is topped with a pressure-treated or otherwise rot-resistant sill plate, above which framing proceeds with normal, biodegradable lumber. The sill plate protects the framing from moisture that might be moving up through the foundation, either by capillary action ("wicking") or, to a lesser degree, by vapor diffusion.

We know from the previous section that vapor diffusion is a process of individual water molecules moving through a material in the vapor state, from an area of higher concentration to an area of lower concentration. Capillary action is a similar process, but instead of vapor it is actually liquid water that moves through the pores of a material. Capillary action depends on pore size; if the pores in a material are large enough, as in gravel, the water molecules cannot fill and "stick" to the sides of the pores, and capillary action does not take place. Likewise, if the pores are small enough, as in aluminum flashing, water molecules cannot fit through them. The pore size in standard concrete is perfect for capillary action, and thus water moves up from the ground and through the concrete, contacting the underside of the framing, or bales. Presumably, it can keep on rising, right into the straw.

How vapor would migrate up from concrete, into the bales, is a bit less obvious than capillary movement. Sometimes the concrete is warmer than the framing above it. In the cool evening of a warm day, for instance, the massive concrete will cool more slowly than the wooden sill or straw walls of the building. If these are in direct contact with the foundation, vapor can then condense out of the concrete onto the cooler wood or straw. Similarly, it is easy to imagine periods when the concrete is colder than the air surrounding it. This happens frequently in spring, summer, and fall, at times of the day when the concrete wall has yet to be warmed by the sun. At such times vapor in the air can condense on the concrete. It is safe to assume that, under these circumstances, any untreated wood or straw in contact with concrete is susceptible to moisture damage.

For all of the above reasons, designers of bale buildings should follow the lead of conventional construction and isolate any biodegradable wall materials from direct contact with concrete foundations. If the bales are to sit on a framed floor, they are already held away from the concrete; details between foundation and framing should follow conventional construction practices. Where a wall rests on a slab, it is crucial that some separation be created. Rigid foam or Roxul boards isolate biodegradable materials extremely well—they also insulate and elevate, forming the toe-up that is so crucial in keeping the bales dry during construction.

Water During the Construction Process

Straw bale builders commonly assume that the top and bottom of a bale wall (including window sills) absolutely must be protected from rainwater during construction. The top is usually protected by a roof or tarps, the bottom by a toe-up that raises the bales off of the floor on which water might puddle (see chapter 5, "Foundations," for more details on toe-ups). If a driving

A sill of rot-resistant black locust separates the bottom plate of the stud wall from the foundation.

rain is expected it is equally important to protect the sides of the walls, because the pressure drop across a windward wall will draw water into the bales. (See "Siding," in chapter 9 for more on pressure drop.) Also, if a significant amount of water contacts the surface of an unplastered bale wall, it may be drawn toward the center by capillary action, both through the straws themselves and through the gaps between the straws. (Have you ever noticed how little effort it takes to draw water up a drinking straw? They didn't call them "straws" for nothing!)

In most cases, surface wetting of an inch or two into the bale will dry quickly in good weather. A bale that is wet to its core, on the other hand, will take so long to dry out that biodegradation may begin. The wetter and colder the climate, the more this becomes a problem. The difference is between a drying process that is carried out primarily by air and a process that is primarily diffusion. Air passes readily into the first inch or two of an unplastered bale, so it is no surprise that a few days of warm, dry weather can remove water from that area. The core of a bale is a different story. It dries primarily by vapor diffusion through the straw, from the damp center to the dry surfaces, where it is picked up and carried away by dry air. This is a much slower process.

The temperature and relative humidity of the air have fairly obvious effects on these processes. The drier and warmer the air, the more moisture it can hold and carry away from the bale surface. Similarly, the difference in vapor pressure driving diffusion from the core of the bale to outside air is greater when the outside air is dry. Toe-ups, therefore, are doubly crucial. Not only is the un-toed bale more likely to find itself sitting in a puddle, thirstily sucking water by capillary action but the bottom and center of this bale can only dry by vapor diffusion toward the surfaces. Soaking up a puddle takes minutes, while drying a soaked bale takes weeks.

Exterior Moisture Sources

Of all the potential sources of moisture, precipitation poses the greatest threat to cold-climate straw bale houses. The bales, therefore, must be protected from rain, and, to some degree, from melting snow. Additionally, as mentioned above, the choice of exterior finish is limited by the need to be kept at least as vapor permeable as that employed on the interior, so that any vapor that makes its way into the walls from the inside has the opportunity to dry to the outside.

> Of all the potential sources of moisture, precipitation poses the greatest threat to cold-climate straw bale houses.

Driving rain and piled snow can cause problems with any building; it follows that current best practices from conventional structures should be applied to bale buildings. It is also becoming increasingly clear that bales, or at least plastered bales, are not appropriate for every site and situation. The careful designer will think obsessively about potential sources of water entry and design details to prevent such entry.

In theory, the matter is simple: First, reduce the amount of rain and snow that strike wall surfaces. Second, employ construction details and strategies that prevent deposited precipitation from wetting the bales. The need to reduce exposure to rain and snow should be obvious, but the basic methods are often ignored. The built-in matters include siting, roof overhangs and gutters, elevation from the ground, and drip-sills and flashing details. Maintenance, however, is at least as important as any of these factors.

Maintenance

One of the unfortunate repercussions of postmodern life is that most people, liberated by machines and telecommunications, are now so busy trying to keep up with their ever increasing responsibilities that they have little time for (or interest in) the simple matters of food and shelter that once helped bond their predecessors to the places where they lived. This pattern is noticeable in many facets of our lives—where we get our food, the distances between our work and our homes—but it really comes to bear on straw bale construction in the matter of building maintenance. Once a source of pride and a sensible part of the annual cycle of life, people now look on maintenance as drudgery—a consumer of valuable time, an obstacle in the way of getting on to more important and profitable activities. Maybe we should apologize for using the word in public; our culture has so little time or respect for maintenance that it has become one of the dirtiest words in the construction lexicon.

This has had serious implications for our choice of building materials, of course. The most obvious example is the spread of PVC (vinyl) siding. This material does one thing superbly well: It sheds weather for years with no need of maintenance. It's also cheap, and looks it. It cannot be painted successfully, which means that when bored suburbanites decide to change the color of their house, they have it all torn off and tossed into a dumpster, and a fresh batch applied. This is absurd and wasteful, but only a minor affront compared to the fact that the stuff was ever put on the market in the first place. PVC is stable in solid form, but in gaseous and liquid form it is one of the most toxic materials we produce. It is tremendously dangerous to the factory workers who make it, and to the environment surrounding the factories. It is one of the great banes of fire-fighters. From an ecological perspective, PVC should not even be produced. By the narrow logic of today's construction industry, however, it is considered (by anyone who can tolerate the fact that it looks like plastic) to be a flawless material. It is applied to thousands of new homes and retrofits every day.

Now, it is possible to apply PVC siding over a straw bale house. It is possible, in fact, to apply any kind of siding on straw bales, and some kind other than vinyl may be a good idea for wooded or very exposed sites, or for homeowners who really cannot abide the idea of annual maintenance. For the majority whose image of a bale house includes a plaster finish, however, there is simply no way out of a maintenance routine. This is because all plasters crack. Try as we might to build perfectly sound buildings atop perfectly stable substrates, some shifting and settling always goes on during the life of a building. Add to this the abusive actions of wind loads and freeze/thaw cycles, and you come to the inevitable conclusion that no masonry finish can be trusted to remain waterproof forever.

In mainstream stucco construction, where relatively brittle cementitious products are the norm, walls are built with a drainage layer of asphalt felt between stucco and substrate. This tar paper "drainage plane" catches any water that makes its way through the plaster, diverting it down and away from the plywood or OSB (oriented strand board) sheathing. The assumption here is that the stucco will crack; the felt acts as insurance against imperfect materials, poor workmanship, and lack of maintenance.

> A person who is unwilling to accept yearly maintenance as part of the long-term package simply has no business considering a plastered straw bale house.

In bale construction, the situation is very different. Installation of a felt drainage plane is impractical for reasons of both mechanics and moisture. There is, first of all, no civilized way to attach tar paper to a bale wall, and no way to attach the then necessary stucco netting over it, without poking the paper full of holes. The long-term problem with this method, however, is that it radically reduces the drying potential of the wall, by removing the possibility of water passing in the liquid state from the straw to the plaster, and then on to the outside. Because the felt works equally well at stopping water coming from either side, any moisture in the straw must change into the vapor state in order to pass through the tar paper, then to the stucco, then to the outside. (See chapter 10, "Cement Stucco," for more details.)

Without a drainage plane, the exterior plaster must be counted on to protect the bales beneath from damage. This is the great question for bale construction in wet climates: Is the exterior finish up to this task? Historical evidence from around the world indicates that the answer should be yes—but *only if the plaster is maintained* to a degree that reflects the weather exposure of a given wall. The maintenance routine varies with site and material choice, but generally involves a day or two each spring, applying limewash or patching cracks. A person who is unwilling to accept yearly maintenance as part of the long-term package simply has no business considering a plastered straw bale house. We will discuss the maintenance requirements of each plaster option in much greater detail in chapter 9, "Selecting Finishes."

Designed in response to local landforms and vegetation, a building positioned for protection from weather will also look like it belongs on its site. Hermitage at Santa Sabina Monastery, San Rafael, California, and Hesla/Bennett home, Wiscoy Valley, Minnesota.

SITING

The level of maintenance required depends on the site, and on the degree to which the building is designed in response to the site. This begins with geographic region; drier and warmer climates are obviously easier on buildings, wetter and colder climates more harsh. Local site conditions become quite crucial for plastered bale buildings in areas where precipitation averages above 20 inches per year. On the ideal site, the building will be protected from the predominant weather by some combination of landforms and vegetation. This is not always as easy as it sounds. Where Paul lives, for instance, most of the winter weather comes from the northwest, while spring storms blow up from the south. Some mean winter storms crash in off the Atlantic Ocean, however, and the hilly landscape can play havoc with any of these patterns, to the point where they can never be completely trusted.

One of the first questions in designing a bale house, then, is about the site. How well do you really know it? Does it conform to regional weather patterns, or does it have a local logic of its own? Can the house be tucked in for shelter among trees and land formations, or must it be exposed to the full force of nature? The answers to these questions will have a profound effect on your choice of exterior finishes, and on the amount of maintenance they will require. They affect what you choose to do to the site, in order to buffer the house, and, in an intelligent design, they affect the placement of overhangs, porches, firewood sheds, and so forth. These issues, in turn, influence your options for interior finishes, and, obviously, how the building will look. If the owner is averse to maintenance, it may even turn out that a plastered bale building is simply not appropriate for a given site. Wood or manufactured siding might be a better choice; or bales might not be appropriate, at all.

ROOF OVERHANGS AND GUTTERS

Roof overhangs on a plastered bale building should be at least two feet wide in wet climates. Three-foot overhangs (or continuous porches) are better yet, especially on a two-story building. Eighteen inches should suffice in dry climates. Ideally, the rainwater should be run into gutters and then away from the foundation, either through a pipe to daylight, or through extended downspouts. Unfortunately, gutters are

Intersecting roofs can concentrate water onto a bale wall; they should be flashed so as to direct the water away from the wall surface.

usually impractical on metal-roofed buildings—sliding snow will often take the gutters along with it. There is no reason not to incorporate them on roofs of all other types, however. In good-quality new construction, the ice dams that are the bane of gutters on older buildings simply should not be a problem (see the "Ice Dams" sidebar earlier in this chapter).

In situations where gutters are not appropriate, Michel has had good luck placing a 2-foot-wide band of small, round stones around the perimeter of a house. When rain hits these stones, the jumble of convex curves breaks the droplets into a fine mist, dispersing it such that only a small percentage splashes back onto the wall, and that in a much less concentrated (and therefore less damaging) form than the typical splashback droplets. The stone bed should be tied into the foundation drain system.

Michel has found an even simpler solution to the problem of snow piling up against walls: He has noticed that in most cases, it turns out not to be a problem at all. Snow does accumulate against the wall during the early part of the winter, but because all walls (even those made of

A drainage board at the dripline prevents water from running or splashing back against the wall. Dadell/Espy house, Guilford, Vermont.

bales) allow some heat to pass through, a narrow channel of air soon forms between the snowbank and the wall, clear down to the ground! (Paul was amazed when he began to actually look at these snow piles, and realized that Michel was exactly right.) As the pile of snow grows higher, the air channel grows higher as well, so that, come spring thaw, the meltwater is really not in contact with the wall. Good foundation drains are obviously crucial with this system as well.

ELEVATION FROM THE GROUND

Given a good set of details for dealing with rainwater, the typical code minimum for biodegradable materials—8 inches above finished grade—should be sufficient for a bale wall. If the site is particularly wet, or if rainwater can be expected to splash back against the wall, then an elevation of two feet or more might be appropriate. Whenever the design will allow it, extra distance between the bales and the ground will serve as health insurance for your bale walls.

DRIPSILLS AND FLASHING DETAILS

One of the main ways to keep the weather out of bale houses is to copy how it was done in the old days, before modern sheet, roll, and caulking materials introduced the option of sloppy workmanship. Have you ever seen an old house in a wet climate without protruding sills below the windows? Dripsills carry the water that sheets off the windows out and away from the building, where it belongs. These sills can be made of wood, or stone, or poured concrete. It is also a good idea to push the window right to the outside edge of the wall. An exterior sill of straw and plaster, even if covered by a dripsill, is a vulnerable point; omitting it greatly reduces the likelihood of water working its way in, over time.

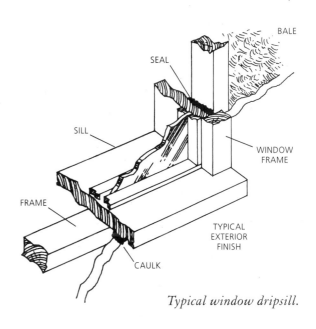

Typical window dripsill.

A wooden dripsill carries water out away from the building, where it belongs. Shirley White and Rosie Heidkamp's studio, Wendell, Massachusetts.

Todd Osman's poured concrete sill is another handsome and durable option. Hesla/Bennet home, Wiscoy Valley, Minnesota.

A stone sill can also work well. Shaw home, Charlotte, Vermont.

Flashing, of course, is as crucial in a bale building as in any other building. Unless the window is right up under the eaves, the flashing above it must be detailed very carefully. Plaster (typically reinforced by some sort of lath) should be run down into this flashing, to create a continuous water-shedding layer. To whatever degree it is possible in a system that does not employ a felt drainage plane, typical stucco details should apply.

Though our long-term experience with straw bale walls in cold (and especially cold and wet) climates is quite limited, it seems that by carefully thinking through the issues of heat loss, air quality, and moisture control we should be able to detail our new bale buildings well enough that, in exchange for some loving maintenance, they will repay dividends of comfort to generations of our heirs.

CHAPTER 3

PLANS, PERMITS, and PROJECT MANAGEMENT

WHILE IT MAY BE VERY EASY FOR YOU to understand the basics of a straw bale project, chances are that, unless you're a building professional or an experienced owner-builder, putting together the many details of design and construction in a workable and efficient way will turn out to be a real pain in the neck. This is normal, considering that lots of new concepts are involved. It might be that good examples from which to take direction have not yet crossed your path, or you might just be feeling the weight of taking as much as possible onto your own shoulders. In either case, you might want to have a look at a few helpful guidelines before you get so far into the project that you need to start thinking about how to repair mistakes.

Establish Priorities

No matter what type or size of building you have planned, some aspects of your project will become so all-consuming that they will threaten to overwhelm those big-picture factors that seemed essential in the beginning. The best way to avoid making poor choices in pressure situations is by establishing a set of priorities that you can refer to during any decision-making process. When many different options are available for the same situation, these guidelines will allow you to evaluate your choices by giving them scores on a comparable scale of values. For instance, if ecological concerns are your top priority, put them at number 1 on the scale. By following such a framework, you build in the opportunity to stop and rest and make an appropriate evaluation, rather than giving up your priorities to a decision rushed by the course of action.

Budget is often the most imposing factor in the major decisions and, because it is a purely quantitative guideline, it can easily overwhelm the more subjective factors. Since your choice for a straw bale house was probably motivated by its performance and its aesthetic qualities, you should carefully detail these in the list; otherwise they may be totally forgotten in favor of other factors that, in the long run, may turn out to feel less compelling than they did during the rush of construction.

If, like many in the early bale revival, you were attracted by the idea of a bale house as a cheap alternative, you should know that for this to be at all possible, many other factors need to be planned carefully. Some savings will appear when you compare the cost of superinsulating a house with bales rather than with conventional materials (for the same R-value); but the com-

parison doesn't stand when you consider all of the costs involved with completing a project. If your house is going to be entirely contractor-built, chances are that it will be, at the best, cost-competitive with a standard house. As in conventional construction, any really substantial savings will have to come from labor savings, by building as much as possible yourself; and on fancy equipment costs, such as in kitchens and bathrooms, where big money can be spent very easily. The finishes of the house can also make the total cost jump sky high! (Read the "Straw Bale Reality Check" section in chapter 1 again.)

Consider Professional Advice

Don't underestimate the invaluable contribution that a professional can bring to even the smallest and simplest of projects. This can be particularly true for a bale project, even if you are an experienced owner-builder. Many people believe that they cannot afford to pay professional wages when their budget is very limited, but people on a tight budget are often the ones who will get the most benefit from advice that is grounded in experience and practical knowledge. Design and construction processes hide lots of subtle intricacies that people inexperienced with a given technique cannot even guess at, until an unwelcome surprise bounces in from nowhere.

Feeling overwhelmed sometimes is normal.

Few design or construction professionals today are thoroughly integrated into the world of straw bale techniques, but any building professional should at least know the basics of construction, and have some and maybe lots of experience in design and project management. They should, at the worst, be able to help you prevent major mistakes. Whether familiar or not with the bale world, a design professional has at least one important quality for which he or she is trained: the capacity to create a design that will suit your own and very personal needs. If this person only helps to properly size your dreamed-of house, he will justify his participation. When budgets are limited, which is unfortunately always the case to some extent, the hardest thing for untrained people to achieve is the design of spaces that not only fit their needs properly, but also keep them in a feasible price range. A design professional should be able to keep you out of the horrendous trap of the 3,500-square-foot fantasy house built inside the limits of an 800-square-foot budget.

Good planning is the best way to prevent mistakes. Detailed plans and construction documents are the only solid basis on which to negotiate contracts and ensure a successful construction process. Even if you're an owner-builder, world champion of improvisation, you will need plans to get the building permit, bank loans, insurance, and so forth. Even for you, planning ahead will be very useful in making equipment, tools, and materials available on-site at the time when they are needed, and that will certainly be more than helpful for the friends coming to give a hand. And how will you keep the contractors fully informed of all the peculiarities of the project without having a good set of plans on hand?

Plan ahead. Here, plastic sheeting has been set up to protect the straw from rain.

Beware of Newborn Straw Bale "Experts"

Though we are strong believers in the usefulness of professional advice, we must also recommend that you proceed cautiously in your appraisal of any self-proclaimed "straw bale construction expert." While there are people out there who have earned some real experience with and feeling for the technique, there are nowhere near enough of them to fill the current demand. As is always the case, two types of persons have flowed in to fill this void. The first is the well-intentioned weekend expert. These people can be very helpful; the danger is that the shallowness of their experience can seriously limit the quality of their advice. They should be treated with gratitude and caution. More dangerous (and thankfully, rarer) is the shady character who latches on to the idea of bales as a marketing tool. These people were the bane of the solar hot water industry during the Carter tax-credit years; they form a consistent portion of the mainstream construction industry,

Who's that masked man? Beware of newborn experts.

and they are likely to cause problems for every new technology that comes along. Obviously, such operators are not to be trusted to do anything other than what is most expedient, so that they may line their pockets with your money.

So, how do you avoid getting burned by bad advice, from either of these quarters? We offer the Four Step Plan for the Preservation of the Sanity and Checkbooks of New Bale Builders. First, plan ahead. Second, find someone who doesn't act like they know everything. Third, beware of one-size-fits-all "systems." Fourth, check references.

Planning ahead is crucial because it allows you the time and mental clarity to take any advice you might receive with a grain of salt. It also leaves time to search out corroborating evidence. Especially if you are receiving free counsel from someone whose experience is only a bit greater than yours, you will want to bounce this advice off other people. If you plan to work with an "expert" through your whole process, planning ahead gives you time to evaluate their experience and instincts before you get into the thick of construction, when there will be pressure to make decisions more quickly.

You must also seek out someone who is willing to admit what they don't know, and to proceed logically, based on what they do know, in trying to figure the rest out. Straw bale construction is a young enough discipline that nobody (emphatically including these authors) has dealt with every imaginable situation. Typically, the most experienced people are the most willing to admit their weak points, while those with less experience try to cover their shortcomings by assuming an air of expert professionalism. The problem with this posturing is that nobody can think clearly or carefully when their primary concern is to quickly state something that sounds authoritative, so they can justify their fee.

Watch out for anyone who is pushing a single "straw bale system." Good systems exist out there, to be sure, but not a single one of them fits all situations. Good design begins with the needs of the occupant, proceeds at a schematic level to the physical attributes of the building, and then settles on the technical matters of an appropriate construction system. Anyone who pushes the idea that one system can suit all needs clearly has no depth of experience.

Most important of all, before you pay anyone for anything beyond preliminary advice on straw bale construction, ask for three references, and call all of them. This action is in no way confrontational—anyone who does good work should be proud to have you call on their past clients. You will learn a lot just by the person's response to your reference request. Odds are, if they can supply references the references will check out, but you must call them to be sure. Checking references also serves an invaluable secondary function: It is your opportunity to learn in advance the fine points of how to work most effectively with your chosen consultant. Don't be afraid to ask (politely) what you need to look out for in working with Mr. or Ms. X. Maybe you will learn that they have good ideas, but don't know how to express them clearly, or that they consistently underestimate how much things will cost, or how much time they will take. Everyone has these honest human failings; the earlier you can learn about them, the sooner you can begin to compensate for them. Any self-

proclaimed expert who cannot provide good references, on the other hand, needs to find more experience or another line of work. Sales might be an appropriate field.

Codes and Permits

Unlike the design and the planning work, which can be fun and exciting, getting your building permit for a straw bale house may not be a party unless you know exactly how to do it. Professionals are usually familiar with the requirements of the respective codes and regulations that prevail in the municipalities where they work. They can help you coordinate the details needed for the application.

If no experienced consultant is available, you should first get a written copy of the applicable local regulations. Then study their specific re-

Many successful projects involve good collaboration between owner-builders and contractors. Here, the pros are pouring a top slab over insulating bales and the radiant heating tubes.

quirements *before* starting any application process. Get to know the requirements and limitations and prepare yourself ahead of time.

It is very easy to confuse everybody, including the building inspector, by just stating flat out that you're building a straw bale house. Chances are that this guy will start telling you the three little pigs story, which will put you in the uncomfortable position of having to smile and act as if you haven't heard this dozens of times before. You have to be much more descriptive about your project, and you should not hesitate to emphasize its conventional aspects. You'll get through the process faster and with better understanding if you submit a complete set of detailed plans with all other documents necessary to prove that your project complies with the regulations and code requirements.

Building permits have been issued for all kinds of bale buildings, even in places where regulations

---

Keep it Small, Keep it Simple

Whether or not you can afford to work with a professional, your design can at least rely on common sense and simplicity, rather than the illogical greed for space that characterizes so many new houses. Unless you are quite well off and have unusually modest needs, some conflict between what you want in a house and what your budget can reasonably support is inevitable. What you must remember is that, while the goal is to get the best possible house for the amount of money available, the process does not need to involve putting yourself through an emotional wringer, to squeeze things down to the last dollar. It is advisable, for instance, to work through the design phase with a budget of 5 to 10 percent less than the total available; this leaves breathing room for cost overruns and fun changes during the construction process. And if you end up with 1 percent left at the end (this never happens) you can throw a great party!

Similarly, the "best possible house for the available money" almost never means "the largest house for the available money." A steel industrial building will probably always be the largest space available for any given amount of money, but would you want to live in one of those? A house that is more or less enjoyable to build and consistently enjoyable to live in will strike a balance between size and character, between quantity and *quality* of space. (This is less true in truly low-budget situations, though these houses, even though they cannot afford delicate amenities, will tend to have a handmade character built in.)

The starting point of a good design process, then, is to simplify your needs. If you begin with the intention of building small and simple, you are very restrictive. Public buildings, which are normally under more severe controls, have been permitted; houses can be found nowadays in major cities. In some jurisdictions, building codes have been amended to include straw bale techniques. Documents and videos on fire resistance and moisture tests, and on structural and insulative capacities of straw bale structures, are available to ease the process of dealing with most authorities. Provide them with as much information as is needed but don't confuse them by overemphasizing the straw bale aspects. Experience has taught us that in most jurisdictions, once the basic safety requirements are fulfilled, the presence of straw in the walls ceases to be a major issue.

In some cases, the easiest route to a permit is to find a registered engineer or architect to work with you on your plans. If a sympathetic professional can be found, their stamp on the drawings removes the onus of responsibility from the

Bales retrofitted around the stud frame of a small cabin. Heaslip house, Saxtons River, Vermont.

can add amenities as the budget firms up, and you find out what you really have to spend. That process prevents you from wasting money on wants disguised as needs and prevents stretching the budget thin on unnecessary space; this keeps the quality of the space high, and saves on heating and maintenance costs.

If, for any reason, you still think you deserve a 3,500-square-foot dream house, give yourself a chance by planning it as a multiphase project that is flexible enough for adjustments in the course of action. Build a small building first, ahead of time, if possible, or in the earliest phase of the project, to get your own hands-on training. In the old days, this would have been the kitchen and bathroom, maybe with a bedroom located above. This will serve as a profitable apprenticeship for you and the other workers. If this is part of a pay-as-you-go schedule, you'll have the option of building in total accordance with your capacities, both physical and financial. You will also be more likely to reward yourself and crew with an enlightening experience while still having fun by keeping in control of the project.

local building department. This can be a practical course in tightly regulated jurisdictions, especially if yours is among the first bale projects in your area.

Basics on Code Issues

For most people, codes seem like a collection of incomprehensible, restrictive rules that pave the road to the impersonal buildings typical of most modern suburbs. In fact, the opposite is the case. Suburbs look the way they do precisely because codes and regulations are not all that restrictive. Codes prescribe performance standards (and sometimes size) for buildings and materials; they become somewhat restrictive for safety purposes in densely built environments, but they seldom put limitations on good taste and harmony. The confusion and sameness derives instead from a general lack of exploration within the scope of the possibilities inherent in the code.

FINDING THE KEY: USING THE ALTERNATIVE MATERIALS SECTION IN YOUR CODE

The great majority of readers of this book are likely to live in industrialized countries, where most of the inhabitable environment is regulated by very similar building codes. These generally do not directly address the use of straw bales and related techniques. Many people think that this absence means they are simply not permitted. This is only half true. In this sense, load-bearing and non-load-bearing structures differ greatly.

In the early projects of the 1980s and 1990s, which were mostly Nebraska-style structures, building permits were hard to get mainly because the structural capacities of the bale-and-plaster wall system were not scientifically known, and thus were not generally considered to be reliable

Consider the advice of those with more experience. Here, the exterior straw surface has been carefully prepared to provide uniform support for plaster.

by authorities. To change that attitude, profoundly dedicated pioneers started to work with local authorities. With a lot of time and patience, some were successful in modifying their local regulations to include prescriptive standards for the use of straw bales as a structural material. Thanks to the hard work of Matts Myhrman and David Eisenberg in Tucson, Arizona, and many others who followed their lead, straw bale walls are now in the codes in many jurisdictions in the western United States. The existence of these codes has also eased the bale permitting process in other locations where code modifications have not yet been made. Not surprisingly, it is easier for a building official to follow the lead of someone in another jurisdiction than to be the first to go out on a limb in support of a technique whose capacities are not yet completely understood.

In the course of all this negotiation and research, it also became clear that it is much easier to get permits for non-load-bearing structures.

This is especially the case with codes that have a section on alternative materials. When the bales are acting only as insulation and a substrate for the plaster, they can often be permitted through such sections, so long as it can be proved that they are not a fire hazard.

Codes in Canada

Building codes in Canada are of provincial and municipal jurisdiction. One general reference code, the National Building Code of Canada 1995, can get legal enforcement in any province and municipality as long as these jurisdictions adopt it. In some provinces, municipalities have the choice of endorsing the code as a whole, or using only some of its sections to create their own adapted one. In some cases, such as in major cities where fire risks are an important issue, some specific regulations are added to the original code. This generally makes it more restrictive.

The NBC's philosophy is explained by this description in the National Research Council's catalog:

"La Maison de Ville," built to code in the center of Montreal.

Widely referred to as the "bible" of the construction industry, the National Building Code of Canada (NBC) is designed to ensure that buildings are structurally sound, safe from fire, free of health hazards, and accessible. The code, prepared by the Canadian Commission on Building and Fire Codes, is used as a model for virtually all regulations in Canada and pertains whether you are constructing a building, or renovating or altering it.

Health and safety are the Code's primary objectives, and it strives to achieve these objectives by establishing model standards. Divided into nine parts and organized using a convenient decimal numbering system, the NBC defines words, terms and phrases, and spells out minimum requirements for fire protection; structural design; environmental separation, heating, ventilating and air-conditioning (HVAC); plumbing; construction site safety; and housing and small building construction.

A number of detailed appendices provide background information that will help you better understand and apply the Code. The NBC complements the National Fire Code of Canada (NFC), and both must be considered when you are constructing, renovating or maintaining buildings.

Local authorities may decide to apply the universal building code to all buildings in a wide diversity of climates, such as humid, mixed heating/cooling maritime areas (Vancouver), or very cold, dry places (Calgary). Such a code has to be flexible enough to provide room for appropriate building standards in very different environments. Unfortunately, there is a lot of misunderstanding and therefore misconception in the construction business regarding how to apply the code locally.

For bale builders, the same rule applies: You have to find out what section of the code addresses your type of project in order to get it permitted.

Section 2.5 on Equivalents is the part of the code that allows for the possibility of permitting a straw bale structure. In only five short paragraphs of description, you can find out exactly what regulations apply and can be used to prove the reliability of your project. It addresses the basic elements of a building—materials and structure (frame)—and their performance. Once you have proven the applicability of each material or technique used and not already described in the other sections of the code, your permit should be issued.

SECTION 2.5 OF CANADA'S NATIONAL BUILDING CODE[1]

2.5.1. General

2.5.1.1. Alternate Materials, Appliances, Systems and Equipment Permitted

1) The provisions of this Code are not intended to limit the appropriate use of materials, appliances, systems, equipment, methods of design or construction procedures not specifically designed herein.

2.5.1.2. Evidence of Equivalent Performance

1) Any person desirous of providing an equivalent to satisfy one or more of the requirements of this Code shall submit sufficient evidence to demonstrate that the proposed equivalent will provide the level of performance required by the Code.

2.5.1.3. Equivalence Demonstrated by Past Performance, Test or Evaluation

1) Materials, appliances, systems, equipment, methods of design and construction procedures not specifically described herein, or which may vary from the specific requirements in this Code, are permitted to be used if it can be shown that these alternatives are suitable on the basis of past performance, tests or evaluations.

2.5.2. Structural Equivalents

2.5.2.1. Structural Equivalents

1) Provided the design is carried out by a person especially qualified in the specific methods applied and provided it demonstrates a level of safety and performance in accordance with the requirements of Part 4, *buildings* and their structural components falling within the scope of Part 4 which are not amenable to analysis using a generally established theory may be designed by

    a) evaluation of a full-scale structure or prototype by a loading test, or
    b) studies of model analogs.

2.5.3. Equivalent Test Standards

2.5.3.1. Acceptance

1) The results of tests based on test standards other than as described in this Code are permitted to be used provided such alternative test standards will provide comparable results.

1. NBC 1990 & 1995. Canada.

Section 9 of the code, which specifically addresses houses and small buildings, will tell you exactly what other limitations are applicable to your project, if any.

Codes in the U.S.[2]

In some parts of the United States, standards for straw bale construction are now included in the building codes. As of this writing, Tucson and Pima County, Arizona, the state of Nevada, the city of Austin, Texas, and several counties in California have adopted codes for Nebraska-style construction, which also apply to bale infill. The New Mexico state code includes a section on infill construction. As time goes by, and maybe by the time you are reading this book, bales will be adopted into the code in many more jurisdictions.

To date, however, bale advocates in cold-climate regions have been slower than their southern counterparts in working for the adoption of prescriptive code standards for bale construction. There are three main reasons for this slower pace. The first is time—the bale revival began in the hot, dry country of the American Southwest, and is really still spreading from there. The second reason is personality—some of the early proponents of bale construction are the sorts of people who made the codes their problem to deal with, head on, rather than finding ways to work within the existing framework. The third factor, however, is the most important—in cold climates, we tend to construct an independent structure to bear roof loads, and such buildings are not all that hard to permit, using existing code language.

2. Credit for much of this material goes to David Eisenberg, of the Development Center for Appropriate Technology, whose Web site is listed in the Resources section. For more in-depth coverage, see his working paper, "Straw Bale Construction and the Building Codes."

The key to all of this is that codes in the United States are truly not intended to prevent the use of any material, but only to protect health and safety, and to guarantee ancillary standards, such as energy use. According to the preface to the CABO (Council of American Building Officials) *One and Two Family Dwelling Code:*

All of the nationally recognized model codes upon which this code is based are comprehensive and flexible and make provision for the use of all safe materials and methods of construction. Consequently, there are construction materials and practices other than listed in this code which are adequate for the purposes intended. These other methods represent either seldom-used systems or performance-type systems which require individual consideration by the professional architect or engineer based on either test data or engineering analysis and are therefore not included herein.

Now, this CABO code is not actually the code that will govern your jurisdiction. Codes in the United States are typically written on the state, county, or city level. These codes take most of their language from one of three larger code organizations: Building Officials and Code Administrators International, Inc. (BOCA) in the Northeast, the Southern Building Code Congress International (SBCCI) in the South, and the International Conference of Building Officials (ICBO) in the West. CABO is an organization made up of representatives of these three organizations, and the CABO code is a compilation of these codes. The above excerpt does, therefore, reflect the intention of all the major code bodies in the United States. Whether or not some language to this affect appears in your local code (and it is

First and foremost, building officials are people, with a job to do. As in any group of people, some are grumpy or petty, some are lively and interested in new or unusual things, and the majority are simply trying to get their job done, so they can get home in time to have supper with their families. Thus, you might be met with a range of possible responses when you walk into the inspector's office with your sheaf of plans calling for straw bale walls. How you are received matters far less than how you act. You must remember that enforcing codes is a useful job and also not an easy job; there are some very obnoxious morons in the construction industry, and building inspectors take flak from them all the time. You must separate yourself from these people; your actions and attitude must make clear that you are not a jerk, that you are not trying to build an unsafe house, and that you respect the official's role in the process and are willing to supply them with the information necessary to see your plans through. Humility and competence are the required qualities, here.

worth looking for), this attitude should be what guides your local officials.

It should come as no surprise, then, that securing permits for bale walls has been simpler when they are acting in a nonstructural capacity. Existing tests prove that they will not burn and that they meet energy codes. Proving that they will not rot might be somewhat more difficult, except for the fact that code officials tend not to ask about this. It seems that they are quite accustomed to wood construction, which is also rather decay-prone. On the other hand, if the bales and plaster are to support the roof it must be proven that they can handle both live and dead loads. In the jurisdictions where bales have actually been adopted into the codes as a structural material, this was typically the result of some significant (even if homemade) test procedures.

In some areas, it will be possible to walk into your local code office with a set of plans for a bale building, and walk out with a permit. This will usually mean that someone has come before you, and done a very good job of informing the local building officials. More likely, you will be the person doing this job, and you had better be willing to handle the task cheerfully and thoroughly. There is also a good possibility that your local or state officials will take the language of the above passage quite literally, and "... require individual consideration by the professional architect or engineer based on either test data or engineering analysis." Some bale enthusiasts chafe at the notion that the simplest (and sometimes the only) route to a permit can come through the stamp of a licensed professional. In reality, this is quite a reasonable stance for a code department to take; in effect they are saying that while they don't want to take responsibility for the safety of this new technique (there are liability issues, unfortunately), they don't want to prevent you from using it, either. Until bale construction develops a track record across many different climatic regions, and until champions emerge to push for amendments to the codes in the corresponding political jurisdictions, we must work with what we have available.

Maybe you will be the one to bring a willing local architect up to speed on straw bale details, or maybe you will initiate the process of writing a straw bale code for your state.

Cost Control and Project Management

As interest booms in straw bale construction, the questions of cost and project management are becoming increasingly important.

You at least need to figure out which aspects of the cost of a straw bale project are most subject to your control. Like in any conventional building, total costs here are twofold: materials and labor. While it is feasible to make accurate cost appraisals of materials and therefore to plan and/or make necessary adjustments, making accurate labor estimates is more challenging.

When planning the numerous tasks that make up a project, there are two major categories to consider: the rough and finishing work. Because the pros and cons of building load-bearing or non-load-bearing structures are discussed in other chapters, we will simply reiterate here that in both types of bale construction the rough work, by which we mean raising the basic structure and putting on a roof, is relatively easy to estimate and control. But needless to say, in a bale project the finishing work, which is mostly unconventional, will use up most of the money, creating the biggest pains in the neck, unless control measures have been planned.

While there are possible savings in doing the rough work yourself instead of paying a professional contractor, if you can afford to spare only a limited length of your own time to work on the project, you should definitely invest this time entirely in the finishing phase, where the big money goes. Carefully allocating the high-cost and low-cost jobs between owner and contractor will eventually help balance your time and money budgets.

Work Organization and Supervision

If you have been involved in construction processes before, you are familiar with the intricacies of dealing with professionals—including architects, designers, engineers, and contractors—and

An organized building site is safer and more likely to stay on schedule and on budget.

with the legal relationships that link these parties. Even though the following advice is mainly intended for owner-builders, certain cautions may also be useful to professionals who have never before worked on a straw bale project.

Because labor costs may amount to as much as 50 percent of the total cost in a standard house—or much more for an unconventional project, substantial savings are possible if the purchased labor is kept to a minimum. Professional and trade workers deserve the wages they ask for when they work in their field of experience, but when learning new techniques and possibly doing experimental or improvised work. They may be willing to negotiate lower fees to gain experience, so that they will be able to charge full fare with future clients.

Don't Just Rely on Goodwill

Goodwill is often the worst source of misunderstanding: on the one hand, a client needs help and presumably has turned to professionals for guidance, and on the other hand, a contractor is willing to make every effort to make the project successful. But unless these teammates are accustomed to working together, and the strength of their friendship and mutual trust can overcome even serious problems, it may happen that at some point communications will fail to satisfy both parties. This will likely bring about the question of liability, with much discussion arising when it may be too late to agree even on the basic issues.

Work Agreements

Efficient communications are the key to success in any business. With clear contractual agreements based on detailed plans and specs, problems should not be any more difficult to solve in a bale project than in any conventional one. Disagreements will frequently arise when key technical information is shared only verbally. Even in the best possible atmosphere of goodwill, the expectations of the owner may depart from what the contractor has understood and the mental image he has been relying on for his work. In a bale project this is more crucial because all teammates—contractor and crew and owner—frequently lack appropriate experience and training.

Unless there is a clear template for discussion between the parties, as the work progresses, discrepancies in understanding can grow into obstacles. As time becomes an issue, progressively less of it may be devoted to communications, further undermining the success of the project.

Expecting contractors to be responsible for techniques they don't know much about puts them in a very uncomfortable position. The fairest arrangement is to agree on a very detailed description of the work, where the contractor's responsibility is linked to the execution of the work as described, while the liability for the long-term performance of the building rests with the owner. There are as yet no standards, no guarantees, no agencies that can back up liability for experimental techniques such as those we often use in our bale projects. These methods are at best perpetually evolving toward higher performance and generating a growing bank of reliable references. While testing proceeds and guidelines develop, we all know that the long-term performance of every new project remains to be seen.

A contractor is usually bound for the execution of the work as described in construction documents, but he has no liability if such documents don't exist or are too vague on the particularities of the technique, due to bad design or simple lack of information. If you can't provide reliable information, let the contractors do what they know best and try to keep the experimental work under your own supervision. Do it alone or with friends, or hire someone willing to charge less for the sake of his own apprenticeship; that person may as well be a contractor, as long as it is understood that he is also learning and only expected to do his best under the circumstances.

> Expecting contractors to be responsible for techniques they don't know much about puts them in a very uncomfortable position.

Separate Responsibilities

Responsibilities in a building project can be split three different ways. The execution of work can be undertaken by the contractor, the administrative work can be supervised by the owner, and the legal issues and general project oversight can be handled by the architect (or designer, or engineer). In some projects, administration can be the contractor's responsibility, but overall supervision of the work should never be left to the contractor's authority. The reason is simple: In the course of the work, he might find himself in the position of judging if his own work complies with the plans and is satisfactory to the owner. This is best prevented by having someone act as an arbitrator between the owner and the contractor in case of conflict. That person will be in the best position to assess such a problem, providing this arrangement has been established by both parties. Normally the project's architect, designer, or engineer or any other designated professional, fulfills the role of arbitrator.

To prevent unpleasant surprises you may be attracted by fixed-priced contracts as security against excessive costs. These can work well in a conventional, predictable project, but in a bale project, they may also encourage the contractor to take a very large markup to cover the unpredictable risks inherent in imprecisely described work. This mistake left a bitter taste for some early-era bale house owners who expected to have their project entirely contractor-built at reasonable cost. Fixed-price contracts for bale buildings are more likely to succeed when designs are simple and efficient, and the execution of the work is closely supervised. The risks involved in small-scale projects are smaller than those in large ones. Think twice before getting into an important project if you can't keep the risky work under your sole control and responsibility; otherwise you might have to become very friendly with your bank manager.

A good way of dealing with the challenge of imprecisely specified work is to hire contractors on an hourly basis. Make arrangements to work with them to learn the technique. Establish that once you have learned, for example, how to do the plastering work, you will take over. That will give you an opportunity to keep labor costs to a minimum, and it will ensure that you pick up the technique properly.

Work Management

If the entire job is not under the responsibility of a general contractor, you will act as project manager, and either your architect or yourself will supervise the quality of the work in compliance with the contract documents (plans and specs, etc.). However, depending on your competence and availability you might want to hire a project manager with adequate background to supervise and coordinate the work of the subcontractors for you. Subcontractors should be given their specific tasks, and the project manager will help to plan their work schedule and their interactions with other workers.

Foundations and roofs are usually best done by contractors because you always want these two jobs to be finished rapidly; they are easily negotiated under fixed-cost contracts and under full liability. If the supporting frame is simple, it may be possible for subcontracted carpenters to build it from detailed drawings. Frames for straw bale buildings often vary from standard techniques, however, so it's crucial that the carpenters understand how the bales will fit into the frame, and what limitations the bale module imposes. The remaining jobs—the bale work, the electrical and plumbing installations, and the finishes—can be carried out by subcontractors or by the owner and various volunteers.

The bale portion of the work always requires some special handling, experimentation, and adjustments; because this demands careful attention and concentration, it is best achieved during a separate phase of the project. Trade workers who are used to working under pressure and with an established rhythm usually don't feel comfortable when things don't move that way. If the bale work is carried out when these guys are off duty, they won't complain and will more easily concentrate on their own work. Thus, let them do their part and work your bales in when no one else is working on the premises. Weekends are ideal for bale work because they are usually the only time when you can get together fam-

> Fixed-price contracts for bale buildings are more likely to succeed when designs are simple and efficient, and the execution of the work is closely supervised.

ily and friends to lend their helping hands. Do all the basic handling with their help, such as unloading the bales from delivery trucks, carrying them inside the house, and stacking them close to their final placement in the walls. These types of tasks are boring for one or two people but become fun when done by an enthusiastic crew looking forward to a pizza party!

The next step is to organize small groups to place the bales into or around the frame. Make sure there is at least one person in each group who knows exactly what to do and how to teach the others. Here it is important to plan ahead about how to transfer the knowledge from its primary source—you, your architect, the project manager, or anyone else with the appropriate knowledge—to the bottom of the production line.

Last-Minute Changes

Change orders are a significant source of extra costs. Major changes introduced during construction always have considerable consequences for the budget and the schedule. In bale projects, changes in finishes are the most common source of these extra costs.

We all dream of the "money is no object" project where everything is possible, but unfortunately the real world works with limited budgets. It is a reality, however, that when the finishing phase comes up, either we become very excited or new options appear that we had not even considered during the planning phase, and most of the time we end up making all kinds of changes. We usually don't mind the additional costs attributable to these changes because they will make us happy for a long time. Nonetheless, the best way to prevent such eventualities is by providing a good buffer in the original budget.

Celebrate a Happy Ending

Keep in mind all along that you will organize a big party at the end to celebrate, and that all participants will be invited. This will force you to keep your relations with everyone smooth throughout the entire process, and will help you to solve problems when they occur. No frustrations will be carried along unresolved and a shared feeling of success will be the most enjoyable gift that you could dream of!

The Bourke House

MONTREAL

by Michel Bergeron

This story is not just about a straw bale house, it's about an architect's dream house for her family—an affordable, comfortable, ecological home in the city. It is also about an enthusiastic straw-baler determined to be the first to build in a major Canadian urban center—not just on the outskirts, but a mere ten minute walk from the downtown center.

I had been fantasizing about building a straw bale house in Montreal for many years. I had met Julia Bourke, a teacher in the Affordable Housing Program at McGill University who was interested in ecological housing. One day she called to ask if a straw bale house in Montreal was a realistic goal and if I'd be interested in working with her on the project. My positive answer was all she needed to start the process right away.

— THE PROJECT —

The house that Julia was living in was located on a property that ran between two streets, deep enough for subdivision into two small lots. The street behind was essentially abandoned. She was aware of the existence of a multitude of similar vacant lots in her working-class neighborhood, and she discovered that the property had originally had two distinct dwellings. Over the years, however, city regulations had changed to favor larger lots than those typical of Montreal's early settlements. With many origi-

nal buildings burnt down or demolished, particularly during the 1970s, these neighborhoods couldn't be reconstructed. Bourke's first objective, designing a sustainable home, became paired with a second one: encouraging urban renewal, or sustainability, through the construction of housing on undersized lots.

The dream house turned into a demonstration project when research funding became available through the ACT (Affordability and Choice Today) program funded by the Canadian Mortgage and Housing Corporation. The first objective was to show that small-lot housing could improve housing affordability, promote choice and quality in the urban context, and revitalize older neighborhoods with a type of housing compatible with the historic architectural fabric of the community. The second objective was to introduce straw bale construction to Canadian Cities.

The small-lot issue was not the only regulatory constraint tackled by this project. The city's regulations, amazingly, prohibited single-family homes in Bourke's neighborhood, as well as affordable, traditional design choices such as stucco facades and pitched roofs. Our design and construction team worked closely with city planners, providing historical analysis, documentation of existing conditions, identification of potential building sites, and design guidelines. The advice of the city's professional design review committee was considered, and public

Accessible and affordable: balloon-frame construction, with bales inserted between studs.

opinion was sought through neighborhood consultations. The scope of this effort underscores the necessity of collaboration among architects, housing and planning specialists, contractors, and community organizers.

— THE DESIGN —

Sustainability was weighed against affordability in the selection of systems and materials for the house. Most important to Bourke were simplicity and accessibility in the building process. It was essential to her that she and her family be able to contribute easily with their own hands; to understand and love the house not only because of its functionality and beauty, but through their participation in the process. She also wanted to show that the experience of

owner-building does not have to be relegated to the countryside.

Based on my prior experience, we decided that the most accessible, affordable building technique would be a combination of a traditional balloon frame with straw bale infill. The house is a two-and-a-half-story, 1,700-square-foot building. It features a hydronically heated, straw-bale–insulated slab-on-grade, with its top slab left exposed and waxed, with a linseed-oil sealant. The second and third floors are made of tongue-and-groove softwood boards simply treated with a natural oil finish. Joists of both floors are also exposed underneath to create a warm, spacious feeling. The roof is constructed of durable galvanized steel, or "galvalum"; the pitch is shifted off center toward the street to create a more urban facade as well as more efficient interior attic space. The roof insulation, originally planned to be straw bale, was changed at the last minute to incorporate R-50 "dense-pack" blown-in cellulose. The front, southwest-exposed, 60-degree pitch was planned to eventually support solar panels hooked to the hydronic system. The gentler pitch of the northeast section of the roof also allows better sun penetration into the backyards of both Bourke's and the neighbor's house.

The balloon-frame structure was built on a standard 10-inch-wide concrete frost wall, insulated with 4-inch rigid rockwool boards covered by cement-fiber panels finished with plaster. Notched bales were inserted in a standing position between studs spaced at 18 inches on center, and attached to them with poly strapping. The 1½-inch x 3½-inch notch along the interior edge of each bale accommodates the stud, making the exterior wall plane a fully uninterrupted straw surface. The familiar balloon frame was chosen for the same purpose of keeping the straw uninterrupted from ground to roof, avoiding the extension of floor platforms into the core of the bales. The second- and third-floor joists are therefore attached to a border joist bolted to the inside face of the studs. Windows were installed in cantilevered plywood boxes screwed to the inside studs.

Both interior and exterior plasters are made of the same 5:1 lime-cement mix. Dry oxide pigments were added to finish coats for color. Graded sands were used in decreasing sizes from base to finish of the exterior coats to reduce moisture capillarity. Chopped straw was incorporated in the base coats for additional cohesion. A narrow strip of expanded metal lath was nailed to the interior face of each stud to hold the plaster.

Another innovative ecological aspect of the house is the use of Isobord panels (see chapter 15, "Beyond the Bale") for all the cabinets, baseboards, and a few decorative wall panels. These surfaces were also simply treated with natural oil-based finishes. Milk paints were used everywhere else where color or protection was desired.

Straw bale construction sites attract curious visitors.

— THE WORK AND RESULTS —

The building permit was delayed due to ongoing municipal elections, so only the site excavation and foundations were done before winter froze hard. As soon as the temperature became mild again in April the framing was started, even though the snow had yet to melt and the ground was not thawed. There were a few unusual details to care for in the structural work: along with studs spaced at 18 inches on center, they also had to span two and a half stories in a single piece. Since you don't find 2x4s that long any more in this prefab world, two lengths had to be spliced together. For wall-raising convenience this was done after the first floor was built. A good set of temporary braces was necessary to hold the frame firmly together during construction.

After the roof was assembled, sheathed, and temporarily waterproofed with tar paper, the straw work could finally begin. A pizza party was organized for the first delivery of bales. Expected to arrive in the late afternoon, the 35-foot flatbed with 350 bales aboard finally got in at 8:30 due to a tire replacement on the highway and a lot of tango dancing with the cars parked along the narrow streets of the neighborhood.

Two workshops were held during the weekend when we poured the straw bale slab (see "The Archibio Sandwich Slab" in chapter 5), and TV and newspaper reporters and photographers assailed us, while a growing number of curious and amazed neighbors suddenly realized that something very unusual was happening. Two kindergarten classes even came along to play with this fantastic new construction material!

During the duration of the bale work we were careful to bag and store the considerable quantities of loose straw produced by the notching. In fact, we ended up packaging no less than 250 garbage bags of the loose stuff. Since mulching materials are like gold in a city, these and some 75 damaged bales were happily recycled by community gardeners.

A few modifications and adjustments were also required in the subsequent work. We had begun the bale attachment procedure by tying the bales to the frame with horizontal metal H pins made from masonry wall-reinforcement rods. These ladder-type, light-gauge wires are easily cut and rigid enough to make good staples. The whole system was too labor-intensive, however, and not always as reliable as we wanted. The pinning would have worked better if done by the same people all the time, but we had such a rotation of volunteers that it was impossible to maintain consistently rigid attachments.

After a short period of investigation we came up with the strapping solution. I bought a tensioner, a crimping tool, crimps, and a couple of rolls of poly strapping from a packaging-tools supplier. The new system made the work progress much faster. Many bales could be placed in a row without any sort of attachment, and then strapped in a bundle while others were installed in the next row, and so on, in rotation. We could adjust the rhythm to the number of people involved. It also appeared that the strapping contributed to the overall stability of the building by making every wall like one huge, rigid panel. We also successfully used the strap-

The characteristic deep window well of a straw bale house.

The Bourke family kitchen.

ping system to retie odd-shaped bales and make new ones, which made 64-inch-long bales as easy to make as 18-inch ones. We even thought for a moment that we could strap together one long bale to fill the entire height of the house and lift it into place like a giant cigar. Yet appropriate tensioning to keep the bale from rippling seemed too hard to achieve, though this idea could lead to further experimentation in the preassembly of entire sections of freestanding walls.

The other problem we had was the plaster mix. We fiddled awhile with a base mix that was always lacking cohesion. No matter what proportions of water or sand we used, the plaster would not stick well to the straw. I finally realized that the lime we were using was probably not fully hydrated and that it needed to be soaked before being mixed with the other ingredients (see chapter 11). As soon as we started to pre-soak the lime, even for just an hour, the mix became easy to work with, directly on the straw. Chopped straw was added to the first and second coats to reduce cracking. Because the weather had been a blessing and the sun was constantly shining hot, special care was needed to keep the fresh plaster continually moist to favor an appropriate cure. Other than a couple of cracks, which seem directly related to expansion of the metal lath supporting the sun-exposed plaster or to joints with wood pieces, the exterior walls are crack-free. The interior plaster didn't fare as well, displaying many superficial cracks, the causes of which are currently being investigated. Fortunately the interior walls are less vulnerable to weather and can wait for the necessary maintenance.

Sensors were installed in the slab at four locations and in the walls at five others to monitor

Voilà!

seasonal as well as long-term moisture fluctuations. Readings should help us understand the seasonal movements of moisture in both slab and walls, if any (see chapter 14 for more on this subject).

The Bourke family moved in after four intense months of work, but it was three more months before all the interior details were finished and an open house was held for the public. No less than a thousand visitors queued up during two sunny weekends in October to see for themselves the feasibility of a straw bale family dream. They probably all went home with a vivid image of the sage green straw bale house as a distinctive reminder of "green architecture" in the city.

CHAPTER 4

CHOOSING BALES

ONCE YOU HAVE DECIDED TO BUILD with bales, one of your highest priorities should be to evaluate the number, type, and size of bales that will best fit your design. The reason for this is easy to understand if you know a bit about farmers, harvesting season, storage, and commercial bale dealers. Because there is no such thing as an official, verified source of construction-quality straw bales, the great majority of projects occur within a market that is unaccustomed to producing bales for this purpose.

Before you start shopping for bales you need to establish a set of standards that you will be able to communicate to the dealer or a farmer. As most of the bales on the market vary in length and density from batch to batch, you may get a lot of useless ones delivered unless they have already been checked for compliance with your standards.

Because this is probably the first time in your life that you will talk with any degree of specificity about straw bales, and the first time you will have to shop for them, you will probably end up doing what a majority of your fellows have done before you: rely on your good luck! As an additional obstacle to your success, the farmer or dealer (though they will know a lot about straw) probably knows even less about your specific requirements than you do. So you'll have to be doubly lucky! And if your luck fails, you may be forced to reject a big delivery of prepaid useless straw bales.

You probably know the main characteristics of good-quality bales: They have to be dry, uniform in size and weight (which means uniform compactness), and tightly strung. But if you don't really know what dry means, how will you determine if the size is uniform enough? How can you tell the dealer or the farmer exactly what you are looking for?

Before considering these refinements, however, you must find a potential source of bales that will be available at the time they'll be needed. The best way of doing this is to negotiate directly with a farmer. By meeting with the farmer before the harvest, you can explain your exact specifications, and the farmer can bale to them. If the farm is nearby, you may as well check in during the first day of baling, to ensure that the quality is what you expect. Farmers who think all this concern for quality is a bit weird are not worth working with, unless you have no other choice. Usually, those farmers who are resourceful enough to have stayed in business are interested in any new market for their products, and they will be quite willing to take the bit of extra time required to meet your needs. You should be prepared to pay a premium of as much as 30 percent if your bales are packed tighter than the norm for your region—a denser bale will contain more straw, which means that a field will yield fewer bales than usual.

If you do not have the opportunity to meet with the farmer before harvest, the next best way of procuring bales is to buy them out of his barn. This still allows you to physically check the bales before purchasing them, and, ideally, to tweak

> Good-quality bales have to be dry, uniform in size and weight (which means uniform compactness), and tightly strung.

your design according to what is available. In either of these scenarios, you should give the farmer a deposit ($100 usually does it) to reserve your lot of bales. This is mostly for your own benefit—it will ensure that the bales you have seen are the ones that will show up at your site.

If you cannot deal directly with a farmer, you will probably have to rely on a commercial straw dealer. The danger with this approach is that, while you can explain your needs to the dealer, he will not be the one producing the bales, so he will, to some degree, have to take what he can get when the time comes. He might have to make a quick decision about whether a given batch is suitable; unfortunately this means that your standards will be diluted by his, and also by his economic need to get some bales and get on the road. He doesn't get paid for time spent rejecting given lots as inappropriate for construction. On the other hand, bales that are intended for shipping are usually packed quite tightly, as this allows more material to fit on a truck. This is especially the case when the dealer buys from the farmer based on weight, rather than quantity. Whether you are paying by the bale or by the ton, you are probably safer buying from a dealer who purchases by weight, because this lines up everybody's interest in packing as much material as possible into each bale and onto the truck.

Of course, you should inspect the bales when they arrive, and you should have made it abundantly clear, in advance, that you are not going to accept a shipment that does not meet your standards. If you are a designer or builder whose prospects include multiple bale projects, you

An experienced straw inspector physically checking the materials.

should go out of your way to cultivate a relationship with a suppler of quality bales. This person will become no less important to you than a good lumberyard or an experienced plaster crew.

Selecting Bales

The bales you need will have two characteristics. They must be dry (no more than 14 to 16 percent moisture content) at time of delivery. This means they will have been harvested in dry weather and will never have been exposed to rain or other sources of moisture. They must also be of the predictable size on which your design has been or is going to be based.

There are also two basic checklists to go through before buying and using the bales: first, a set of questions to ask the farmer or the dealer before visiting the site, in order to narrow down the field of potential suppliers; second, a set of simple physical tests that you can carry out on the farmer's premises and possibly repeat on your site when the bales are delivered.

Questions to Ask

We have devised a list of some standard questions to ask the farmer or bale distributor, which will help you to ascertain the suitability of the bales under discussion.

TYPE OF CEREAL

It is sometimes useful to know the type of cereal the straw is harvested from. The glassy texture of rice-straw fibers can make it even tougher than most straw on the hands, for instance, but rice is also quite durable and highly fire resistant. Barley is known to resist moisture quite well. Flax is thought to be the most rot resistant, but it is also more flammable than others, due to its high oil content.

You also want to know if the bales are of pure straw or if they are a mix of straw and weeds. Theoretically, the presence of those green weeds should have no detrimental effect on the performance of bales, but under severe moisture exposure, green material is less resistive to decay. So, in the long run, the higher the content of straw fibers, the healthier your walls will be.

UNIFORMITY OF BALES

Width and thickness are normally quite uniform for two-string or three-string bales, so length is the only dimension to really check for variation. Depending on the design of your walls, accuracy may be a real issue, because too much variety might require a lot of retying and therefore result in a significant waste of time. Bales are never perfectly consistent, and your design will have to accommodate some variations in length. The key is to find out what the average length of the shipment will be, and also how much the bales can be expected to vary in either direction from that average.

MACHINE ACCURACY

Modern baling machines, when maintained properly, make a greater percentage of uniform bales than older machines. The accuracy of the settings on older equipment may have relaxed over time; this can result in sufficient size variation to render the bales unsatisfactory for a precise design.

STORAGE PERIOD AND CONDITIONS

A reasonable storage period is usually a few months after harvest season. A longer period may suggest that bales are no longer in their best condition. Further investigation is needed.

Short-term storage conditions will not matter much, so long as the bales are protected adequately from rain. But for a longer period, ambient damp conditions may become risky. For instance, bales stored in the attic of a barn full of cattle may pick up a lot of moisture over time and therefore not be as dry as required at the time of delivery. Well-ventilated structures are preferred for long periods of storage, especially when damp conditions prevail.

HARVESTING TECHNIQUE

Undoubtedly, the ideal harvesting technique would be the traditional hand cut, which leaves beautiful straw with long fibers, the best quality for making perfect clean bales. Unfortunately,

it seems that cereals are now often harvested by conditioning machines that break those long stems into much shorter pieces. The multiple machine handling sometimes creates bales with a hairy look of loose fibers that make direct surface plastering a bit difficult.

WEATHER EXPOSURE

Straw harvested in dry weather will have a better chance of staying in good shape over a long storage season than straw that was exposed to rain.

MOISTURE CONTENT

The moisture content of the straw is a very useful figure if you can get it. It is measured with a hay meter, and should be 14 percent or less. If the figure is not available, then the other questions and simple tests described below can serve as reliable guidelines.

ORIGINAL DESTINY OF BALES

Farmer's own use. A farmer who makes bales for his own use (generally for livestock bedding) won't pay as much attention to the baling, handling, and storage requirements described above. For this reason, a high percentage of these bales may be totally unsuitable for construction purposes. On the other hand, they might also be smaller and shorter than commercial bales. This can be a positive factor if you don't want to play around with heavy bales, though their size may become a design issue.

Commercial use. Because they have to survive multiple handlings, and to fit the maximum possible amount of straw on a truck, bales intended for shipment are generally very compact and tightly fastened.

PRICE OF BALES

Because the price tag can vary substantially from one supplier to another, it's always better to check with a few sources to determine the average for the season. Low prices are related either to low quality or to abundant harvests. Commercial bales are generally more expensive because of the intermediary costs involved.

DELIVERY

You'll have to make sure the bales will be protected from rain during transportation. It may be advantageous if you take responsibility for the delivery, particularly if you deal directly with a farmer, as he may not be interested in selling directly to you unless you *do* take on that responsibility. You might also be able to get a better deal if you pick them up directly from the field.

Buying from commercial dealers, on the other hand, removes these responsibilities from your shoulders. The drawback is that most of the time you have to count increments by the truckload. Depending on the size of the truck and the size of your project this may force you to buy more bales than you really need. You also must specify the need to protect the bales from rain during transportation. Some dealers use closed-box trucks, but most transport their materials on a flatbed trailer. Such a load is likely to show up without a tarp on it, unless you clearly state that you will not accept any bales that become wet during transport.

BALE EXCHANGE

Even after all your questioning and checking, it may happen, for reasons out of your control, that the bales you get are different from what you were expecting. In that case you should be able

Bales must be dry and fairly consistent in shape and density.

to exchange them or return them. This is really only possible if you have been very clear about what you need, and about your unwillingness to accept a different grade of material. It can also be very helpful to make arrangements to get small quantities of bales, in case of shortage during construction. (The easiest way to deal with this potential problem is to order more bales than you think you'll need. Ten percent extra is a good margin.)

Simple Physical Tests

Once you've chosen a potential supplier, the next step is to go to the premises and check the quality of the material for yourself. Start by carefully inspecting the storage location and evaluating the possibility that the bales were exposed to bad weather conditions. First see if they all look similar, then select some bales at random from different places and perform the following tests on them:

Visual Tests

Check the bales for these features first:

Size. Measure the length of a few bales to evaluate whether they are uniform enough for your purposes. There should be no noticeable difference in width or thickness, only in length.

Shape. It's easy to notice any variation in the overall shape of the bales. Curved, uneven or odd-shaped bales may be so because of careless handling. Maybe they were already in bad condition when stored, or they might have deteriorated during storage. Whatever happened to them, this is a sign that they might not be in good enough condition for construction.

Weight. Weight uniformity in a batch of bales can be evaluated by hefting a few of them. Too much variation in weight is definitely a sign of low quality. Excessive moisture content, looseness, or a combination of the two conditions may be responsible for the weight variations; either of these is a good reason for rejection.

Color. Bright gold straw is the sign of a recent harvest, of straw baled under good weather conditions and stored adequately. Pale yellow is the result of long storage. A smooth gray color on the surface means the bales may have stayed awhile in the field, exposed to sun and probably some rain. Maybe it's just a minor surface problem, but this can also indicate problems deeper inside the bales. Further tests should be carried out. A dark color is usually the sign of decay due to moisture exposure.

Live Organisms. Green sprouts or mushrooms growing on a bale are signs of high moisture content; these bales should be directed to the compost pile. Large populations of insects are generally reliant on a moisture supply, so that sign should also be investigated.

Odor

Smelling the straw is also a good way to detect moisture damage. Any kind of stinky smell should be investigated. Molds have a strong odor, especially when they grow inside a bale, and this is not something to be lazy about since some health hazards may be caused by the presence of a toxic mold called *Stachybotrys* (with a name like that, you certainly don't want it to grow within your walls, do you?), a slow-growing saprophytic fungus that seems to grow very well on decaying straw. Good straw should smell sweet and clean.

Dryness to the Touch

Feeling the straw on the bale surface and sticking your fingers into the bale should tell you, more or less, whether it is dry or not. If you have any doubts, ask to break open a bale, so that you can examine the center. Very fine dust should be inspected, as it might be dried mold.

Compaction

The density of a bale can be checked in a number of simple ways:

Stepping. A solidly compacted bale won't be affected by your stepping on it, while a loose bale will depress significantly under your weight. If you have a feeling of not being evenly supported by walking gently on it, this is also a bad sign. Bales are commonly used as scaffolding during construction, so they must be able to stand up to this kind of abuse. A bale should bear the weight of an average-size person without slumping.

Lifting. Lift a bale in the air by its strings. The tension on the strings should not loosen more than the thickness of your fingers between the string and the bale. A little more may be acceptable if they don't get looser by shaking them. Bales that have been pressed wet and have dried afterward in the field or during storage will have looser strings than average; they definitely will be hard to handle and many may have devel-

oped molds. Check carefully in their cores for other signs of moisture damage.

Shaking. Shake the bale around by one string—it shouldn't even think about coming apart!

Fingers. Push your fingers down into the bale, parallel to the straws, between and perpendicular to the strings. You might or might not be able to slide the whole length of your fingers in; you definitely should not be able to insert any more of your hand, beyond the base of your fingers.

Dropping. Lift a bale up and drop it on a solid surface, such as a wooden or concrete floor. It should rebound gently. If it has a tendency to collapse, again that means it's probably too loose.

Kicking. When you kick at the butt end of a bale laid on the ground, your foot should normally rebound a little. If it gets very far inside the bale, that is another sign of looseness.

Pressing. Put the bale in an upright position, bend it gently, press down with both forearms, and feel how it supports your weight. It should be difficult to loosen the tension of the strings this way; if it becomes possible to easily slide the string off the bale with one hand, it's probably too loose.

Embracing! Hold the bale in your arms and give it a big hug, and feel if it is hard or gentle! A bale should keep its original shape during this manipulation.

Now that you are familiar with the design questions, project management issues, and the basic building blocks of straw bales, you are ready to lay your foundation. Read on.

Shaking a bale will tell you if it's tightly tied or not.

PART 2

Straw Bale Structures

CHAPTER 5

FOUNDATIONS

Like all foundations, the main purpose of the foundation under a cold-climate bale building is to carry the loads of the roof and walls down to stable, frost-free soil. On many sites, the ideal foundation will also serve a second function: It will isolate the bales (and any wooden framing members) from the deleterious effects of damp ground and rainwater splashing back up off the ground, against the walls.

Soil can freeze at depths varying from a few inches to many feet, depending on climatic conditions. Pressures as high as 19 tons per square foot (1,820 kiloPascals) have been registered from freezing soils, in one case raising a raft foundation (a specialized floating slab used in commercial construction) under a seven-story building a total of 2 inches in one season![1] Frost-related heaving will result from the conjunction of three conditions: soil must be capable of holding water, water content of the soil must be sufficient, and temperatures must be low enough to induce soil and water to freeze. Lacking any one of these three conditions, ground heave will not happen.

Most foundations work by extending down to naturally frost-free soil, or to solid rock. This is an obvious choice if you want a basement, but in other situations, it can be unnecessarily expensive. The rubble trench and grade beam works by allowing water to drain out

1. K. N. Burn, "Action du Gel sur les Fondations," *Digest de la Construction au Canada* (Conseil National de Recherches Canada, Division des recherches sur le Bâtiment, CBD 182F, April 1977).

Shallow foundations will not move if resting on solid rock.

from below the foundation so that it cannot freeze in place and heave. An increasingly popular third choice is to temper the soil below the house, so that it never gets cold enough to freeze. Such is the premise behind the shallow, frost-protected foundation. As we look at foundation options through this chapter, we'll consider these various approaches to avoiding ground movement, while also explaining moisture control and the suitability of a given option to bale construction.

Foundation Walls, Basements, and Bales

When you move into a house with a full cellar, you pretty much move into a house, workshop, and storage space all at the same time. A basement is the ultimate in what Stuart Brand calls "low road"[2] spaces: areas of a building that are so utilitarian that it really doesn't matter what you do in them. They are supremely flexible

2. Stuart Brand, *How Buildings Learn* (New York: Viking Penguin, 1994).

spaces, to which every layer of use adds character. We've seen basements used as workshops and offices, as play rooms for kids and exercise rooms for their parents, as a space to relegate the TV, as an extra bedroom, in a pinch, and (yes, Paul really did see this) as a place to throw the garbage. Basements in farmhouses have historically been used for food storage. In Quebec, it was once common to find sheep and pigs housed through the winter in a basement. In the days before the central furnace, they probably served to keep the rooms above from freezing.

Advantages of Basements

Basements hold three great advantages for bale builders. First, and most important, they offer a simple way to pick up the bales away from the ground. Second, they provide a place to run utilities. Third, they serve as a warm, dry place to store tools and materials during construction.

Elevate Those Bales!

On some sites and with some roof configurations, splashback and direct rain can cause periodic wetting of the lower portions of the walls. One of the simplest steps you can take toward keeping your bale walls dry is to elevate them above these ground sources of moisture. In such cases, basement walls are typically brought up one to two feet above finished grade, and sometimes higher, if the basement is to have some real win-

Why Do 1 Need a Strong Foundation?

Foundations serve the same function in every building—they anchor the building to the ground. The taller the building and the colder the climate, the more crucial this function becomes. Tall buildings require a firm foundation for fairly obvious reasons: The effects of wind and earthquakes are amplified by height, and the more stories you stack on top of each other, the more weight is concentrated at one point on the ground, increasing the per-square-foot workload of the foundation and the soil upon which it bears.

If tall buildings need strong foundations because they spend their lives conducting kinetic energy (wind) out of the air and into the ground, then it could be said that cold-climate buildings need strong foundations for exactly the opposite reason. In cold climates, the ground cannot be trusted to stay still. Each time wet soil is subjected to below-freezing temperatures, the water held in it freezes, and expands. This happens every winter, to some degree, the total depth of frost being determined by a combination of temperature and snow cover. Cold temperatures freeze soil, snow insulates. It is not uncommon to dig through three feet of snow and find thawed soil underneath. During a cold and open winter, on the other hand, soil can freeze to four or five feet of depth at the U.S./Canadian border, and deeper farther north.

When the water in the soil freezes, it expands. Expanding water needs more space, and the direction in which space is to be found, as any astronomer will tell you, is up. Anything in the way of this expansion will be carried right along, that is, will be pushed up. The rock farmer, therefore, has chosen an effortless profession: He simply waits for each winter's freeze to push up some more rocks!

Your house, ponderous though it may seem, is really no different from a rock. Its weight is much less than the force of expanding water, pushing skyward. If the frost were simply to increase the elevation of your home by an annual increment, no harm would really be done, especially as the local shrubbery could be expected to grow at a better than equivalent rate. The problem is that frost can be counted on to push unevenly against the underside of your building, resulting, before long, in cracked foundation walls, cracked plaster, windows that don't open, water in the basement, and the rest of the litany of structural problems that have plagued homeowners since the dawn of the permanent dwelling (not all that long ago, mind you). This is why cheap bale houses on minimal foundations, which are not inappropriate in desert settings, are usually not a good idea in cold climates.

dows and eventually end up as a finished space. The floor framing system, plus a toe-up for the bales, will add another foot or so of separation between the straw and the ground, for a total of two to three feet. In situations where harmful moisture sources are an issue, this should be sufficient distance to isolate them from the straw.

UTILITIES

Basements provide an ideal location for a building's mechanical room. The space and hot-water heating equipment, if located in a basement, need not compete with the domestic functions of the home for valuable floor area within the living space. Basements also offer a space in which to run pipes, electrical and telephone wires, ducts, speaker, television, and computer cables, and any other accessory of postmodern living that you or your descendants may dream up. Electrical wires can be run in the basement and stubbed up into your bale walls, making future modifications to the electrical system relatively simple. Basements also do not usually freeze, which is an excellent quality in a space that will house pipes. A building's entire mechanical system, from delivery through appliances and back through return lines, can be left visible in a basement, with no effect on the aesthetic qualities of the spaces above. A basement is basically a giant chase, with the added benefit that you only need look up in order to see where everything is. This is the type of arrangement that remodelers dream about.

STORAGE DURING CONSTRUCTION

Basements offer a dry place to store bales, plaster ingredients, and other moisture-sensitive materials. A basement is not necessarily the ideal place for such storage, because the materials must

Graded stone and piping can ensure that water drains from below a foundation, so water will not freeze in place and heave.

Electrical wires can be run in the basement, and stubbed up in conduit into the bale walls.

be lugged upstairs before they can be used; but in a situation where a house is to be built slowly or in stages, the flexibility offered by a dry, relatively secure space for tools and storage more than offsets the hassle of having to haul things up and down the stairs.

Moisture Control with Basements

When we talk about basements as useful spaces, by no means are we talking about damp, smelly caves ruled by trolls whose eyes would be put out by the light of day. Useful basements are dry basements (and, ideally, partially daylit basements).

Moisture appears in basements by three processes: bulk leakage from groundwater sources, wicking through capillary pores in concrete, and vapor migration from both interior air and exterior soil. (See chapter 2, "Design Challenges," for definitions of these terms.) Each of these sources must be dealt with, if basement walls are to be kept dry.

LEAKAGE

Bulk leakage is best avoided by keeping standing water away from foundation walls. Backfill material should be free draining, composed of gravel or coarse sand. A perforated drainpipe should be located at the perimeter of the foundation footing; this should be surrounded by a coarse gravel, and the gravel layer should be wrapped top, sides, and bottom with filter fabric, to keep fine material from migrating in, clogging the pores of the gravel, and eventually blocking the pipe. The pipe should be sloped to daylight. Ideally, this whole array should be covered by a relatively impermeable, clay-based soil, with a slope of at least five percent away from the building (see diagram at right).

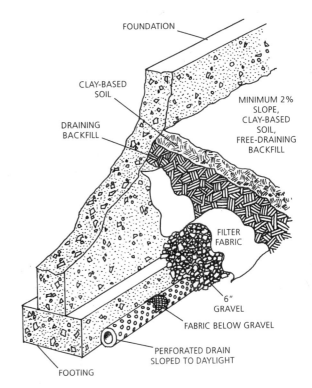

Foundation drain.

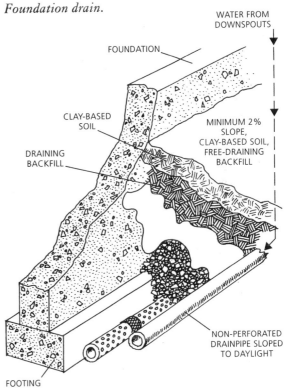

Gutter drain.

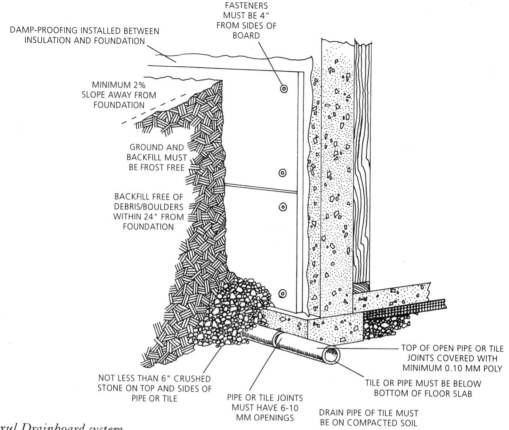

FASTENERS
MUST BE 4"
FROM SIDES OF
BOARD

DAMP-PROOFING INSTALLED BETWEEN
INSULATION AND FOUNDATION

MINIMUM 2%
SLOPE AWAY FROM
FOUNDATION

GROUND AND
BACKFILL MUST
BE FROST FREE

BACKFILL FREE OF
DEBRIS/BOULDERS
WITHIN 24" FROM
FOUNDATION

NOT LESS THAN 6" CRUSHED
STONE ON TOP AND SIDES OF
PIPE OR TILE

PIPE OR TILE JOINTS
MUST HAVE 6-10
MM OPENINGS

TOP OF OPEN PIPE OR TILE
JOINTS COVERED WITH
MINIMUM 0.10 MM POLY

TILE OR PIPE MUST BE BELOW
BOTTOM OF FLOOR SLAB

DRAIN PIPE OF TILE MUST
BE ON COMPACTED SOIL

Roxul Drainboard system.

Roof gutters should not be run into the foundation drainpipe. The net effect of this practice is to dump all of the water that comes off the roof directly at the base of the foundation wall, the exact area from which the gutters are supposed to divert it. Gutters should either be run into extended downspouts, which carry the water a minimum of four feet away from the building, or into a separate set of below-grade, nonperforated pipes, and then run out to daylight, alongside the foundation drainpipe.

Straw bale builders in Canada and the United States are lucky to have available a product called Roxul Drainboard; Canadians also have access to RXL panels. Roxul is a rigid mineral wool (reprocessed slag) that possesses a remarkable

pair of qualities for foundation builders: an R-value of 3.5 per inch for the Drainboard (available in 1- to 4-inch thicknesses) and as much as 4.08 per inch for RXL 80 (thicknesses of 1 to 5 inches), combined with the ability, due to the orientation of the mineral fibers, to drain water freely. Even after being soaked, these boards dry out and keep their insulation value. (A report in the magazine *Innovation* [winter 1999, vol. 4, no 2] by the Canadian National Research Council on tests of foundations insulated on their exterior with this type of insulation proves that their thermal properties are not affected by water exposure.) Roxul boards used as exterior foundation insulation should be flashed top and bottom, to keep rainwater from running into the top, and to direct water running out the bottom away from the footing, toward the foundation drainpipe. In Canada, Roxul Drainboard is less expensive than extruded polystyrene insulation; it can also save on fill costs, as it can be backfilled with native soil (though a proper foundation drain system is still required).

Stay-in-place foam forming systems (discussed later in this chapter) typically employ a tough, bituminous waterproof membrane on the exterior of below-grade walls. Such a layer blocks moisture entry by all three transport mechanisms (bulk leakage, capillarity, and vapor migration). At roughly 75 cents U.S. per square foot, however, such a layer is rather expensive, especially where it is serving as backup to a free-draining backfill. Many other self-adhesive or torched-on membranes made of modified bitumen, PVC, or EPDM are also appropriate for those who are looking for a fast and easy job, or are in a risky situation and ready to pay a little more.

CAPILLARITY

Capillary wicking in basement walls is typically controlled by rolling on a dampproofing layer of black bituminous liquid, which fills the capillary pores on the surface of the concrete. An alternate method, employed for years by Todd Osman of Gays Mills, Wisconsin, uses bentonite clay. Bentonite expands dramatically in contact with water, increasing to as much as nineteen times its dry volume at full saturation. (If your cat litter is of the swelling type, chances are it's made of bentonite clay.) It is used for lining irrigation ditches, and also by well drillers as a combination lubricator/sealant. It is often available from well-drilling companies.

Todd's method is to mix the bentonite with water until it reaches a trowelable, gelatin-like

consistency. He then spreads it over the wall, followed by a sheet of 6-mil polyethylene. (Some builders of underground houses will sandwich the plastic sheet between two thin coats of bentonite plaster.) The bentonite takes on any water that makes its way through or around the porous backfill and plastic layers, presumably swelling to fill the capillary pores in the concrete, in the process. An added benefit of this method is that it should work as a gasket-like seal over any small cracks that might appear in the foundation wall over time. Composite bentonite/geotextile membranes are also available on the market; these are used for foundation waterproofing in large commercial structures, but would be equally appropriate in houses.

VAPOR

The dampproofing layer, be it bituminous or membrane or bentonite and plastic, should also serve as an effective barrier against vapor diffusing into the foundation from the soil. The more pressing issue here is condensation of vapor from interior air, on the surface of or at some point within the depth of the foundation wall. This phenomenon is prevented by one of two insulation strategies.

The basement wall can be insulated on its outside, thus raising the temperature of the wall to the same as that of the interior air, and thereby removing the dewpoint from the wall to some location in the backfill soil (see diagrams on page 92). This method offers the benefit of turning the entire concrete wall into a substantial thermal storage medium. Foam-formed walls work on the same principle.

Alternately, the wall might be insulated on the interior, and detailed as if it were an exterior wall, with a continuous poly air/vapor barrier behind

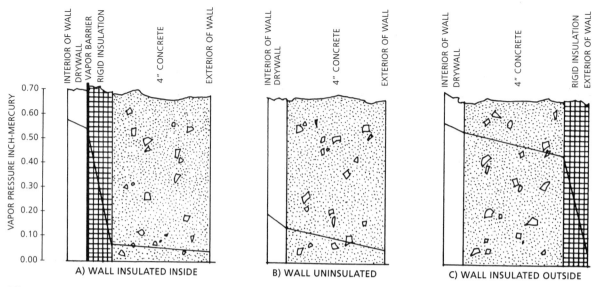

The vapor pressure inside a wall is related to the location of insulation. Adapted from J. K. Latta, Murs, fenêtres et toitures pour le climat canadien (Ottawa: Division des recherches sur le bâtiment, 1975: p. 71).

the drywall. Airtight drywall finished with a vapor-barrier paint would also be an option. It is not a bad idea, in the case of interior insulation, to also dampproof the interior surface of the foundation wall. Even though such a layer is outside the air barrier envelope of the building, it is still safest to avoid the use of any material that might adversely affect the air quality inside the building. A vapor-retardant paint would be a better choice than foundation sealer here, though you must make sure it is capable of adhering to concrete (see diagram on page 93).

The interior surface of bale-insulated foundation walls (see "Foundation Walls," below) should be treated with a vapor-retardant paint. Unlike in above-grade walls, any small amount of vapor that does make its way into the bale core of the wall will have no way of escaping to the exterior, because this surface will have been sealed against ground moisture entry. The best strategy, in this case, is to detail the wall as carefully as possible to exclude all potential sources of moisture.

BASEMENT FLOOR SLABS

All of the same concerns that apply to basement walls apply to basement floors. Because floors are often detailed less carefully than walls, they typically tend to contribute a disproportionate share of moisture to basements. Basement slabs should be detailed exactly like concrete floor slabs. (See "Concrete Slabs" below for more information.)

Builders on a tight budget are often tempted to cut corners on the basement floor insulation, especially in situations where the basement is not expected to be incorporated into the living space. Except in a very dry climate, this is a serious mistake, which can ultimately saddle the owner with a choice between running a dehumidifier or accepting a damp basement. It also effectively rules out the possibility of using the basement floor as the floor of a finished living space, because it will always be cooler than the basement air, and thus a surface that collects dampness. In order to safely finish such a space, without risk of unhealthy molds in area rugs or other floor

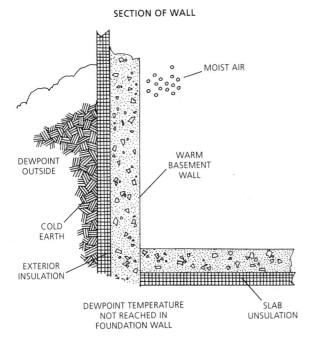

SECTION OF WALL

MOIST AIR

DEWPOINT OUTSIDE

WARM BASEMENT WALL

COLD EARTH

EXTERIOR INSULATION

DEWPOINT TEMPERATURE NOT REACHED IN FOUNDATION WALL

SLAB UNSULATION

Dewpoint for exterior-insulated basement walls.

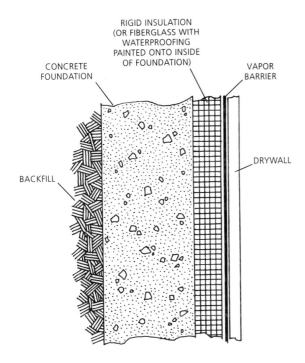

RIGID INSULATION (OR FIBERGLASS WITH WATERPROOFING PAINTED ONTO INSIDE OF FOUNDATION)

CONCRETE FOUNDATION

VAPOR BARRIER

DRYWALL

BACKFILL

Typical foundation with interior insulation.

coverings, the prospective remodeler would need to fur up with framing lumber and insulation, and install a second floor. As headroom tends to be at a premium in a basement, such a solution would often not be practical.

TOE-UPS

If your bales are to sit upon the floor of the building—that is, unless your bale walls sit atop an independent foundation wall or grade beam that is made just for them—then you must think about toeing-up the bale wall from the floor level. This will certainly be the case in a bale house over a basement, where the bale walls will sit upon a framed floor, which rests on the basement walls. The purpose of this toe-up (typically 1½ to 2 inches) is to protect the bales from inundation, either during the construction process, or if ever the plumbing in the house explodes. (See "Concrete Slabs" below for more information.)

Foundation Walls

Most people, when they think of basement walls, think of conventionally formed concrete, or concrete blocks. While these two systems do account for the vast majority of basement walls, some alternative systems merit attention. Because these alternatives tend to be wider than standard foundation walls, they can also be useful in situations where, within the same story, a transition must be made from a below-grade wall to a bale wall.

STAY-IN-PLACE FORMING SYSTEMS

Stay-in-place foam forming systems, now available almost everywhere, can be used to advantage in bale houses. Various manufacturers have each developed their own twist, but the basic idea is a simple one. Hollow blocks of rigid foam (or, in some cases, sheets of foam held six to ten inches apart by plastic spacers) are stacked like giant Legos, creating a freestanding foam wall with an empty center. Rebar is added as necessary, typically snapping into chairs molded into the spacer component of the blocks. The entire cavity is then poured solid with concrete, the exterior sealed with a waterproof membrane, and, presto! you have a basement wall that is insulated to somewhere between R-25 and R-35.

These forms do have a few disadvantages. They're somewhat expensive, though they allow the owner-builder or small contractor to do his or her own formwork, with a minimum of purchased or rented equipment. They use a lot of foam, and foam is not too high on the list of ecologically preferable materials. You can assume that such a forming system will use between two and three times the 2 inches of rigid insulation that is typically applied to the exterior of a foundation wall. (Of course, this also means two or three times the R-value.)

One particular brand of these forms, the Rastra block, is quite interesting. It is made from 100 percent recycled beadboard—ground up packaging material from the electronics industry—held together with cement. It is vapor permeable, yet nonabsorptive. The cores are poured in a grid pattern, rather than as a solid wall, so less concrete is needed than with most other systems (although a substantial amount of cement is used to bind the foam beads together, raising the embodied energy of the material). The widest block is 14 inches, exactly the width of a two-

string bale laid on edge, and also sufficiently wide to support a three-string bale laid on edge, or a two-string bale laid flat (especially if the 4-inch overlap is held to the inside, and a wiring and plumbing chase is framed in below it).

The manufacturer's stated R-value of 3.5 per inch is somewhat difficult to believe. Still, given a margin for error, a Rastra wall should have a higher R-value than the typical basement wall, with its 2 inches of exterior extruded polystyrene insulation. The two major drawbacks to Rastra panels are the need for a small crane in order to install them, and the long shipping distance to any cold climate, anywhere in the world. Plants are located in Ciudad Juarez and Mexicali, Mexico, and in Las Vegas, Nevada, U.S.; transporting these panels to your site may add significantly to the cost of the product, both in terms of dollars and embodied energy.

The Faswall block is a substitute for concrete block, made of waste wood chips treated with a mineral solution, bonded with cement. As with foam-form systems, the cores are grouted solid, to create a very strong wall. Blocks measure 16 inches long, 8 inches high, and 11.5 inches wide, weigh 22 pounds, and are rated by the manufacturer at R-13. Produced in Arkansas, this product can be a good choice for Midwestern-state and prairie-province bale builders.

Both Rastra and Faswall, with their highly textured surfaces and cement component, take plaster quite nicely. This allows for a seamless visual transition from bales into foundation material.

Foam-formed basement walls have been used as a basement-wall-and-floor-support system, as

> Stay-in-place foam forming systems, now available almost everywhere, can be used to advantage in bale houses.

Crawlspaces

The crawlspace was a popular foundation in the days when cellar holes were dug by hand, and lined with the stones that were a product of the excavation. Removing soil from an 8-foot-deep hole would have been a very different scale of operation from digging to the frost line, and since a crawlspace stores potatoes quite nicely, many settler houses, regardless of region, rest upon such a foundation. These people did not have the luxury of thinking about where they might store their Christmas decorations. Their houses also tended to suffer from such extreme ventilation that a damp crawlspace would have had little opportunity to cause moisture-related problems within the fabric of the building.

For the vast majority of buildings today, however, crawlspaces simply don't make any sense. The problem is summed up in the name: A crawlspace is a 3- to 5-foot-deep space under your house through which you must crawl, in order to get at your pipes, wires, potatoes, or Christmas decorations. Subcontractors will curse you throughout the construction process, and you will probably curse yourself, once you realize that with a bit more excavation and concrete, you could have built a usable space under your house. Have you ever tried to set up a sewing machine or table saw in a crawlspace?

Other issues come into play, as well. Crawlspaces must be detailed like minibasements, which is what they are. You have two basic options: Either the foundation walls and floor must be insulated and the crawlspace heated somewhat, or the crawlspace ceiling (the framed floor of the main building) must be detailed like an outside wall. If the floor of the crawlspace is soil, it should be covered by a continuous sheet of polyethylene, to keep ground dampness in the ground, where it belongs. Unless you are in a very dry climate, the crawlspace should not be vented to the outdoors in summer, as venting will cause water to condense out of warm, humid air onto the cooler crawlspace floor. This is less of an issue if the floor of the main building is detailed as an outside wall; in neither case is it ideal.

Crawlspaces share with basements and piers the benefit of picking up the bales a fair distance from the ground. They do make sense in isolated situations—specifically when ledge or groundwater is close to the surface, or if you live in one of those peculiar areas of shallow frost depth (2 feet) based on the assumption of a snow cover through the winter, or if you want a wood-framed floor but really have no interest in a basement.

A crawl space is not usually a good foundation choice, but can be convenient and economical for a large building sitting on rock.

in Jonathan Stevens' and Nancy Simons' home in Leverett, Massachusetts, and also to support bales directly, as a wrap around a post-and-beam structure. Laurie Smith, an experienced and inventive straw bale builder from Shelburne, Vermont, used the Blue Maxx brand of forms, which offer the option of a flared-out top course, designed to support a brick veneer. This flared foundation, including foam, finishes out at 15½ inches of width, ample support for a wall of two-string bales, laid flat.

Michel's Bale-Core Stem Wall

Michel's innovative system was tried experimentally on one project in Quebec, in 1994. It was intended to be used for the whole house, a six-level building on a sloping site. The first phase was a 13-by-15-foot storage and work space with two walls completely buried in the ground. A modified post-and-beam structure made of 6-by-rough-sawn hemlock posts spaced 6 feet apart topped by 6-by-6 beams was raised on a previously poured straw bale slab. Two 36-inch bales were jammed on edge in rows between the posts. They were secured together by forcing down onto their top a 1-by-2 furring strip running horizontally on each side of the posts and fastened to same. Nails were driven through the 1-by-2s into the bales to hold them firmly in place.

Flakes were then laid between the 1-by-2s and additional rows of bales were stacked and fastened the same way until the 7½-foot-high walls were completed. As regular form panels were placed on each side of the walls and tied with conventional 18 inch spacers, vertical 1-by-2s spaced at 12-inch intervals were slid along the bales inside the forms to keep a regular gap for the concrete to be poured. These stakes were going to be pulled back up as the pouring progressed.

The intention was to pour a fluid concrete to fill the 1-inch gaps on both sides and completely enclose the bales. The 3-inch-deep joints left between rows by the 1-by-2s were also going to be filled with concrete, thus making horizontal running ribs every 18 inches. The bale walls were going to be sandwiched by these 1-inch-thick, occasionally ribbed skins. Surface waterproofing was then to be worked onto the walls to be backfilled.

The pouring was done before Michel could get there to supervise the work and a few mistakes were made that called for later adjustments. The first mistake was inadequate cross-bracing of the formwork to hold it firmly in place. High pressure created by the pour made some panels wave slightly and burst open at a couple of places but, fortunately, without much damage. Second, the pour was done with a 4-inch pump and a vibrator was used to drive the concrete to the bottom of the walls, thus putting too much pressure on the formwork. Third, the pour could not be done on both sides at the same time because the special splicing funnel specified for that purpose had not been made; thus the pressure created by the heavy vibrated concrete on one side made the bales move outward against the facing form at several locations, preventing the subsequent concrete pour from filling these parts of the walls.

So, at removal of the forms, though many spots were bare, amazingly the very thin skins still held quite firmly to the bale surface and were so hard after just 24 hours that they couldn't even be broken with a hammer. The structure was sound. These thin areas were covered with a strong cement plaster reinforced with chopped straw. The dried surface was then thoroughly brushed with a cementitious sealer and back-

Bales held with horizontal 1-by-2s nailed to posts.

Forms placed with 1-by-2-inch spacers.

Walls after removal of forms.

filled as planned, the structure being sturdy enough to support the lateral loads imposed by the backfill.

The rest of the building was not built with this technique because of a tight schedule and because the site topography made scaffolding too labor intensive.

Comments and adjustments. The main purpose of Michel's experiment was to find a way to raise an infilled modified post-and-beam structure in the shortest time possible with the smallest crew available. Even with the subsequent plastering necessary to cover the bare patches of bales, three people were able to raise and finish 464 square feet of wall in only three days. A conventional basement is usually prepared and poured in the same amount of time.

The speed of execution combined with the relatively small quantity of concrete required makes this approach more than appealing even for regular walls, providing the necessary equipment is available on-site. The pump is essential in this case, and we wouldn't recommend doing without; hauling buckets of concrete to the top of the wall would be too burdensome.

To get a still more rigid wall by using the same idea, we would suggest sticking the form panels against the interior face of the bales and leaving a wider space on the outside, perhaps 2 or even 3 inches. For a very sturdy wall, horizontal rebar could be laid in the row joints and wire mesh attached to the exterior surface of the bales and spaced away with 1-by-2s or any other suitable device. That way the pouring could definitely be fast and most effective without the use of a vibrator (which is not recommended in vertical spaces), and without any risk of moving the bales out, because the forms will keep them stable on the other side. The resulting exterior reinforced skin would be uniform and ready for backfilling after waterproofing, which could be done in a conventional way. On a risky site a very safe waterproofing could be achieved with the use of a membrane.

The interior side of the walls (bare straw) can then be plastered by hand once the roof has been completed! Even with the extra cost of the pumping equipment, the total cost of this superinsulated basement (or even regular) wall

Structure built upon bale wall.

would be incomparable to any conventional one. This alternative might also be the best choice for an exterior-pinned load-bearing wall. The vertical pinning stalks (bamboo, saplings, 1-by-2s, or even rebar) would hold the wire mesh away from the bale surface. This would bring the total cost even lower.

Concrete Slabs

The concrete slab has been the most popular foundation option for straw bale houses. This popularity derives from a pair of important qualities: A slab is a relatively inexpensive foundation that provides a very durable floor surface. The benefits of a slab floor extend beyond pure practicality, however. A well-finished slab can be a very beautiful floor surface. A concrete slab is also the ideal medium in which to lay radiant heating tubes. Until you have walked barefoot across a warm floor in midwinter, you cannot understand the therapy that this kind of heat provides to tired feet and ankles.

Slabs do have one drawback as cold-climate foundations, which is their tendency to hover close to the ground. This can be an issue on sites with seasonal high groundwater or in any design that does not include ample roof overhangs or gutters to keep the rain that hits the roof from splashing back against the walls. Most codes require that biodegradable materials be held 8 inches above finished grade. On questionable sites, we usually aim to keep the bales a minimum of 1 foot above finished grade; 1½ or 2 feet is safer yet.

Conventional Slabs

Conventional concrete slabs fall into three categories, according to the method employed to keep the slab from heaving. A slab with frost walls is the most common variety; in this case, foundation walls are poured to a frost-free depth, and the slab is poured inside these walls. The frost-protected shallow foundation works on the same principle, except that the frost-free depth is raised by a perimeter skirt of insulation. The "monolithic" or "Alaskan" slab accepts the possibility of the ground under the building moving slightly. Such a slab is built strong enough to float atop unsteady soil.

SLAB WITH FROST WALLS
A slab with frost walls is the conventional way of pouring a slab, and still the most common method. In cold-climate construction, this tech-

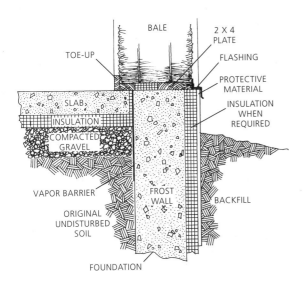

Typical frost wall with slab.

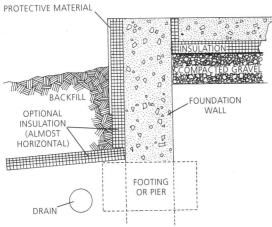

Typical frost-protected shallow foundation.

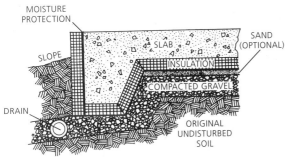

Typical monolithic slab. Some frost-protected shallow foundations also end up looking like this.

nique involves excavating a trench to four or five feet below grade, and pouring a footing and foundation wall. The whole system is usually detailed as a basement wall would be, with footing drains and free-draining backfill. The main benefits of this system are that it is approved by code bodies everywhere, and that concrete contractors are quite familiar with it. This method involves enough excavation and concrete that the old argument for basements—dig down another four feet and create a usable space—often applies.

The slab is typically poured within the area demarcated by the foundation walls. Paul likes to use a thermal and expansion joint of 2-inch extruded polystyrene or mineral wool board between the edge of the slab and the foundation wall. See "Floor Slab Moisture Control," later in this chapter, for other slab details.

FROST-PROTECTED SHALLOW FOUNDATION

The frost-protected shallow foundation is another kind of slab with frost walls. The only difference is that the frost walls need not extend nearly so deep, because the frost level is raised by insulation.

Design of these foundations is very specific to local climatic conditions. In some cases, insulation is run vertically down the foundation wall, and across the top and down the outside edge of the footing. In colder climates, a below-grade skirt of insulation extends two to six feet out from the foundation wall, in all directions. Design details are different for fully heated, semi-heated, and unheated spaces. See the bibliography for the National Association of Homebuilders' design guidebook.

ALASKAN SLAB

In the case of an "Alaskan" or "monolithic" slab, the working assumption is that the ground below the slab will move, over time. Standard drainage precautions are still used, but the slab is built strong enough so that if the ground does move, the building can float, like a boat, to wherever it lands when the ground solidifies. This strategy was developed for Alaskan terrain above permafrost, which cannot be kept frost-free, and which suffers substantial movement during each spring thaw.

A thermal expansion joint of extruded polystyrene separates this concrete slab from the perimeter grade beam.

Floor Slab Moisture Control

Liquid water contact with basement floors is typically prevented by locating the foundation drain system at a level below that of the floor slab. Because any groundwater that rises to the elevation of the drain will be carried away from the building, this technique effectively drops the groundwater level to a point below the bottom of the slab. The site for the floor slab is next prepared by laying down a minimum of 4 inches of coarse gravel, as a capillary break, and also to help drain any water that rises under the bottom of the slab. This gravel layer should be continuous with the gravel surrounding the foundation drain, so that groundwater has an uninterrupted path away from the building. A layer of rigid insulation, 4 inches thick, is installed above the gravel, to keep the slab at a warm enough temperature so that it does not become a condensing point for vapor held within interior air. This is a good place to spend some extra money up front—there is no such thing as retrofitting insulation under a slab.

A layer of 6-mil polyethylene is sometimes installed above the insulation, as a vapor and radon barrier. An increasingly popular replacement for this practice is to tape the seams of the insulation board material.

In mixed heating/cooling climates, it is common to insulate only 4 feet at the perimeter of floor slabs. This technique is also sometimes used in cold climates, where it is a particularly bad idea. All through the year, the uninsulated portion of the floor will remain at a lower temperature than the air in the house. In winter, this results in cold feet and higher heating bills, while in summer (in humid climates) this cool area of the floor can cause water to condense out of the air, resulting in molds and an unhealthy indoor environment. Though it may save a few dollars during construction, poor detailing of this sort will increase heating bills and reduce comfort throughout the life of the building.

Toe-ups

Bale walls must be elevated off the surface of a slab, away from any water that might puddle on the floor during construction, and also as a protection against future plumbing leaks. An excellent toe-up detail employs a combination of wood (for nailing) and rigid foam, rigid fiberglass,

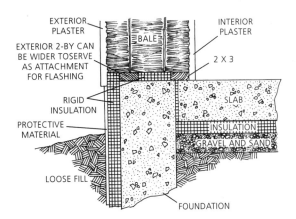

Typical toe-up.

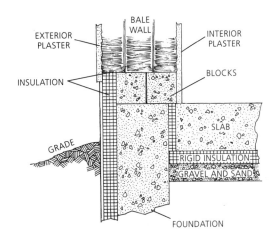

Toe-up with blocks.

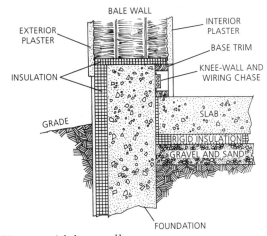

Toe-up with kneewall.

blocks of autoclaved aerated concrete, or RXL panels (for insulation). The 2-by-3s or 2-by-4s are nailed on the flat along the inside and outside planes of the bale wall. The gap between these two is filled by a strip of rigid insulation, which has the capacity to bear the weight of the bales above. At least one of the two wooden nailers (and typically the one that is on the air barrier side of the wall) is caulked or gasketed to the floor, as a defense against air leakage through the seam between it and the subfloor decking material. (This is crucial if the building is to receive wood siding, less so if exterior plaster is to be carried down over this seam.) If wood is not needed for nailing, the toe-up can be made entirely of rigid insulation.

Some people replace the foam in the toe-up with gravel. The problem with gravel is that it does not insulate, and the resulting cold surface at the base of the bales provides a potential point for condensation. If external foundation or rim joist insulation can be carried up to cover the outside of the toe-up, thereby keeping it warm, this system should work well.

A wood and foam toe-up over a slab or floor deck protects the bales from water that might pool on the floor during construction or a plumbing explosion.

Elevation of Bales

Contrary to common assumptions, a "slab on grade" need not be built at the original grade. In the case of a slab with frost walls or a shallow frost-protected foundation, the foundation walls can easily be extended one to two feet above grade. The area inside the foundation walls can then be backfilled, and the slab poured atop this fill. This is the simplest way to raise the level of the bale walls away from the ground. The only drawback is that it also raises the floor level, which is not always desirable.

Codes typically require some step-up between the finished grade and the floor of a house. In cases where a large step is not desirable, it is possible to elevate the bale wall on top of a built-up base of a nondegradable material.

Two courses of doubled-up concrete blocks, faced with 2 inches of rigid insulation, work quite well. This would yield a 16-inch-high, 18-inch-wide wall. Faswall or Rastra blocks might also be of use here, as might gabions (stone-filled wire crates used for riverbank retention), railroad ties, stone, sandbags filled with earth or soil-cement, or anything else you might dream up.

Alternately, you might bring an 8- or 10-inch-wide foundation wall up to a height of one to two feet above the slab, and frame a wiring chase to the inside of it, atop the slab, to create the extra width necessary for full support of the bale wall. This detail accomplishes two jobs at once, elevating the bales while creating a large and convenient area for running cables of all sorts. Guy and Alice Snyder, of Snyder and Snyder Architects, Portland, Oregon, came up with a similar detail for a project in Washington County, Oregon. Their design does not include a wiring chase, but instead builds out the foundation wall with rigid insulation to the exterior and a framed and insulated kneewall to the interior. This detail could easily be modified to include a wiring chase.

Some bale builders, instead of elevating bale walls, have attempted to protect them by lapping asphalt felt or housewrap over the first course of bales, behind the exterior plaster. This is not a great idea. Though asphalt felt is somewhat vapor permeable (about as much so as cement stucco), it is quite impervious to liquid water. This is exactly the reason for employing it here, of course. The problem is that the felt blocks the movement of liquid water in either direction, so that if this bottom course of bales should ever become wet, a major drying mechanism—wicking into the plaster followed by evaporation into the air—will not be available. In order for liquid water to leave this bale, it must first change into a vapor state, so that it can pass through the felt layer. As always, the site must dictate the most sensible course of action.

The Archibio Sandwich Slab

Straw bale–insulated slabs have gained some popularity in recent years. Ecological and economic concerns have motivated a few pioneers to experiment with bales as insulation under concrete floors. Although not very well documented and not yet backed by scientific data, the observed performance of these slabs can make them attractive for very-cold-climate situations. With almost no other alternative to petroleum-based materials, bales represent an ideal low-cost solution to bring concrete slabs to the quality of comfortable floors.

Because the Archibio technique was described in *The Straw Bale House* (Chelsea Green, 1994), it became very popular. Reports from different sources revealed that casual misunderstandings of the technique had resulted in some very unfortunate experiments. The original procedure has been improved over the years, and Archibio hopes that a new, updated document will lead to a better understanding, not solely of the slab, but of the environment required for it to function adequately. We highly recommend that you check with Archibio for any more recent version of the plans for the sandwich slab.

Slab Description

In climates where winters are long and demanding, nobody wants a cold and uncomfortable uninsulated concrete slab floor. While conventional insulation is usually provided by expensive petroleum-based rigid boards, no satisfactory natural material exists as an efficient and cheap alternative for those who want to live in a chemical-free environment. Because bales can be used in walls to create a high level of insulation, why not do the same with the floors?

Economics

The straw bale–insulated slab uses approximately 20 percent more concrete than a 6-inch-thick conventional slab for an equivalent floor area. But at a cost of between 50 cents and 1 dollar U.S. per square foot of R-50 straw insulation, no other insulated slab can ever be so affordable.

While the Archibio slab is like a big sandwich made of two concrete slices with a layer of bales in between, we know that some people in Mongolia, in order to save on concrete, labor, and cost, have experimented with straw-insulated slabs without a bottom layer of concrete. Similarly, to save even more, the top slab could be reduced to a thin layer of concrete and finished with an earthen floor (see "Earthen Floors," in chapter 13).

SLAB PERFORMANCE AND MOISTURE CONTROL

The key to good performance of the sandwich slab is to build it to be free of water and moisture damage. To clearly understand this issue, simply picture a straw bale wall tilted onto well-drained ground; if no moisture is present on the surface of the slab, it should behave like a wall. Some people would be tempted to lay a plastic sheet underneath the slab to prevent moisture migration from the ground; we don't, for three main reasons. First, we create 100 percent water and damp-free conditions prior to slab pouring. Second, common sense and building science say that a vapor barrier should always be installed on the *warm* side of the building envelope. We think this rule should apply for floors or slabs as well, and in this case it would mean on top of the slab, which seems useless. Third, if water ever gets between the slab and the plastic, it could wick up through the concrete base slab and eventually damage the straw. It would actually be more advisable to lay the plastic underneath the drainage layer of gravel.

As explained in chapter 2, moisture may enter slabs by three processes: bulk leakage, capillary action through pores in the concrete, and vapor migration. Bulk leakage and capillary wicking are prevented by backfilling and draining in such a way that it is impossible for liquid water to remain in contact with the slab. Vapor can move out of the soil and into the slab at a very slow rate because concrete has a low perm rating. Because we suggest finishing the floor with materials that are at least as vapor-permeable as the slab (natural sealers and wax rather than epoxy sealers and the like), vapor should migrate the same way through the top slab and thus not present a problem. In addition, the slab is at the same temperature or warmer than the soil, and the vapor is coming out of the soil. No cold spot, no condensation. Similarly, vapor from interior air will not condense on the slab, because the slab is insulated, so its surface should be warm. With a radiant heating system in the slab, the possibility for condensation is further reduced.

> Moisture may enter slabs by bulk leakage, capillary action through pores in the concrete, and vapor migration.

IMPORTANT WARNING

Since our first experience, in 1984, Archibio has supervised the construction of more than fifty slabs with a total of 60,000 square feet of floor area. Although no visible moisture problem had ever been reported for any of the slabs, Archibio had the opportunity to test for potential moisture effects in four slabs in November 1999 under the close supervision of Canada Mortgage and Housing Corporation's (CMHC) experts. In brief, it was found that water infiltration inside the sandwich occurred almost inevitably on risky sites, with some degree of bale deterioration as a result. In the worst case the straw was almost completely composted. In a few other cases, just a small amount of straw had deteriorated by direct contact with water, while the remaining straw was sound although with a high moisture content. In the best case, the bottom half-inch layer was decomposing while the rest was sound throughout but with a higher than normal moisture content. Sensors were installed in the tested slabs and in a recently built one, so more data should be available in the future to evaluate long-term performance.

A fuller discussion of these tests is reported in chapter 14 of this book. The complete detailed results of the tests are available directly from CMHC or Archibio. We strongly recommend that you consult these documents and/or contact Archibio before building your own slab.

PHYSICAL COMPONENTS

The basic sandwich slab is made of full bales laid flat, side-by-side, on a 2-inch layer of concrete; the rounded butt corners where bales meet are filled with poured concrete pillars. Spaced according to the size of the bales, the pillars form a grid of 18 inches on one axis and of bale lengths (usually about 3 feet) on the opposite axis. These are intended to carry the weight from the top slab down to the base slab on the ground. Because we don't want to create a Faraday grid effect by reinforcing with wire mesh, we add chopped straw in the concrete mix before doing these two pours. (The "Faraday effect" is a change in electromagnetic field caused by conductive materials used in certain grid configurations. Some experts consider it to be unhealthy to humans.) A 3-inch-thick top slab is then poured on the bale surface, with or without chopped straw in it depending on its desired final texture.

This design is based on the low-cost plunger pile slab developed by Dr. Billig of the Central Building Research Institute of India and described in Ken Kern's *The Owner-Built Home*. Dr. Billig's light-duty floor, which was subjected to loading stresses of up to 450 pounds per square foot without showing any sign of distress, was a 1-inch-thick concrete layer poured on a piece of fabric laid across piles that were spaced on 3-foot

centers. These had previously been poured in predrilled holes in a lightly rototilled soil. The later settling of the soil made the floor rest only on the piles, separated from the ground by a very shallow crawlspace.

Because our top slab is at least three times thicker and rests on a tighter grid of piles, we believe that any bale settling after the final setting of the concrete would be of no significant consequence to the system's structural performance. In the worst case, bales collapsing inside the sandwiched slab would create a small airtight crawlspace without reducing the structural integrity of the floor slab. The tests conducted in the autumn of 1999 confirmed that rotten collapsing bales do not affect the structural capacity of the slab system.

SITE PREPARATION

As previously mentioned, because we want our slab built in the best possible conditions, our first concern is site drainage. We start by installing perimeter drains below the bottom slab level. On sloping sites we suggest building reversed V-shaped diverting berms on the upper side of the slope, behind the building, to drain water away on the sides.

We always make sure there is no underground source of water or rising dampness under the slab. When such risks exist, such as on soils with high contents of clay that could wick water from any nearby source, we suggest removing as much of that soil as possible under the projected base slab. (In one particular project, we removed as much as 4 feet of soil.) The hole is then filled with pure sand or gravel, compacted mechanically, and topped with at least 6 inches of coarse gravel to block capillary action and to ensure superior drainage.

When there is no risk of water infiltration, the topsoil and subsoil are removed to 6 inches under the depth of the desired base slab level (approximately 14 inches below the exterior finished grade so that the finished slab level will be at 6 inches above grade), and that 6 inches is filled with compacted gravel before pouring.

SLAB COMPOSITION

We use a 3,000 psi concrete mix for all our pours except when a stronger bearing capacity is needed, whereas then we use a 4,000 psi mix. For best workability we use half-inch net aggregates that fill thin surfaces and small gaps effectively. Low-slump mixes are also easier to work with, for the base and top slabs. Unless conditions are unpredictable, we always try to avoid using chemical additives in the mixes.

POURING THE SLAB

At the arrival of the truck mixer on-site, we add chopped straw in the amount of one-third of a bale for every cubic yard of the concrete mix. It is then left spinning for a few minutes. (Because mixer drivers are unfamiliar with this idea and sometimes quite skeptical about it, this proce-

dure should definitely be checked beforehand with the dispatcher when the load is ordered.)

The idea, of course, is to use the truck to thoroughly mix the straw into the concrete. The straw has to be previously chopped into loose fibers no more than 4 inches long. A good and quick way to chop the straw is by making two chain-saw cuts along the strings through the bale. When large amounts of fibers are needed, we shred loose straw in a garden mulcher. The straw is added by small handfuls, in order to allow it to mix well. Because overtime is always charged, it's better to have the chopped straw ready and handy in bags or buckets before the truck arrives.

Because the added straw eats up a bit of water, the driver has to add water as the mix thickens. Make him add just enough to be able to pour, otherwise the water weakens the concrete.

When the mix is ready, we pour the straw-reinforced concrete on the gravel base; 2 inches is usually enough to uniformly cover the entire surface. At this stage two options are possible depending on the size of the project and the number of helpers available. For small projects, the concrete is left to set for a few hours before bales are laid on it to cover the entire surface, we then

Pouring the base slab.

Bales laid on the base slab.

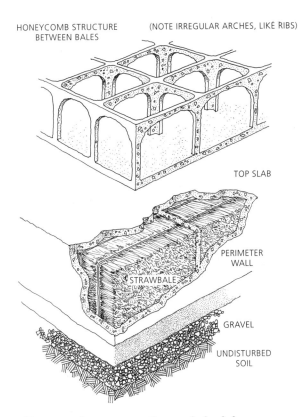

(NOTE IRREGULAR ARCHES, LIKE RIBS)

TOP SLAB

PERIMETER
WALL

STRAWBALE

GRAVEL

UNDISTURBED
SOIL

Honeycomb structure of straw bale slab.

proceed with the next step. For large projects with frost walls to bear the framed baled walls, in which the roof has to be finished before any sort of bale work is started, the base slab is left uncovered until the roof is up.

It is worth mentioning here that the frost walls built to support the framed walls need to be insulated to at least the same depth as the straw bale slab in order to prevent the concrete from freezing and becoming a potential thermal bridge and a good spot for condensation. We usually apply Roxul rigid panels on the exterior side of the concrete wall and finish them with netting and plaster. A 10-inch-thick wall with 4 inches of insulation will allow for alignment with the plaster applied on the bales and thus make a vertical continuity in the plaster finish.

In cases where capillarity is a concern it is possible to create a capillary break by making a horizontal saw cut across the plaster, after it has set well, a few inches below the top of the rigid insulation. The kerf can then be sealed with regular caulking material. This stops any rising moisture from getting to the bales at the base of the wall. This method is also much easier than trying to insert regular continuous flashing at the base of the curvy irregular surface of the plastered bale wall.

PLACING BALES

The bales are laid by placing them side-by-side, barely touching each other, making sure there is a vertical gap left at the corners to pour the piles. When the void seems insufficient, the corners may be beveled with a chain-saw cut or the gap simply widened with a stick. Bales that would be inappropriate for walls because of inadequate length may be used for this application. At spots where supports are needed for chimneys, posts, and other structural elements, pads are poured and sufficient space is left open to place these elements between the bales.

POURING PILES

This next operation requires very special care.

Chopped straw is once again combined with the concrete in the mixer. This time approximately 25 percent more concrete is needed than for the base slab. Once well mixed, the straw-reinforced concrete is either dumped, carried along, or pumped *on top of the bales*, and tossed carefully into the corner cavities with thick sticks such as 2-by-3s, making sure they are completely filled from bottom to top, thus forming strong piles to carry the weight of the top slab. Because of the uneven shapes of the bales there are usually lateral gaps between the piles. These gaps are filled loosely from the top, with the intention of forming small arches spanning from pile to pile like a honeycomb structure.

Because this operation is time consuming, it is best carried out by a large crew of people. The piles are the structural key of the sandwich slab, so it is critical that they be poured with care.

To prevent damaging the bales from the volume of traffic on them, we suggest laying plywood sheets or wooden boards as walkways.

The pour is stopped after the top of the bales are covered by a fine layer of concrete. The work is then left to firmly set overnight or longer, according to conditions.

These first two operations can be done on the same day or on two separate days, depending on the size of the floor. At this stage, some plumbing equipment, such as sewage pipes or electrical conduits, may have to be installed before any further pouring is done. Usually, we have previously notched the bales with chain-saw runs to create the channels needed for these purposes.

Mechanical floating of the top slab.

We make these on the top part of the bales, just below the interior top slab level, so that they still have some insulation left underneath while being easy to reach for maintenance, if ever necessary. Then, if the floor has been planned with a radiant heating system, the tubes are installed on top of the slightly covered bales before the last pour is done.

The final step is to pour the top slab. We use a 4,000 psi, low-slump concrete mix with finer aggregates when the concrete floor is to be left exposed. Depending on the desired finish, this pour may or may not contain chopped straw (see "Floor Finishes," in chapter 13). There are various curing methods, but the easiest one is to cover the entire surface with a plastic sheet immediately after the floating has been completed, and to keep it protected for a minimum of seven days, and ideally as many as twenty-eight days. This step is critical for an exposed slab.

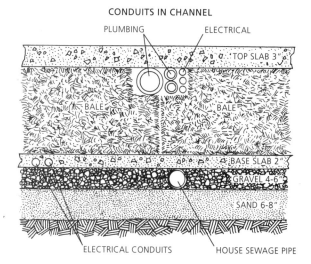

Ditch or channel cut into bales for pipes and conduits.

When the slab is not going to be left exposed and has no heating tubes, this final pour of concrete may be approximately 2 inches thick and simply bull floated. (A bull float is a 4-foot-wide steel trowel with a very long broomstick-type handle, used for the initial surfacing of a concrete slab.) Otherwise, a total of 3 inches with the tubes are a minimum for the slab to perform adequately as a heating system.

Other Types of Foundations

Depending on the size of the project, the conditions of the site, and the building resources available, some other less conventional foundation options may be worth an evaluation. Because all of the following systems have proved their reliability, there is no reason why they couldn't work with bale walls, properly detailed.

Piers

Poured concrete piers use very little material and can easily be owner-built; they are, therefore, among the least expensive foundation options. Piers also accommodate uneven terrain and high water tables. As the holes are typically dug by a small backhoe or by hand, site disturbance is minimal. Piers are an excellent foundation option for sites that are difficult to access by machine, because they can be poured with concrete mixed on site, either in a portable mixer, or by hand in a wheelbarrow. Piers need not necessarily be made of concrete; rot-resistant wood species, pressure-treated poles, or salvaged telephone poles can also work well.

On the negative side, a house on piers tends to look rickety and disconnected from its site. This effect is exacerbated in the case of a plas-

tered bale building; a structure with such a massive feel really wants to be anchored to the ground. Thermally, a cold-climate building is better off having one of its sides in contact with 50°F (10°C) earth than with cold winter air. The ecological tradeoff, here, is that the floor of a building on piers can be insulated with blown cellulose, rockwool batts, or even bales, rather than rigid foam.

Piers typically support carrying beams, which, in turn, support a framed floor system of joists and decking, upon which your bales will rest, high and dry. Whenever possible, Paul likes to cantilever beams 1 to 2 feet beyond perimeter piers, and likewise cantilever floor joists a similar distance beyond perimeter beams. The idea here is to recess the piers, so that you don't have to look at them. (Horizontal shear can be an issue in this situation. Be sure to take this into account in your load calculations.) You might also

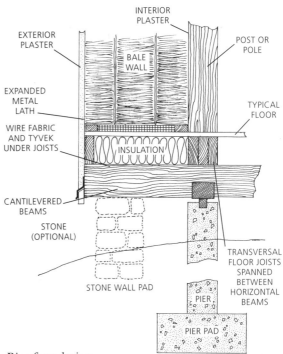

Pier foundation.

Wooden piers accommodate a severely sloping site. Chapin home, Phillips, Maine.

choose to dry-lay stone outside the piers, at the building's perimeter; this strategy combines the beauty of stone with the strength of concrete, removing the need to pay careful attention to the structural integrity of your dry-laid stone wall.

If the bales in your building are to be wrapped around an internal post-and-beam system, then the cantilever of your floor deck should be sized such that the structural columns within the living area are placed directly over the piers—the structural columns that will carry the weight of your building down to solid soil.

The floor of a building on piers should be detailed as if it were an outside wall. This can be tricky, because the plane at the bottom of the joists is regularly interrupted by carrying beams. It's not a bad idea, if this plane is to become your air barrier layer, to lap a strip of plastic or housewrap over the beams, before setting the joists. This can then be caulked to whatever sheet material you apply to the underside of the joists. Even if your air barrier is to the interior, you will want to cover the underside of the joists, to prevent massive

wind-washing through the floor insulation. In combination with blown cellulose insulation, GreenSpace has had good luck with ½-inch homasote (commercially produced pressed-paper board, suggested by Tony Walker of Cellu-Spray Insulation, Shelburne Falls, Massachusetts—the missionary of cellulose). A combination of housewrap and hardware cloth (to deter rodents) also works, as does plywood, or boards.

Experience tells us that the greatest problem faced by buildings on piers is not structural—it is frozen pipes. Horizontal plumbing lines must be run either in the upper third of the joist zone, or in interior walls. It is a fact of physics, however, that if you have running water in a house, then the water needs to both enter and leave. Unfortunately, in a house built on piers, this means that the main supply and waste lines must pass through the open air, as they make their way between the building and the ground. Waste lines are not a major issue, as the water in them is usually moving along at a pretty good clip. In a supply line, however, water will often sit overnight, and occasionally for days or weeks, without moving; this means that the pipe will freeze solid, and burst.

The safest way to avoid the prospect of frozen pipes is to accept the need for a small crawlspace or cellar under a portion of the building. This space can be as small as 4 feet by 4 feet. It should have insulated walls, and should extend below the frost line. Aside from protecting the plumbing lines, larger versions of this space can house wine and potatoes, or double as a mechanical room. The boiler or furnace, in this case, would provide waste heat, as added insurance against frozen pipes.

Special attention must also be paid to traps under tubs and showers; these can often end up far enough down in the joist zone that they will be separated by insulation from the heat of the building. You might need to bump down an insulated area below such traps. By all means, avoid insulating above them. And don't expect plumbing or insulation contractors to be thinking about such things; they have lots of other problems to worry about. The responsibility is on the designer to ensure that such important details end up on the house plans.

Moisture should not be much of an issue under a building on piers, as the space below is typically in continuous conversation with the out-side air. In situations where this is not the case—when the building is close to the ground, for instance, or when the space between the ground and the building is carefully filled with stones—and where the ground under the building is wet for long portions of the year, it can be a good idea to lay a sheet of polyethylene over the soil, to block moisture from moving up and challenging the integrity of the building's components. Also be aware that by closing in the area under a house on piers, you are creating a very nice home for the local rodent population.

Pole Framing

Pole framing is similar to building on piers, in that columns bear all loads down to a frost-free soil depth. Whereas piers end at the floor carrying beam, however, poles typically run all the way up through the wall, to the roof framing system.

A pole-framed building can sit comfortably close to the ground. The completed Haeme home, Kempton, Illinois.

Pole framing: Buried poles run all the way to the roof, and bolted-on beams support floor joists. Haeme home, Kempton, Illinois.

Floor framing is hung from the poles, so the floor can be set at any height that seems appropriate, given local weather patterns and land forms. This system, therefore, offers the option of raising the bales a significant distance above the ground.

The second benefit of pole construction to bale builders is that in one-story construction, the fact that the poles are buried 4 to 5 feet in the earth provides all of the necessary lateral bracing to the wall. This means no diagonal braces to interfere with bale laying or window placement.

Poles are typically of rot-resistant or treated wood, though they can also be made of poured concrete. Such a system could mesh quite nicely with the depth of the bale wall.

Rubble Trench and Grade Beam

The grade beam is like a floating slab, without the slab. It might be called a floating beam, though it is specifically designed never to touch water; it is a beam of concrete poured on top of a rubble-filled trench. Water drains down through the rubble, and the beam is left high and dry, immune to heaving, floating on a piling of air.

A grade beam allows for flexibility in your choice of floor material. The floor might be stone, or brick, or the increasingly popular poured adobe. It might be concrete, poured in small panels. Because concrete sets up more evenly when it is not exposed to direct sunlight and heat, it is not a bad idea to pour your floor after putting on your roof, even if you intend to pour in a continuous slab. A slab poured late in the construction process will not suffer the chips from dropped hammers that inevitably plague the monolithic slab.

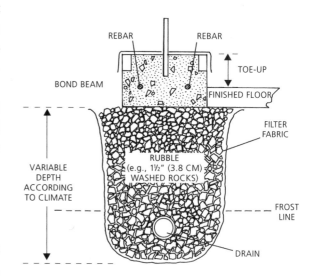

Rubble-trench footing.

This grade beam sits on a 4-foot-deep trench filled with rubble and drained by perforated pipe, so it should be safe from frost heaving even in frigid New York State.

It is quite possible to use a foam-form product, or Rastra or Faswall, to create a 2-or 3-foot-high grade beam/wall, sitting atop a rubble trench. Such a hybrid beam would elevate the bales nicely, with minimal use of concrete.

Stone and Earthbags

No rule says that the beam above your rubble trench needs to be made of concrete. The monolithic nature of reinforced concrete adds strength to the structure, of course, but those willing to experiment can certainly come up with other material options. Stone, either dry-laid, mortared, or slip-formed with concrete can be an

excellent choice for sites where lots of it is lying around.

Some builders have also had success using sandbags as forms for tamped-in-place soil-cement blocks. This technique, known as earthbag construction, was first developed by Nader Khalili and others at CalEarth, in Hesperia, California, where entire structures—walls and vaulted roofs—are being built by this method.

The soil mix is typically filled into bags, which are then set in place in the wall, and tamped to create a solid mass. Barbed wire is often run between courses of bags, to keep them from sliding, and rocks are also sometimes placed to form a key. Alternately, a groove can be pounded into the center of each bag, parallel to the direction of the wall, so that each course of bags can nest down into the course below.

If the soil on your site is between 15 and 20 percent clay, it can work with little or no cement stabilization. Lower percentages of clay require

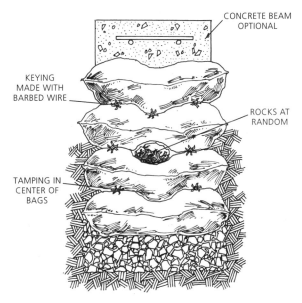

Three ways of keying courses in earthbag foundations.

An earthbag wall, partially covered by foam insulation.

Paul pours a concrete bond beam atop an earthbag wall, to create a level surface for framing. Note separate foundation for poles supporting the roof. The earthbags will support only the bales and windows.

that cement be added, as a binder. Proportions are typical of rammed earth construction; a 10 percent clay mix would want 5 to 10 percent cement, while a soil with no clay content would want 10 to 20 percent cement. If the soil is damp, sufficient moisture should be available to set the cement; in dry conditions, the wall can be soaked after it is built, to help the cement to set. The main drawback to this method is that the tamp-

ing requires quite a lot of rather brute labor. While it is possible that Paul was somewhat more compulsive than necessary in his bag tamping, he feels compelled to warn anyone considering this method to avoid its use at times of the year when spinach is not available in abundant quantities. Regardless of how burly you may consider yourself to be, pounding these bags will leave you quite sore by the end of the day!

An alternate approach is to assume that the bag will last indefinitely as a structural component of the wall. In this case, the fill material need not be compressed or stabilized into a cohesive block. Gravel-filled bags have sometimes been used as a foundation material under bale buildings; the gravel serves the secondary purpose of forming a capillary break between the bales and the ground. The trick with this approach is to find a bag that will not begin to photodegrade during the construction process. Because sandbags are typically made for temporary installations, they are generally not designed for durability. Depending on your local supply of bags, you may find it necessary to plaster the foundation immediately after stacking it. It can also be quite difficult to acquire strength ratings from the manufacturers.

Earthbag or stone walls can work particularly well in a hybrid foundation system, where either poles, or posts on piers, bear the roof load down to the frost line, while stones or sandbags, atop a rubble trench, support the bale walls.

It should be clear that no one foundation system is most suitable to bale construction. Most foundations will work fine; once the need to support the wide walls is covered, other aspects of the design, including the site conditions, are really more important than the bales.

CHAPTER 6

NEBRASKA STYLE
Load-Bearing Bale Walls

A BALE-WALLED BUILDING is said to be built in the "Nebraska style" when it follows the structural pattern of the early bale houses, most of which are found in the Sand Hills region of Nebraska. The defining characteristic of these buildings is that no vertical support columns are employed in holding up the roof. The roof load, instead, is borne directly onto the walls, and carried to the foundation by some combination of the bales and the plaster skins.

Origin of Nebraska Style

This early form of bale construction was a very specific response to the need for shelter produced of locally available materials. Trees were few and far between across much of the western plains, and the lumber that came in by train was expensive. The archetypal response to this situation was the sod house—literally a house whose walls were built of the sod that homesteaders cut as they settled the prairie. These were (and continue to be—many still survive) fine houses.

In the Sand Hills region of western Nebraska, however, the soil was not well suited to construction. The sod/sandy soil composite was simply too crumbly to form a stable wall. Luckily, at about the time this region was settled, the mechanical baler was beginning to come into use. A scattering of homesteaders, the early owner-builders of

Built in 1925, the Martin-Monhart house, Arthur, Nebraska.

forcing mesh act in concert to support the various loads to which the wall is subjected. We have clear theories, underscored by testing, about how the wall functions in its two most extreme forms—without any plaster, and with wire-reinforced cement stucco—but we know little about the more appealing options that fall between these two.

The three main issues that affect the practicality of Nebraska-style methods for cold climates are structure, moisture, and construction efficiency.

bale houses, came around to building of what they had—large blocks of dead grass.

While many of these homestead dwellings were made obsolete by the consolidation of Sand Hills land into large ranches, those buildings that have been consistently used and maintained are in excellent shape today. More important, the people who live in them almost always report that they consider their bale house to be more comfortable than a conventional frame house (not a surprise, on the cold and windy plains). So, what we know is that bales can work structurally, for periods approaching one hundred years, in relatively modest buildings that are well maintained.

How Does a Nebraska-style Wall Work?

The fact of the matter is that the straw bale construction community is not really sure, yet, just how a Nebraska-style wall works. We understand that the bales, the plaster, and any rein-

Structure

Nebraska-style walls are often referred to as "load-bearing," which is intended to mean that the bales are supporting the compressive loads typically associated with a roof: the dead load of framing and roofing materials, and the live loads of snow, roofing crews, dance parties, and so on. This is certainly true until the plaster goes on. It is also not unreasonable to think it true for the life of the building, given that most people look at a plastered bale wall as just that—a bale wall covered with two protective skins of plaster. Engineering tests performed in 1996 by Linda Chapman and Bob Platts of Fibrehouse Ltd., Ottawa, Ontario, suggest otherwise, however.

STRESSED-SKIN PANEL

The Fibrehouse tests indicate that the typical Nebraska-style wall actually functions as a structural sandwich composite, or stressed-skin panel. In most situations, therefore, the primary role of the straw is to maintain the rigid skins in a vertical position. The bales do initially carry the dead load of the roof; the extent to which they continue to do this over time might depend on the tightness of the bales at the outset, and also on the extent to which the wall is allowed to compress (or is forced into compression) before the plaster is applied. As a general rule, it is best to assume that the bales will simply creep to the point where all compressive loads are carried by the skins.

Live loads are most certainly taken up by the plaster. The reason for this is very simple: The bales are softer than the skins. When a live compressive load is applied to the wall, say by a foot of snow on the roof, the bales are willing to compress a bit under the extra weight. The plaster

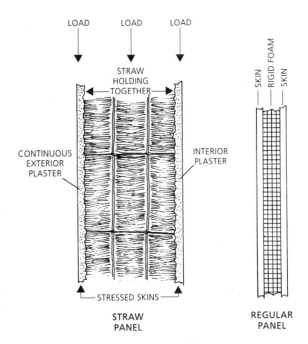

Stressed-skin panels.

skins, on the other hand, do not compress (or at least do not compress as much or as willingly as the bale core) and are, therefore, forced into bearing the snow load.

The very important job of the bales, at this point, is to keep the skins from buckling. They share this job with any steel mesh that may have been used as a reinforcing material. This is a role for which the bales are aptly suited; their rough surface texture allows the plaster a very strong mechanical bond. Separating the plaster from the bales is quite difficult.

LIVE LOADS

It follows that in areas of minimal snow load (and assuming those rooftop dance parties don't get too wild), the skins should have a relatively easy job; they aren't asked to do much beyond protecting the wall from the weather, and coming to bear or share the weight of the roof, as the

Using saplings for exterior pins, which creates a very rigid wall.

bales settle, over time. The rigidity of the skin, therefore, is not a major issue, and designers in such climates are free to choose plaster materials based on other criteria. Clay plasters, which have been popular in the southwestern United States, have not suffered excessive cracking on Nebraska-style buildings in that region, presumably because they are not typically called upon to bear any substantial loads.

In climates with significant snow accumulation, on the other hand, the story is quite different. The plaster skins of Nebraska-style buildings are required to accept these loads, and it would seem that they must be more rigid. Interestingly, cement stucco is the plaster that has been most commonly employed in snowy climates, presumably on account of its ubiquity, but maybe also because of builders' intuition regarding its structural role. Because cement makes the most rigid plaster available (and as it has often been applied to both sides of the wall), bale builders in snow-load climates generally have been constructing walls that seem to perform quite well as structural panels. It is also crucial that the ce-

---

How a Stressed-Skin Panel Works: A Lunchtime Experiment

You can probably imagine that a freestanding, 1-inch-thick by 8- or 12-foot-high wall of any kind of plaster material could not be expected to bear much of a load, on its own. It would quickly topple or buckle, depending upon how perfectly vertical the applied load was. How, then, do the plaster skins of a bale building come to accept snow loads, without buckling?

A stressed-skin panel, or structural sandwich composite, is composed of two relatively rigid outer materials, such as plaster (or toast), spaced apart and fastened by a core material, such as bales (or peanut butter). Here's an experiment you can try at lunchtime, to demonstrate to yourself how it works:

1. Toast three slices of squarish bread, until dark, dry, and rather stiff. (You might need to lop off the top edge of each slice, if it's rounded.)
2. Stand up one slice on its edge, and try to rest something on top. Tough to do without having it fall over, eh?
3. Stand the toast back up, and, while holding it loosely in a vertical position, put something heavy on top, like a 28-oz. can of tomatoes. Did the toast buckle under the weight? If not, keep adding cans until it does. (At this point, this piece of toast is toasted, as far as this experiment is concerned, so slather on some butter and eat it before it gets too cold.)

ment stucco be reinforced with wire, which takes up tension loads (shear, typically generated by wind) in the same manner as rebar in poured concrete. Cement stucco is probably too brittle to handle these forces without wire. (The trick here, according to Bruce King, is that wire fastened tight to the face of the bale doesn't reinforce nearly so well as wire that is sandwiched into the plaster. This is difficult to achieve, in the field.)

It is unclear whether lime- or clay-based plasters possess sufficient compressive strength to work, over the long term, as a skin material on Nebraska-style buildings that will be subjected to a snow load. There is no question that lime plaster sets up quite hard—but is it rigid enough? And should it be reinforced with some sort of continuous netting, or does the addition of hair or milled straw or synthetic fibers provide sufficient tensile strength? Should it be applied thicker than the usual inch? Is the key into the flexible straw substrate substantial enough to hold the lime in column over 50, 100, 300 years? Maybe the lime plaster's combination of strength and flexibility will turn out to be just perfect for this

4. Make a sandwich of the remaining two slices of toast and about a half inch of good-quality, stiff peanut butter. (This is pure science, and no place to skimp on materials.) You might have to smear half the peanut butter on each slice and then stick them together, in order to achieve proper cohesion.

5. Stand the sandwich up on its edge, and put the can of tomatoes back on top. Does it bear the compressive load of the can of tomatoes? Unless you got hungry and took a bite, it should!

6. Apply a very slight pressure to the sides of the sandwich with your fingers, to make up for the fact that peanut butter is not really all that effective a glue. Now start piling up more of those tomato cans. Can your little stressed-skin lunch panel bear more weight than the bread alone? Of course it can! It is performing in a manner very similar to the two thin skins of plaster held in by bales.

7. Open your sandwich up, and add in something sweet (or maybe a pickle?) with your peanut butter. Since this experiment is definitely not your first step up the ivory tower of scientific research, you may as well enjoy your rewards immediately.

A structural composite sandwich can bear more weight than any of its components alone (good thing you didn't try stacking the cans atop the peanut butter, eh?). Why is this so? There are two basic reasons. First of all, the panel has a wider base than any of its individual components; it is therefore inherently more stable. The second factor is that the core material, which serves as both spacer and glue, holds the skin materials (the elements typically responsible for bearing the load) in column. Toast is remarkably strong when tied in to this upright position; the same is true for oriented strand board (OSB), which forms the bread around a foam filling in structural insulated panel systems, and for some common plaster materials (which are held apart and in column by bales) in a Nebraska-style straw bale wall.

task. In the absence of both traditional examples and modern tests, we don't yet know how such a wall will react to live loads.

All of these same questions apply to clay plasters, but since they are less rigid than those bound by lime, the odds that they will work under severe loading are lower. Still, nobody knows. It could be that 2 inches of straw-reinforced and lime- or cement-stabilized material over each side of the wall is sufficient to bear significant snow loads, and maybe even seismic loads. Once again, until someone does the tests (or until we wait fifty years), nobody really knows.

TWO-STRING VERSUS THREE-STRING BALES

An interesting factor in all of this is that the dense three-string bales that are common in some parts of the western United States are probably quite capable of bearing both dead and live compressive loads on their own, with no help from the plaster. They might depress a bit under heavy snow loads, and may show a gradual creep over the years. The first round of structural tests in Tucson, carried out by Matts Myhrman, David Eisenberg, Lance Durand, and Ghaline Bou-Ali (commonly known as the Bou-Ali thesis) were purposely made on unplastered bale walls, so that the structural capacities of the bales themselves would be tested, and the resulting prescriptive code language would not specify the use of particular finish materials. In this test, 8-foot-high walls of well-pinned three-string bales were determined to be capable of supporting the compressive and shear loads required by the Tucson codes.

Lime-based plaster ready for a final coat. Jocelyne Henri's Nebraska-style home, Chénéville, Quebec.

The Tucson code does not require the wall to withstand snow conditions, of course, but based on our experience with them, it seems reasonable to assume that walls of three-string bales are capable of bearing these loads without some sort of catastrophic failure. (We are not talking about earthquakes here.) Stringing one assumption after another, it also seems a reasonable guess that the worst-case scenario in the use of softer plaster over such a wall is that the plaster would crack excessively. Is this the end of the world? That is an individual decision, based on a person's tolerance for maintenance.

Two-string bales, on the other hand, are an entirely different material. Because they are narrower and less dense than three stringers, they form a less stable wall, which is less able to bear loads. In this case, the skins are crucial to the ultimate strength of the wall assembly. The skins also stiffen the wall to where it feels safe enough to walk around, but unfortunately, the plaster does not usually go on until after the roof, at which point the walking-on-walls phase is over. Unless your design is for a very small building, or you can integrate a system for stiffening and stabilizing the walls early in the process (see "Prestressed Nebraska," later in this chapter), we cannot recommend the use of two-string bales for Nebraska-style construction.

SEISMIC LOADS

California, of course, is where most of the earthquake research is taking place. California has development, rice straw, and seismic activity, all in excess. Thankfully, it also has a very talented straw bale community, and these folks are pursuing designs that mesh these three components, hoping to dampen the negative effects of each.

Thus far, the key really does seem to be in the mesh. In their tests to this point, engineers David Mar and Bruce King, the designers and builders at Skillful Means, and the architects at Daniel Smith and Associates, have determined that a bale wall that is held tight within a cage of steel hardware cloth is capable of absorbing a tremendous amount of energy. What happens is that because the bales are prevented from shifting under load, compression struts (like shock absorbers) are set up all through the bale wall, running at diagonals from face to face. Because the straw can compress and rebound at an uncountable number of points throughout the wall, it is capable of absorbing tremendous quantities of energy, without cracking (as a brittle masonry building will) or experiencing severe fiber or connector stress (as a wooden building will). In other words, the straw core of this bale-and-wire wall seems to be able to shimmy around a bit, without failing catastrophically. The amplitude of shimmy is limited by the wire, and the plaster. These components hold the top of the wall within a reasonable degree of plane with the bottom, so that it doesn't fall over.

Though most of this testing has been done on bale walls (and arches—see chapter 1, "Why Straw Bales?") covered with wire mesh and cement stucco, David Mar's theoretical work leaves open the possibility that because the wire and bales are really handling the shear loads, the choice of plaster may not really matter, so long as the two curtains of mesh are fastened tightly together, through the bale core. Choice of plaster will still affect the wall's ability to handle compressive loads, of course. Once again, we don't yet have the complete set of answers to how these systems function, and what the possibilities and limitations may be.

Moisture

Moisture control is obviously a major issue in Nebraska-style construction. Because the bales and plaster are supporting the roof, the bales had better be kept dry and sound, and the plaster maintained. The big issue here is the fact that one component—the skin—is called upon to do the two most important jobs of the wall: holding up the roof and keeping out the weather. Stuart Brand, in his groundbreaking *How Buildings Learn,* makes a strong case for separating the various functions of buildings, to whatever degree is possible. This simplifies the inevitable remodeling; it also makes the building more durable by allowing each component to be tailored to its role. By merging structure and skin, we raise some obvious durability issues.

Wet Climate

In cold and wet climates, Nebraska-style construction seems like a risky proposition. This is because the most conservative plaster choice for handling structural loads (wire-reinforced cement stucco) is the most dangerous choice for preventing moisture-related damage. A person who chooses this route must decide whether to take their risks on structure or on moisture; an unpleasant quandary, indeed. The seriousness of this dilemma will be determined by the site and the design, of course. If the building is well protected from the elements, or if it will be sheltered by porches, sheds, and the like, the reinforced cement stucco seems like a better gamble. If, on the other hand, the building is completely exposed to the weather, it might make more sense to try a lime plaster, and take your chances on its ability to bear compressive loads, over the years.

Compounding this problem is the fact that there is really no consensus of opinion on how best to apply cement stucco over bales in wet climates. While it is clear that the stucco must be bonded directly to the bales if a Nebraska-style wall is to function properly under snow load, some people maintain that for the stucco to perform its other major task—protecting the bales from the weather—a drainage plane of asphalt-impregnated felt paper should be hung between it and the bales. This is how stucco is typically detailed over wood-sheathed structures, mainly because cement stucco always cracks, and allows some water entry. While your friendly authors do not believe that felt is a good choice in bale construction, we could be wrong. (See chapter 10, "Cement Stucco," for a more detailed exploration.)

The safest response to this moisture-versus-structure conundrum is to avoid Nebraska-style construction on exposed sites in wet climates. Wet climates grow trees, and trees are a renewable resource. Use a few to hold up your roof. More on this later.

Interior moisture is also an important issue in wet climates, because the drying periods—the times of the year during which the exterior air will thirstily suck moisture from walls—are limited. It is therefore crucial, in Nebraska-style houses in cold or wet climates, especially those finished with cement stucco, that very careful attention be paid to air-sealing details at penetrations. Keep that moist air inside the living space, where it belongs! With cement stucco on the exterior, a vapor-retardant paint finish (two coats of any alkyd latex paint) is a smart choice for the interior (see chapters 2 and 10).

There are two other possible options for handling this dual problem. The first is to use a cement stucco on the interior, and a lime plaster on the exterior. Such a finish makes sense from a moisture point of view, but would it work structurally? It would seem that a truss could be designed to bear primarily on the inside portion of the wall; indeed, when a snow load hits a truss, this is probably what is happening on a wide bale wall. Things seem much dicier with rafters. This is one for the engineers.

> In cold and wet climates, Nebraska-style construction seems like a risky proposition.

The second possibility is to develop a two-ply, rainscreen-style plaster system for the exterior. The bales would be covered by a base and brown coat of cement stucco, and vertical spacers formed or troweled into the surface of the brown coat. Alternately, some rot-resistant plastic or metal or cementitious furring-strip material could be nailed to the stucco, as the brown coat cured. Or, as suggested by Tim Lambert of Port Townsend, Washington, a tie could be fabricated out of stainless steel, and hung from or through these first stucco coats. Expanded metal lath or felt-backed stucco netting could then be affixed to the spacers or furring strips , and a three-coat stucco applied. The resulting ½- to 1-inch gap between the plaster layers, if properly vented, should act as a rainscreen. (See "Siding," in chapter 9.)

This idea might be most practical on a wall that was to be finished in brick. The bales could receive a two-coat stucco treatment, with standard or modified brick ties laid into the stucco. These would then secure a brick curtain wall; details would be fairly typical of commercial brick facing.

Dry Climate

In areas of low precipitation—say 20 inches per year or less—moisture is much less of an issue for walls of bales and plaster. Assuming careful detailing around openings, good flashing details, a reasonable roof overhang (18+ inches), sufficient separation between the walls and the ground, and regular maintenance, well-applied cement stucco should be adequate for these climates. As always, this depends on the site; if most of the weather arrives on the horizontal, the windward walls might need to be protected by porches, sheds, or some other structure.

The beauty of dry climates is that rain storms or seasons are usually followed by long periods of drying weather. This means that the small amounts of water that might pass through the stucco should have ample opportunity to dry out. Similarly, interior moisture is much less of a concern, though attention to air sealing at penetrations is still a good idea. So is vapor-retardant interior paint, when the exterior is finished in cement stucco.

Construction Efficiency

Unlike infill construction, where the builder can erect the roof first, and then work at a relaxed pace with relative lack of concern for the weather, the Nebraska-style builder must move to get her or his bale walls under cover as quickly as possible. If rain is common in your area during the construction season, this need becomes a driving force behind the design of the building.

The most critical element in such a case is that the building's footprint be kept small and simple. Large buildings with many windows, and especially with complex roof lines, are a recipe for disaster in Nebraska-style construction. The

A Tent
Big Enough
for All

If the site is in the woods, and the building is small enough, you might think about buying a large tarp of good quality, which can be hung from the trees, to cover the entire site. By removing the pressure to get the walls up and the roof on quickly, such protection increases your range of options, both in terms of design complexity and construction process. It will pay for itself, in time savings and stress reduction.

A contractor who was cranking out bale houses in one area might do well by investing in a plastic bubble structure, of the sort that is used over tennis courts and, recently, over driving ranges. (Apparently golf addicts need their fix, even in winter.) Such a structure would seal out the two main problems that slow progress on any site—rain and cold fingers—resulting in a more efficient operation. If a contractor could keep this bubble in constant use, by moving it from site to site as roofs went on, the payback period might not be all that long.

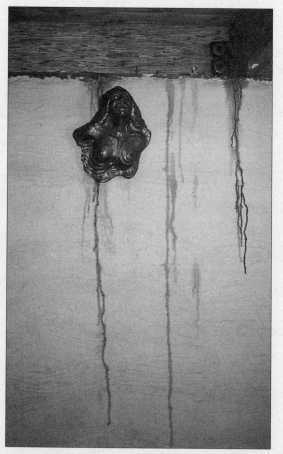

A leaky tarp above caused these stains on a beautifully plastered bale wall. When it comes to keeping bales dry, there is no substitute for a roof.

building does not necessarily have to be a box, but the shape should allow for a simple roof structure. Unless you are in a very dry climate, we would not recommend, for instance, trying to frame an octagonal roof atop a Nebraska-style bale wall. (Though on a small building, it might be possible to assemble such a roof structure on the ground, and lift it into place with a crane!)

While it is hard to determine a fixed limit on the practical size of a Nebraska-style building, we can come up with a couple of guidelines. If the crew is to be small, or the work is to progress at an on-and-off pace (we really do not recommend this), one limiting factor is the size that can be covered by a single tarp or 6-mil poly sheet. Don't even consider overlapping smaller tarps; it doesn't work. And these tarps must be configured such that the water that runs off of them doesn't sheet down the walls.

If the bale and roof work is to be done in a burst, by a large group, the following questions are relevant: What size building can the expected group wall and roof within a typical period of dry weather? How accurate are the local weather reports? How flexible is the anticipated crew—must the date be set a month in advance, or can the builders watch the weather, and call an assembly on a few days' notice?

Think Twice before Jumping into Nebraska-style Construction

By this point it should be fairly clear that these authors have strong reservations about Nebraska-style construction. We love the simplicity of the idea: stack up some bales, toss a roof on top, shoot on some plaster, and you've got a house. This is the concept that draws most of us into bale construction in the first place. The problem is that this image is a drastic oversimplification of the real process of building a bale wall. Laying bales is easy; laying them well—in such a way that the walls and corners are plumb, the top of the wall is level, and the whole configuration is capable of properly supporting a roof—is hard. Bales resist such linearity. They resist measurement more precisely than by the nearest inch, which means that each stretching of a tape introduces a margin of error somewhere between sixteen and thirty-two times greater than would be acceptable to any decent carpenter. Neither does a bale wall form a planar surface against which to lean a level. Often, by the time enough bale courses have been stacked to establish a de-

cent average among the various bulges that form the wall, one corner or other will be so hopelessly out of plumb that the reluctant builder will have no choice but to reconstruct it—typically by cutting open each of the corner bales, removing material, and retying. This is never fun, because inherent in each opportunity to improve your technique is a tacit admission of your continued lack of mastery over those damned ornery bales.

The bale's nonlinear nature is also one of its greatest attributes as a construction material, of course. This complexity of character reveals itself on the surface of the wall, creating a texture that no concrete masonry unit could ever dream of. Bales make beautiful walls. They do not, however, make a beautiful job of providing the level, square platform that is necessary if ordinary, human carpenters are expected to frame a roof on top, in the time typically allotted for such

Rigging tarps over a Nebraska-style building can be complicated.

work. Add in the fact that the tremendous compressive strength of wood (or concrete) means that very little of it is needed to support a roof, and you (or, at least, we) come to the inevitable conclusion that inserting a few columns makes a lot more sense than trying to bully the bales into a job that they wholeheartedly resist.

Part of our attitude is a function of where we live. In the wet eastern portion of the North American continent, wood is a highly renewable resource. One could make a strong case, in fact, that wood production is less ecologically destructive than straw production. Growing and harvesting timber involves no tilling, herbicides, pesticides, fertilizers, or monocultures. Cuts in well-managed forests cover areas smaller than most grain fields. So there is no great ecological imperative to avoid the use of wood; the imperative is to use it responsibly, by which we mean sourced as locally as possible, and in quantities and dimensions appropriate to the task at hand. We have seen Nebraska-style buildings on for-

ested sites, whose owners burn wood for heat, and who think they did something admirable by not inserting a dozen posts to hold up their roof! Honestly! What about all of the poly sheeting that was required to keep the building dry as they built it? Did they produce that on-site, or did they keep a few bucks in the local economy by buying it off their neighbor's backyard plastic mill?

We certainly recognize that wood is used in egregious and disgusting ways on this continent, to build unnecessarily large, ugly buildings that will survive a deplorably but mercifully short lifespan. And old-growth Western forests are massively abused, in order to make this happen. True enough, but this doesn't mean that wood is an ecologically inferior building material. It means that wood is a straightforward and cost-effective building material, and that many people are greedy and have poor taste. There's no sense in blaming wood for human shortcomings, especially as we witness a bloom of straw bale trophy houses.

Architect Chris Stafford conceived of this collection of small, square-shaped, Nebraska-style buildings, built in an interlocking pattern to create a more intricate structure. Burnett home, Whidbey Island, Washington.

We do recognize that the situation is different on the high plains, where wood is not a native resource; but then it is not so clear that the wire and cement typically used in Nebraska-style construction are native resources, either. These are also very energy-intensive materials, whose production involves strip mining and other ecological damage. They are caught up in the same human consumption game as wood; they're very useful materials, and in our greed, we use too much of them. The point here is that the ecological difference between a framed or Nebraska-style load-bearing structure will be small. It will be much less important than the size of the house, or how far the owner needs to drive to get to work in the morning.

There are other good reasons to avoid Nebraska-style construction. How do you plan to protect those walls from weather, during construction? Will your tarp system be anywhere near as effective as a roof, in keeping rain away? What about snow loads? How do you plan to frame windows and doors? Might you not make more efficient use of smaller-dimension lumber if the openings could be framed in, as part of the load-bearing structure? Will you be able to get a permit for this type of building?

Many readers of this book will no doubt feel compelled to try their hand at Nebraska-style construction, simply because they have never done it, and are admirably unwilling to take our word on its limitations. We must implore these readers to restrict their first effort to a situation where Nebraska-style construction can actually make sense. A shed or studio is a great place to start. Cold-climate Nebraska-style buildings are simplest if limited to one story, and to small floor areas. They should also possess straightforward roof structures that can be framed and covered quickly.

Load-bearing interior walls made of bales create dramatic features, such as this arch leading into a library. Burnett home, Whidbey Island, Washington.

Now that we have something of an understanding of how these buildings work, and what their limitations are, let's look at some specific design details.

Types of Nebraska Style

Nebraska-style construction techniques break down into two categories. In the traditional method, bales are stacked in such a way that the bale component of the wall has a substantial degree of integrity, on its own: Bales and corners are often pinned or tied together, and windows receive lintels or boxes strong enough to bear compressive loads. Compression of the walls is achieved by roof load, and an independent system is employed to fasten the roof to the foundation. Only after each of these steps is completed (not to mention a whole host of other details, such as windows, interior floors, etc.) is the plaster applied. The two main structural components, bales and plaster, are viewed, during the construction phase, as functioning separately. It is only once the building is completed that they are considered to be integrated.

Under the Prestressed Nebraska method, the bale walls are never required to perform any structural function independent of the plaster skins. The bales, therefore, can be stacked more quickly. Pinning is not required; window boxes and roof-bearing assemblies are sized down substantially. The walls are compressed—even plastered, if the people and equipment are available—before the roof goes on.

Traditional Nebraska Style

Three issues, all of them having to do with weather, drive Nebraska-style details in cold climates. First and foremost is the need to get a roof over the walls, as rapidly as possible. The second and third issues come into play over the longer term; they involve the ability of the bale-and-plaster wall to bear snow loads, and the ability of the exterior skins to keep water out of the walls

Roof Design

Especially in wet climates, it is crucial that Nebraska-style roofs be kept simple, so that they can be installed quickly. Trusses are a good choice, as their delivery can be timed so that the

rafters are ready to go up as soon as the roof-bearing assembly (RBA) is leveled and squared into place. If a large group is assembled to stack the bales, it is possible for these same people to lift the trusses into position. Otherwise, a crane can be ordered for early in the week following a weekend wall raising.

ROOF-BEARING ASSEMBLIES

The roof-bearing assembly performs the same function in a straw bale wall as a top plate in a stick-framed wall: It ties the entire wall structure together, and forms a continuous (and, ideally, level and square) surface on which the roof will bear. Straw bale designers and builders have experimented with many different configurations of the roof-bearing assembly, but all of them fall under one of two categories; they are either rigid or flexible.

Rigid assemblies are typically box beams, whose sides are made of 2-by-6s, 2-by-8s, 2-by-10s, or 2-by-12s (or the equivalent in engineered

A box beam is a very rigid roof-bearing assembly, capable of bearing weight across openings in the wall.

Unless it can be framed in advance and lifted all in one piece, a complicated roof such as this octagon is not a good idea over Nebraska-style walls in a rainy climate.

Eisenberg/Myhrman

A flexible, ladder-type roof-bearing assembly.

lumber), and whose top and bottom are made of ³/4-inch plywood. Box beams are capable of spreading roof point loads (discussed later). They are also capable of spanning right over window openings, acting, in effect, as lintels. The size of framing members is best determined by the length of the spans over openings.

Flexible assemblies are of a lighter construction, typically a "ladder" of 2-by-4s either sheathed on its underside with plywood, or doubled up like two conventional top plates, and blocked apart to sit 2 inches in from each edge of the bale. This assembly is not capable of bearing any loads that cannot be borne directly down into the wall, therefore it cannot be expected to span window or other openings. (However wire-reinforced cement stucco will often serve as an adequate lintel, so this concern may vanish once the stucco has cured. On longer spans, this RBA might require temporary bracing.) The main benefit of such a plate-type assembly is that it can be tweaked into level, before the roof is applied. High spots in the walls can be cinched down with cables and gripples (or a similar system), creating a more or less level surface on which the roof can bear.

The main drawback to a rigid roof-bearing assembly, on the other hand, is that it is not adjustable to so fine a degree. A box beam may still be cinched down by means of external cables, but it spreads the cable load over a longer stretch of wall,

If the roof is to be conventionally framed with rafters, you will save yourself time later in the process by cutting them before the bales go in. The roof-bearing assembly (RBA), likewise, should be built in sections on the ground, before a bale ever comes out from under a tarp. Laying out the RBA on top of the foundation makes very good sense, as it allows you to be absolutely sure that it will be of the proper dimensions to top the wall. Both of these measures raise the ante on the need to stack bales precisely, however. If they are allowed to wander more than an inch or two out of plumb, the RBA and precut rafters will not fit correctly, and you'll be kicking yourself for not kicking those bales into place as they were stacked.

effectively increasing the wall's resistance to compression in the specific area where it is needed. Piling lots of people and heavy objects on top of the offending point in the wall can help.

Paul is generally inclined toward the rigid RBA approach, because of the design flexibility of a beam-and-window header in one unit. Leveling can sometimes become a complicated procedure, but once a box beam is fastened together all around the building, the walls begin to feel solid and durable.

The width of the roof-bearing assembly should be sized down by an increment (generally 20 inches for a 23-inch-wide bale) as a means of building in an acceptable margin of error for the plumb of the walls. This way, if a wall flares out by a bit, the RBA can sit toward that wall's inside edge, while still retaining the square or rectangular shape required by the roof framing system. This functions as a built-in hedge against time spent fiddling with the walls, in order to get them to line up properly under the roof-bearing assembly.

Probably the most solid of all possible roof-bearing assemblies is the concrete bond beam. In theory, a bond beam sounds like a simple way to knit together all the walls of a building, while providing a level surface for roof bearing. In reality, however, forming a bond beam can become quite complicated, because the bale wall does not supply any ready attachment points. A form must be floated and squared atop the wall, and shimmed up to level. This process takes time. The concrete must then be allowed to cure, and forms must be stripped, before roof framing can commence.

The bales also have an annoying habit of beginning their settling process once the weight of the bond beam is applied. (This is more of an issue with two-string bales than with the more rigid three-string bales.) This means that if the forms do not lap far enough over the faces of the bales, concrete can actually blow out of gaps between the form and the newly settled top of the bale wall. Worse yet is the fact that the bales do not settle all at once; they continue to creep downward during the curing period of the concrete. Unset concrete, not yet rigid enough to bridge over less dense areas of the wall, can actually settle with the wall. This does not make for the strongest possible bond beam; neither does it make for the perfectly flat roof-bearing assembly that will allow roof framing to proceed efficiently.

Bond beams also use a lot of concrete, which must be pumped or bucketed up to the forms. This process is expensive and energy intensive. We really do not recommend a bond beam, but if you do decide to employ one, it should be insulated well, and only on its exterior. Insulating the interior will do nothing but make the concrete cold, and increase the risk of condensation.

PRECOMPRESSION

What is typically described as the precompression of bale walls is a procedure whereby the bales are squeezed down by mechanical means, so that the compression that would otherwise be created slowly, by the roof dead load, can be achieved quickly. Two intentions are at work here: to create a level plate at the top of the wall on which the roof will bear, and to move the walls directly to the plaster stage, omitting the traditional six- to eight-week period of waiting for the walls to settle.

In various attempts at systematizing Nebraska-style construction, a wide range of compression procedures have been employed: wires with gripples, heavy-duty plastic strapping, steel strapping, and all-thread rod. (Another possibility is the Chapman/Platts Prestressed Nebraska system, described later.) Each of these systems is capable of the first task described above: the creation of a level plate from which to frame the roof. None of them, however, succeeds in significantly precompressing the wall; in each case, the tensioners, which are typically tightened to near their breaking point, end up hanging slack after a few weeks (or sometimes a few days) under roof load. It may be that this doesn't matter; if the skins are primarily responsible for bearing compressive loads, they can probably be applied at any point. This would certainly be true with cement stucco; once it sets, settling is over.

Wire and gripples form the best of these systems, in our estimation; it is fast and easy, rela-

Stomp those Bales! (Carefully)

Three-string bales should be stomped as they are put in place. Because these big brutes are not concrete blocks, they do not sit perfectly against their neighbors, and they are not always fully compressed. By jumping on them, you settle them into the wall. This is one of those practical absurdities that makes bale construction so enjoyable. Two-string bales want to be snugged and tamped into place as well, but depending on their density, stomping can deform them, and end up bulging the corners and generally pushing the wall out of square.

tively inexpensive and relatively strong, and is infinitely adjustable. While the gripples are not capable of truly precompressing the wall, they do work well as a roof tie-down system, because they can be periodically snugged up as the wall settles under roof load. Poly and steel strapping are not as efficient or flexible. Since the fastening clips are permanent, an extra length of strap has to be spliced in, in order to retighten, once the wall has settled. The initial investment in tools for these systems is also rather high. All-thread rod, a popular material in the early days of bale construction, is both expensive and difficult to install.

An interesting possibility for reducing compression comes from Tom Rijven, of France. Tom dips the faces of his bales (those sides that will eventually receive plaster) in a clay slip before stacking them into the wall. Paul has used this system on a couple of buildings, and has found that once it dries, the clay seems to stabilize the bale into a more rigid unit. Architect Tommie Thompson of Litchfield, Connecticut, has made the same set of experiments with a thinned-down lime putty, with similar results. A cement slurry would be a better choice for a building that is to receive cement stucco.

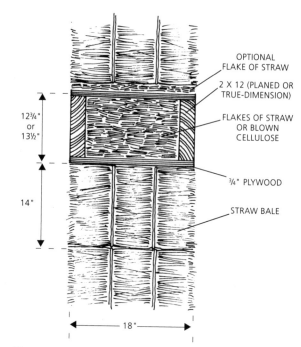

Typical box beam.

Roof Loads

Roof loads on Nebraska-style houses are best borne across substantial lengths of wall. Point loads, such as those generated at a valley or at the end of a carrying beam, should be avoided to whatever degree is possible; where they do occur, it is crucial that they not fall over narrow columns of bales. Point loads cause uneven settling of the bales and cracks in the plaster. Openings of any sort should be kept at least 4 feet away from either side of such a load. If a rigid, box-

beam-style roof-bearing assembly is to be employed, this should be stiff enough to spread the point load over a sufficient area of bale wall.

If, on the other hand, the design calls for a lightweight, flexible plate, you will probably want to stiffen the plate for 3 to 4 feet in each direction from a point load. There are two ways to do this. Each edge of the plate can be reinforced with steel "angle iron." This is typically drilled and nailed twice per foot, to both the inner and outer edges of the plate. As these two pieces of steel run only along the inner and outer edges of the wall, and are not connected, thermal bridging and resultant condensation problems should not be a concern.

The second option is to replace some or all of the top course of bales with a box beam. The sides of such a beam are usually framed of 2 x 12 stock or engineered lumber, and the top and bottom are framed of ¾-inch plywood. If built of rough-sawn lumber, this box finishes out at 13½ inches in height, while the planed-lumber version comes to 12¾ inches. The gap between the box beam and the RBA can be shimmed, and insulated with flakes of straw.

Interconnection of Bales

In the early days of the straw bale construction revival, it was assumed that bales needed to be pinned together. As we have come to recognize the primary role of the skins in the wall assembly, however, it has become increasingly clear that the main reason to pin is to keep the wall stable enough to work on top of, as it goes up. Unless the walls are to be built from scaffolding, this is still an important function.

Several methods of interconnection are common. At the fore is pinning, either at the interior or the exterior of the wall. Tying bales together can work, as well. A thin mortar bed is another option—Pascal Thepaut has had good luck with this system in France. Finally, bales that have been dipped in slip or putty seem to glue together.

PINNING

In the majority of bale buildings, rods of some sort have been pounded down through each course of bales, to help affix them to their neighbors below. This procedure holds the bales in place, more or less, and does add some stiffness to the wall panel. It is also labor intensive, and does not give a truly positive connection between bales. We never use rebar for this purpose; it is expensive, energy intensive, hard on chain saws during remodeling, and a potential point for condensation. We also don't usually use bamboo, as it is imported from Southeast Asia, which seems

silly. We use wood. Saplings work fine if you have time to cut them; Paul follows the lead of Juliet Cumming and David Shaw of Dummerston, Vermont, and uses 1-inch-square hardwood surveyors' stakes, which are locally produced at a reasonable price. A similar item could be milled on-site, from dimensional lumber. While we no longer employ pinning of this sort as a primary system of interconnection, it is useful to have a couple of bundles of stakes on hand, for problem situations.

EXTERIOR PINNING

Exterior pinning, or "corseting," as Matts Myhrman rather gruesomely describes it, is a system developed by the Steens and their collaborators in the "Casas que Cantan" owner-built housing initiative in Ciudad Obregon, Mexico. In this method, pairs of vertical saplings, furring strips, rebars, or bamboo stalks are attached to the inside and outside face of the wall, as it is stacked.

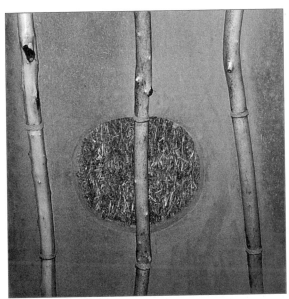

Exterior pins left exposed. Fox Maple School Library, Brownfield, Maine.

The vertical members are then tied one to the other, through the bale wall, squeezing the bales in, as in a corset. Twine for tying can be threaded through the bales, though it is usually easier to tie off between courses. Lightweight poly strapping also works well for this job.

The main drawback to this system is that it is difficult to get the pins to snug back into the bales, and out of the plane of the plaster. Round stock works somewhat better than milled stock for this purpose. Pounding the rods with a sledgehammer also helps, but is unpleasant and time consuming. If the bales are to be laid flat (such that the strings are in the wall) a better option may be to rout out a channel on each edge of each bale, wide and deep enough to accept the pins. This can be done with the standard electric chain saw, but a faster and more precise option is a router fit with a large bit.

The exterior pinning method creates a very stiff, stable wall. It is also reasonable to conclude that exterior pins (or ribs, as Kelly Lerner has called them) are capable of bearing some portion of the roof loads. Just as the plaster skins in a Nebraska-style wall are held in column by their bond with the straw, the vertical pins, in this case, are kept from moving by the fact that they are wedged tightly against the bales, and tied through from interior to exterior. Though it might be difficult to get a building inspector to buy into the idea, it seems that in such a hybrid structure, these vertical ribs might protect the plaster from live compressive loads, thus making softer plasters a more reasonable option for Nebraska-style buildings in snow-load climates. In a well-designed wall, the external pins might also serve as a connection point for the roof, removing the need for some ancillary tie-down system.

TYING

Bales can be tied one to the next, either from twine to twine or by sewing through with the baling needle. Lightweight strapping, available through packaging supply catalogues, also works well for this job. This is useful at corners and other places where the bales might become ornery. It is not commonly used vertically, from course to course, though this technique can also be useful to help stabilize narrow columns of bales.

MORTAR

One of the early bale construction systems, engineered in the 1980s by Louis Gagné in Quebec, involved laying bales within a matrix of 1-inch-thick, straw-reinforced mortar joints made of 2 parts cement to 1 part lime. The bales, in this case, acted like a provisory formwork waiting for the matrix mortar to set firm. Pascal

Curved, load-bearing, matrix-style bale structures designed by Michel Bergeron to serve as retaining walls at the north side of a house. Coated with waterproofing and backfilled, then bermed entirely. Roy-Brassard home, Lanoraie, Quebec.

An old silo houses a root cellar in its basement, a bathroom on the first floor, and a meditation room on the second floor. Jocelyne Henri home, Chénéville, Quebec.

Exterior view of the incorporated silo on the north side of Jocelyne Henri's Nebraska-style home.

Thepaut, in France, modified this system by replacing the cement with lime putty. Tests run in 1982 by Scanada Consultants on a Gagné demonstration wall measuring 12 feet long by 8 feet high and 20 inches thick found such a wall capable of resisting compressive and shear loads of 79 kN (17,760 lbs) and 3.2 kN (720 lbs), respectively. Load capacities were evaluated to be 1.9 kN/m (1,400 lbs/lf) for dead loads and 2.5 kN/m (1,845 lbs/lf) for snow loads. The wind resistance of the wall was estimated at 0.67 kN/m^2 (7,210 lbs/sf) and permanent loads at 2.0 kN/m^2 (4,838 lbs/sf). The test report also notes that the resistance of the walls is directly affected by the composition of the mortar, the size of the bales, the geometry of the wall, and the quality of the plaster (Louis Gagné's mix, bound with a 1:1 blend of cement and lime).

On their Roundhouse, Paul and Amy have experimented with a much thinner lime-straw mortar, applied as a 2-inch-wide by 1- or 2-inch-high bead near the interior and exterior edges of the wall. Because this mixture is kept near the edges, it can set much more quickly than a full-width mortar joint. By gluing each bale to those above or below it, this technique stabilized the wall quite nicely. The main drawback to the lime mortar is that it takes several days to begin to set; a small percentage of cement or pozzolan would be helpful for a Nebraska-style project, where the walls need to be stacked quickly. A clay-straw mortar should also work well.

BALE DIPPING

Bale dipping provides a very tight connection between bales, while also substantially reducing the compressibility of any given bale. Though the bales are dipped predominantly on their faces, 2 or 3 inches of slip is allowed to lap over into what becomes the joint between courses. This material glues the bales together, creating a wall that, once it dries, is very solid. For situations where the work crew doesn't mind getting seriously muddy, this can be an excellent option. (See part 3, "Straw Bale Finishes," for more details.)

Windows

Window framing is one of the great challenges of Nebraska-style construction. In fact, the ideal Nebraska-style building would include no windows at all: nothing to interrupt the running bond of the bales, no weak holes in the wall that need to be reinforced. Maybe an above-ground cave for curing cheeses? This would be a project to get excited about!

Unfortunately, the building that you are designing will probably include windows. These can be approached in three basic ways. First, you might use a rough opening box that is strong enough to bear any loads (primarily compressive) that might be applied to it. Second, you can span across the opening with some sort of lintel. Third, you may choose to top the wall with a roof-bearing assembly that is rigid enough to bridge across openings, and hang window frames (and any bales above the window) from this box. On normal-sized windows, wire-reinforced cement stucco will also form a lintel; the trick is in providing enough support that the stucco will not be forced to take loads during the curing process, as this will cause cracking. It may be possible to temporarily support the center of openings, until the base coats of stucco have cured.

Roof-Bearing Assembly as Header

Of these three methods, the rigid RBA with hung window boxes is the simplest. It allows for the use of small-dimension framing stock, which means that the interior window wells can be nicely rounded. Of course, the boxes must be installed as the wall is stacked, and then attached to the roof-bearing assembly, once this is in place. The trick here is to design the box to be strong enough to survive the process of bale laying, and also to be short enough so that it is not forced into compression as the bale walls settle.

In this system, a typical window box is built of 2-by-6 stock. Wherever possible, we like to hold the window down a foot or so from the underside of the RBA, and use the extra height to angle the plaster up from the window (at the outside of the well) to the ceiling, at the inside of

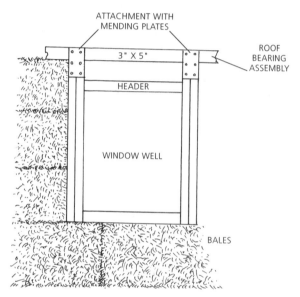

Hanging window box.

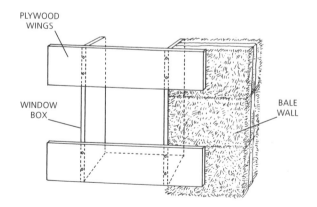

Window box with temporary plywood wings.

A wooden windowsill contrasts beautifully with plastered bale walls. The Permaculture Institute of Northern California.

the well. This allows light to spill up onto the ceiling, providing better illumination to the room and also making the window more inviting to the occupants. The resulting gap can be insulated with blown cellulose or whatever will be used in the ceiling. Alternately, the window can be designed such that a single bale fits above it, and this bale beveled to match the sides of the windows. A sling of expanded metal lath, spanning from the window "header" (it need not be a true structural header) to the ceiling, cradles this bale tightly into place. Vertical window framing extends up to meet the roof-bearing assembly, while the actual rough opening is headed off a foot or so below the RBA. The window framing can be connected to the roof-bearing assembly with steel mending plates.

During construction of the bale walls, the windows must be comprehensively braced, either by diagonal members or by wide strips of plywood that are nailed across the exterior of the window, top and bottom. The plywood is preferable, as it does a better job of preventing the window's midsection from bulging in as the bales are laid tightly against it. (A length of 2-by-4 jammed horizontally across the center of the window box serves this function, as well.) Also, the plywood can be run past the outside edge of the window by a foot or so; by holding the resulting "wings" tight against the outside face of the bale wall, the window box is automatically flushed into place.

Window boxes are sized such that, once the connection to the RBA is made, they will end up hanging somewhat above the bales below them. This ensures that the window box will not be forced into compression as the wall settles, which could cause long-term difficulty in getting windows to open. Typically, the height of the frame is undersized by ½ inch per bale of window height. So, the box for a window that was four bales high would be undersized by 2 inches. As the walls compress, some

Angling plaster at the top of a window allows more light to flow onto the ceiling, so the window is more inviting. Willson house, Massachusetts.

of this gap below the window will disappear. The remaining gap can be insulated, and the area to the interior filled with a sturdy sill of wood, stone, or poured concrete.

LINTELS

In some cases, such as gable-end walls, you will find that the bales will not always sit below an RBA. Lintels are an option here. Unfortunately, the narrow-profile steel lintels that work well for bridging small openings in warm-climate construction are simply not appropriate in cold climates. Any moisture that is present in the wall will condense out onto the cold steel, causing an area of wet straw adjacent to it. You want to avoid this.

A good option for small openings is a wooden lintel of similar construction, sort of a site-built wooden I-beam, laid on its side. It consists of a length of ¾-inch plywood edged with equivalent lengths of 1-by-6 (or better yet, grooved 2-by-6) that are glued and screwed in place. This entire assembly is as wide as the bale wall, so the

bales above and below it should have their edges trimmed off, to fit snugly inside. Such a lintel should be sufficient to span any length opening that would receive a 2-by-6 header in frame construction. As always, the lintel should extend beyond the opening by a distance of one-half its span.

For larger openings, we have sometimes employed a box beam lintel. See previous discussion, under "Roof Point Loads," for a description of the design of such a lintel.

In either of these cases, a lightweight window frame, of the same construction as would be suspended from the roof-bearing assembly, is installed below the lintel.

LOAD-BEARING WINDOW BOXES

Load-bearing window boxes are an inferior system, for two reasons. First, they are somewhat redundant in a stressed-skin panel wall. Their primary job is to keep the straw above the window from sagging down toward the opening; their secondary function is to bolster the ability of the stucco above the window to act as a header, thus reducing the likelihood of its cracking. Whether this second function matters at all probably varies with the thickness of the plaster, how well it is applied and bonded to the straw, how well it is reinforced, and what it is made of. In many cases, the strong window box may not be doing any real work, once the finishing materials are set.

The most annoying feature of these boxes, however, is that they must be built to nearly the full depth of the wall. This requires a lot of lumber and picky framing work, and it also removes the possibility of splaying the bales at the top and sides of the opening. Sure, the box can be flared (yet more picky framing work), and each bale can be modified to fit against this angled framing. This adds up to a lot of effort, only to create window openings that will probably end up covered in sheetrock. Hardly an inspiring outcome.

Load-bearing boxes work better in drier climates, where the window need not be pushed toward the outside of the wall. If centered in the wall, the box really only needs to be half the depth of the wall; this leaves room to bevel the

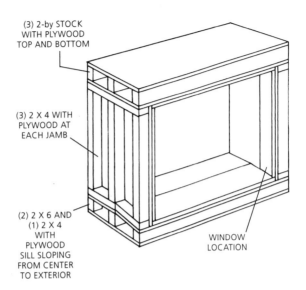

Sheathed window box.

opening, both inside and out. In rainy or snowy climates, where an exterior sill of straw is in consistent danger from weather exposure, the window should be pushed toward the outside edge of the wall. For any load to be distributed evenly, the box should be brought quite near to the inside edge of the wall, as well. This leaves little room for a bevel, resulting in a window that, unless it is quite wide, feels like a slot.

These frames can be built in two ways. The first is to frame the sides with true-dimension 2-by stock. As the boxes require wider stock than is typically available off the stack at the lumberyard, each side is built up of two pieces, butted edge to edge and joined with a mending plate. The top and bottom of the frame is a box beam, sized according to span.

Alternately, the sides and bottom of the box might be built as a miniature framed wall, of 2-by-4s sheathed with plywood. The plywood faces toward the opening; the gaps between the studs are stuffed with loose straw as the bales are stacked against them. The top of the box is still

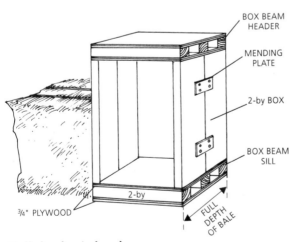

Full-depth window box.

a box beam. This system has the advantage of providing a wide (4-inch) surface around each window to attach flashing, casing, and/or a plaster stop.

WINDOW PLACEMENT AND DRIPSILL

In cold climates, it is best if all windows on plastered bale buildings are pushed to or near the outside surface of the wall. The recessed window and rounded stucco sill that is popular on bale buildings in hot or dry climates is not suitable to cold- or wet-climate construction. Before too long, such horizontal plaster—exposed in the best cases to periodic inundations of rainwater, and in the worst cases to freeze/thaw cycles and piles of snow and ice—will begin to chip and crack, allowing bulk water to enter the wall.

It is also crucial that all windows, even those that are pushed right to the outer edge of the wall, receive a dripsill. This might be built of wood or stone, or of concrete formed in place and reinforced with steel mesh—but in any case it should extend at least an inch beyond the exterior finish, to carry water out and away from the wall. A kerf must also be cut or formed into the underside of the sill, near the outside edge, to prevent water from clinging to this bottom surface and inching back to the wall. When water hits the kerf, it drips harmlessly to the ground (see photos in chapter 2).

A secondary benefit of pushing the window to the outside edge of the wall is that it removes the need to install any sort of membrane as a secondary layer of water protection, as is typical between a straw sill and the plaster material that covers it. Impermeable membranes are dangerous in bale construction, because they inhibit drying. This is especially the case when they are

In wet climates, an exterior sill of straw and plaster is an invitation to trouble.

installed on the cold side of the straw. Solid details—such as a good dripsill and no horizontal straw on the exterior of the building—provide better insurance against water entry, without the negative side effects.

FLASHING

Flashing is as important in bale buildings as in conventional buildings, though its role is a bit different. When you drive around and look at older stuccoed houses, the most noticeable problems are at poorly flashed window and door openings. This is surprising, because flashing on framed buildings, where a drainage plane of as-

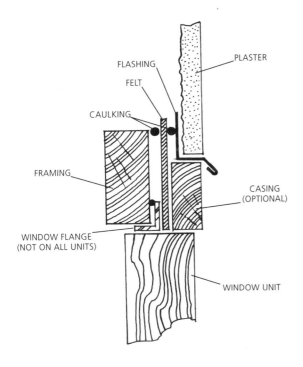

Flashing at header level.

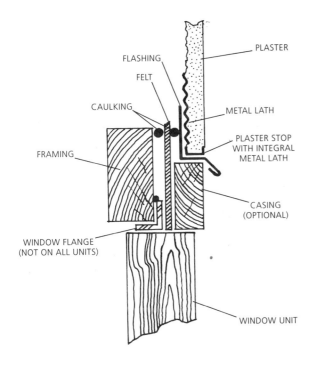

Flashing and plaster stop.

phalt-impregnated felt is typically applied between sheathing and stucco, is relatively simple. The felt is installed shingle-style, and it laps down into the flashing. Any water that makes its way through cracks in the stucco runs down the outside surface of the building paper, until it meets a flashing, at which point it is directed out and away from the skin of the building.

When stucco is applied over felt paper and sheathing, its back side is truly formed into a smooth plane, suitable for the transmission of water downward, by gravity. The plaster does not physically adhere to the felt. The felt, though it does have the capacity to absorb some water, is technically waterproof, in that it prevents liquid water from passing through to the sheathing that backs it. It is easy enough to see how any water that makes its way through cracks in the plaster will be diverted downward at this juncture. This water will eventually either reach the bottom of the wall, reach a flashing point, or dry back out (as vapor) through the stucco.

When we apply plaster over straw, we create a situation that is inherently quite different. First off, the back side of the stucco is in no way planar. On the macro level, it will dip and roll with the contours of the bales, while on the micro level, its conformation to the profiles of individual straws and straw ends will create a serrated surface. It will, likewise, be intimately bonded to the straw. Add to this the fact that straw is not waterproof—that it seems to act, instead, as a reservoir for moisture—and you have a situation that is the farthest possible from the drainage plane that is typical of conventional construction.

What does this mean, as far as flashing is concerned? We cannot really expect the flashing to catch any water that gets through the plaster. We must rely on maintenance to mostly prevent that, and on the ability of the straw and plaster to dry out, when the weather changes. The role of the flashing is to catch any water flowing down the surface of the wall, and divert it out into the air, away from the window, door, or whatever else might be below it. Our typical detail is to nail the flashing to the framing above the window. As a nod to convention, we also cover any wood at the exterior of the structure with felt paper, so a strip of felt would be stapled to the outside face of the header, and lapped down into the flashing. The edge of this felt is typically caulked to the framing, as insurance against water entry.

If a plaster stop is to be used, this is caulked and nailed in place within the flashing. We assume that the flashing is, in essence, a plaster stop, so this joint is usually finished with a piece of expanded metal lath, nailed in place over the felt. The lath extends into the flashing, and also out an inch or two beyond the edges of the felt, into the plane of the straw.

Prestressed Nebraska

Earlier in this chapter, we mentioned the engineering tests performed by Linda Chapman and Bob Platts of Fibrehouse Ltd., which demonstrate that a plastered bale wall bears loads in a manner characteristic of a stressed-skin panel. This understanding of traditional Nebraska-style building was actually gleaned out of a much deeper investigation into an improved construction method, the core of which is a simple system for precompressing the bale walls. Thus the name "Prestressed Nebraska." Here is how Linda Chapman presents their system:

Straw: How Green Can We Go?

Fibrehouse Limited was created to do research and development on straw and other renewable fibers for use in construction. The architect and engineer partners, Linda Chapman and Robert Platts, have been working in this field since 1993, but both have been involved in construction and building science for many years. We have participated in the construction of well over a dozen straw bale buildings and have published structural and moisture studies on the subject.[1]

We have sought to push the "green" envelope of straw as far as it can go. We are not there yet. The guiding parameters are the particular circumstances of the Canadian environment. Snow loads, the availability of mostly 18-inch-wide and poorly compressed two-string straw bales, a fast and efficient wood-frame construction industry, a temperate climate, and a short and wet construction season all contribute to the complexities of simplifying load-bearing straw bale construction.

We have been developing load-bearing straw bale walls as the least resource-intensive way to build. With the help of CMHC we have tested 18-inch-wide stuccoed straw bale walls and found them to be very competent stressed-skin wall structures. The stucco skins take all the loads, acting as very strong and thin columns that are kept from buckling by the transversely oriented straws bonded into the stucco on the inside and outside faces of the wall.

We have pushed the boundaries of load-bearing straw bale wall construction by creating several tools that compress the straw bale wall while tightening chicken-wire mesh on the inside and

1. Contact the Canada Mortgage and Housing Corporation for full copies of the reports. See their Web site: www.cmhc-schl.gc.ca

Bob Platts and Linda Chapman in 1995, in front of the first precompressed, load-bearing building. Bales were stacked eleven high, then compressed with one of their first-generation compression tools. Wakefield, Quebec.

Stuccoed straw bale walls are very strong indeed. A post-and-beam superstructure using straw bales as infill is clearly not necessary. However, due to the frequency of rainy weather, the susceptibility of straw to moisture rot, and the increased time and labor required to build with and stucco straw, often a post-and-beam structure is the wisest choice.

We have several goals, then, working with load-bearing straw bale walls in this climate: to reduce the time and labor involved; to apply good building envelope thinking—get rid of air gaps, cracks, thermal bridges, capillary leaks, and use of doweling; and to reduce the amount of lumber used in top plates and door and window bucks, as well as the quantity of stucco required to get a level wall finish.

outside faces of the bale. The tightened chicken wire is then used as reinforcing for the stucco skins. We call this a Prestressed Nebraska wall.

Our test rig could not fail an 18-inch-wide straw bale wall with 1-inch cement-based stucco coatings at 5,000 pounds per linear foot (plf). This load is 3.7 times the typical loading for a two-story house in the snow belt. (Our test rig was not strong enough to try higher loads.) Structural analysis suggests that axial strength is at least 10,000 plf and probably 15,000 plf. Hurricane wind load testing was also impressive. The test panel was able to withstand wind loads of 153 psf, more than seven times a hurricane design load. The test panel behaved much like a floor structure, not just a vastly overstrong wall. In theory, these prestressed walls are strong enough to be used as floors and roof structures.

The Prestressed Nebraska System

The current preferred method of creating a Prestressed Nebraska straw bale wall uses an 8-inch-diameter pneumatic tube on top of the wall. The tube requires simple but specially designed and reusable prestresser plates that provide a rigid surface for the tube to push against.

After the straw bale walls are stacked, running-bond fashion, to the desired height—usually seven or eight bales high—a permanent wood-frame top plate is installed on the top of the wall. Our system requires a minimal top plate fabricated from ⅜-inch particleboard and 2-by-4s nailed flat to the underside of the particleboard. The inflatable tube is then uncoiled over the top plate and laid along the full extent of the wall to be compressed.

Dowels are not required for the construction or stabilization of these walls as they go up, but some exterior wooden stud braces are used temporarily, especially at the corners, and do double duty by holding up rain tarps.

The prefabricated prestresser plates, made in 2-, 3-, and 4-foot sections and 18 inches wide to correspond with the width of a straw bale wall, are placed over the inflatable tube. These plates can be made a number of different ways. The most advanced way we fabricate them is with ⅝-inch plywood that has an 18-gauge steel claw plate fixed to each edge. The claw plate is designed to allow 1-inch hexagonal-grid chicken wire to hook on and off with ease.

Precut sheets of 20-gauge galvanized chicken wire are then stapled to the wooden sill plate at the bottom of the wall and brought up and hooked over the prestresser plate claws. (Do not use 22-gauge chicken wire, the prestressing loads will break it!) The chicken wire can be in 3-, 4- or 6-foot widths, depending on availability. This meshing procedure is repeated on both sides of the wall for as much length as you have tube and prestresser plates. This sandwichlike wall configuration holds the tube and whole wall assembly snugly in place.

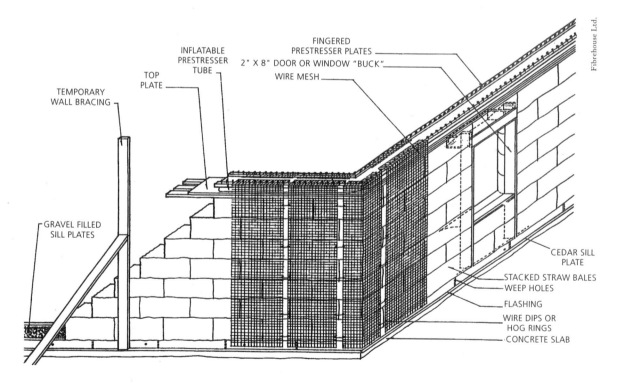

The Fibrehouse Limited system for using chicken wire and a pneumatic tube to precompress a load-bearing bale wall.

1) *The pneumatic tube is unrolled over the top plate in preparation for precompression of the wall. Note the air valve and the wood-block ends on the tube, which was fabricated from agricultural irrigation hose, with valves, stops, and seams added.*

2) *Hooking chicken wire over protruding screws, which hold the wire in place over the precompressing plates. Note the pneumatic tube sandwiched between the precompression plates and the top plate of the wall.*

3) *The tube inflating and the bale wall compressing. The wooden blocking nailed over the window header prevents that section of the wall from compressing the desired 3 inches.*

4) *A load-bearing kneewall on the second floor, with 2-by-4 struts to hold the top plate rigid. The pneumatic tube is compressing the wall.*

Air is blown into the tube with a commercial air compressor or hand pump. The tube is fully inflated in minutes, compacting the straw bales downward while tensioning the chicken-wire mesh upward. The tube is rated for a maximum of 30 psi and normally requires only about 5 to 10 psi to fully inflate. This air pressure produces an approximate loading of 800 pounds per linear foot. The wall quickly compresses anywhere from 1 to 3 inches depending on the quality and type of the straw bales used. We like to use a precut measuring stick hung from the top plate and moved around to check for level compression throughout all the walls.

Once the walls are compressed to the desired level, the wire mesh is stapled to the top plate, while the tube is still inflated. After the wire mesh has secured the wall to its final height, the air is let out of the tube and the tube and prestresser plates are moved to another section of wall or to another house.

The excess wire mesh left atop the wall (which was hanging over the steel plate claws) can then be used to connect to the second-story wire mesh or can be overlapped and stapled to the roof trusses as a superior hurricane tie-down connection right down to the sill plates. The strong and straight wall is now ready to receive floor joists, roof trusses, hand-applied stucco, or the heavy impact of shotcrete finishing.

Because of the significant loads imposed on the wall, we reduce air gaps between bales in the wall, and hopefully prevent sagging from future imposed snow loads. Our goal is to keep the stucco stress- and crack-free.

The heavy loads imposed on the straw bale wall during the prestressing process have led us to develop simple but particularly strong door and window bucks, which are considered to be an integral part of this system. Currently we are using 2-by-8s as the vertical members and 2-by-6s as the lintels. A load-bearing straw bale wall only develops its full strength when the cement stucco coatings inside and out have cured. The door and window bucks have to be overdesigned to take the prestressing and imposed dead loads until the stucco is cured enough to take them all.

We have used this system successfully on one- and two-story houses, but we are not yet satisfied with the results. We recently prestressed the walls on a house, added a second floor, and prestressed the second floor wall and then added a

This air-bag-compressed, Nebraska-style studio, finished with cement stucco, withstands heavy snow loads. Millard residence, Sandpoint, Idaho.

roof. We discovered that the bales still had some creep. The wire mesh became slack before the stucco got applied. The stucco went on and the house is in great condition, but the stucco job took longer than necessary because we did not achieve our goal of tight wire-mesh reinforcing.

In the next go around we developed precut, removable 2-by-4 struts that were inserted between the edge of the sill plate and the top plate, in the gaps between the 3-foot-wide panels of chicken wire. This worked well. It kept creep from occurring after prestressing and before stuccoing. The stucco must be applied around but not over the struts so that they can be removed and used in the interior partition walls. It works but it adds one more labor step to the process. We have not yet achieved our goal of reduced labor.

The greater issue is that load-bearing straw bale wall systems still use as much lumber as a comparable wood-frame wall. The very thick walls use up extra lumber and labor in the top and bottom plates, the window and door bucks, inner and outer headers or lintels, and the extra roof framing needed to cover the wall top. It also uses extra lumber or concrete to support the base of the wide wall. When we also include the extra roof overhang needed for crucial moisture and mold deterrence, we see that straw bale walls can use more lumber than smartly-designed wood-frame houses. Again, we chip away at this issue, but have made no great breakthroughs.

Where Do We Go from Here?

We know that straw bale construction can be further developed into a significant contributor to green, sustainable housing production. More radical steps could give it a much better chance,

and more research and funding is badly needed.

The following is a summary of new ideas we are currently pursuing:

1. Place the bale the right way: *on edge*. It's much stiffer that way, in vertical compressibility, and much more stable against creep—more like wood. It's more precisely sized and readily built into a level wall. It won't sleaze around on its mates or distort in its vertical plane; readjustments for those distortions are a big drain on labor. Its thermal value is greater despite the thinner wall. And it doesn't stick thousands of straw wicks into the stucco to invite in water. (The Canadian and American technicians who so carefully tested straw bales and concluded that on-edge orientation is not as "strong" as flat placement, and therefore wrong, missed the point: That aspect of bale strength has nothing to do with final wall strength or stiffness.) On the other hand, shear strength (diagonal tension) and stiffness are not inherently improved. Through-the-wall tying of mesh to mesh will be necessary. We need to go back into the lab to ascertain exactly how much of this procedure is required.

2. Replace the galvanized steel mesh—a most laborious and awkward component—with polymer mesh. Perhaps try out mesh made from recycled plastics, or even hemp. These are not as stiff or strong, but the wall will be more than strong enough. Labor will be cut substantially, as will the fear of potential corrosion of steel mesh.

3. Replace the present prestressing process with heat-shrinking or other post-application tensioning of the mesh. "Settling" the stacked

bales over a long period of time should not be necessary; one-step shimming of the top plate should do the leveling job; the top plate should be only a light lateral beam and temporary struts should be unnecessary.

4. The wall core is now 14 inches rather than 18 inches or 24 inches thick. Wood usage in the top plates, window and door bucks, floors, and roofs can be reduced accordingly; headers and lintels can be designed into the door and window bucks or set into the roof trusses.

5. Investigate the potential of a three-layer "rain-screen" stucco system.

6. Investigate creating better baling equipment.

There is indeed much to do in the world of sustainable construction research. There are many dedicated researchers out there, all striving to make sustainable building work within the constraints of a financially driven world.

Hundreds of straw bale and other "alternative" houses are built across North America annually. Let's see what we can do about turning those hundreds into thousands of sustainable houses every year.

Afterthoughts

In the time since Linda submitted this piece, Fibrehouse has moved somewhat away from the prestressed method, until such time as a group of houses will be built all in one place (such as a housing development). This is on account of the setup time required for the pneumatic tube, but also because their main premise—that the bale-and-stucco wall should be treated as a stressed-skin panel—can be respected with the use of more commonly available equipment. Specifically, they have moved to cables:

Cable systems do work. We place them on initially (every 3 feet along the wall length) to secure the top plate in place. We still use the same minimal top plate. Shim the top plate as level as possible. Hand tighten cables or use a come-along or a blue tube, whatever the weather or your budget permits. We compress and try to level to the nearest ¹/₂ inch. Then build your roof or second floor. The walls will compress under the dead weight and the cables will sag. No problem. We like compression. Dead weight is enough.

My experience has been that the initial settlement is about all you are going to get. When the roof or floor is completed (i.e., the dead load is complete) tighten up the slack on the cables and shim the top plate to level again if required. Then stucco. Stucco right away! Do not wait for snow loads to arrive. Do not wait for one month or even one week. Stuccoing locks the straw bale walls into place and prevents them from compressing or creeping any further. Lock that bale wall into place while it is level, man. When the stucco is cured, loads are fully taken by the stucco, not by the straw, and so there will be no more creep. Unstuccoed straw bales are plastic, rather than elastic. You keep putting new loads on 'em, they will keep creeping downwards. They sure don't bounce back.

The idea of locking the bales into place as soon as they have settled enough to stiffen does seem to have significant potential. The most important new issue raised by this approach is how the

Panoramic view of the Sivananda Yoga Center in Quebec, a straw bale lodge where one hundred guests can attend retreats and workshops.

A luxurious perennial "meadow" has established itself on the 8,000-square-feet of living roof.

Julia Bourke's "Maison de Ville" in the city of Montreal is a balloon-frame construction with bales inserted between the studs. The exterior stucco has a warm green pigment that contrasts nicely with the urban surroundings.

The pioneering "Hay House" built by Ben Gleason in Connecticut in 1975. The overhanging roof design and consistent maintenance have protected the building from New England's wet weather for nearly three decades.

The Brissette-Panfili house at Ile-Saint-Ignace, Quebec, designed by Michel Bergeron. This is a timber-frame structure with straw bales used as infill in the walls. Exterior walls are plastered with lime and a small quantity of cement, and interior walls with gypsum mixed with lime, plaster of Paris, and silica sand. The roof is red cedar shakes with copper ridges and flashing.

Fran Izermans

Fran Izermans's owner-built home and carpentry workshop in Dingle, Sweden, has a timber-frame structure with straw infill and recycled roof tiles and windows.

(Far left) Custom tailoring bales to fit within a frame, using an electric chain saw.

(Left) A stud-frame construction with bales used as insulating infill. With this supporting frame, the roof can be added to protect the bales during construction. In the foreground is a straw bale house built by children visiting the site.

(Above) The exterior pinning system developed by the Steens for load-bearing walls. In Arizona, locally available reeds are used to provide this additional structural support.

Old rope can be chopped into the lime mix to give the plaster additional texture.

Cement slurry is thrown on the fluffy straw surface to harden the surface of the bales and favor a better bond with the base coat of plaster.

Pre-soaking lime for a while before mixing in the other ingredients will give the plaster better cohesion.

Color samples applied to a wall — experimenting with tones for the final coat of plaster.

The colorful exterior plaster finish of Ken Geisen and Laura Corbin's home north of Minneapolis, Minnesota.

The Kirk/Starbuck house in New Hampshire is a replica of a traditional Japanese timber-framed farmhouse. Instead of solid clay, however, the walls are made of bales finished on both sides with a clay plaster.

Kelly Lerner

This vault in Mongolia shows just how adventurous you can be with a load-bearing structure. Designed by Kelly Lerner of One World Design, and built by local tradespeople.

The Fox Maple Library's beautiful timber frame, visible from the interior, was wrapped with bales to provide warmth in the cold Maine winters. The wooden roof structure is covered with thatch.

A lovely painted finish over gypsum plaster at the Panozzo house in Bonfield, Illinois.

Contemporary bale builders have made a tradition of creating "truth windows" that show a glimpse of straw behind the plastered finish, as here in the Park/Zimmerman house, near Sandpoint, Idaho.

The handsome lime-plastered interior of Clark Sanders's straw bale cabin in upstate New York.

Built-in shelves at Paul Dadell and Alice Espy's house in Guilford, Vermont.

Roald Gunderson's home in southwestern Wisconsin was built of bales laid against a frame of poles, and invited this local tree right inside.

Some plasterers get quite creative, as in this evocative gypsum face in the Comstock home in Charlotte, Vermont.

stucco will be integrated with other components such as windows, trim details, interior floor surfaces, mechanical, and the smaller details that are usually dealt with after the walls are built, but before they are plastered. It may be possible to apply only the first coat, or the first and second coats, at the outset, holding the mud back from crucial intersections. Picky work (such as installing windows) could then proceed as usual, followed by patching of gaps in the plaster. Finish stucco work should then be able to cover any cold joints, resulting in a seamless finish. Since this pattern is a substantial shift from the usual jobsite order, it is crucial that the designer think through the details of how the various phases of work will be affected. Innovation of this sort is healthy, but it shouldn't fall to the builder to have to figure out whether the process can actually proceed as drawn.

We have some serious reservations about Nebraska-style construction for cold, and especially wet, climates. Both during construction and once they are occupied, these structures possess less insurance against catastrophic water damage than their framed cousins. On the right site, and with the right combination of a good design, a fast construction schedule, and careful maintenance, these buildings have performed well, and should continue to perform well. We only ask that before you jump into Nebraska style, you ask yourself why you want to go this route, and be sure that your reasons mesh with your design goals and your construction schedule.

CHAPTER 7

FRAMED STRUCTURES

The key feature of a building that possesses a framed structure is that the bales and plaster are not called upon to bear the loads of roof and floors. In some designs, the bale walls share the job of resisting shear loads, but in most cases they act simply as insulation, and as a support for the plaster finishes. In this chapter we will look at several practical framing systems, but first we must address the question of why you should consider these methods.

Why Framed?

The choice between framed and Nebraska-style systems is basically one of design flexibility. While simple Nebraska-style buildings can be elegant and useful structures, they also come with a substantial set of design restrictions (see chapter 6, "Nebraska Style"), which limit the range of situations over which they are practical. In the vast majority of cases, a framed approach is better suited to the demands that we and Mother Nature place on cold-climate buildings.

These demands fall into two categories: those that come into play during the construction process, and those that affect how the building will perform over the long term. The three main issues facing bale walls during the construction phase are weather, inexperienced contractors, and nervous (or occasionally obstinate) building officials.

A visible interior wooden structure beautifully complements the soft curves of plastered bale walls. Wisbaum home, Charlotte, Vermont.

comes to the ability of the wall to accept snow loads, to go up two or three stories in height, to include lots of windows to let in scarce winter light, and to maximize the owner's investment, infill designs typically outperform Nebraska-style designs.

Construction Phase

Because the essential material in straw bale construction is extremely vulnerable to rainy weather and because of the unusual set of skills required to put a bale wall together, the bale phase of a project tends to become a project in itself. Let's see how framed structures simplify the bale work.

Rain during the Construction Season

Unlike most rough-stage materials, bales must be kept dry throughout the construction process. On small projects, tarps tossed over the walls—or even a large tarp strung over the entire site—can be effective. On larger buildings, however, tarping can just about become a subtrade of its own, sapping time, energy, and money that is best reserved for actual construction. Plus, complex tarping systems always leak.

A sophisticated straw bale house design will take these factors into account, and will plan the construction process accordingly. While it is not essential that the roof go up before the walls go in, this pattern certainly simplifies the job of keeping the bales (and the builders!) dry. This is primarily because the roof sheds vertical rain, but it also provides a handy nailing surface from which to hang tarps on sites and in construction schedules where the walls need to be protected from wind-blown rain.

Framed approaches simplify the relationship between the building process and these three constituencies. A fourth issue comes into play here, as well. Laying bales into a frame is a smoother, simpler process than dry-stacking them into a wall. Because there is less to worry about, it's more fun.

The factors influencing the long-term success of the building are somewhat more complex. They involve a set of trade-offs between the structural capabilities of the bales, and the needs and wants of the building's occupants. When it

Providing effective rain protection can be a construction project in its own right.

Jon Haeme, of Kempton, Illinois stakes the bottoms of his tarps at a distance out from the building, creating pitched tent walls all around the perimeter, under which he works with minimal interference.

Of course, the best way to protect the bales from this horizontal rain is to get on a first coat of plaster, as the walls go up. In any work party, some people will prefer mudding to the heavier and pickier bale installation. If you can round up and are capable of managing a large group (thirty or more people) it is realistic to have both of these processes happening at once. This is not practical on a Nebraska-style building, where the walls are usually allowed to compress somewhat before the finish is applied.

In situations where there will be a time lag between bales and plaster, a fallback is to nail a scrap board to the bottom edge of each tarp; the tarp can then be rolled around the board and up to the roof, leaving free access to the outside of the wall. At the end of the workday the tarps are allowed to fall back into their nighttime position, blanketing the walls. Jon Haeme, of Kempton, Illinois, came up with an improved version of this system; he stakes the bottoms of his tarps at a distance out from the building, creating pitched tent walls all around the perimeter, under which he works with minimal interference.

The wetter your climate, the more compelling rain protection becomes, not only because

Plaster going on the first story as the bales go into the second, all under a roof as the rain comes down! Gould/Crevier home, Leverett, Massachusetts.

the bales are more likely to get wet, but also because they will be harder to dry out if they do get wet. If you live in a place where an occasional thunderstorm comes ripping through a generally dry environment, you might chance the possibility of a storm catching you with your tarps down, as any water that gets into the bales should have ample opportunity to dry out. If you live in a place with consistently humid and rainy weather, on the other hand, your design had better assume that the bales require continuous protection. An unprotected bale wall, in our experience, summons rain clouds about the same way a trailer park attracts tornadoes.

Permitting

Code officials tend to freak out at the idea of a wall of bales supporting a roof. The concept of a conventional structure of wood, concrete, or steel, infilled with bales, is easier to grasp, especially if yours is among the first bale projects in the area. The bale walls, in this case, simply need to hold themselves up, resist fire, and provide acceptable compliance with electrical codes, all of which they are substantially documented as being capable of doing. (They also need to resist damage from moisture, of course, but even in this case, a frame makes permitting easier. Your inspector will be happy to know that in the unlikely event that the bales were to fail, you at least still have something holding up the roof.)

Inexperienced Contractors

Lack of local construction expertise can be the downfall of any well-designed building. It is typically easy enough, nowadays, to find a contractor who is willing to build a bale house. This does not, however, mean that he or she is actually familiar with the process. In the best case, an inexperienced contractor will be learning on the owner's time; in the worst case, he or she will fail to grasp a major issue (such as the need to keep the bales dry), which can result in hundreds or thousands of dollars wasted on remedial efforts.

If the frame of the building is constructed first, the contractor will inevitably feel more at home

with the process, because the most essential element will have been built according to a familiar method. A lot less can go wrong. Since most contractors do not enjoy risks, they tend to work more efficiently when they are confident of the success of their endeavors.

More Fun, in Some Ways

Stacking bales is pretty well a right-brain operation. Inches and feet, plumb and level, on the other hand, are left-brain concepts, at least when measured to the tolerances typical in building construction. Paul has found that while stacking bales, most people really don't feel like worrying about whether the walls are plumb. The level seems a party-crasher, spoiling the good time.

So, by framing out the building in advance, the left- and right-brain functions are separated. You get in the framing mode, and put up the structure. Then you get in the kid-with-blocks mode, and lay in the bales, without having to

Building a roof before walls is crucial in projects that will progress slowly. With a complete roof, the bales can even be stored over winter.

worry about gross errors in judgment resulting in corners that flare out like the bow of a ship. Such corners can induce seasickness a thousand miles inland. You still need to pay attention to how you are stacking the bales, of course, and you still need to consult occasionally with the level; but with a structure in place outlining the work to be done, the majority of the bales can safely be stacked by look and feel. This construction pattern is also very well suited to wall-raising parties, as the opportunity for major errors is greatly reduced. Likewise, any unevenness that might creep into the bale-laying process poses no structural problems, which means it can be chalked up to "character."

At the Park/Zimmerman house in northern Idaho, the north wall is sometimes completely obscured by snow!

Long-Term Issues

The long-term differences between Nebraska-style and framed construction generally revolve around the design limitations of the former method.

Snow Loads

In snow country, roof framing design can be based on significant live loads of 30 or 40 or more pounds per square foot. Because a "load-bearing" straw bale wall is really, in most cases, acting as a stressed-skin panel, this load is being transferred to the stucco and plaster skins. While wire-re-

inforced cement stucco seems capable of picking up these loads, as demonstrated by the Fibrehouse Ltd. tests (see chapter 6, "Nebraska Style"), there is some danger in requiring one wall component—the skin—to do the two most important jobs of the wall: keeping out the weather, and holding up the roof. In situations where at least one of these jobs is not difficult (no snow loads, for instance, or no driving rain or serious freeze/thaw cycles), this system seems practical, and durable. In cold, wet, snowy climates, on the other hand, Nebraska-style construction on the scale of a house might be a more dangerous bet.

Furthermore, it is unclear whether the load-bearing system will work well with lime or clay plasters, under snow-load conditions. The rigidity of a thin column of masonry held in place by wire and straw is what we are counting on, here. Lime might be rigid enough, clay probably is not. If the plaster is too soft to bear this kind of weight, then presumably both it and the bale substrate will flex under load. At the very least such flexure will open seams in the building envelope; at worst it will lead to serious cracking or spalling of the plaster, and moisture entry. (Then again, if the owner were to carefully maintain the plaster, there might never be a real problem. It is forever amazing how designs that seem as if they should not work turn out just fine. Try it on a shed or guest house, maybe, and in fifty years we'll see how it's held up.)

If a strong structure is holding up the roof, the concerns mentioned above no longer apply. The skin now has one major job—to keep out the weather—and the designer is free to choose whatever surfacing material is most appropriate to the particular site and building. The structure, meanwhile, can be designed according to documented standards, so that it can be counted on to withstand centuries of winters.

Two Stories

Roofs and foundations are expensive, in cold climates. Therefore, it typically makes sense to stack at least two stories of floor and wall between the foundation and roof. Given the same total square footage, it is also easier to achieve a pleasing quality of light in a taller, narrower two-story house, versus a low, spreading one-story version. Bales, and especially two-string bales, do not seem to be made to go two stories, in a load-bearing situation. They simply are not rigid enough. In addition, the inherent unevenness of individual bales, compounded over 16 or 20 feet of height, can make for a very uneven wall top, leading to problems in leveling and squaring the roof-bearing assembly. Add to this the wobbliness of bales at this height, and you find people in a potentially dangerous situation trying to maneuver roofing members into position while the wall

Framed structures allow variety. Here the first story walls are infilled bales and plaster, the second story is built of conventional materials. Weiss home, Charlotte, Vermont.

on which they stand sways below them. (The Prestressed Nebraska system does seem to minimize some of these problems. Two stories are possible, and the wall is rigidified before the roof goes on. See "Prestressed Nebraska," in chapter 6.)

If the bales are stacked around or into a frame, these issues are avoided. Bales have no problem going two or three stories if they need only support themselves. Balloon-stacked around a frame, the bales provide a continuous layer of insulation over the entire wall. If the bales are stacked into a frame, such that each course of bales sits on a floor deck, there is pretty well no limit on how high they can go. One could, conceivably, infill a skyscraper with bale walls.

Lots of Windows

Unlike desert houses, whose main function is to shelter people from the sun and heat, cold-climate houses should be designed to let in the sun for heat and daylight, and to maintain the sanity of the people who will probably be inside the house for a good portion of the year. This means that cold-climate houses usually have lots of windows, which break up the masonry structure of the bale wall. A common experience has been that the supplementary framing required to box out window openings, to shore up narrow columns of bales, and to bear roof point loads, ends up being so extensive that the supposedly Nebraska-style wall turns into a disconcerting mishmash of structural systems. Such designs are difficult to build and difficult to remodel. They also make building inspectors uneasy.

One of Paul's favorite structural systems, first detailed in print by Paul Weiner of Design Build Consultants in Tucson, Arizona, actually employs the framing at the sides of the windows as load-bearing columns. Instead of acting as pesky holes in the fabric of the wall, frequent windows, in this method, bring a rational rhythm to the building's structural support system. More on this later in this chapter.

Less Expensive

Infill bale construction tends to be less expensive than Nebraska style, because of what Paul calls the "fiddle factor." One of the reasons bale construction is so much fun is that it is inherently imprecise; measurements are necessarily estimations, exact plumb and level can be hard to determine. If any significant percentage of the labor is to be paid, however, all of this fiddling with bales can drive the cost of the walls through the roof, or at least through the roof-bearing assembly, which really does want to be square and level, so that the roof framing, sheathing, and cladding can proceed in an efficient manner.

If the roof and its support structure are already in place before the bales go in, then a roof-bearing assembly is no longer necessary. Additionally, if the windows and doors are framed rigidly in place, then these become reference and anchor points for the bale wall. Assuming the structure is designed so that

> There is really no "best" way to frame a bale-walled building. Some systems are used more often than others, but no one method applies in every case.

Bales being stacked around a heavy timber frame.

the bales do not require excessive modification, the walls can be laid up relatively quickly, and therefore, at a lower cost.

We often hear claims that Nebraska-style bale construction should be less expensive than infill because, since vertical columns are omitted, less material is used. This is not necessarily the case. Because wood (or concrete, or steel) is very strong in compression, very little of it is required to stand vertically, in order to support a roof. Also, in Nebraska-style walls horizontal wooden members (roof-bearing assembly, window framing) tend to be quite wide, on account of the width of the walls. Since these components are much narrower in a framed structure, wood use tends to be fairly comparable between the two systems.

Methods

There is really no "best" way to frame a bale-walled building. Some systems are used more often than others, but no one method applies in every case. This is one of the great joys of bale construction—it is flexible enough to allow the designer a wide range of responses to variations in site, neighborhood, needs of the client, and locally available materials and skills. Designers and owner-builders should be wary of self-described straw bale "consultants" who promote a particular construction system. This is an inevitable sign of inexperience. (See "Straw Bale Reality Check," in chapter 1.)

Non-load-bearing bale systems break down into four general categories, depending on the relationship between the bales and the structural frame. The first three methods typically employ a heavy frame of timber, concrete, or steel. In the "bale wrap" system, the bales are stacked around the outside of the frame, such that the frame is left exposed to the interior. In the "infill" method, the bales are stacked between the framing members; the frame disappears completely into the wall. If the frame is allowed to "float," different strategies are employed in different walls, such that the load-bearing members are sometimes exposed, and sometimes hidden. The fourth method meshes bales with conventional stick framing. The bales can be stacked inside, outside, or between the light-gauge framing members.

The Bale Wrap

We have had good luck wrapping bales around timber frames, basically using the bales as a replacement for the foam-core, stressed-skin panels that have come to dominate the timber-frame enclosure market. The frame, in this case, does not need to be made of joined timbers; heavy wooden members, laminated or engineered beams, or built-up 2-by stock, connected by hardware, can also work well. Some builders also like the idea of a steel frame wrapped with bales; the contrast between the plastered wall and the machined steel could be quite striking.

When it comes to long-term durability, the wrap might be the safest of the bale construction systems. As Stuart Brand points out, timber-framed buildings tend to be more durable than stick-framed buildings because "the wood structure is protected from the weather, it is massive, and it is exposed. Air and eyeballs can get at it to keep it dry and inspected."[1]

1. Brand, *How Buildings Learn*, p. 120.

Foundation

Many foundation systems are possible with the bale wrap. The key point is that the foundation (or at least the floor deck) must be extended beyond the load-bearing structure, to carry the weight of the bale wall. This extension will vary between 14 and 24 inches, depending on the type and orientation of the bales.

If the building sits on a slab, the matter is simple. The bearing points (where columns come down to the slab) must be sufficiently thickened to carry the loads associated with the structural frame. The width and depth of these bearing pads will vary with design loads and soil type, but their pattern will follow the standards for interior bearing walls (or posts).

If, on the other hand, the bales and structure are to sit atop a framed floor and over a basement or crawlspace, the most common course of action is to place the foundation wall at the perimeter of the floor deck, as in a normal house. The bales and plaster, which also come to the outside edge of the floor system, bear directly through the framing, onto the foundation. This means that an ancillary system must be installed to support the interior frame, which will otherwise rest on top of an unsupported section of floor. Usually, a set of columns are added in the basement, directly below the bearing points of the frame, to carry the structural loads of the building straight down to pads poured integrally with the basement floor. These can be steel-and-concrete lally columns, or if the basement is to be finished, they can be of wood. They do not generally get in the way, because they are quite close to the walls. Wooden columns are actually very convenient as places to fasten and hang the many accessories typical of basement life.

If your bale wall is relatively narrow, and you are blessed with an adventurous concrete contractor, you might substitute pilasters for these columns. (A pilaster is like a giant, structural shelf bracket.) These would, presumably, be poured integrally with the basement walls.

If the building is to sit on piers, the only way to support a bale wrap is to cantilever the floor, so that the structural columns bear down onto the piers, while the walls sit out on the cantilever. This is not a bad idea over a basement or crawlspace, either. It is one very direct answer to a complaint sometimes leveled against bales by those who are accustomed to skinny walls—that they take up too much floor space. Here the foundation footprint is the same as what it would be under a thin-walled building, and the thickness of the bale wall hangs out beyond. The floor framing and roof still need to be extended, of course, but this is a small price to pay for the beauty and insulation of the bales.

Working with a design load of 22 to 25 lbs/square foot per course of flat-laid bales and plaster, the load imposed by a standard 6- to 8-course bale wall should be well within the tolerances for a cantilevered 2-by-10 or 2-by-12 floor joist system. The assumption here is that the interior plaster skin bears directly through the framing, onto the carrying beam or foundation wall. If the building is more than one story high, each floor will have to be cantilevered, in order to divide the weight of the bales and plaster. This strategy offers the fringe benefit of providing a band of framing halfway up the wall, a handy attachment point for porch roofs, decks, swimming pool slides, Batman poles, additions, scaffolding, or anything else that may be invented by present or future collusions between homeowners, designers, and builders.

The main drawback to a cantilevered floor is that it can look rather strange. It might not be a bad idea to stack stones at the perimeter, if light to basement windows is not an issue. Insulation and air sealing in a cantilever can also be tricky—the overhanging portion of the floor deck should be detailed pretty much like an outside wall, with proper attention to air tightness and insulation.

DEAD LOADS ON FLOOR OF BALES AND PLASTER

2-STRING BALES, 36" LONG X 18" WIDE X 14" HIGH

Laid flat: 10 pounds per square foot per course
On edge: 13 pounds per square foot per course

3-STRING BALES, 46" LONG X 23" WIDE X 16" HIGH

Laid flat: 11 pounds per square foot per course
On edge: 16 pounds per square foot per course

Sand-based plasters: 10 pounds per square foot of wall area (or 80 pounds per running foot of 8-foot wall)

Gypsum plaster: 5 pounds per square foot of wall area (or 40 pounds per running foot of 8-foot wall)

Window Framing

Framing windows in bale-wrapped walls can be simple or complicated, depending on the design. In a one-story structure, window framing is easy: 2-by-4s run up each side of the window, from the floor to the soffit. Single verticals work fine, structurally; you can double them to provide a wider nailing surface for casing or lath, or to make your building inspector happy. Doubled-up framing makes a more natural reveal around the window; with single members, the bale returns can feel as if they are crowding in against the window unit. Single or double horizontal 2-by-4s work as sill and header. The header is not actually bearing any load, just holding the win-

Whenever possible, size the window framing to a bale length, so that bales can be stacked in a column below the window.

A frame rigged out and ready for the bale infill. The bale in the photo is a temporary bench. Stevens/Simons home, Leverett, Massachusetts.

dow in place. Cripple studs are omitted, as they wouldn't be doing anything but getting in the way of the bales.

Whenever possible, it is best to size the window framing to the bale module. This allows the bales below the window to be stacked in a column. Depending on the character of the bales and whether the framing is doubled, the bales' outside corner might or might not need to be shaved off, so that they can slide between the studs. Given the 3-foot-length typical of two-string bales, the framing is easily enough spaced to yield the 33- to 34-inch rough opening that is required for a 32-inch window. Standard rough openings are 1 inch larger than the window unit, but here it is best to go a bit wider. This leaves room both for a bead of spray foam, and for any tweaking the framing may take during bale installation. If the windows will have nailing flanges, be sure they can accommodate the increase in rough opening width!

Window framing is not always more complicated in a multistory, bale-wrapped structure. If the upper-floor decks are cantilevered out over the first floor, window openings on each floor can be platform-framed. If the upper-floor framing is not extended, but all or most of the windows on each story are made to line up vertically with those above or below them, then the windows can be balloon-framed, from the floor deck to the soffit. This may sound strange at first, but it is quite common on old houses, and lends an organized appearance to the building's facade. On the interior, the rhythm of the windows will mesh quite naturally with the regular pattern of exposed framing members. If most of the windows are kept to such a pattern, the occasional oddball can be scabbed in according to one of the methods described below, or allowed to float in the bale wall.

If the windows are not to be stacked on top of each other, things get more complicated. The first-floor window frames can be built to the height of the beam separating the first and second floors; horizontal outriggers can then return to the beam, where they are hung in joist hangers, or toe-nailed. The attachment between window frames and horizontal returns can be made with a plywood gusset or mending plate. Needless to say, this unit is built on the ground, in one piece; it is then stood up and nailed down to the floor deck and in to the beam. It's not an ideal system, but it becomes quite stable, once the bales are in place.

Framing second-story windows is a further challenge. One option, which can be practical on walls with a lot of windows, or where the

Aligning windows vertically simplifies the framing and gives the facade an organized appearance. Earth Sweet Home, Dummerston, Vermont.

building is to be furred out for siding, is to create a full-height skeleton of 2-by-4 framing at the window plane. The first-floor windows would be framed to beam height, and topped with a doubled-up plate. Second-floor window framing would then rise from this plate to the soffit. Ancillary studs between window openings will probably not be necessary, as this superstructure is not bearing any real loads. The plate should be tied back to the beam every 6 or 8 feet, depending on the length of bale used. The course of bales at the plate height will need to be grooved to accept the plate. Though it will slow the bale-laying process somewhat, this grooving should not be a major concern if the bales are to be laid flat. If the bales are to be stacked on their edge, however, you had better make sure that the plate falls

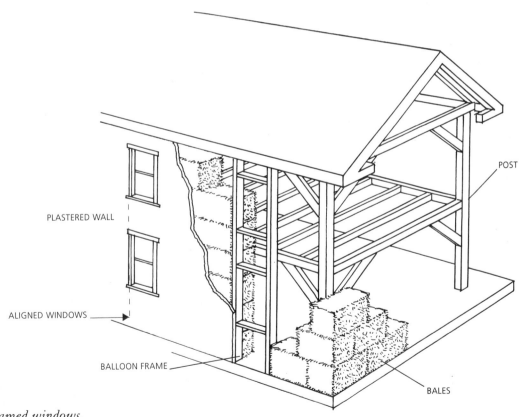

PLASTERED WALL

ALIGNED WINDOWS

BALLOON FRAME

POST

BALES

Balloon-framed windows.

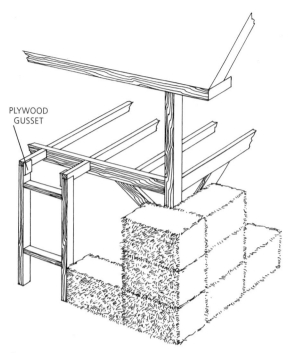

PLYWOOD
GUSSET

One-story window frame.

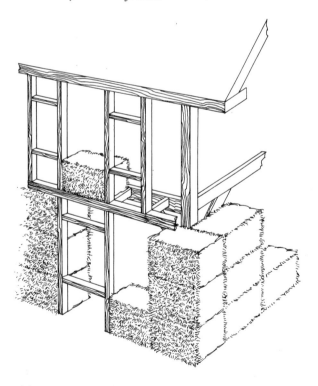

Two-story window framing with studs and plate.

at a break between bale courses. If you've ever attempted to groove the string face of a bale between the strings (or worse, at a string) you will understand the impracticality of doing so.

The bales, in this configuration, will also need to be slipped between the tie-back framing members. This should not be particularly difficult if the returns are placed on centers that approximate the length of the bales. Don't worry about throwing off the bales' running bond at this point; the rigidity imparted by the framing makes the bale wall very stable. From the point of view of bale laying, this intersection can pretty well be treated as the starting point of a new wall.

Another option is to place a wide plate (platter!) in the bale wall at the beam height, to provide a base on which to nail the frames for the second-story windows. Such a device serves a secondary function, as a way of fastening the bale wall to the main structure. This platter is also useful as a means of attachment for porch roofs, or any other exterior accessories. Indeed, it may be worth installing one just to ease remodeling. Architect Guy Snyder of Portland, Oregon, employed a wooden I-joist laid flat for this purpose. You might also fabricate your own version of it, sometimes known as a "track." A track is basically a series of strips of ¾-inch plywood cut to the width of the bale, with a series of 1-by-6s (or better yet, grooved 2-by-6s) screwed and glued to each edge. It would be best if the I-joist or track could be laid directly into the bale wall, at the appropriate height: this would simplify the problem of having to wedge the top course of first-story bales up and under this collar. Unfortunately, if part of its job is to hold the top of the first-floor window framing out away from the main structure, there is no practical way to avoid

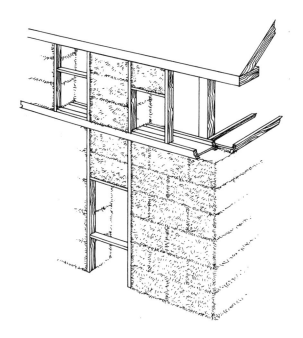

Window framing with "track" or wooden I-joist.

installing the collar as part of the process of standing the window frames. One other low-end detail is possible, here: extending the upper-floor decking material out into the bale wall. It could be beefed up by gluing and screwing a second layer of material on top, to yield, presumably, a 1½-inch-thick collar, all around the building. The build-up will double as something of a toe-up for the second-story bales.

FLOATING WINDOW BOXES

Windows can also be allowed to float in the wall, as in Nebraska-style construction. This method inevitably involves more fiddling than its framed-in counterparts, and it removes the window frames as a reference and attachment point for the bale walls. Nonetheless, this can be a reasonable solution if you have only a few windows, or some oddball windows, on the upper story. Floating window boxes work best in situations where the load above them is minimal; if the box doesn't need to support much beyond itself, the framing members can be scaled down substantially from the 2-by-12 and greater material that is typical of Nebraska-style construction. But 2-by-6 framing is the minimum here; just enough to allow for some attachment into the bale, inside the outer string. And 2-by-8 framing (or 2-by-4s sheathed with plywood, and the plywood extended back 8 or 10 inches into the opening) is better. The plaster, especially if it is wire-reinforced cement stucco, can be relied upon to do a portion of the job of holding the window in place.

If you really want to experiment with floating window boxes, the best place might be on a small window. Framing from floor to beam in order to place a 2 x 2 window, for instance, is not so obviously worth the trouble, because the bales above and below will need to be notched around the framing. The amount of bale displaced by the window, in this case, is so small that the window box can be kept quite lightweight, without any real concerns about settling. Such small windows can even be cut in with a chain saw after the wall is built.

Support of Bales above Windows

Because the window framing in the bale-wrap method is typically kept quite light, any bales that fall above a window must be supported by an ancillary system. There are four possible methods. The first and simplest is to omit the bales entirely. Second, these bales can be hung from the frame. Third, they can be supported by a simple lintel. As a last resort, the window box can be beefed up to where it can support the weight of the bales above.

OMIT THAT BALE!

Typically, there is no more than one bale above a window, in any given story of a building. Borrowing a detail from Edwin Chapin of Phillips, Maine, Paul usually omits this bale, substituting instead a piece of metal lath or sheetrock angled or curved from the top of the window up to the ceiling. It meets the ceiling at the plane of the inside face of the bale wall. This opens up the top of the window, allowing light to spread up onto the ceiling, and thus into the room. Except on very tall windows, this looks better than the heavy brow that is created by placing a bale above a window; it also makes the window opening feel more approachable for tall people. The hollow area behind the angled-forward plaster is blown with cellulose insulation, or stuffed with loose straw or fiberglass.

HANG THAT BALE!

Bales above windows, if you do choose to employ them, are often best hung, rather than stacked. Framing can almost always be found not far above a window; a sheet of metal lath nailed to the window header and looped up to the framing at ceiling level makes a fine, tight hammock for suspending a bale. The inside bottom edge of this bale will want to be rounded, anyway, to match the flare of the window openings and allow more light into the room; the natural curve of the lath conforms well to the bevelled bale. Furthermore, this surface will probably need to receive lath anyway, if you ever wish to get any plaster to stick to it; so you may as well allow the lath to do two jobs at once.

The potential difficulty with employing this technique on first-story windows of a two-story house is that the lath and window frame end up bearing a portion of the weight of the bales above.

This is not necessarily a problem, for two reasons. First of all, if you have built in any sort of interstitial framing at the height of the beam between the two floors, then this framing picks up a good portion of the load from the second-story bales, and carries it in to the main structure. Second, this lath hanger system is really quite strong. If the lath must be assumed to be carrying the weight above, then the window header should be bulked up from a doubled 2-by-4 to standard header size for the size of the opening, and you should be sure to use the heavier gauge (3.4 rather than 2.5) of lath. We have had no problems with this system.

LINTELS

If you do find yourself in a situation where you have lots of bales over a window, and no ceiling or beam to attach the wire lath to, then you pretty well have no choice but to support the bales above with some sort of framing. If the rough opening is of ordinary size, say 3 feet wide or less, then a simple solution can be to insert a section of I-joist or track as a lintel above the window. This lintel should extend at least 18 inches to each side of the window, to properly spread the load of the bales above. (The general rule of thumb is that the overlap onto the wall at each side of the window opening should equal half the span of the lintel, over the opening.)

Across larger spans, you will need a heftier lintel. A box beam works well in this situation, framed (typically of 2-by-12s and ¾-inch plywood) to come as close as possible to the depth of the bales it is replacing. (Extra depth can be filled with scraps of rigid foam, or shimmed up with wood and stuffed with loose straw.) Paul considers this type of box lintel effective for spans out to 6 feet; following the rule of thumb from above,

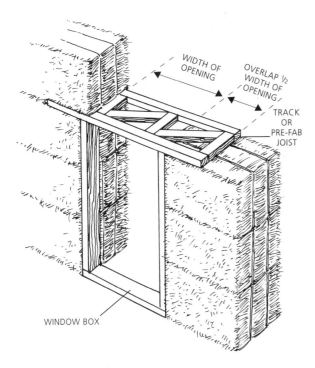

WIDTH OF OPENING

OVERLAP ½ WIDTH OF OPENING

TRACK OR PRE-FAB JOIST

WINDOW BOX

Using a prefabricated joist as lintel above a small opening.

there should be 3 feet of overlap onto the wall, on each side of the opening. Thus, a box suitable for spanning a 6-foot opening would be 12 feet long.

The steel lintels that are sometimes used in warm-climate construction are not appropriate to cold climates. Steel creates a thermal bridge between the inside and the outside of the wall, robbing the building of heat and creating a cold spot, an excellent point for mold growth, on the interior of the wall. The cold steel also creates a tremendous opportunity for condensation of any water vapor within the bale wall.

HEAVY-DUTY WINDOW BOXES

A final option is to build the window box itself strong enough to bear the load from above, as in Nebraska-style construction. The major drawback to this method is the depth of framing re-

quired around the windows, and the resultant loss in ability to round out the window openings. See chapter 6 for details, if you choose this route.

Bale Attachment

While attaching the bales to the frame is not absolutely necessary in the bale wrap method, it is obviously a good idea. This is especially true for buildings of more than one story in height. In cold-climate buildings we generally avoid attachment systems that involve running bolts from the inside to the outside of the wall; this is somewhat unfortunate, as they do provide a very positive connection. We have heard of threaded rods made of nylon, but we have never seen them. These could offer the perfect solution.

In the interim, however, the ever innovative straw bale community has devised some other workable systems. The operating assumption here is that the structure will be exposed on the building's interior, and that, therefore, we cannot go wrapping twine or strapping around the framing members.

The most effective method is a variation on the Steens' exterior pinning system (see chapter 6, "Nebraska Style"), where the interior pins (usually 1-by-3s) are attached to the outside of the frame, as part of the preparation for the bales. As the bales are laid in against this cage of vertical strapping, matching small-dimension members (1-by-3s or round stock) are added on the exterior of the bale wall, and fastened through, locking each bale into its position in the wall, and the entire wall tightly to the frame. The connection between inner and outer pins is usually made between the courses of bales, with every second course being adequate. This can be done with baling twine or with poly strapping.

If the bales are to be conventionally pinned, or not pinned at all, then the connection must be made directly between the bales and the frame. (It is possible to tie conventional in-wall pins to the frame, but this is an unpredictable and picky process, best reserved as a secondary method.) The simplest method we have found is to use either baling twine or poly strapping, fastened off by means of large fencing or electrician's staples, and tied around individual bales. The trick here is to use two staples for each bale to be fastened, one at the top and one at the bottom. This assures a stronger connection by dividing the tension in the fastening material; it also eliminates the sloppiness that inevitably results from trying to fasten a malleable rect-

(Top) Frame at a demonstration building, strapped with 1-by-3s and ready for bales. Aiperon Foundation, Coventry, Rhode Island.

(Left) As bales are installed, vertical strapping is added to the exterior and attached through the wall to the interior straps.

Bales secured in place, with plastering commencing.

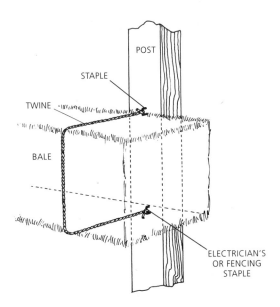

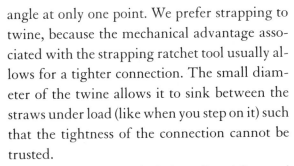

Fastening bales to the frame with twine.

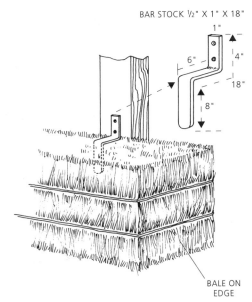

A homemade bale fastener.

angle at only one point. We prefer strapping to twine, because the mechanical advantage associated with the strapping ratchet tool usually allows for a tighter connection. The small diameter of the twine allows it to sink between the straws under load (like when you step on it) such that the tightness of the connection cannot be trusted.

A collar placed in the bale wall and fastened to the frame, at the break between stories, can also serve to stiffen and attach the bale wrap. This method works well in conjunction with periodic tying, as above. (See the discussion of platters under "Window Framing," earlier in this chapter.)

A final option is to fabricate hardware out of steel bar stock. When working with bales set on edge, we have had success with a custom fastener made from $\frac{1}{8}$-inch-thick, 1 inch wide, 18-inch-long material, bent in two places to form an L with a leg added to its bottom. This 8-inch bottom leg is pounded down into the bale, a bit more

than 6 inches from its inner edge. The 6-inch horizontal portion of the bracket heads back toward the post, and the 4-inch vertical is nailed to the post, through two predrilled holes, drawing the bale tight to the frame. A large quantity of these fasteners can be bent in a vice, in fairly short order; and if the bales are dense they form quite a firm connection. This method would not work with bales laid flat, as the bracket leg would approach the straws in an inappropriate orientation.

Plaster

Plaster techniques do not vary much between styles of bale construction. The one unusual detail, in the case of the bale wrap, is that the exposed framing makes for a difficult job of maintaining a continuous air barrier layer over the entire wall. To deal with this issue, we have borrowed a detail from Building Science guru Joe Lstiburek. Before the bales are laid in, the back

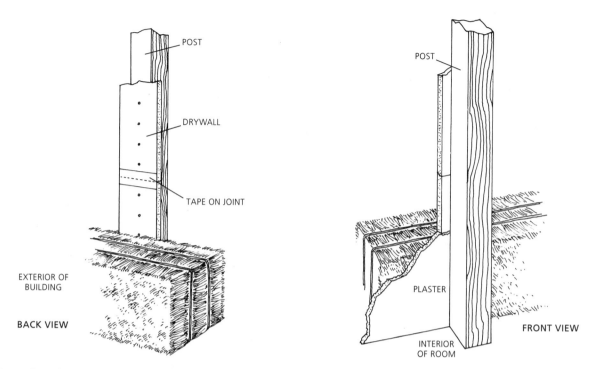

POST

DRYWALL

TAPE ON JOINT

EXTERIOR OF
BUILDING

BACK VIEW

POST

PLASTER

INTERIOR
OF ROOM

FRONT VIEW

Providing for continuity of interior plaster with an exposed frame.

sides of all framing members that are to contact the bale walls receive a strip of sheetrock or plywood, which extends out an inch or more beyond each edge of the framing, into the plane of the plaster. Any joints are taped. The plaster is then run across the bales, and lapped over the protruding fins of sheet material, thus providing air barrier continuity behind the framing members.

Siding

An internal frame is not the most efficient structural system to use on a bale house that is to be sided. The infill post-and-beam and stick-framed methods described below would be a more ideal choice if siding is to be used.

Nonetheless, timber-framed bale buildings have received wood siding. If the siding is to be horizontal (clapboards or shiplap), the most popular procedure is to run 2-by-3s or 2-by-4s on the flat, from the floor framing (or a nailer shot into the slab) to the soffit, or to a nailer that is rigged out from the beam supporting the second-floor deck, and then on up to the soffit. Window and door framing, obviously, must be coordinated into this nailer system. We typically use 2-by-6s

The frame is furred-out with strips of plywood (or drywall) and ready for bales. When plaster is run onto these protruding fins, air-barrier continuity is maintained between frame and bales.

for the window and door framing, in this case, and hang the frames out 1½ inches beyond the floor deck, to bring the framing to the same exterior plane as the nailers. In this manner, we avoid having to pad out the framing. It is usually necessary to add a nailer at each side of the framing, however, because the window casing will typically cover the nailing surface available from the frame itself. An ancillary benefit of this system is that the siding nailers become an attachment point for the bales.

Vertical siding can often be simpler. If the siding boards are of true-dimension material and a nailing surface is available (or can be made available) at the top and bottom of each story, then an additional nailer is only necessary at the midheight of each story. This can typically be fastened to the window and door framing, if the framing is sufficiently stout and sufficiently frequent. (Extra nailers will still be necessary around the windows.)

Under less ideal circumstances, you might find that to install vertical siding, you must first fur out vertically, as for clapboards, and then cross-hatch with 1-by strapping material. This is a rather material- and labor-intensive method, but it does work.

Bale Infill

In general straw bale parlance, "bale infill" means any system in which the bales are acting in a nonstructural capacity. For the sake of clarity, we have substituted "framed structures" for

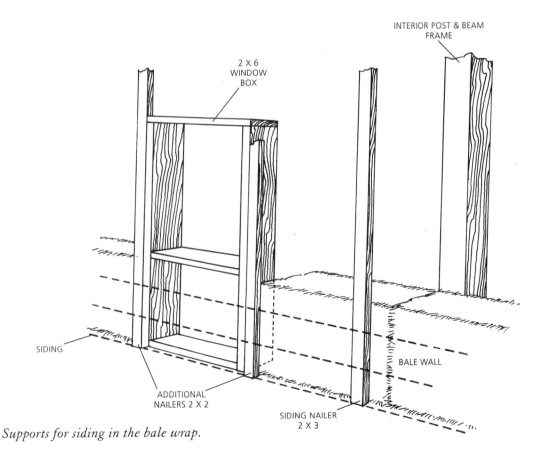

Supports for siding in the bale wrap.

In the big picture, bales function similarly to foam-core, stressed-skin panels, in that they form an unbroken envelope of insulation around both the load-bearing structure and the conditioned interior space. On the detail level, however, the two systems could not be more different.

Panels are the ultimate in expensive, factory-produced, site-labor-saving materials. They show up on the site and are often installed with a crane in one day. The roof and walls are instantly dried in. The interior plaster-board layer is mudded and taped, the exterior is sided, and the walls are complete. The home-owner and builder are happy—the job has been done well, costs have been strictly controlled. Unfortunately, very little of the home-owner's money has entered the local economy; it has mostly gone to the panel manufacturer, who has sent a large percentage of it to foam and OSB manufacturers.

If the walls are made of bales, the job can be done equally as well. The process will certainly take longer, especially if the plaster is applied by hand. Costs will be roughly compa-rable—probably 10 to 20 percent less for the bales in a tight design with volunteer-applied plaster, 10 to 20 percent more if too much time is spent in fiddling. Of the money spent, however, a much higher percentage will go to the people engaged in the work of constructing the walls. Of the sums spent for materials, at least a third will go to the farmer who produced the bales, the rest to production of framing and plaster materials.

The walls produced will look wholly different. If you like thin walls, flat planes, and crisp corners, the panels are for you. If you like deep, rounded window wells and soft surfaces, then bales are the way to go.

Which material is more durable is an open question. If bales get wet and stay wet, they'll rot. Panels, on the other hand, are a home of choice to mice, termites, and ants. And nobody can tell you for sure that the glue that holds panels together will still be functioning a hundred years from now.

In the case of a fire, any sensible person would choose a bale-walled house over a panel-walled house every time. The plastered bale walls would ignite much less quickly than the panel walls, and the gaseous by-products of any combustion that did take place would contain far fewer chemical toxins than would be emitted by the foam and OSB panels. Addi-tionally, far fewer toxic substances are re-quired for the production of the bale walls. This makes them a superior choice from an ecological point of view. Finally, the bales can be composted at the end of their useful life. Depending on your choice of plaster, it may be able to accompany the bales to the compost pile. The panels, on the other hand, become garbage; they will never biodegrade, and their composite nature makes unlikely the possibil-ity that they will be recycled as feedstock for other manufactured materials. Of course, maybe in some future of technological bliss, foam-fed ants will become a prime part of the human diet.

A bale-wrapped, timber-frame structure which has 2-by-3 vertical nailers and 1-by crosspieces to support the pine siding. The Auberge "À la Croisée des Chemins," Mont-Tremblant, Quebec.

this wider category, reserving "bale infill" for systems in which individual bales or panels of bale wall are built between the structural members, such that the framing system disappears into the wall. There are many ways to do this; the remainder of this chapter will look at some of the most popular and practical options.

Structural Window Frames and Box-Column Corners

Paul's favorite in-the-wall structural system for bale construction is an adaptation of the "modified post-and-beam" system first detailed by Paul Weiner in an appendix to *The Straw Bale House*. His system is a hybrid in that vertical columns (extensions of the window and door framing)

bear the load of the roof, while the bales (or bale-and-plaster panels) provide the diagonal bracing. The windows and doors are framed to the full depth of the bale, to maximize the ability of the bale-and-plaster wall to resist shear.

Paul Dadell, for his home in Guilford, Vermont, developed a variation on this design. (And no, your name does not have to be Paul to use this method.) The door and window frames are still treated as load-bearing columns, but the framing is reduced to doubled-up 2-by-4s or 2-by-6s (or 4-by-4s or 4-by-6s) at each side of an opening. This framing is held flush with the outside of the bale wall, the plane in which the windows are most safely hung. The header and sill are typically framed of the same stock (doubled 2-by-4 or 2-by-6) used for the verticals, to create

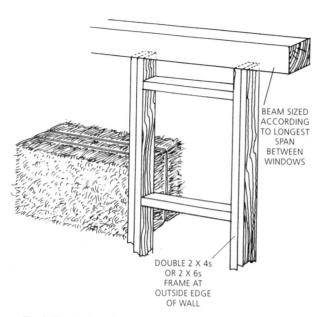

Dadell window frame.

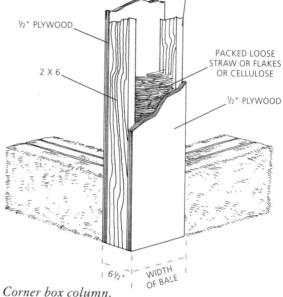

½" PLYWOOD

2 X 6

PACKED LOOSE
STRAW OR FLAKES
OR CELLULOSE

½" PLYWOOD

6½" WIDTH
OF BALE

Corner box column.

BEAM SIZED
ACCORDING
TO LONGEST
SPAN
BETWEEN
WINDOWS

DOUBLE 2 X 4s
OR 2 X 6s
FRAME AT
OUTSIDE EDGE
OF WALL

consistent nailing surfaces for fastening windows and casing. The assumption is that these need only support the window.

Corners are framed with box columns, typically built of 2-by-6's and ½-plywood or OSB. Finished dimensions are 6½-inches wide by 18 inches deep (for two-string bales, laid flat), by the height of the wall. The bales do not overlap at the corners; instead they butt into this hefty column, and are tied one to the other, and to the column itself. This detail eliminates one of the trickiest points in bale construction: the overlapping bale corner that always tries to lean out, as it goes up. These corners are very solid; they also provide a nailer that is an excellent attachment point for both siding and trim. Corner trim is a great aid to exterior plaster (especially cement stucco), because it serves as a control joint in an area that is particularly vulnerable to cracking.

A beam runs across the tops of these vertical members, sized according to the longest span in the building. To control this longest span, a box

Box column and structural window frames, with plywood (covered by house wrap) for diagonal bracing below windows.

"Barn-Raisings"

Bales and plaster work well with timber frames, because they fit nicely into the "barn-raising" tradition. Rarely is an owner-built timber frame erected on a weekday with a crane; raising day is almost always a Saturday, and it inevitably involves lots of friends and lots of good food and beer. Owner-built bale walls, of course, are usually put up in the same fashion. A marriage of the two makes obvious sense. The real Tom Sawyer trick is to lure those people back for a plastering party. Odds are, if they had a good time with the frame or the bales, you can get them to bring others along to help with the plaster. Then, not only will the work get done more quickly, but you'll make a bunch of new friends in the process!

A barn-truss system raised with the help of friends. Gabriel Cornu studio, Saint Germain, Quebec.

With the frame up and the roof on, installing the bales is a party.

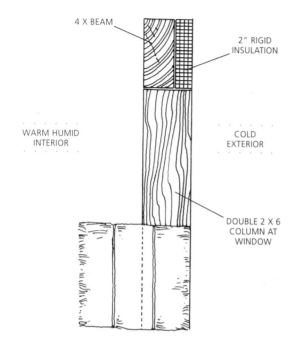

WARM HUMID
INTERIOR

COLD
EXTERIOR

4 X BEAM

2" RIGID
INSULATION

DOUBLE 2 X 6
COLUMN AT
WINDOW

If the framing is 2-by-6s, the 4-inch beam can be set toward the interior edge of the frame, and the exterior-side space filled with rigid insulation.

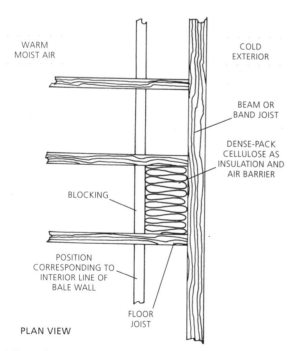

WARM
MOIST AIR

COLD
EXTERIOR

BEAM OR
BAND JOIST

DENSE-PACK
CELLULOSE AS
INSULATION AND
AIR BARRIER

BLOCKING

POSITION
CORRESPONDING TO
INTERIOR LINE OF
BALE WALL

FLOOR
JOIST

PLAN VIEW

The Seldon dense-packed floor joists, plan view.

column may be inserted into any run of wall (a north wall, most likely) whose length is out of scale with the rest of the wall panels in the building.

The slightly tricky detail here is how to insulate this beam well, especially avoiding making it cold enough that it becomes a point for condensation. If the vertical framing is of 2-by-6s, it may be possible to hold this beam in 1½ to 2 inches from the exterior of the wall, and wrap it with rigid foam insulation. An alternative (and rather more elegant) detail comes from innovative carpenter Gary Seldon of Greenfield, Massachusetts. Gary's method is to frame a cavity at the interior of the beam, by blocking in the joist system, more or less in line with the interior edge of the bale wall. The resulting cavities are then dense-packed with blown cellulose insulation. Unlike fiberglass batts or loose straw, dense-packed cellulose acts as an air barrier, so even though the beam is kept cold by the interior insulation, it is also kept out of contact with warm, moist interior air. Thus, condensation should not be a problem. The cellulose also acts as a defense against exfiltration at this very vulnerable location. Where a floor-joist system sits on top of the beam these same concerns apply, and the same details work for insulating at the band joist.

DIAGONAL BRACING

Though Paul Dadell did so in his one-story house, we typically do not rely exclusively on the bale/plaster panels for diagonal bracing in the structural window frame method. Steel-strap cross-bracing is the most common choice for shear resistance, because it can be held to the outside plane of the wall, and thus requires no notching of the bales. Nils Smith employed sheets of plywood at the corners and under the windows of Roberta Nubile and Oliver Kiehl's house in Charlotte, Vermont. A hybrid of plywood (or OSB) and steel strapping is also possible, as at the Gould-Crevier house in Leverett, Massachusetts.

L-shaped steel brackets placed in the joint between the columns and the beams would work well to reinforce this or any other post-and-beam-type system. The danger is that when framing is held to the outside of the wall, the steel will be cold, and therefore a potential point for condensation. Wooden diagonal braces are also an option. These can be the knee braces that are typical of timber-frame construction, or 1-by braces let into or nailed to the outside of the framing. All of these methods have their drawbacks. The timber-frame-style and let-in 1-by braces both require notching of the bales, while the outside braces exactly occupy the plane of the exterior plaster. We generally steer away from this type of bracing system, for these reasons. An

Plywood and steel strapping can be combined to diagonally brace a building. The Gould/Crevier home, Leverett, Massachusetts.

exterior bracing system could, however, be compatible with wood siding.

All of this said, it should be obvious to anyone who has built with them that the bale-and-plaster composite walls are quite capable of reinforcing a building against shear loads. The extent to which they can do this without cracking depends more than anything on how windy a given site is, and whether earthquakes are an issue. It may be that the most important job of the official bracing system is to keep the building steady until the bales and plaster are installed.

Tests undertaken in 1998 at the University of Washington by David Riley and his students show promise for the ability of wire-and-cement-stucco panels to provide diagonal bracing to infill bale buildings. In the UW tests, bales were filled into an 8-foot-high, 6-foot-wide frame of box columns and beam. One surface was professionally plastered with cement stucco, the other with gypsum plaster, each over 17-gauge stucco wire. An in-plane lateral load (parallel to the wall surface) was then repeatedly applied to the top of the wall. The wall performed well within Uniform Building Code standards, requiring a load of 6,100 lbs (762 lbs per linear foot) to achieve the maximum deflection allowable for stucco veneer, 0.64 inches at the top of the wall.[2]

A load of 8,000 lbs was required to move the top of the wall 1 inch, and 10,000 lbs created 2 inches of movement. At 13,500 lbs, the wooden frame was experiencing severe fiber stress, the wire component of the plaster panels had detached from the frame, and the plaster panels had also largely detached from the straw. Neither the cement nor gypsum plaster showed any

2. David Riley, Gregory MacRaw, and Juan Carlos Ramirez, "Strength Testing of Stucco and Plaster Veneered Straw-Bale Walls," *The Last Straw,* 24 (winter 1998): p. 8–9.

serious cracking. According to David Riley, this adds up to a highly promising system, with the weakest link being the connection of the wire-and-plaster panels to the framing and the straw. The role of the wire both in reinforcing the plasters and in making a positive connection between plaster and frame was demonstrated quite clearly in these tests. It is reasonable to assume, therefore, that bale walls with unreinforced finishes would be less ideal for bracing frames, and that cracking (especially in the case of cement stucco) would be more of a problem.

Foundations

In most bale infill systems, the foundation choice is simple, because wall and roof loads are borne at or near the building's perimeter. In this particular system, the roof loads are carried down through the outer 4 or 6 inches of the wall area; foundation design, therefore, is exactly the same as for a conventional stick-framed wall.

Laying Bales

Bales lay very easily into the structural door and window frame. Maintenance of the running bond between bales is not particularly important. If the window framing has been sized to something like the length of a bale (see "Window Framing," earlier in this chapter), we typically stack the bales below a window in a column. The runs of wall between vertical framing members also tend to be fairly short—rarely more than three or four bale lengths. Depending on the pinning system, it is possible to stack these bales in columns as well, or, at the very least, to minimize the number of half bales required, by laying up two courses of full bales to one in which half bales are used at each end.

Keeping wall runs to the bale module is not crucial here. The consistent framing provides a wealth of attachment points for the bales, so cutting and pasting becomes as smooth a process as cutting and pasting can ever be. Bales can be inexpensively tied off to the framing with baling twine or light-gauge poly strapping available through the packaging industry. L-shaped bends of metal lath also work very well, providing a stiff connection between bales and frame. The back of the L, in this case, is nailed to the framing; the base is then pinned down into the top surface of the bale, with ground staples or "Robert" pins.

The bales can often be compressed, rather than fastened, into place. John Swearingen of

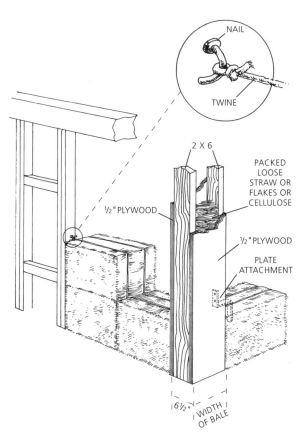

Another way to fasten bales to framing.

Skillful Means, an experienced straw bale design/build company in California, recommends driving wedges between the top course of bales and the beam. Paul has experimented with this system and has found it to be very fast and easy. It also snugs the bales very tightly into place. This is now Paul's favorite system for any infill situation where the beam rests directly above the bales.

This framing system is particularly well suited to cold, wet climates because it brings the windows right out to the exterior surface of the building, where they should be in order to best shed the weather, but it leaves the window wells free for rounding, to bring in maximum light. Window finishing is easy. Standard extension jambs can be applied, and the interior of the window trimmed out. Plaster is then run around the rounded end of the bale, and butted into the window casing. This joint is sealed either by caulking the intersection between the plaster and the casing, or by running the plaster into a stop, which has previously been caulked in place, on the face of the trim. Alternately, the extension jamb and casing can be omitted, and the plaster wrapped all the way back to the window unit.

The structural window frame method offers tremendous economy of materials, by taking advantage of framing that is there in any case, and employing it to support the roof. It uses small-dimension lumber to great advantage, and simplifies the carpenters' job by standardizing the location of all framing, at the outside of the wall. Furring out such a structure to receive wood siding is a simple process.

Other Infill Systems

Employing the window framing to support the roof is not always the best choice. In a building that has few windows, for instance, it would simply not be an option. Or, in a case where the load-bearing posts are to be sunk in the ground or borne directly upon concrete piers, it would probably make sense to separate the structural and window framing, rather than subordinate window placement to column interval.

In these situations, we typically use 4-by-4 dimensional or 6-inch round columns, held to the outside plane of the bale wall. Corners, in square and rectangular buildings, are often still built as box columns, in order to avoid notching at this location. Posts are typically let into the bale, except in the case of multisided structures (such as an octagon), where bale walls are treated as panels, with the columns placed to the outside of the wall, in the notch created where wall panels meet.

One benefit of this method is that it allows separate foundation systems to support the roof and the bales. For their roundhouse, for instance, Paul and Amy worked with engineer Murray Solomon to design a simple way to meet local code, which requires that foundation footings be laid at 4 feet below grade. The roof-bearing col-

> The structural window frame method offers tremendous economy of materials, by taking advantage of framing that is there in any case, and employing it to support the roof.

Windows can be finished with an extension jamb and casing, and the plaster butted into the casing.

In this case roof- and wall-foundation systems are separate, the roof supported by a pole frame, while the bales sit atop earthbags. The bale walls are allowed to "wander" in relation to the frame. Lacinski/ Klippenstein roundhouse, Ashfield, Massachusetts.

umns, in this case, extend 4 feet into the ground, where they rest upon concrete pads. The walls, meanwhile, sit atop soil-cement blocks, formed in place by tamping sandbags full of dry material into their positions in the wall. These sandbag blocks rest on a 4-inch pad of gravel, at a depth that ranges from 6 inches to 3 feet below grade. A combination of foundation drains and well-drained native soils ensures that the area under the walls should remain quite dry, but even if water did get in and cause the walls to heave a bit, the roof would not be affected. It was thus possible to meet code without pouring a continuous frost wall to 4 feet of depth.

The "Floating Frame"

No rule demands that the load-bearing columns in a bale-walled building must stand everywhere in the same relationship to the walls. Bales are unique among insulation materials because they are capable of standing upright, on their own, independent of a supporting structure. This opens tremendous possibilities to the designer. Ted Butchart of GreenFire Institute, Winthrop, Washington, has evolved some very original designs, based on the practical idea that structure (in this case, the roof and the columns that support it) and walls can be allowed to join or separate in different areas of the building, to maximize the potential of each.

In his design for Nancy Simmerman's house on Lummi Island, Washington, Ted employed a slightly different system in each of the four main walls. The south, with its large windows, is stick framed, and includes no bales. The north, east, and west are framed in a post-and-beam system, but the 4-by-4 posts, in each, stand in a different relationship to the walls. On the east, the columns are buried within the walls. To the north, the posts are held 3 feet out from the wall, creating a substantial overhang to protect the wall from the prevailing weather. (When Paul visited, the north soffit was hung with dozens of bunches of drying flowers and herbs. Nancy is a brilliant gardener.) To the west, the gable-end roof and supporting columns are carried out 14 feet, to shelter an outdoor sitting area from the coastal Northwest drizzle.

Looking at the roof and interior floor of this house in plan view, you realize that they are two separate units, one superimposed over the other. Excepting the fact that the roof must be kept, in all directions, larger than the area enclosed by the walls, there are few limitations on the variety of indoor and outdoor spaces that can be economically enclosed using such a system. Ted also employed a creative variation on this idea on the Thrune massage studio. (See the Thrune profile following chapter 12).

Here the bale wall extends in alongside the front door, creating a covered entryway. Miner/Stromberg home, Darby, Montana.

Stick Frame and Bale Walls

Stick-framed structures and bale walls are highly compatible; it is surprising that so few buildings have been designed this way, to this point. We think the reasons are primarily emotional. First of all, people are in the habit of thinking of bales as a masonry material, as blocks to be stacked. Using them individually between framing members requires a departure from this mind-set. Second, stick framing is just not alternative enough for a lot of people. The boiled-down, mainstream stick-and-sheet industry is what is wrong with our buildings, right?

Five advantages proceed from the idea of using a stick-frame structure with bales as insulation. First, similar to any other framed structure, is the fact that you have a roof over your head before starting to play around with bales. The second advantage is the presence of abundant nailers wherever needed for openings, cabinets, siding, bracing, and so on. Carpenters (the people responsible for most construction) love this, because it's what they're used to, and it's what these other components are designed to mount to. As a third benefit, stick framing is one of the most conventional and cheapest forms of construction available in areas where wood is an abundant resource, as is the case in many northern countries. The technique is well known, and trained carpenters or moderately skilled

The north and west walls of this house are extended, to shelter the building and create an outdoor sitting area. Simmerman home, Lummi Island, Washington.

owner-builders can raise a complete structure (including the roof!) quickly, so that they can then concentrate on the real thing everyone's been dreaming of: the bale work! Building inspectors also like the fact that stick framing is standard; at worst they are likely to regard the bale component only as a bit eccentric.

The fourth advantage comes with the spacing of the studs. Because of building code requirements, the maximum allowed spacing of studs for snow-load conditions is relatively narrow, which works well with placing single bales, stuck between framing members. A fifth benefit is the numerous ways the bales can be tied to the frame; they can be stitched to the studs with twine, pinned by several methods, wrapped with strapping, or even fastened with hardware. All of these techniques, alone or in combination, will also add some stiffness to the structure. Bales can be stacked either inside, outside, or between framing members.

Well-planned stick framing can use very little wood. Gary Seldon's design employs a beefed-up band joist as window header, allowing single-stud construction all along the wall, greatly simplifying bale notching. Gould/Crevier home, Leverett, Massachusetts.

Bales Inside Frame

Bales inside a stick frame can be the ideal system for a house that is to receive wood siding, because the required nailers are already present. The frame would be stood first, and the roof installed. The frame might be sheathed on the inside with plywood, or preferably braced with the T-shaped device called "Windbrace" nailed across the studs' faces, the T pointing away from the wall so that no kerfing is required on the stud and bale surfaces. This allows the bale to receive at least one rough coat of plaster on their exterior, as a protection against fire and rodents, and to maximize R-value (see "Siding," in chapter 9).

The bales would be stacked against the interior of the frame, and tied periodically to the studs. A rough coat of plaster would then be blown onto the exterior surface of the bales, windows and doors would be installed into their conventionally framed openings, and the wall would be ready for siding. It would be possible to ventilate this wall cavity, essentially creating a ventilated rainscreen cladding system (see chapter 9, "Selecting Finishes" for more details on rainscreens).

This system has only one major drawback: the bales take up what, in a conventional building, would be usable floor space. In reality, of course, this is always the case with bale walls; their depth means that the design must include an extra band of floor area, out beyond what would be required if the wall were only 4 or 6 inches thick. This fact seems particularly obvious in the stick-framing case, since the bale wall is being built entirely within the space enclosed by a standard structural system. We think that to focus too intently on this fact is to fall into that old consumer trap of placing quantity before quality. Who would not gladly choose a smaller, more vibrant bale-walled space over a larger, thin-walled box of sheetrock, anyday? The fact remains, however, that integrating the bales into the frame is often a better choice, to preserve the maximum amount of floor space.

Bales Outside Frame

In this technique, a bale wall is built as a wrap around a conventional stud wall, on its exterior plane. An objection to this system could be made on the aesthetic grounds mentioned above. What would be the point of placing bales outside a sheetrock wall?

Technically speaking, however, this method does have some merits. Wires and plumbing can be run within the stud-wall cavity, and a polyethylene air/vapor barrier can be placed behind the drywall. Such features would ease the minds of many designers, builders, and code officials.

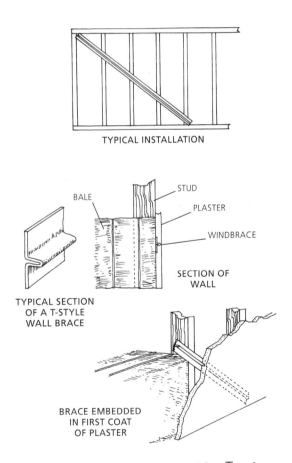

TYPICAL INSTALLATION

BALE   STUD
PLASTER
WINDBRACE

SECTION OF WALL

TYPICAL SECTION OF A T-STYLE WALL BRACE

BRACE EMBEDDED IN FIRST COAT OF PLASTER

Providing extra lateral support with a T-style metal wind brace.

If the interior walls of the house were to be paneled with wood, this system might prove quite practical. The contrast between interior wood and exterior plaster, a reversal of the usual configuration, could be quite interesting.

Bales between Framing Members

People have experimented with inserting bales between studs in various ways with fairly good success. This seems to be the most promising variation on stick/bale construction. Because stud spacing can be varied to accommodate different designs and environments, the bales can be positioned in many ways. To fully understand these we have to review the nomenclature of a bale: A regular bale laid flat has a bottom and a top (the two string sides), two edges, and two ends. For any type of bale, the length is measured from end to end, its width from edge to edge, and its thickness from bottom to top. While length regularly varies 6 to 10 inches within a shipment of bales, the two dimensions that remain constant with any type of bale are the width and the thickness. Because studs are usually spaced quite closely, typically between 16 and 24 inches apart, these narrower dimensions are the best suited to fit between studs.

This means turning the bales up on their ends. Knowing that the R-value per inch of a bale is higher across the grain (through its thickness, rather than its width), we often find it beneficial, in terms of saving floor space, to place the bales such that their narrower, thickness dimension is in the wall. Bearing this in mind, we find several ways of inserting the bales between the studs.

> People have experimented with inserting bales between studs in various ways with fairly good success.

UNADULTERATED BALES

The first option, which requires the least prep work, is to snug unmodified bales tight between the studs. Stud spacing would depend on whether two- or three-string bales are used, and on the orientation of the bales. Studs are placed so that the thickness, or more likely the width, of the bale will fit exactly between them. Thus, a two-string bale that is to be set on its end and so that its strings are exposed on the face of the wall will need an 18-inch space between the studs, which means a framing layout of 19½ or 20 inches on center, depending on whether planed or true-dimension stock is used. If thicker stud material is used and the top plate beefed up into a lightweight beam, the bales could even be laid horizontally, either on their edge or flat.

This technique is fast, doesn't require any notching of the bales, and allows the studs to be positioned wherever most appropriate in the section of the wall. Studs placed flush with (or, more likely, 1 to 2 inches proud of) the exterior plane of the bales would provide nailers for siding; held to the interior they would work for fastening drywall or paneling. They could also be hidden anywhere inside the section of the wall, leaving the two bale surfaces available for a plaster finish.

The main drawback of this method is the need to stuff the vertical cavities left between the stacks of bales. This stuffing needs to be done very carefully in order to maintain the full integrity of the wall. It must be made to achieve a compaction and insulation value comparable to that of the bales. If the plaster is to be applied directly over the straw, without reinforcing, then the stuffing must also be capable of supporting this material. The ideal stuffing is probably a very light straw-clay mixture, but densely packed straw flakes, possibly covered with some netting material, would also work well in most situations.

MODIFIED BALES

The next options involve notching the bales for stud insertion. The main advantage of this method is that it dramatically reduces the need for stuffing, because any cavities left between bales and framing will be small. Placing the bales on their edge is impossible, in this case, because the strings would interfere with the notching. Laying them flat is annoying because each bale usually has to be measured and marked before it can be notched, and the strings sometimes still end up in the way of the cuts. In this case it usually makes the most sense to place the bales in an upright position, on their end, with the strings showing on the face of the wall. This leaves ample room both for notching at the edges of the bale and for rounding or beveling at the window openings.

Notches can be made on one or both sides of each bale. This decision depends on the design and on the attachment system, but as a general rule one notch per bale means a cleaner job with half the work, and less time spent squinting and coughing through a haze of straw dust.

Unless someone can be very accurate at eyeballing regular cuts with a power tool, a jig should be used to cut precise notches. The process of mating the bales with the studs is difficult enough, without notches that are too fat in some places and too thin in others. Obviously, it is crucial that the framing be laid out on a very regular pattern, and that doubled-up studs be avoided, wherever possible. This is not a framing plan for those who are content to copy their details out of books of standards. It should be possible for the great majority of the bales to be notched on the same pattern, without any form of measurement. Some corner bales will require a second notch, to accept studs on two faces. Bales at windows might require custom treatments as well, though it is far better if window openings can be made to correspond to the larger framing cadence.

At the Gould/Crevier house, where Gary Seldon allowed the bale dimension to completely rule the framing layout, bale insertion was still difficult. Because the notches were cut with an oversized circular saw to exactly the 1½-inch width of the studs, each bale usually needed to be pounded quite forcefully, to be able to slide between its neighboring bale and its let-in stud.

Notching a bale with an oversized circular saw and jig. Note the single-stud framing at all locations.

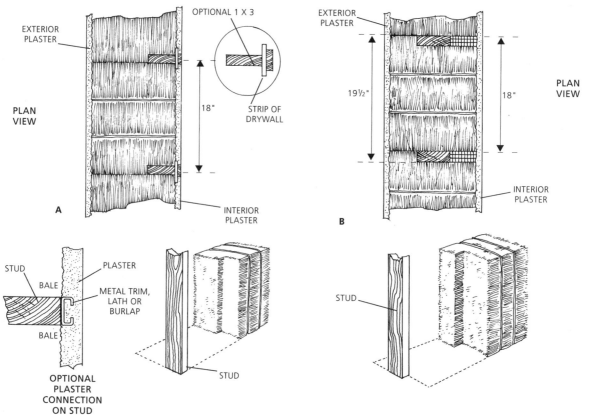

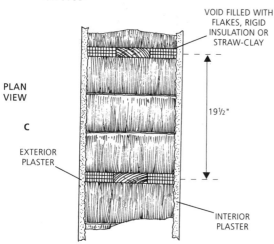

Notching options. A) One-edge notch for position-ing studs either toward the interior or exterior of the bales. B) One-edge notch for positioning studs in the center of the bales (gaps are filled with loose straw, straw-clay, or rigid insulation. C) No notching, for positioning studs anywhere.

This problem tended to increase as the builders progressed down the wall. It was also inevitably compounded by bowed framing members; in fact, these may have been the source of most of the trouble. Considering this experience, it seems prudent to oversize the notches by a small mar-gin, say ½ inch, to allow some breathing room during the insertion process. This would be less necessary in the first few columns of bales in any given wall, which tended to go in easily. Because the gap created would only be as deep as the framing member, typically 3½ or 4 inches, it could be filled with a straw-rich lime or clay plas-ter. This would be much easier work than the pounding that was required to install most of the perfectly notched bales. The substantial com-pressive strength of such plasters would ensure that the bales and studs would ultimately be pressed tightly together. As an added bonus, the resulting ribs of plaster would anchor the finish very securely to the bale substrate.

In most cases, notching will occur at the corner between the edge and the face of the bale, because the framing will be held at either the inside or the outside face. This is easier than cutting a groove down the center of a bale surface; it also leaves the wood available as an attachment point for all manner of other building components. It is possible, however, to conceal the studs anywhere within the wall. Gabe Prost of Ladysmith, Quebec, built his house with such a system. Gabe's is a 2-by-6 frame with studs spaced at 19 inches on center. Using an angle grinder fitted with the Lancelot chain saw wheel, he made a 6-inch-wide running kerf down the middle of each edge side of his bales, and then forced them between the studs, such that the studs keyed into the wide grooves. Some stuffing was needed to fill a few gaps, due to the irregularities of the bales. The main drawback of this method is that additional framing was needed to accommodate cabinets and other similar items. (See profile, "The Bourke House," in chapter 3.)

Steel and Concrete Frames

Although it is not yet a trend in the bale world, steel framing is considered by many people to be a valuable alternative to wood framing, and a few projects have been built with steel frames. Without getting into a detailed evaluation of the ecological and economic factors of using steel, it is worth mentioning some of the particularities of the straw-steel relationship.

First and probably worst of all is that working with steel usually means using torches, or power tools that throw off a great deal of sparks. Neither of these can be recommended on a site where piles of bales or loose straw are ready to catch fire. In the arid West, where the moisture content of bales is typically very low, a couple of disastrous mistakes have resulted from the use of torches around straw. If you're going to head down this road, you should schedule all possible metal cutting before the bales go in or after they are plastered. If any steel work must be done in the interim, the bales must be carefully protected, and any loose straw must be removed from the building. (This is a good idea in any case, of course.) You could also spray your walls with a fire-retardant mixture made of Borax and boric acid (see the sidebar "Recipe and Example of the Borax Application and Results" in the Sivananda profile, which follows chapter 8).

As far as owner-builders are concerned, steel is certainly not as user-friendly a material as wood. With occasional or inexperienced volunteer help, the risk of injuries can also become very real. Workers who are experienced with the material and the tools involved are not always available, and because they tend to work in the commercial construction industry, their time may be unaffordable.

In cold-climate construction, the major potential drawback of steel is the risk of condensation, if the details of the relationship between steel and straw are not carefully worked out. This should not be too difficult in the walls—steel framing should be held either inside the living space, as in a bale wrap around a heavy steel frame, or to the inside portion of the bale wall, as in a steel 2-by-4 stud system let in to the inner 3½ inches of the bale wall. Obviously, no steel members should span from inside to outside; the detailing could get tricky at the windows. Roof details

A French Farmer's Hint

Thierry Baffou and Catherine Dubourg, who paid a visit to Quebec straw-balers after a one-year world tour of straw bale structures, taught us about a very interesting peculiarity that makes bales somewhat self-protective from rain when stacked in a certain position.

A close look at a bale is all we need to understand this characteristic. In fact, we can quite easily notice that the tips of the fibers are all oriented in the same direction, as if every surface of the bale were combed in the same fashion. This is due to the baling process. In the machine, loose straw is packed inside a closed chamber into flakes that are all equally compressed in the same fashion; these are tied together and then pushed along a tray to the exterior. Every step of this process forces the fibers to slightly bend in the same direction. With clean bales this is visually pretty obvious.

On some types of bales with fluffy surfaces, this has to be checked in a different way; the trick is to rub a hand on the bale surface, lengthwise: you get either a smooth or a scratchy feeling, which tells you exactly the orientation of the fibers. Like on a thatched roof, the orientation determines how water can be shed away.

In their native Bretagne, Thierry, Catherine, and most of the other farmers traditionally stack their bales in the fields with this notion in mind. They make bundles with six or seven bales sitting back-to-back in an upright position, making sure the fibers are oriented downward. Each bale is patted, as a check. Piled in this fashion the bales can stay in the field for days under pouring rain without any major damage to the straw.

This knowledge could also assist in the placing of bales in your walls. If the design is made for bales to be placed upright between studs, for instance, the Breton fashion could make your bales equally self-protected until the roof and/or the plaster goes on. Even after the house is completely finished, the bales would still be protected from water infiltrating behind the plaster.

You will also find that this positioning is quite beneficial if you're plastering directly onto the bales. If, like most people's, your plastering technique is an upward movement of the trowel, having the bales stacked in this fashion will make the fiber tips tuck up under the pressure of the trowel, while letting the plaster snug into thousands of small niches. Applied on bales turned in the other direction, the plaster is thrown back at you, as the thousands of tips are pressed down under the pressure and then swing back up when released, like miniature catapults!

The tips of the fibers are generally all oriented in the same direction on the surface of the bale.

might also be difficult, because roof framing has no choice but to span from the ceiling or attic to the outdoors.

Reinforced concrete framing is an option as well. As with steel, some insulation and condensation issues are relevant, but these can be solved in a straightforward manner with exterior insulation of the concrete structure. In areas where wood is plentiful, it is certainly preferable to concrete, from an ecological point of view. For large buildings in cold dryland regions (where size, rather than weather, might make Nebraska-style construction impractical), concrete framing might be the way to go.

Retrofits

Retrofitting and remodeling comprise an even larger component of the building industry than new construction. This makes ecological sense.

Retrofitting an existing structure by snugging bales between the 2-by-6 studs and extending roof overhangs to protect the straw. April Heaslip home, Bellows Falls, Vermont.

An old hospital building was delivered to this site on a flatbed truck, then one room was outfitted with bales to create climate-controlled conditions for seed storage. Winthrop, Washington.

A New Life for an Old Stud Frame

Let's say your old house has a conventional stud frame and the interior finishes are in good shape, but the old sawdust has settled a bit in the wall cavities (or the walls never had any insulation at all) and the exterior siding needs a serious face-lift. Air leaks through the walls make the place impossible to heat, and drafts make you sneeze all winter long. So you figure it's time to do something about it.

You first remove the siding, then the sawdust, and sort out the salvageable siding, storing it for reinstallation. You then fur out the existing floor platform by 19 inches (18 inches for the bale extension and 1 inch for the plaster) and build new overhang extensions to accommodate the extra thickness of the walls and provide valuable rain protection. Then, from the platform up, you start nesting bales against the interior drywall. Finally, you fill the vertical cavities facing the studs, between the stacks of bales. The bale wall is now ready for finishing.

You have two sets of finishing options: You could reinstall the old siding, with necessary repairs and replacements, or put on a brand-new one; in either case you'll have to add nailers on the exterior plane of the bale wall. The other option would be to finish your wall with plaster and get the real bale look that you've been wanting without really believing it was ever possible!

The main drawbacks of this method are the overhang and floor extensions that you'll have to build. Otherwise, if you can afford to lose the required interior floor space and you don't want to fiddle with the overhangs and platform extensions, you're well advised to consider retrofitting from the interior. You will then have a great opportunity to get rid of that boring drywall and preserve the original exterior look of your house, which, after all, was what you had fallen in love with when you bought the place. The other advantage here is that you will be working in total protection from the weather.

A final option is also possible if both exterior and interior finishes are in too bad a shape to be salvageable, and if you also want to add more windows or make other renovations. If the frame is in good condition, then you can strip it bare naked and fill it with bales in any of the options described before. Compared with new construction, you will have certainly saved substantially on framing and roofing while having the opportunity to do most of the work protected from the rain.

Beginning to plaster interior walls.

Paul Bélanger of Living Design Systems has developed an efficient way to make octagonal buildings by using eight prefab columns to support the roof beams. Bales are stacked between the columns then plastered. The roofs are conical steel caps usually used on grain silos. Also note the modular windows.

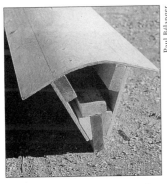

Detail of the Bélanger column made of ³⁄₈-inch plywood and regular 2-by stock. Curving the plywood is too difficult, and the plywood had to be cut anyway so the column would have a slot in front. It's far easier to use ¹⁄₄-inch plywood in two sections.

Remodeling is also a key to maintaining the fabric and character of our communities.

Considering that one of the main reasons for retrofitting an old building in a northern climate is to improve the quality of the insulation, a bale retrofit becomes an interesting option for almost any kind of structure, providing the additional floor and roof space required by the bale walls is available or can be added at a reasonable cost.

It is possible to retrofit many types of buildings with bales; this usually happens by wrapping the bales around the outside, or, in the case of a barn, by stacking them inside the existing boards, with a supplementary backplaster already installed.

Stick-frame structures are probably the best suited for retrofit. We find that a two-string bale placed on its end such that the strings are hidden in the wall (and the wall is 18 inches thick) fits quite nicely between 2-by-4s conventionally spaced at 16 inches on center. If either one or both sides of the wall can be stripped down and refilled with bales, this can work perfectly.

Framed structures offer many advantages for bale builders. They dramatically increase the range of available design options, while allowing for a slower construction process, and protection from the elements, during this process. In areas where trees are a native resource, it usually makes sense to use them (or concrete, or steel) to support the roof of a bale-walled building.

CHAPTER 8

ALTERNATIVE ROOFS

ALTHOUGH THE ROOF is probably the most crucial part of a house, it often seems that the attention devoted to it is inversely proportional to its importance. After all, don't we symbolize a shelter by the expression "put a roof over our head"? Maybe we don't look at roofs enough, or pay attention to the way they can make a house look either protective or frail, how they make a building fit into its environment.

Roofs over straw bale buildings are no different from roofs over more conventional walls. We have, therefore, omitted a general discussion of roof framing and membrane options, which can be found in any book on construction. We have chosen instead to include a brief description of some less common roofing materials, which fit unusually well with the look and spirit of bale walls.

If we care so much about the aesthetics of our walls, we should also care as much about our roofs. Of course, there is an incontestable obligation to make that part of the structure absolutely waterproof, and while there are not many techniques that work effectively with natural materials, some do exist that can enhance the beauty of a straw bale home. These are old techniques that have passed the test of time in the worst weather conditions, so they are capable of enduring harsh winters and rainy summers.

Clay tiles, slates, and wood shingles (or shakes) are the most familiar natural roofing materials throughout the world. Thatched and sod roofs are better known in European countries, where they have a strong tradition; these are also found in clusters of less industrialized countries. Although it is beyond the scope of this book to offer detailed descriptions of these roofing techniques, we will remind the reader of some of their most striking qualities and disadvantages.

Tiles, Slates and Wood Shingles (or Shakes)

The building technique for tiles, slates, and wood shingles, all small-size materials, is the same. Nailers are laid across a conventional frame of trusses or rafters to receive successive overlapping layers of the roofing material. While the structure can be built by any carpenter, these roofing techniques require some special training and are often more labor intensive than the industrial alternatives that have replaced them during the past quarter of a century.

Réjean Cimon's unusual log home, designed by Michel Bergeron and built in 1996 on a straw bale–insulated slab. Constructed mostly of materials found on-site, including the roofing shakes, which were hand-made with a chain saw in a jig. Saint-Côme, Quebec.

Qualities

Roofs covered with wood shingles or shakes are a tradition in many northern countries. They often outperform their asphalt cousins when laid on roofs with an appropriate pitch. They age to a beautiful gray color and are a perfect match with almost any light-colored plaster.

Slates and clay tiles are still available for salvage at competitive prices in areas where they used to be the most common roofing material. These materials are fireproof and durable: The life span of slates ranges from one hundred to three hundred years.

Disadvantages

Shingle and shake roofs have a few disadvantages. They can be prohibited in some urban areas or restrictively permitted unless treated with an appropriate fireproofing material. They are not well suited for low-pitched roofs in wet climates, as they may favor moss growth and accelerated decay of the wood. Strong windy rains would also infiltrate too easily under low-pitched shingles.

The disadvantage with slates and tiles is the weight they add to the structure. In areas with heavy snow loads, that means an increased load capacity for the entire structure, which could be a major issue when load-bearing bale walls are considered. The extra cost of a stronger frame

Réjean Cimon

Slate makes a beautiful roof, durable for hundreds of years with proper maintenance. Clark Sanders home, East Meredith, New York.

thus becomes another disadvantage. Like their wooden cousins, low-pitched tile and slate roofs are problematic in wet climates.

The modern construction industry, instead of rehabilitating these traditional techniques using noble materials, has created an extraordinary hodgepodge of simulated wood shingles, tiles, and slates made of all kinds of mixed industrial residues that have nothing to do with the originals they're trying to replace. If they resulted in any substantial savings, they might be worth considering, but most of the time they are merely a poor competitor to their traditional counterparts. Often, their manufacture serves only to enrich distant multinational corporations.

Thatched Roofs

One of the best performing ancient roofing techniques composed of purely natural raw material, thatched roofs have a very long tradition on many continents, in all sorts of climates. And as contradictory as it may seem, they are still an important part of the rural landscape in countries where rain is abundant and the climate very humid most of the year, such as Belgium, northwestern France, and the British Isles. "All of us like the look of a village with thatched roof cottages gathered around the church and those snug collections of thatched farm buildings remaining in lonely combes or far off on the downs. These traditional and attractive ornaments of our landscape, seen in England in most counties south of a line joining the Mersey and Humber rivers, have come to be accepted all over the world as an essential part of English country scenery—what Henry James called 'unmitigated England'"[1] In Japan, thatched roofs are characterized by striking crest designs made with combinations of straw, bamboo, rocks and clay.

The basic technique is so simple (although labor intensive) that it is hard to understand why, although farm buildings were often thatched, it was not also used for cottages and townhouses in cold regions where most settlers originated from these thatchers' countries. The massive look of a thatched roof is exactly what a northern home needs to feel and look more protective and comfortable.

1. *The Thatcher's Craft* (London: Rural Development Commission, 1960).

Minimalist straw roof, which insulates this simple shelter from the heat of the day.

Qualities and Advantages

Although most modern thatched roofs are built with the most suitable material, the water reed (*Phragmites communis*), cultivated barley and wheat or rye straw make a decent second choice. But even before those grasses were available, wild vegetation such as rushes, heather, broom, and even bracken were also used in various regions. Other native species are also possible. There is a beautiful sample of thatch made with a wild plant called "Bear Grass" at the Canelo Project, in Arizona, Bill and Athena Steen's living laboratory.

Water reeds grow abundantly in marshlands in dense patches, varying in height from 3 to 8 feet, and are easily recognized by their brown feathery seed heads, growing on a single stem and having broad spearlike leaves. In Quebec, for instance, they grow in ditches along highways, where they form an undulating colonnade. This material is usually free for collecting. It would even be possible to collect by hand enough reeds to thatch a small building. Some municipalities have ordinances requiring landowners to cut dried reed fields before they become a fire hazard when they grow too close to densely-built suburban areas.

One advantage of roof thatching is its simplicity: collect the material, attach it in small bundles and haul it to the site, build a roof frame of rafters, nail purlins across those rafters, and then lay the bundles in a shingle fashion, stitching them solidly to the purlins. Except for mechanical collection of the material for larger projects, the installation itself requires only a few hand tools, some of which are similar to those becoming standard in working with bale walls.

In addition to its capacity to shed water very efficiently, thatch also has a high insulation value, thus making attic and roof insulation unnecessary and allowing for substantial savings on that part of the job. In fact, an average thickness of 12 to 14 inches of thatch, which is about the thickness of a normal roof, would presumably give the same R-value as the walls of a bale house, because the material is also a type of straw.

Disadvantages

The lack of popularity of thatch in most countries today is probably due to a lack of skilled thatchers, rather than to a shortage of the mate-

A light structure of purlins is nailed across the rafters, and thatch follows the resulting curves.

rial itself. Perhaps if the technique was dependent on a long list of expensive power tools that are hazardous to operate, noisy, and highly polluting, then governments and corporations would push its use. Because it can contribute only to small-scale local economies, there is no incentive to preserve thatch in a corporate economy. The main disadvantage in a short construction season is obviously the time required to finish a thatched roof. Thatch is labor intensive, so when labor is paid, that translates into high costs. This is probally why thatch has disappeared from the construction market.

Another serious issue is undoubtedly the urban emphasis on fire hazards, which is certainly justified. In many localities, a sprayed coating of a certified fireproof material should make the

Thatching a roof. The reeds are gathered in bundles called "yealms," which are laid similarly to shingles, with successive overlaps.

thatched roof compliant with the law. But this shouldn't be a concern in rural areas, nor even in low-density suburbs where some realistic prevention programs and design features, such as long chimneys topped with spark arresters, would be sufficient to ensure a minimum of safety.

A final concern is that *Phragmites* is not native to the Americas. A continuing story in the long history of European colonization, *Phragmites* has overrun many thousands (maybe millions) of acres of wetland in eastern North America, from the mid-Atlantic states to Quebec. It is a fierce competitor, driving out the great plant and animal diversity of native wetlands before its monocultural march. (Sound anything like agribusiness grain production?) While harvesting may be a useful way to control *Phragmites,* careless builders can also spread seed, both intentionally and unintentionally.

Green Roofs with Sod, Turf, or Straw

As an alternative to conventional roofing, the idea of a green cover over a house can be very attractive. You might choose a living roof for aesthetic reasons, or to help buffer the building from the heat of summer sun, to grow flowers, herbs, or other edibles, or simply to blend the house with its environment. Covering a roof with soil may be the most natural way of not wasting the earth removed by the imprint of a new house. Take the turf or sod removed from the ground while excavating and put it back on your roof; instead of robbing the earth of its potential life-producing surface you will actually contribute to the planet's life equilibrium, which is increasingly debilitated by the constant spread of asphalt roads, parking lots, and tar-covered roofs. Put-

A living roof on a round shed built of straw bales to shelter batteries for a solar-electric system. Earth Sweet Home, Dummerston, Vermont.

ting your local soil back on the roof is like a lung transplant for your environment.

Sod- or turf-covered living roofs will last almost indefinitely if laid over good-quality waterproofing membranes; in turn, they will prolong the life of the membrane by protecting it from sunlight and weather.

Construction Techniques

Sod or turf roofs and other living roofs don't differ much in the way they are built up. They are quite simple to construct. Build a low-pitched roof frame, cover it with a solid deck, stick on a waterproofing membrane, and lay the organic material on top of the membrane. Little maintenance will be needed over the years to turn it either into a rooftop garden or a long-lasting shaggy blanket.

Archibio developed another living roof system. A basic substrate made of second-quality straw bales, laid side by side with the twines cut to loosen the straw, is placed on top of the waterproof membrane. Then a thin coat of manure, compost, leaves, or any other organic material is spread over the surface and left to grow on its own, or planted with edibles and flowers. The only maintenance required, besides the usual gardening work, is to add more straw periodically as the original layer decomposes and becomes thinner.

Advantages

The temperature moderating effect caused by 5 to 6 inches of earth on the roof helps keep a house cooler in summer and warmer in winter, especially in extreme climates; 14 inches of decomposing straw will have the same effect while adding some insulation for a while. Such roofs are therefore a prime choice for cold-climate houses built with a high degree of insulation for maximum comfort.

The wind and noise protection qualities of a living roof are also worth considering in specific environments. A city house built with bales and covered with an organic roof will become a peaceful retreat at any time of day, even in areas with dense traffic. On particularly windy sites, such a roof anchors the house to the ground physically as well as visually.

Durable roofing membranes such as EPDM, Hypalon, neoprene, PVC, or modified bitumen are the best choices for low-pitched roofs. In conventional construction, these are left exposed to weather. Although they have some type of protective coating, they will nevertheless slowly but surely degrade under ultraviolet light exposure, and some of them will also erode over time from continuous heavy rains and ice buildups. In both cases the protective coat of organic matter will considerably increase their life expectancy.

Using a much lighter growing medium than soil, with enough volume for plant roots to stay healthy, was the origin of Archibio's straw bale concept. Earth, the original base material for sod roofs, is ten times heavier per volume than baled straw. Moisture impregnated composted straw was tested to weigh approximately 30 pounds per cubic foot, while moist earth ranges in the vicinity of 100 pounds per cubic foot. With the addition of compost or manure on top, the straw roof will weigh a little less than the 5 to 6 inches of sod roof. It also seems to give more protection to roots in the winter because of its greater volume.

An interesting alternative to both of these heavy systems would be to lay down 4-inch-thick flakes of straw. That wouldn't add more than 10 pounds per square foot to the whole structure, and it would still protect the membrane while offering the same natural look.

A "living roof" on Randy Schnobrich's sauna. Grand Marais, Minnesota.

Disadvantages

The main drawback of building a heavy roof is the additional 50 to 60 pounds per square foot that the structure will have to support. This might be too much on certain load-bearing walls and designs, so the bearing capacities will have to be thoroughly investigated. The need to shore up the structure would obviously increase the building costs, so that prospect should be cross-evaluated with the positive aspects of the roof.

Although it may be reduced to a minimum, some seasonal maintenance will be required on a living roof. The type of maintenance will depend on the degree of refinement you want in the appearance of the roof. All the usual activities associated with gardening—weeding, watering, mulching—will be required if your roof is going to be some kind of garden. Otherwise you just need to keep a sufficient cover by peri-odically adding some material to the original layer. At worst, if no maintenance is performed, the membrane might eventually become exposed, as it would have been if not covered at all.

The last disadvantage derives not from the performance of your organic roof, but rather from your relationship with your neighbors. Social conformity may be something to consider in some areas. Taste and common sense may also be a factor in deciding whether such a roof will look completely out of place in a given site. If you go forward with a living roof, your design should emphasize integrating the building into its surrounding environment.

The Sivananda Lodge

QUEBEC

by Michel Bergeron

In September 1994 the twenty-five-year-old summer accommodation building at the headquarters of the International Sivananda Yoga Center, in the Laurentian Mountains of Quebec, burned down. A couple of months later the directors of the ashram contacted me to see if I would be interested in designing and supervising the construction of a replacement building. They outlined a proposal for a new, ecological building to fulfill their current and future needs.

Straw bale construction was already an option in their minds but many questions remained unanswered. Would the use of straw be permitted for a public building? Were there any particular issues related to the climate of Quebec if the building was to last for at least as long as its predecessor? Because the size (in the range of 10,000 square feet) and complexity of the project made it essential to work with an experienced contractor, would it be possible to find one willing to take the risk of jumping into such an unusual experience?

I had been working with straw bales on relatively small housing projects for ten years and had been considering moving on to larger-scale

The Sivananda Yoga Center's straw bale lodge.

buildings when this opportunity came up. I could not refuse. I had previously dealt with restrictive codes and large conventional projects while working for an architectural firm, and I knew the Sivananda project would be a new challenge.

— FEASIBILITY —
AND PLANNING

My two biggest challenges were obtaining the building permit, and designing the structure to be built by conventional tradespeople, without giving them any special training. I knew that the use of straw bales must not become a major issue at any phase of the project.

For both reasons, load-bearing walls had to be rejected. I wanted everyone to work as usual, without making too many adjustments for the bales. Carpenters would do carpentry; electricians: electricity; plumbers: plumbing; roofers: roofing, *alouette!*

The straw bale work involved unloading the bales off delivery trucks, stacking them, placing and fixing them within the structure, and preparing them to receive the plaster. In all my previous projects, these tasks had been mainly undertaken by the owners, who sometimes even plastered the bales themselves. In this case, we were talking about maneuvering ten thousand bales, which would certainly require more than a couple of owner-volunteers. Paying workers to do the job would have become quite expensive. Fortunately, the ashram is run by volunteers working together in the spirit of selfless service as part of their yogic lifestyle, and they wanted to participate actively in the building process. We decided that the volunteers would take responsibility for all the bale work, while leaving the framing, utilities, and plastering to professionals.

In Quebec large-scale public buildings have to be built by registered tradespeople. Normally, nobody else is allowed to work on the premises apart from the owners and authorized personnel. We had to find a legal way to have all those volunteers on-site. Negotiations with the building inspectors permitted members of the community to be considered part of the owners' "enlarged" family, provided that they were not paid for the work and that they would comply with the usual security code and wear the prescribed safety gear.

Because it was not a good idea for the volunteers to interfere with the trade crews, and because many more people would be available on weekends, we decided that unless otherwise impossible the bale work would be done when the contractors were off duty, during weekends or late afternoons and evenings.

This procedure became an integral part of the general contractors' time planning and task dispatching. His cost estimate was therefore much easier to work up, because he had no unknown factors to deal with, just conventional work with normal costs and a small buffer for necessary adjustments. The only issue remaining was the stucco work. Because of the scale of the job, skilled conventional plasterers would be required, even though they would probably not be experienced with straw bale work.

The subcontractor selected for the job was used to working with a crew of young, very dynamic stucco applicators. These young guys were familiar with modern premixed acrylic-based stuccos, but their work was supervised by an old man who had done a lot of traditional stucco work in his early career, some fifty years previously. He was not familiar with straw bale work, but the challenge of mixing and applying old-fashioned recipes on bales did not appear to bother him. His only concern was the direct application of the stucco on the bales. He wanted to use some type of netting, but was finally convinced to experiment before rejecting direct application when I insisted that the expense of the netting material and installation work seemed unnecessary to me. He agreed to wait until tests could be carried out on the real walls.

The project schedule was already very tight because the building was desperately needed for July—no more than seven months after our first meeting. A rough draft had to be drawn right away and engineers hired immediately to work on the structural and mechanical components. A full set of construction plans had to be submitted by the end of February at the latest, for the project to start in April. It soon became evident that we were not going to be ready that quickly because the process was so complex. To speed things up, a preliminary design was filed for permit in late February, hoping that we would at least receive comments. Nothing happened until we hired a code expert (who had worked at the permit department) to prepare a document highlighting the code issues and how the project was complying with them. In spite of this, the permit was only officially granted on May 31st, a little too late for the building to be delivered on time.

In hindsight, this was probably the best thing that could have happened. The Sivananda staff were convinced that sufficient time should be given to build under the best possible conditions. Had the permit been delivered when we wanted it, the extremely short building schedule would have been a nightmare for everybody involved.

> We decided that the volunteers would take responsibility for all the bale work, while leaving the framing, utilities, and plastering to professionals.

— DESIGN PROGRAM —

Designing the building was a challenge. The organization wanted a building that respected the environment in accordance with the yogic principle of "Right Living"; it had to be simple in shape and modestly finished. Because the budget was limited it also had to be very easy to build. Wherever possible, raw materials of natural provenance were to be used, ecology and sustainability being the main concerns. The local economy was to be favored.

The space needed to accommodate sixty to eighty guests, and to include a large multifunctional room serving mainly as a dining room and for yoga classes. A commercial kitchen connected to that large room was also required, as were a laundry room with adjoining linen storage room and a small boutique. The whole building had to guarantee a maximum of physical comfort and a peaceful atmosphere. Passive solar heating was an additional desire, and people hoped that some living roofs would be part of the design.

Rebuilding on the site of the burnt building was ruled out because of its bad sun exposure. A new location was selected: a small hill situated at the heart of the ashram with beautiful views of the surrounding countryside, easily accessible. The first building ever constructed on the land, a log house, had stood there for over seventy-five years and had also been the victim of a fire some twenty-five years previously. No wonder most of the questioning among the community members with regard to using straw for the new building concerned the issue of fire!

— DESIGN PHILOSOPHY —

To me, appropriate design means the creation of a living environment capable of fulfilling all the mental and spiritual needs of the occupants. For this project I wanted to create an atmosphere supportive of the yogic lifestyle, which everyone agreed was seriously lacking in the buildings they were currently occupying. The Sivananda ashram has a precise goal to which all energy is directed: healing body, mind, and spirit through a yogic life. I have always seen a house as an energizing sanctuary where one should enjoy being no matter what daily life involves. Most industrialized buildings today, including houses, function contrary to that principle. They threaten our health. Modern architecture has developed buildings like machines. They are no longer environments. I wanted to create a living environment that would not be detrimental to the healing processes taking place inside the new lodge and yoga center.

Two main activities guided my design: yoga classes and vegetarian meals that take place in the same room at different times, and overnight rest, which has to be quite efficient because it is relatively short: The wake-up bell rings at five-thirty in the morning!

For eight months of the year, most of the yoga activities are held inside. I have never designed a building that did not provide maximum direct sun exposure to living areas, and this was to be no exception. Yoga classes take place in the early morning and midafternoon; therefore, the main room had to be situated to get early morning and late afternoon sun. This enabled me to design for a maximum of direct heat gain in the bedrooms during the daytime by placing them on the long south-facing slope of the hill. They would be warmed by the sun during the day when unoccupied and would stay comfortable overnight without need for much additional heating.

I wanted every bedroom to be a small sanctuary, peaceful, silent, and warm, insulated from the main rooms as well as from the other bedrooms. We had agreed that the exterior walls would be made of straw bales—stuccoed on both sides—and I could not see how the undulating feeling of the bales that we all preferred would be perceptible inside the building when obscured by numerous partition walls. I strongly believe that a building's exterior should reflect its interior and vice versa. I do not like flat drywalls and my clients did not either. It became obvious that the interior partitions should also be made of stuccoed straw bales.

The quality of air in an airtight, heated building is directly affected by the type of heating system in operation. In an environment used for healing and exercise, fresh air is essential. Convection systems have a bad reputation for moving air around, burning most of the oxygen, and increasing the concentration of pollutants. During the summer, Sivananda guests get plenty of fresh air, as most of their physical activities take place outside. During the winter, opening windows is the most natural way of purifying the air, but it's not always comfortable to feel a cold breeze caressing your back when attempting to meditate in the "crow" position. Maintaining a constant comfortable temperature at floor level with a convection system would require the air to be very warm at eye level—not an ideal condition.

The best option in this situation is radiant heating. Radiant heat warms bodies and materials by direct exposure without the need to warm up the ambient air, as in convection systems. The air stays relatively stable, hardly moving, and can be at a lower temperature without creating any sense of discomfort. Every molecule of oxygen is available for breathing. Once a group session is finished, you can open windows, allowing a good supply of fresh air to enter, which will still be available when the next session begins.

Yoga exercises require light clothing and are best performed barefoot. For cultural reasons, shoes are generally not worn inside the ashram buildings, with the exception of barns, workshops, and other utility buildings. We had briefly discussed using concrete floors as the most economical choice for the entire building, and more specifically, insulated straw bale slabs such as the ones I had already used on numerous projects. Hydronic heating buried in the floors seemed an excellent solution. Heat would be directly available where most appropriate: at floor level. Since the bedrooms were to be autonomous cells, such a system would permit isolating sections that didn't require as much heat during low-occupation periods. Heat provided by that system, in conjunction with direct solar gain, would also make the massive floors and the thick stucco of the walls useful as an enormous heat storage medium.

Another issue concerning the quality of interior air was that of building materials and outgassing, which brought up the question of paints. One of the project coordinators was a former artist whose health had been affected by exposure to chemicals. She was well aware of the problem and wanted the most ecological approach possible. We explored the possibilities of milk paints, *alises,* and limewashes. There was another possibility that I had not yet experienced, and we all agreed that this would be the simplest and most economical way of dealing with the problem. Since perhaps 98 percent of the finished surfaces would be a plaster or concrete base, why not just completely eliminate the use of paint? We had two options: leaving the material raw as applied or coloring it with dry pigments. Nobody wanted the gray finish of the concrete, so we decided to color the floors. The exterior walls were also to be colored, but all the interior walls and ceilings could stay white until maintenance was required, at which point other options could be examined. I had only to ensure that the finishing mix for the interiors was composed of lime, neutral-colored sand, and white Portland cement. Exposed wood was to be stained with natural products. Floors would be sealed with linseed oil and waxed with a natural resin-based compound.

> The quality of air in an airtight, heated building is directly affected by the type of heating system in operation.

As the outline of the building became more precise, the shape and size of the roof—8,000 square feet—emerged as another issue. Flat roofs represent a significant economy at this scale, compared to pitched roofs; however, a flat roof is not usually very appealing. We had previously discussed the possibility of creating living roofs. This idea now became the most attractive option. The building was taking away an important gardening area. With the aim of creating living roofs not only for aesthetic purposes but, if possible, for gardening, we began to look for the most useful and easy-to-grow edible crop, ideally a perennial, to grow on straw. Because the living roof concept needs straw to be added periodically to keep it "alive," the selected crop should be able to withstand that addition. Strawberries seemed highly appropriate, and as soon as this idea was mentioned it was immediately adopted.

— THE BONES AND THE FLESH —

Having determined the philosophical aspects of the design, I was still left with the main challenge of creating the most easily workable system for a project of this scale. My main concern was that such a system would allow foundations, frame, and roofs to be built before introducing a single bale. I had already struggled with enough tarps on windy sites to know that this was out of the question for this project. I was also aware that using an inexperienced group of rotating volunteers for cutting, notching, reshaping bales, and pinning and stitching work—usually considered normal in bale projects, and maybe fun for small ones—would in this case take forever. We were already talking about three thousand bales, just for the walls!

Although it would have been a beautiful feature, our tight schedule ruled out timber framing; instead I was looking for a lighter structure that could be raised by ordinary carpenters using conventional tools and less expensive lumber. After considering many ideas, I decided to go for a modified post-and-beam frame made of locally milled 6 x 6s, rough hemlock. Posts spaced at 4-feet on centers would offer a perfect fit for 42-inch bales laid in between, and, if the fit were tight enough, attaching the bales would not require any notching or intricate devices. These 42-inch bales are not very common in

two-string format but since we needed 3,000 of them—and in the middle of the harvesting season—we figured it would not be difficult to have them custom-made for us. It would be quite easy to pack the gaps in front of each post with loose straw and hold it in place with netting bridged across and tied to the adjacent bales.

The building took its final shape on paper: An overall 4-foot x 4-foot grid was the basic layout from which all the rooms were designed. Foundations of 8-inch stem walls on appropriate footings poured onto the existing rock enclosed the straw bale-insulated slabs (see chapter 5, "Foundations") and supported the frame and the bale walls. The structure was topped by flat living roofs (1:48 pitch) waterproofed with high-quality modified bitumen membranes on a plywood deck. Ordinary 2-by-10 and 2-by-12 joists with straw bales inserted as insulation made the roof structure.

The straw bale partitions would provide perfect sound insulation between rooms on the same floor level, so I decided that the same principle should apply between floor levels. The second floor of the bedroom wings was therefore designed with the same intercalary system as the roofs, but instead of using a wood decking, the bales would be topped by a concrete slab with hydronic tubes buried in it. This way the entire building was to have the same type of floor finish, the same radiant heat system, and the same insulation material. The main benefit of reducing the list of different components was that a minimum of trade workers would have to adjust their work for the presence of the straw bales.

The final floor plan ended up with twenty-two bedrooms distributed on two levels along a slightly curving axis, following the natural profile of the south-facing slope of the hill. To preserve

A poured footing intimately married to the existing rock cliff.

Persuading a bale into place.

the tranquillity of the sleeping area, the multipurpose yoga/dining room and attached kitchen were isolated from that section by the main entrance hall, the library, and the laundry room. The overall floor plan of the building thus developed into a T shape in which the wings accommodate the two levels of bedrooms. Altogether the floor area is a little over 12,000 square feet.

— ACTION! —

Excavation finally started in July. Although we had planned not to, some blasting was required under the projected bedroom wings. The foundation work took a while because of the uneven and irregular rock surface onto which the footings had to be poured. Then the post-and-beam frame started to grow, suddenly defining the volume of the building.

At the same time, a minimum of 6 inches of granular material was compacted over the rock bed to make it level for the base slab that was poured on it afterward.

Next came the roof frame, deck, and membrane. Before starting the deck work, we realized we should try out fitting the bales between the roof joists by pushing the bales in from underneath, since that work was scheduled for after the membrane job. Joist spacing had been made purposely tight—19 inches on center—so that there would be no empty gaps in the insulation. We discovered that the insulation would be very tight and efficient, but too tight to allow us to raise the bales into position from below—certainly not 2,500 of them. This was clearly demonstrated when we switched to inserting from the top, because most of the bales had to be stomped down!

This was not a very helpful modification to our original plan. It was certainly easier to stomp the bales down than to lift and push them up into place, but we were now in a different situation for work planning. With clouds and rain looming in the distance, the bales had to be covered immediately with the decking and tarps until at least the first membrane layer could be installed. The bale work was no longer a part-time job.

After the decking was complete and protected with tarps, rain poured intermittently for a few days. Because of the very low pitch of the roofs and the intensity of the rain, puddles were forming and water started to infiltrate the tarp seams and into the bales. Fortunately, most of the infiltrations channeled along the panel edges, dripping down between the joists and the sides of the bales. We decided to wait until it was time for the ceiling installation before replacing the damaged bales, hoping that some would dry out, since they were not badly impregnated. We marked the spots where signs of moisture had been noted and hoped that the temporary heaters installed in the building would cause the moisture to disappear. Two months later we took very careful readings with a moisture meter throughout the whole surface of the ceiling. The task took a full day of investigation, and luckily only fifty bales needed replacing.

After that short but very stressful period, the roof was properly waterproofed with the first layer of membrane, and work could start on the walls. A day had been planned to check how the bales would fit between posts and how we would fix them to the frame. Before long we realized that the bales fit so tightly between the posts that it was very hard to squeeze them in by hand and, once in, even harder to take them out; most of the 42-inch bales were in fact closer to 43 inches and many were even 45 inches. Because the posts were positioned in the middle of the wall, they prevented the bales from sliding either in or out. I was now convinced that the stucco, once finished and set, would be enough to brace the bales solid, but it would still be advisable to prevent them from moving under accidental collisions during construction. We secured them by driving 6-inch spikes through the top edges of the bales diagonally into the adjoining posts.

For the enthusiastic group of volunteers who found themselves on duty for the next several weekends, building bale walls quickly became a routine part of their yoga life. Delivery vans with loads of up to 1,500 bales would arrive on Friday night and, be unloaded right away, and the bales would be stacked immediately inside the building or under tarps and placed in the walls during the weekend.

Finally, after the first bale wall was erected, the moment of making stucco samples arrived, a crucial juncture because the final look of the building, inside and out, would be dependent on the quality of the rendering.

One morning the first team of stucco applicators

The Sivananda project involved close collaboration of alternative and conventional tradespeople. Here, plumbers do prep work before the top layer of the slab is poured over the embedded bales.

Fireproofing and Mold-repellent Recipe

Paul Bélanger of Living Design Systems in Edson, Alberta, uses a special spray on the straw bale walls of the houses he builds whenever fire could be a problem during the construction process. He also uses it as a mold repellent. On one occasion he worked with flax straw, which has a very high content of natural oil (linseed oil) and therefore can be quite flammable. Apparently a single spark can ignite a stack of bales made of flax straw, especially in dry hot weather. The recipe is very simple, made with nontoxic ingredients. He uses a borax and boric acid mixture combined with heated water and sprayed onto the straw walls or, in high-risk situations, directly onto the bales prior to installation. Two parts of borax are mixed with one part of boric acid and added to near-boiling water to the point of saturation—when the powdered ingredients do not dilute anymore—and then sprayed, usually with a pressurized garden sprayer. It doesn't take very long to spray an entire structure this way, and it certainly makes everybody feel much safer until a base coat of plaster is applied. A mix of 10 pounds of borax and 5 pounds of boric acid is normally sufficient to spray a house. Borax is available in quantities as small as one pound, but boric acid is better bought in 25-pound sacks from chemical suppliers, since it's quite expensive. A quick check with the supplier of the premixed material used by the cellulose fiber industry to treat their material confirmed that these people are willing to sell it to individuals.

showed up on-site with their equipment—more skeptical than worried. After my short explanation of the basic principles of the "bale-and-plaster philosophy," they started to apply patches on the wall, looking amazed at what they didn't yet believe they were playing with. After adjusting their mix to different consistencies and a few minutes of plastering, they finally agreed, to their astonishment, that this was something they could do. In addition, the solidity of the bond between the plaster and the straw resolved the question about the use of mesh. With signs of winter ahead, plastic lean-to walls were built so the exterior plaster work could advance as fast as possible and enable us to seal the building and install temporary heaters. The heaters became very helpful when nighttime temperatures threatened to freeze the fresh plaster.

Later on an accidental test proved the strength of the bond. Almost all the walls had been filled and the exterior plaster had received the final render. Roofers were busy torching the second membrane layer on the roof deck. One of them was pointing his bazooka flame along the exterior plastered wall near a doorway, and all of a sudden the adjacent interior wall caught fire. Fortunately, one of the masons working with a hose nearby was fast enough to extinguish that mighty flame. It was unbelievable! Because floors had to be poured before walls could be plastered and ceilings finished, unprotected straw was exposed over the entire building surface—2,500 bales laid for the slabs, 2,500 in the ceiling, and the 3,000 in the walls still unplastered inside—altogether some 8,000 bales, or to put it more simply, 40,000 square feet of exposed dry straw!

When all was said and done, a section of just seven bales between two posts had been charred. They were removed, leaving a thick layer of fibers woven like a fabric to the exterior stucco skin. The 4 x 8 section of plaster stood solid like a shaggy rigid carpet stretched between the posts. Instead of knocking it down to make room for the replacement bales we just coated it with a thin layer of plaster and installed the new bales against it.

This proved to be the most sensitive phase of the project. For a while the fire risk prevailed, and the hundred people who were sometimes at work at the same time had to be extremely cautious. A lot of preparation work had to be done by the plumbers and electricians who were handling soldering irons, torches, and grinders; sparks had to be controlled and the straw had to be carefully protected. Fortunately no other accident occurred. I now know of a simple borax-based recipe to make the straw fireproof until a first coat of plaster is applied (see page 206).

Finally we were ready to pour the slabs. This was scheduled to take a day for each of the three different sections of the building, at one-week

A patch of living roof.

intervals. This time the challenge was to get the finish we wanted, a rusty color inspired by the color of the existing rock face—150 feet long—that we had decided to keep exposed along the north wall of the first-floor corridor. I wanted to re-create its special variegated earthy aspect by mixing very small amounts of yellow and red dry pigments (iron oxide) into the concrete surface. The experienced workers who were going to do the job couldn't understand why we didn't want a uniform color. After a great deal of talking they finally agreed with this unusual way of working. The final color of the concrete slab is one of the warmer features of the building. The corridor in the room's pavilion matches particularly well with the exposed cliff.

After each slab pour, the plaster of the interior walls and ceilings was finished. With more than two dozen incredibly enthusiastic young applicators, we passed from rough structure to finished walls in no time. Because no painting had to be done, this was the last important phase of the project. By Christmas 90 percent of the finishing work was complete, roughly five months after starting work. Unfortunately, it took another five months to complete the remaining 10 percent of the work, mainly finishing touches. Management problems with the contractor and perhaps a lack of motivation made everything slow down considerably. Instead of Christmas 1996 as originally planned, the official opening was finally celebrated in June 1997.

— AFTERTHOUGHTS —

If the building were to be designed again, there isn't much that I would change apart from a few details. The whole system worked out pretty efficiently and the finished building performs quite well all year round after three years of service.

Perhaps I would use another type of netting in place of the metal lath, because the expansion of the metal under severe sun exposure and hard freezing is possibly responsible for some cracking of the plaster. Alternatively, I would design walls that would not need any netting, as a homogenous straw support seems to work best for exterior plasters.

I would also definitely make sure that samples be made for unusual finishes, such as those we used for the floors. Samples were specified in the contract, but I must admit that I was skeptical that they were necessary. Samples would have revealed to the workers the special care demanded by the technique, and would have tested their capacity to do everything right. Because of coordination problems, and probably because not

Closed in—in time for the Quebec winter.

enough people were assigned to finish the concrete, the workers were caught short of time to
make the control joints prescribed on the plans.
Being short-handed, they could hardly finish the
troweling before the concrete started to set hard,
and they abandoned making the control joints.
The first slab was finished in the middle of the
night and when we inspected it the next morning, cracks had already begun to travel their random journey. Despite my repeated cautions for
the two sections that followed, they were caught
short again. Fortunately there were not too many
cracks and their wavy patterns may look better in
the rustic environment than straight control cuts.

—AGING WELL—

At the end of the construction Sally "Shambhavi"
Thirkettle, one of the staff responsible for the
lodge, reported: "After more than eighteen
months of intensive teamwork, we have a beautiful and unique new building that in many
ways goes beyond our expectations. . . . The finished lodge is inspiring. The use of natural, untreated materials, white stuccoed walls, and
large windows opening onto spectacular views
creates a fitting environment for the practice
and teaching of yoga according to the timeless
principles of 'simple living and high thinking.'"

Straw Bale Finishes

CHAPTER 9

SELECTING FINISHES

OST OF THE DESIGN AND PLANNING PHASE of a new house is spent in resolving technical questions of size, shape, structure, site, and services. If the answers to these questions are carefully thought through, the building should work efficiently. But beyond technical performance, what we are really looking for is a place that reflects something of ourselves, a place we can call our home. A well-designed house will serve both of these functions: It will please our minds by working well, and please our senses by feeling just right.

The relationship between functional efficiency and aesthetic sensibility becomes most apparent in how a building is finished. Like the skins of our bodies, the typical plastered skins of a straw bale house play both essential roles. The quietly undulating surfaces of a plastered bale wall, which most of us choose for their beauty, are also responsible for protecting the bales from the hazards of rain, snow, and interior moisture. In most of the original bale buildings, designed according to the opportunities and limitations afforded by the Nebraska Sandhills, the stucco skins were also called upon to reinforce the building against the racking forces of high plains winds, and to bear at least a portion of winter snow loads.

As the revival of interest in straw bale construction has spread, so has the range of available finish options. And as bale construction has migrated into wetter climates and toward more sophisticated designs, the range of demands placed on the buildings' skins has also increased.

Because this modern history of straw bale construction is so recent, and therefore lacking in accepted standards, it is still necessary to think carefully about the finish system for each project, if we hope to predict how it will perform over time.

While the original Nebraska walls were mostly covered with cement stucco, recent builders from different parts of the world have worked with a range of mixtures, using cement, lime, gypsum, or clay binders in their plasters. The diversity of framing systems now in use has also led designers to investigate other finishing options, such as siding or paneling. As structural systems multiply, so do the options for surfacing. As we look at the different finish options available for cold-climate straw bale construction, we must bear in mind that any decision regarding one side of a wall will have a substantial effect on finish options for the opposite side of the wall.

We must admit a bias toward earth and lime plasters over cement stucco. We have found them to be far more pleasant to work with, and to yield a better looking finish. We also believe, based on traditional buildings in Europe and the American Southwest, that they are less likely to cause moisture problems within a straw bale wall.

At the same time, we recognize that cement stucco has some advantages, most notably its structural strength and its familiarity to mainstream contractors. The following chapters will explore these issues in much greater detail.

"Breathability" and Drying Potential

The idea that bale walls need to "breathe" has become something of an axiom in straw bale construction. This term is a difficult one, because its meaning in a building is different from its meaning in most every other situation. Strange as it may seem, when we speak of a wall that can "breathe," we are not talking about a wall that allows air to leak through. What we are talking about is a wall that is open to the passage of water vapor. (Presumably, the wall is also open to the diffusion of other gases whose concentration is higher inside than outside. See sidebar later in this chapter.) This distinction between vapor diffusion and air movement is very important. It has been a major source of confusion in the design of straw bale walls.

Because "breathing" is a confusing concept, it is simpler to speak in terms of a wall's drying potential. Bale walls dry by two processes.

Ferns pressed into the wet plaster accent this wall niche.

Water vapor is only one of the many gases that make up the life-sustaining air of biosphere Earth. It is also only one of the many gases that can accumulate to unhealthy levels within buildings. Aside from the obvious carbon dioxide, which is a by-product of human respiration and all combustion appliances, the air in our homes tends to collect trace quantities of the many substances, both naturally occurring and synthetic, with which we build. Many people are concerned (and rightly so) about the potential effects of formaldehyde emitted from the glue in some plywood, OSB, and particleboard. We often do not realize, however, that softwoods offgas formaldehyde as well; people with severe chemical sensitivities often cannot live in homes built of softwood tree species.

Carpets, vinyl flooring, and paints are recognized culprits. What about unvented gas stoves and heaters, or the myriad plastic products that most of us haul into our houses, day in and day out?

There is no question that the two most important means of dealing with these pollutants are to 1) not bring them inside in the first place and 2) provide a consistent change of air, through mechanical ventilation or regularly opening windows. It seems reasonable to assume, however, that walls built to be relatively open to the passage of water vapor will also be somewhat open to the passage of these other gases. Presumably, these other gases will be inclined to diffuse from areas of greater concentration (indoors) to areas of lower concentration (outdoors). While the rate of this diffusion will not be significant enough to avoid indoor air quality problems if either of the two main control strategies is neglected, it should serve as an insurance policy to the healthy performance of a well-designed and operated house.

The more important process is vapor diffusion—the passage of water in its vapor state from an area of higher concentration to an area of lower concentration. (See "Moisture" in chapter 2 for a more detailed discussion.) The second process is the movement of liquid water (by capillary action) from the straw into the exterior plaster, from which it can evaporate into the air. Whether this water appeared in the bale as condensed vapor or from an exterior leak makes little difference—the key is that it must be able to dry out. A wall can be said to have a high drying potential if it is capable of efficiently moving moisture out by both of these processes.

In most conventionally built cold-climate houses, drying potential is not a major design factor. Some attention is given to keeping the cold side more vapor permeable than the warm side, but this is a secondary strategy. The primary defenses against moisture damage, in these houses, are an interior poly air/vapor barrier, which is responsible for keeping water vapor out of the walls, and a tarpaper- or housewrap-backed cladding layer, which is responsible for keeping liquid water out of the walls.

The interior finish, in this mainstream case, can be of any material at all, because it is not doing anything other than providing a visual surface. It hides the poly, which is doing the actual work. To a lesser degree, the same is true for the exterior finish; the housewrap is responsible for keeping wind from blowing into the walls, and the housewrap provides the final (if not the primary) barrier to rain and snow. The crucial point here is that because of the barrier membranes, current mainstream construction requires no relationship between the vapor permeability of the interior and exterior surfacing materials.

In a bale wall, the situation is utterly different. In almost every case, the aesthetic finishes and the functional finish are one in the same. It becomes crucial, therefore, that the interior and exterior surfaces be coordinated into a coherent system. The choice of these finishes is one of the most important decisions to be made in the design of a bale house.

Factors Affecting Choice of Wall Finish

Four main factors influence the choice of finishes. The first is taste—what kind of finish do you like? The second is whether a cement-based stucco is needed for structural reasons. The third is the site—what kind of weather exposure is this

building going to endure? Additionally, what is the character of the neighborhood? The fourth consideration is the relationship between inner and outer surfaces. In a cold climate, the outside should be at least as vapor permeable as the inside, and possibly more so.

Aesthetic Concerns

What do you want the building to feel like? Do you like the earthy feeling of a clay-plastered interior, with its visible bits of sand and golden straw? Do you like the soft luminescence of a limewash? Maybe you like to get creative with paint, and would be happy with a gypsum substrate on which to apply it. Do you prefer some sort of wooden siding to plaster?

These questions, and others like them, form the basic set of parameters for your choice of finishes. Technical issues are important, but there's not much point in a finish that doesn't feel right.

Structural Concerns

Larger Nebraska-style buildings, and those in seismically active or heavy snow-load areas, may require a wire-reinforced cement stucco for their structural integrity. Some infill buildings also rely on reinforced cement stucco to resist shear loads. Where possible, structural cement stucco should be used on the interior, rather than the exterior, of a cold-climate building. At a perm rating of 3.2, this interior cementitious layer will likely be less vapor permeable than any material chosen for the exterior (the higher the perm rating, the more vapor permeable the material is). Cement stucco need not comprise the finished surface, of course; it can be painted, with or without a skim coat of gypsum plaster.

It is also possible that lime (and even clay) plasters are capable of fulfilling these structural load-resisting tasks. These materials have simply not been tested, and therefore their structural abilities in certain high-load environments are not known with certainty.

Site Concerns

Local weather conditions are a crucial factor in the selection of exterior finishes. We must remember that rainwater poses the greatest threat to bale walls. The finish, obviously, must protect the bales from water intrusion. The site will determine what finish is appropriate. Earth plaster, for instance, is not the best choice on a site that receives lots of horizontal weather. Cement stucco might not be either, unless the climate also provides substantial drying periods. Lime seems to work everywhere, though the maintenance requirements vary. Siding can be an excellent choice on wet and windy sites.

The character of the neighborhood is also a concern. In areas with a wood-building tradition, a plastered bale building can look out of place on an in-town site. It is always a good idea to pull in some elements of the local vernacular (trim details come immediately to mind) to anchor the building within the traditions of the locale.

Relationship between Inner and Outer Finish

The relationship between the inner and outer finishes is an issue of tremendous importance in the design of bale walls. The key assumptions here are that any moisture that makes its way into the wall must be allowed to leave, and that most (though not all) of the drying of cold-climate walls happens through the exterior skin (see "Moisture" in chapter 2 for background). The design decisions that flow out of these basic assumptions can be simple or complex, depending on the nature of the building.

In the simplest scenario, the interior and exterior would be built to be equally vapor permeable. This is typically accomplished by finishing each surface with the same materials. History is on the side of this approach; many European walls of straw and earth have survived for centuries with a lime finish on each surface. It may be that this system works so well because these walls are monolithic (built of solid material all the way through), which means that air leakage is not much of an issue. It may also be because the plasters are very permeable, and because the straw is coated with clay, which helps keep it dry. With careful detailing and the correct materials, it may be possible to replicate the first of these two conditions, air tightness and vapor permeable finishes. The closest we can come to the third is to apply a base coat of clay plaster over the bales, maybe combined with dunking their faces in clay slip (see chapter 12, "Earth Plaster").

Once we get into more modern materials, permeability tends to go down. This makes things trickier, so we need to think more specifically about ideal relationships between interior and exterior finish. According to John Straub of Building Envelope Engineering and the University of Waterloo, Ontario, Canada, current research into moisture physics allows for an educated set of guesses at ideal relationships between interior and exterior wall surfaces, for various climates.

Vapor permeability is measured in units called "perms." Materials with a "perm rating" of 1 or below are considered to be vapor retarders (more commonly known as "vapor barriers." See perm rating chart in chapter 2). In a cold climate (10,000+ heating degree-days), the permeance of the interior plaster should be kept above 2 perms, and the exterior about five times higher. In a cool climate (6,000–10,000 heating degree-days) the inner layer should be kept above 4 perms, and the exterior three or more times higher. In mixed climates, the 1:1 ratio is best. Currently, it is only possible to apply this approach to industrial materials, because perm ratings for the older materials do not yet exist. (These materials have been used successfully for thousands of years, but no one has yet determined where they fit into our modern classification system.) What all of this boils down to, for cold and cool climates, is that if you use cementitious materials on the exterior (and especially if they are painted or treated with waterproofing agents), you will probably want to paint the interior. A specifically vapor-retardant paint (perm rating less than 1) would be ideal, though any manufactured paint ought to work fine.

Maybe the most important thing to remember is that bale walls are different from those on which our design history is based. They are somewhere between filled cavity walls and monolithic walls of stone or cob; they might act like one or the other, or like neither. We really are not yet sure how moisture migrates through a straw bale, and we are not sure what happens at the interface between bales and plaster. Our decisions about plasters, therefore, are nothing more than educated guesses. These authors (and most people in the straw bale construction community) believe that maximum vapor permeability is the safest way to go, but we could certainly be wrong.

As time goes by, careful studies will certainly be made of bale buildings with various finish systems. These will be very useful. What will be even more useful, however, is if every person who builds a bale house installs at least a few moisture probes in the walls, and checks them on a regular basis. This is anarchist science; learning by experience, and without corporate funding. Moisture probes also serve as insurance for the decisions made on any given project. If readings are normal, you'll know everything is fine. If readings are consistently high, you might be able to solve the problem before the straw begins to fail.

Plaster as Moisture Protection

Water, we know from chapter 2, gets into bale walls by four methods: capillary action and leaks from the exterior, and by air leakage and vapor diffusion from the inside, which can result in condensation. This section examines some specific ways of dealing with these sources, in the plaster stage of a project.

Capillary Action

When an exposed rendered[1] wall is hit by rain, a thin layer of water tends to adhere to the surface of the render; this is known as adsorption. Because they form such a thin layer, and because water sticks so well to surfaces, these adsorbed water molecules will tend to move, with no respect for gravity, into the pores of the render. They simply crawl along the various surfaces, migrating back

---

1. Throughout this and the following chapters, "render" will mean exterior work, while "plaster" will be used more generally to describe the basic material, regardless of which side of the wall it will be applied to.

in. This process is known as capillary action. The rate at which capillary action occurs is determined by the size of the pores; in a plaster, pore size is a function of grain size. The degree to which a material is capable of adsorbing water by capillary action is called its hygroscopicity.

If the capillary action is not blocked, water will continue to migrate into the material until it is saturated. If that material is in direct contact with another porous material, the water in the first material will move into the second one until it is also saturated, and so on until there is no more water to be adsorbed or until all the materials become saturated, and excess water has to find its way somewhere else.

> If the capillary action is not blocked, water will continue to migrate into the material until it is saturated.

But what happens if the second material has a smaller adsorption capacity? Less water will be able to move in. If many materials are bound together with a decreasing capacity of adsorbing water, chances are that from layer to layer less and less water will be adsorbed. The control of capillary action in renders has been developed over time to include two essential components: appropriate choice of aggregates and plastering technique.

CHOICE OF AGGREGATES

There are two main reasons why plastering is commonly done in three different coats. First, thin layers do not crack as badly as thick ones. Second, the capillary action of water through the plaster can be broken by selecting a different size of graded sand for each coat.

In a porous material such as sand, water molecules migrate at a rate inversely proportional to the diameter of the sand grains. The smaller the diameter, the larger will be the adsorption surface, and the more water will get in. With a coarser grain, the total surface will be smaller and the potential hygroscopicity reduced. Capillary action, therefore, is favored from a coarse grain toward a finer one; it is slowed down as soon as water hits a coarser grain again. Because sand is the major component of plasters used on bale walls, it is obvious that this phenomenon can be beneficial if an appropriate size of graded sand is chosen.

This means that on the exterior wall the capillary action will be blocked at the finish coat if it has the finest sand of the three render coats. If the intermediary coat has a coarser grain than the finish coat but a finer grain than the scratch coat, it will add additional breaks to the capillary action through the render. If capillary action is blocked by the second coat of render, the saturated exterior coat will act as a screen and shed the water away.

Picture three boxes, each the size of a room. We completely fill every box with balls, three different size ranges for each room. The first one is filled with fine-grain balls, from marbles up to Ping-Pong balls. The second room has coarser balls mixed in, from marbles up through baseballs. The third room contains larger balls yet, from marbles all the way up to softballs and basketballs. Now for every room we take out all the balls and paint them (since this is a lot of work we don't suggest you try it, we implore your confidence!). Without intricate calculations, we can easily figure that the Ping-Pong ball box will require a lot more paint than the baseball box, and the baseball box will need more paint compared to the basketball box. You've already guessed it: In a three-coat render, the balls are the aggregates and paint represents the water molecules. Smaller grains provide more surface area, and thus require more paint, or water, to cover them. What happens if we keep filling the rooms with fluid paint? Because there is no more surface to cover, the fluid will fill the empty space; but for the fluid to be trapped there until the void space is completely filled, the room has to be perfectly waterproof, otherwise the fluid will just leak out. If the room is watertight, however, how can water molecules get in there?

Wind-driven rain, melting snow, back-splashing rain, and other similar sources of water may, therefore, cause very little damage to the bales, unless the render becomes permanently saturated. Even under these circumstances, as soon as the rainy conditions stop, a reverse capillary action will start working in its most efficient way, dragging all the moisture from inside out through the decreasing size of the aggregates.

RENDERING TECHNIQUES

The other efficient way of reducing the amount of water hitting the exterior surface and minimizing capillary action is by shedding incoming rain away from the plastered wall. Despite appropriate architectural and landscape features, some lower sections of walls may still be exposed to heavy wind-driven rains. How can we ensure at least a minimum of protection to these plastered surfaces without using impermeable coatings? The answer is by creating mini-waterfall effects. If you have ever looked carefully at the action of water coming down a waterfall, you will have noticed that at every object sticking out

of the cliff—a rock, a branch, a fallen tree—water droplets hitting their surfaces bounce back into the air and are eventually projected away. If you create mini-falls on the surface of an exposed wall, water molecules hitting them will turn into mini-mists and bounce back away from the wall; this means that less water will be prone to adhere to the surface of the plaster. Because these falls also slow the motion of water down the wall, they decrease its erosive power. This reduces maintenance requirements.

These mini-falls can be created in many ways, the simplest being the incorporation of loose fibers such as polypropylene or fiberglass into your mix. (Unfortunately, chopped straw, which works very well for this purpose in warm or dry climates, is not a good idea in cold and wet climates,

Exposed straw in an exterior finish can absorb water and then freeze, cracking chunks of plaster right off the wall.

because it can take on water and eventually freeze, blowing off and crumbling sections of the plaster.) Textured designs worked into the surface by hand or trowel can also be effective. In Britain, a runny lime render is often thrown, or "dashed" onto the wall, creating a very bumpy surface. With limewashes, sand is often added to the first coat. These techniques increase the area hit by a given amount of rain, automatically reducing the potential percentage of adsorbed water.

Water Infiltration

In addition to migration of water through the render by capillary action, the worst damage will be caused by direct infiltration into cracks. Cracks can be the result of an imbalance of components in the basic plaster recipe, of poor rendering techniques, or of bad weather conditions during rendering that have influenced the cure of the render. Because the construction world is never perfect, some degree of imperfection will probably enter into any project, and especially in the case of cement stucco, will cause cracking.

Cracking can also be a function of inappropriate design, such as the juxtaposition of incompatible materials with the render. For instance, the widespread practice of placing control joints around every 150 square feet of cement stucco works very well on conventional walls, where the stucco is always backed by a drainage plane of some sort, and solidly attached to a rigid panel. Transplanting that practice onto soft and uneven bale walls, where there is no backing paper, however, doesn't necessarily prevent cracking; it may even increase the risk of infiltration (see chapter 10, "Cement Stucco").

In this context, very special care should be taken in planning and placing any joints, and in sealing them adequately. The same advice goes for the normal construction cracks that are created around doors and windows, adjoining walls, changes of plane, and the like. Where render meets other materials, cracks tend to form. The safest design strategy is to limit such intersections; where they exist, careful workmanship, sealing of joints, and consistent maintenance are crucial to the health of the straw beneath.

Vapor and Condensation

As discussed in chapter 2, water vapor in walls can turn into liquid when it hits a cold surface; this is known as condensation. Because it is difficult to check for condensation everywhere inside the walls, we have to take all possible measures to prevent it. In a conventional house, special care has to be taken with holes and seams—electrical outlets, utility runs in framing, small spaces between frame members, gaps around openings—that create points for exfiltration.

All of these holes and seams can also present problems in a bale building. They will obviously be a matter of concern in any framed partition, but air leakage can certainly happen through the bales, as well. The first line of defense against this problem is the plaster skins—the fewer the cracks, the less air can leak through. Interior plaster should mate well with ceilings and floors, and every effort should be made to have it be continuous, behind partition walls, exposed framing, or other intersections. (See "The Bale Wrap," in chapter 7.)

Stuffing gaps in the wall is also very important. Even if bale walls are very thick, voids do exist in numerous places. Because of the shapes of bales and the various stacking methods used, many horizontal and vertical joints need to be stuffed, to eliminate cavities in which air can circulate freely. This is particularly crucial when bales are placed between frame members. Wherever bales butt together, though you don't necessarily see openings, when a wind blows against an unplastered bale wall you can feel a certain discontinuity of insulation. All of these joints may form irregular gaps, which can turn into cold labyrinths ideal for condensation parties!

Comprehensive stuffing also preserves the insulative integrity of your walls. Tests at Oak Ridge National Laboratory demonstrated that the R-value of an incompletely stuffed bale wall would drop dramatically. A third motivation behind this filling will become obvious at plastering time. Because the plaster needs a continuous support, particularly when applied directly on the bales, it is impossible to apply it over holes left unfilled.

Gaps can be filled in many ways, depending on the size of the holes. The idea is to stuff as much material as possible in them, making sure all of it will stay in place and be strong enough to support the plaster that will be applied to it. Flakes and bundles of straw are normally appropriate to fill bigger gaps, while loose straw will serve for thinner spaces. Loose straw is best twisted and bent into small bundles before it is stuffed in; these bundles will serve as a much better plaster support than loose wisps of straw. Another good way to support the plaster is to complete the exterior parts of these gaps with a thick straw-clay or straw-lime mixture that will set firmly. When the gap is too wide and there is not enough of a key to support the weight of the plaster, it is advisable to use some sort of netting to bridge the gap. Metal lath, chicken wire, hardware cloth, burlap, plastic netting, or even sticks—anything that can be tied firmly to adjoining bales with some sort of pinning should be satisfactory.

To review, the three-step process to an airtight, well-insulated wall is: first, fill all gaps with an insulative material for insulation integrity; second, make sure the bale surface makes a continuous and integral support for plaster; third, plaster carefully and under proper conditions, to minimize cracking and seams, and make the wall as close to airtight as possible.

Plaster Application

Application techniques vary a bit among the different plaster materials, and these details will be covered in the individual chapters that follow. Generally speaking, however, plasters (and renders) are applied in three coats. These go by different names in different regions, but they are most commonly known as the *scratch, brown,* and *finish* coats. In bale construction, an additional plaster coat is often necessary. This *fill* or *patching* coat, applied either before or after the scratch coat, is used only in the deepest holes in the wall. It prevents any one coat from being applied too thickly, thus reducing cracking, and ensuring a good set. The normal first, or scratch coat, is so named because it is scored with a multitoothed scratching tool, or with the back side of a rake or the edge of a trowel. Scratching is usually in a square or diamond pattern, at intervals of ½ inch or so. The resulting toothy surface allows the second, or brown, coat to form a strong mechanical bond to the first. While cracking in the scratch coat will often be substantial, the thinner brown coat should show only hairline cracks.

The very thin (⅛ inch) third coat serves as a finish, or color, coat. In the ideal world, it should seal over all cracks, while providing a consistent color.

Mechanical Application of Plasters

Paul has begun to work with a stucco pumping machine, the Quick-Spray Carousel, and feels that it offers several benefits for backing-coat plaster application. Presumably, these attributes would extend to other brands of equipment as well. Foremost among the benefits of mechanical application is the fact that the mud can be applied to the wall at quite high pressure, between 80 and 100 psi. The pumper literally blows the plaster between the outer fibers of the bale, quickly working it farther into the wall than is possible by hand. This results in a very strong bond between the plaster and bale substrate.

The pumper also applies material at a much faster rate than is possible by hand. Since plaster is the most labor intensive part of the bale wall process, owners who are not prepared to do the work themselves sometimes find the plaster phase prohibitively expensive. Since a pumper is capable of applying base coats well and quickly, it allows the plaster budget to be stretched into the more detailed finish work, where the skills of experienced plasterers can be put to better use.

There are some drawbacks to mechanical plaster application, of course. First is the fact that the equipment is noisy and dangerous. While hand application of plaster is quiet, rather meditative work, the arrival of a large, engine-driven compressor on the site instantly transforms the work into an industrial production process. If the pumper is to be kept in action, it requires at least one and ideally two mixers be cranking out mud. (With lime and clay plasters, it is possible to stockpile mixed material, in advance.) Someone must be constantly ferrying buckets or wheelbarrows of material to the machine, while another person keeps the hopper filled and makes any necessary modifications to the volume or pressure at which the material is delivered to the spray nozzle. One person must work the spray nozzle, of course, while at least two more come behind with a trowel, smoothing off the work. Add to this busy scene the inherent danger of a high-pressure system, and you have the makings of the sort of intense day that is just not for everyone.

The real drawback to stucco pumping equipment is that it requires sand that is perfectly screened. We were pleased to find that the pumper handles milled straw just fine, but any stones present in the sand or clay—whether they arrived through holes in the screen or through scraping the base of the sand pile—will clog the pumper's delivery nozzle. If this happens often, it slows the process to where it is no faster than hand application. Also, if the person operating the pumper end of the machine is not paying close attention to what is going on at the spray nozzle, a dangerous buildup of pressure is possible. In some cases all materials must be screened before mixing.

Siding

Siding is a common finish throughout the world, used on framed houses on several continents. The system is pretty much the same everywhere; the main variation is the type of material used, which is mostly a matter of local custom. In some parts of northern countries, a majority of houses are finished with wood siding, either in the form of shingles, shiplap boards, boards and battens, or even paneling. In other areas, we find extensive use of industrial materials such as vinyl and aluminum cladding, or asphalt or asbestos shingles, which were invented as maintenance-free alternatives to the traditional materials.

There are four good reasons to pick any of these siding materials as a finish for exterior straw bale walls. First, you may prefer the look of wood or some other siding. In many northern regions, it fits the local vernacular better than any render. Second, in areas where it is common and plasters are not, siding can be less expensive. Third, on sites where the exterior finish will be required to shed large volumes of wind-blown rain (and especially in climates that do not experience long periods of drying weather), a rain-screen siding system is probably the safest finish for bale walls. Fourth, if a manufactured product is used, or if wood is stained, oiled, or left bare, it can also be a low-maintenance finish.

This straw bale building fits a local style of camp house. Bascom guest house, near Sandpoint, Idaho.

The rainscreen siding approach described below also allows for tremendous flexibility in the choice of interior finish material. Because the exterior is quite vapor permeable, we need not be so concerned with the quantity of vapor passing through the interior surface. The great thing about the rainscreen exterior is that it will be at least as permeable, and probably more so, than anything you put on the interior. Any moisture that gets into your walls should have a very easy time of drying into the cavity behind the exterior cladding.

Rainscreen

In conventional construction, siding is usually nailed directly to the sheathing, with a drainage layer of felt or housewrap hung between. In better-quality work, the cladding is held away from the sheathing by furring strips. This is known as a rainscreen system.

Rainscreens are usually, but not always, vented. In the unvented variety, the siding is simply furred out from the wall. The resulting gap mostly works as a capillary break between the cladding and the material behind it. Except in the wettest climates, this is probably sufficient to protect the walls from water infiltration. We prefer the vented rainscreen, however, because for a small amount of extra effort, it builds in tremendous insurance against both water entry and trapped condensation. In a straw bale building, insurance of this sort is at least as valuable as the kind you buy from an agency.

The vented rainscreen combines two principles—pressure moderation and ventilation—to keep a wall dry. Of these two, the control of wind pressure is both the least obvious and the most important. How does this mechanism work? The wall finish is composed of three parts: a cladding layer that is relatively open to the passage of air, a wall surface layer (a backplaster, in this case) that is relatively airtight, and an air channel between the cladding and the wall. This channel is typically connected to the outdoors by a screened opening at the bottom, and a connection to the soffit at the top. Some manufactured cladding products are built with weep holes that allow air to move through; in these cases, special openings are not necessary.

Brian Willson's house furred out for siding. The bales should have received a true coat of backplaster, rather than the thin clay slip shown here. Franklin County, Massachusetts.

When a wind blows against the wall, the exterior surface of the siding becomes positively pressurized. (Wind pressure works like any other type of pressure, the wind is, quite literally, pushing against the wall.) In a conventional wall, whose cladding is mostly closed to the passage of air, the back of the siding cannot easily come up to the same pressure as the front. The back side of the cladding, therefore, is said to be negatively pressurized, relative to the front side. In an attempt to equalize this difference, air will blow with great force through any small holes in the cladding surface. Thus, when the wind comes with rain, significant volumes of water will be pushed through any imperfections in the finish surface.

In a vented rainscreen, on the other hand, the air space behind the cladding is linked to the outdoor air. When a wind blows against such a wall, the air on both sides of the cladding is positively pressurized. The rainwater that is deposited on the cladding, therefore, will not be driven through. The pressure doesn't drop (become negative) until the backplaster layer, where it can do no harm, because no water is being deposited there.

Of course, being the sneaky stuff that it is, some water will inevitably make its way through the cladding, and to the wall. It is also a good bet that water vapor will be transported through the wall from the interior, by some combination of air movement and diffusion. The air space serves a secondary purpose as a ventilation channel, providing the backplaster layer (and also the back side of the cladding) with exposure to a column of air, into which any accumulated moisture can dry. Taken together, therefore, the pressure regulation and wall ventilation components of the rainscreen make for a very forgiving system.

The backplaster layer in a rainscreen system wants to be as airtight and as vapor permeable as possible. Ability to shed weather is not a major concern; this is the job of the outboard cladding. A plaster based on clay or lime therefore, is the best choice. Cementitious products are less ideal, as they reduce the wall's ability to diffuse out any moisture that may have originated at the interior. Of course, cement stucco protected by a rainscreen cladding is a far safer system than cement stucco left exposed to wind-driven rain. If cement stucco is required for structural reasons, it can be integrated into the rainscreen.

The tricky issue here is that the plaster should form a continuous skin between the bales and the nailers, but the nailers will typically want to be placed first, so that the bales can be stacked and fastened to them. One option, of course, is to forego this use of the nailers, by placing them after the bales have been stacked, and a single coat of plaster applied. Unless an attachment point can be fashioned at the midheight of each story, these nailers will want to be of 2-by-3 or 2-by-4 stock, on the flat (wide side facing out). Because it would be very difficult to bend this material over bulges in the wall, this approach would only be practical if the bale crew were to include a few seasoned troubleshooters who can keep the walls going up straight.

More often, the nailers are attached to the wall first, and the bales affixed to them. Two backplaster options are available in this case. The first is to dunk the outside surface of each bale in a clay slip before stacking them into the wall, then follow with a thin coat of earth plaster, between the nailers. Assuming the slip soaks into the first inch or two of bale surface, this combination should provide adequate air tightness.

Alternately, the back sides of the nailers can be furred out with strips of drywall, plywood, homasote, or any other sheet material that might be available as scraps around the site. These strips should be cut 2 or 3 inches wider than the nailers, so that they extend an inch or so beyond the nailer, on each side. Once the bales are laid in, a single coat of plaster can be run over the bales and onto these protruding fins, creating a relatively seamless surface, across the wall (see "Plaster," in chapter 7).

A hybrid approach (which GreenSpace plans to employ on our next wood-sided project) is to incorporate the nailers into an exterior pinning system. This could go one of two ways. The bales could be stacked, a rough coat of earth plaster applied, and then the nailers (pins) attached to the interior and exterior, and sewn through to each other. In this case, it may be possible to get by with 1-by stock. Alternately, the bales could be dunked in slip and the pins tied through as the walls are stacked. A rough coat of plaster would follow between the pins. This method would probably require that the pins be made of 2-by material.

Thinking Like a Clapboard

The rainscreen idea can also be applied to buildings that will receive a plastered finish. On a particularly exposed site, it may be possible to build a sacrificial wall between the house and the prevailing winds. This might be a screened or glassed-in porch; it might be a wall of firewood or a latticework covered with growing vines. It might be a planted windbreak, augmented for the first ten years by a temporary wall of boards built out at the perimeter of a porch, or a temporary fence, some 8 or 10 feet from the house. The idea here is to modify the local environment, so that the house

<table>
<tr><td>

The Patry House

</td><td>

In early January of 2000, Michel got a call from Peter Blose, who had built a straw bale house in western Pennsylvania, saying that he had heard about a house in St. Albans, Vermont, that had straw in its walls, and which had some history behind it. Within a couple of weeks Peter took us to meet the owners, Paul and Peg Patry, to see what we could find out.

</td></tr>
</table>

This cozy, unassuming house on a residential street was built sometime in the 1910s, and looks very much like its neighbors. When the Patrys did some remodeling a few years back, however, they found that the exterior stud walls were stuffed with straw, as insulation. Paul Patry says that the straw was "in very

good condition, slightly discolored but still in very good shape." He also says that the house is "warm in winter and cool in summer," a common refrain among old-time straw bale house owners. The house was built by the Lecuyer brothers, as was the one next door, which may have straw in the walls, too.

Judging from the Patry house, wood siding seems to be a very safe finish material for straw walls. After more than eighty years, the straw in the Patrys' walls was in nearly as good shape as when it was first installed, and this only a few blocks from Lake Champlain in northern Vermont, certainly a cold and weather-prone location. As time goes by, it seems likely that we will uncover more clusters of houses built with this same technique. Any farmer would know that straw is a good insulator; it seems obvious that some others would have had the idea to use straw as a filling in stud cavities.

The clapboarded Patry house (left) in St. Albans, Vermont, is insulated with straw stuffed into a stick frame. The house next door was built by the same builders, and also might be insulated with straw.

proper does not take the full brunt of the weather. In all cases, the screening mechanism should be held at least 6 to 12 inches away from the wall. This leaves enough air space for circulation and drying, and also for the occasional inspection for rodents and other uninvited neighbors.

Pre-Plaster Preparations: Michel's Tips for Owner-Builders

The wonderful undulating textures that plaster naturally allows on bale walls are the reason that a plaster finish has become the authentic signature of straw bale homes.

Those same irregular textures, however, are also the reason that plastering over bales has not been a favorite of most builders. Professional plasterers tend to aim for a perfectly flat surface; trying to achieve this over bales can be quite frustrating. For inexperienced plasterers, on the other hand, the work becomes much more attractive on a bale wall than on standard flat surfaces. Because the end result doesn't have to be perfectly uniform, beginners can learn the basics easily and any owner-builder can feel secure enough to take the job on as his or her own responsibility. With very few simple tools and a minimum of handworking skills, these basics can be learned from many different sources, including hands-on workshops, professional plasterers, or plaster parties on other bale houses. Plastering gives an inestimable opportunity to imprint one's personal signature on to the building while making substantial savings on labor costs. Friends and family members can participate under a minimum of supervision. Plastering can turn into a wonderful group experience, the type of activity that bonds people together more efficiently than any politician could dream of.

Rounding bales with a bread knife. This is not nearly as fast as using a chain saw, but it works, and is much quieter.

While smoothing the faces of the bales is not usually worth the effort, an angle grinder fitted with a braided wirewheel performs this job admirably well, and is also useful for cutting decorative niches and holes for electrical boxes.

Wall Preparation

Preparing bale walls for plaster work means a lot of time consuming small tasks that must be undertaken with the care they deserve. The degree of care invested in this operation will eventually make the plasterers happy enough to achieve a fine piece of work, or angry enough to curse themselves for being there. Trimming work on bales; installing and attaching netting (where required); preparing openings, headers, sills, and corners; filling gaps and voids; installing supports for equipment and appliances; carving niches for electrical outlets; these are all labor-intensive tasks that professionals might find boring, and might not do carefully. If left as the builders' responsibility, this work can chew up a significant percentage of the finishing budget. So it's better to assign yourself or a third party to the preparation, making sure that the person is happy doing it and will perform with the greatest care possible. These details will have a very real effect on the look of the finished wall.

Plaster Samples

If you've never done it, or your coworkers don't know much about it, or your project has some innovative aspects, you may not want to get started on the plastering job without some practice. It becomes particularly important if local clay and/or local sands are going to be used in your mixes, because their characteristics vary significantly from place to place.

At some point it will become obvious that a simple description of the plaster composition will not be sufficient for everyone to get the same picture of its desired texture, its exact color, and

Learning the basics of plastering during a hands-on workshop at the Sivananda Yoga Center.

how exactly to achieve these features. The resulting misunderstanding may create an atmosphere of frustration that could be detrimental to the quality of the work. The best way to avoid this problem is to establish your standards through samples, as many as needed, until everybody is satisfied with the result. These samples can be applied to some bales, either in their storage shed or under a tarp on the construction site. Even if the walls are ready for plaster, it is a good idea for the people who will be doing the work to make some samples so that all parties agree on the different features. Samples cost very little compared to the time involved in redoing an entire wall!

Making Tests and Samples for Colored Finish Coats

The only way to judge the color of a finish coat, particularly if it's colored by the addition of dry pigments to the plaster mix, is by making samples on the wall. Since plaster always appears darker when wet, especially lime plasters and limewashes, you'll have to wait until it is completely dry to appreciate the final intensity of the color. You can either wait for the natural drying process to take place, or use a hand dryer to accelerate it.

In the case of cement stucco, white Portland cement should be used in the mix to preserve the quality and brightness of your color, especially if a bright tone is expected. The usual gray Portland cement used in stuccos absorbs light and makes all colors look dull. Even if the cost of white cement is higher, the total extra cost attributable just to the finish coat will be amply justified.

If your local climate is highly variable (which might be the reason why you're reading this book . . .) the color of your finish coat may influence the performance of your sun-exposed bale walls. Because colors absorb or reflect the sun's rays to a certain extent, you might be best advised to use absorbent dark colors in cold climates and bright reflective ones in warmer climates. A sun-exposed bale wall will act as a solar collector, and the warm surface temperature will help any excess moisture in the wall to evaporate by creating a suction effect. The warm exterior surface of a dark-colored wall will also reduce heat loss, because the temperature difference between the interior and exterior surfaces of the wall will be less. In a warm climate, it is better to have a reflective color to keep the heat away.

SOLAR ABSORPTION COEFFICIENT OF COLORS

(0 is 100% reflection and 1 is 100% absorption)

White	0.2 to 0.3
Yellow, orange, light red	0.3 to 0.5
Dark red, light green, light blue	0.5 to 0.7
Brown, dark green, bright and dark blue	0.7 to 0.9
Dark brown, black	0.9 to 1.0

CHAPTER 10

CEMENT STUCCO

CEMENT STUCCO IS PLASTER (or render) made with Portland cement, sand, and water. It is the plaster that was eventually applied to all of the original bale houses (some began their lives with a mud plaster), and for years it has been the most popular finish material for straw bale walls. As experience grows with other types of plaster, however, the appropriateness of cement stucco applied over bales is now being questioned, mainly because of its tendency to crack and its low vapor permeability.

Advantages of Cement Stucco

Cement stucco has three advantages, which have made it such a popular choice of finish for straw bale houses: structural strength, ubiquity, and the ability to accept conventional paints.

Structural Strength

Cement stucco, especially when reinforced by wire, makes a bale wall measurably stronger, increasing its ability to resist both compressive and shear loads. According to a 1995 round of tests by Fibrehouse Limited, a cement-stuccoed, wire-reinforced bale wall actually performs as a stressed-skin panel. The plaster skins, in this case, take up most of the load; the role of the bales is to hold them in a vertical position. This assembly is quite strong. (See chapter 6, "Nebraska Style," for further details.)

Wire-reinforced cement stucco also adds a substantial degree of shear resistance to straw bale walls. This is obvious to anyone who has worked with the materials; tests performed by David Riley and his students at the University of Washington have also begun to prove it in the laboratory. (See chapter 7, "Framed Structures," for further details.)

Ubiquity

At least in North America, cement is a common product, available at every lumber or mason supply yard, and at a good many hardware stores. Though cement stucco is far more common in some regions than in others, plasterers who are familiar with the material can be found in every corner of the continent. Lime and clay plasters, on the other hand, have achieved no such distri-

A stucco-pumping rig.

bution; even in the areas where they were once well known, they had been almost entirely replaced by cement until a recent resurgence of interest. This development resulted from some pretty savvy marketing by the cement industry in the early part of this century, which billed cementitious products as more durable than their predecessors.

Ability to Take Paint

If bright colors are your thing, then a cement stucco will be your exterior finish of choice. Many painting contractors claim that stucco actually holds paint better than wood does. This makes sense: paint seems to soak deeper into stucco than into wood, and stucco doesn't move as much as wood in reaction to changes in temperature and moisture levels.

Vapor-permeable latex exterior paints may actually improve the performance of cement stucco in wet climates. These paints reduce the amount of liquid water absorbed by the stucco during periods of heavy rain, while (theoretically, anyway) maintaining whatever degree of vapor permeability is present in the wall. (See "Coloring.")

Disadvantages of Cement Stucco

We believe that cement stucco has many drawbacks as an exterior finish to bale walls. These include a relatively poor drying potential, the higher probability of water intrusion from the exterior, the difficulty of working with the material, the high embodied energy of the cement, and the fact that cement-stuccoed buildings in cold, wet climates always look dingy after not too many years. These, in fact, add up to a strong case against cement stucco, except in very dry climates and in situations where its rigidity is required as a structural element in the building.

Poor Drying Potential

Of all the finish materials available, cement stucco is clearly the least vapor permeable. This means that any moisture that gets into the wall—from the exterior, as liquid water, or from the interior, as vapor (or, ultimately, condensed vapor)—will have a harder time drying through cement stucco than through any other render. For all of our attempts at devising perfect construction systems, we generally do not succeed in completely excluding moisture from walls. If we think in the time frame of fifty or one hundred or four hundred years, rather than the ten or twenty years to which conventional construction has become accustomed, it becomes clear that the safest course of action in building design is to allow maximum opportunities for any moisture that enters a building envelope to escape. Thousands of historical examples from Britain and northern Europe bear testament to the inappropriateness of cement stucco over biodegradable materials.

Choosing cement stucco for an exterior finish will require an interior finish that has either a lower or the same perm rating of 3.2 for a 1-inch thickness. If you're going to apply gypsum plaster on the interior, which has a perm rating of 15–20, you will definitely have to paint the interior walls. A paint with a perm rating of 1 or less (the generally accepted definition of a "vapor retarder") is the best bet. In this relatively vapor-closed assembly, the air tightness of the envelope (which is not to be discounted in any

Eisenberg/ Myhrman

In areas where cement stucco is common, it should be possible to find a crew who can apply the material by machine—often coating the whole house in one day.

wall configuration) becomes particularly crucial. Because a cement-plastered wall can only dry slowly, it is less forgiving of point condensation loads than a wall whose exterior skin is made of a more vapor-permeable material.

Cracking and the Maintenance Illusion

All plasters other than the commercially produced gypsum mixes shrink as they cure, and thus are prone to cracking. Cement stucco, however, produces larger shrinkage cracks than any other plaster. This is partially a result of the chemistry of the material, and partially a function of its short curing time. Whereas lime and clay plasters are usually reworked when they are firm but still green, cement stucco sets up so quickly that such intervention seems to do more harm than good, rupturing the structure of the plaster.

Cement is also the most brittle of plasters, so the normal stresses of wind and snow loads, freeze/thaw cycles, and slight shifts in foundations and wooden framing members also lead to cracks over time. These cracks, large and small, inevitably admit some amount of water. On the windward side of a building, or in particularly high water-load areas (under windows, for instance), cracks can allow substantial volumes of moisture to enter. Once this water enters, it will not dry nearly as quickly as it would through a more vapor-permeable finish.

Cement stucco has an annoying tendency to crack at the worst possible locations, near windows and at the corners of buildings.

This problem is compounded by the fact that people tend to think of cement stucco as a low-maintenance finish. Because the stucco itself is so hard and durable, it is very easy for a homeowner to ignore what is going on behind the finish. Stories abound—even from the arid American Southwest—about cement-stuccoed earthen buildings that looked fine for years, until one day a large sheet of render fell free, revealing a completely eroded substrate. This phenomenon is well documented across thousands of buildings, public and private. If the illusion of a maintenance-free exterior finish can cause this type of problem in a hot and dry climate, imagine how much worse the consequences could be in a cold and wet climate, when cement stucco is applied over a biodegradable substrate and not subsequently maintained!

Looks and Sounds

In wet climates, exterior cement stucco looks dingy after only a few years. Lime renders, on the other hand, which are consistently renewed by limewashes, maintain a fresh appearance. This factor may not seem all that important during the construction of the building, but in ten years' time it will become quite significant, in terms of both occupant enjoyment and resale value.

When used on the interior, hard cement stucco reflects sound, often creating a tinny or echoing space. This problem is greatly exacerbated by poured concrete floors; it is reduced by rugs and furniture, especially padded furniture. It also seems that a skim coat of gypsum plaster, or even joint compound, over the stucco can help somewhat, though wooden floors and sheetrock ceilings are probably the most effective built-in sound dampeners.

Energy Consumption

Cement is a very energy-intensive material. Its manufacture is responsible for 8 percent of all the CO_2 released into the atmosphere by human activities. (See the "Embodied Energy in Cement Production" sidebar in chapter 5.) Lime is also an energy-intensive material, but less so than cement. Clay, on the other hand, is used in more or less a raw state; the only energy involved in its manufacture is spent in digging, transportation, and, in some cases, milling.

Difficult to Work With

Of all the available plaster materials, we find cement stucco to be the most difficult to work with. Because it is not very sticky or plastic, it

Windows can be surrounded by expanded metal lath. This sometimes controls cracking near their corners. Galvanized plaster stops can also be used to create a clean edge.

doesn't trowel easily. It doesn't adhere well to straw, and its alkaline nature makes it very tough on the hands. Cement also sets up quickly, which means that the mud, rather than the plasterer, is in charge of the pace of the operation. Tool cleaning requires more time and effort than with other materials. Professional plasterers are accustomed to working within these limitations, of course, but they can present some real challenges to inexperienced and volunteer crews.

Design and Application Details

Even though cement stucco has been the most popular plaster on bale buildings so far, many design issues have to be carefully worked out if it is to become a reliable finish material. Here are the major ones, in our experience.

Metal Reinforcement and Control of Cracking

It is a general rule in construction that the more rigid a material is, the more brittle it is. Cement stucco (all cement-based products, in fact) is quite rigid, and also quite brittle. The standard method of gaining tensile strength in cementitious materials is to reinforce the mix with steel. In the case of cement stucco, this metal is some combination of 17-gauge stucco netting, 20-gauge chicken wire, 2-inch hardware cloth, and expanded metal lath. Typically, the stucco netting, chicken wire, or hardware cloth is used over the field of the wall, while the lath is used in trouble spots: around doors and windows, at corners and any bale ends, and anywhere the stucco must be applied in an upside-down position.

A great debate rages in the straw bale construction world over whether metal reinforcement is necessary in cement stucco applied over bales. On the one hand, it seems logical that if the stucco is well keyed into the straw, the straw should be reinforcing the stucco, to some degree. On the other hand, stucco and wire is a designed system. The wire reduces cracking due to structural stresses and it is the fact of being held in column by wire that gives stucco much of its structural strength.

The relationship between the stucco and the netting is also tricky. In order to provide the ideal reinforcement, the wire should be held out away from the bale wall, such that it is embedded in the center of the 1-inch thickness of plaster. (Official stucco netting is made with a profile that furs it away from conventional flat sheathing, so that this type of embedding can occur.) Unfortunately, it is difficult to apply plaster if the netting is not tight to the bales. Any loose spots in the wire tend to spring out from the wall as the trowel is run over them, flinging the plaster back at the plasterer. This can be very frustrating.

If the stucco netting is pulled tight, on the other hand, stucco application is easier, because the tautness helps hold the material in place. Cement stucco, remember, doesn't adhere all that well to straw. While the goal is still to work the plaster into the straw as well as possible, having the wire in place to help hold everything together can make a big difference. Though there is a general consensus that reinforcing wire is not necessary on the interior of the wall (except in certain designs where the wire is an integral part of the structural system), those who use cement stucco on the interior often employ wire to make the plaster application easier.

Metal lath is usually used to control cracking at areas of the wall where the stucco is subjected to concentrated stresses. The primary examples are at the corners of windows and doors, and at the corners of the building. This technique works, to some degree, assuming the stucco is applied at a sufficient thickness. If the stucco is too thin over the lath, the combination of high-expansive metal and low-elastic stucco in freeze/thaw cycles will definitely make it crack. This tendency is exaggerated on walls exposed to sun, where freeze/thaw cycles are always more numerous. (Even in the best applications, some cracking is inevitable in these locations.)

A good compromise in crack control for cold climates might be to use polypropylene fibers as reinforcement in the scratch and brown coats, and concentrate on working the material well into the bale. These fibers are gaining popularity as reinforcement in concrete flat-work; they are also a common ingredient in so-called one-coat stucco mixes. While we do not recommend these additive-intensive one-coat mixes, it does seem sensible to borrow the fiber technology that makes these products possible. Fibers should not pose any of the temperature-related cracking problems caused by metal. Because the fibers will not anchor the material to the wall, however, their use in place of stucco wire makes working in the material thoroughly all that more important.

A final technique hails from Duncan Echelson of Dripping Springs, Texas. Duncan says that

> A great debate rages in the straw bale construction world over whether metal reinforcement is necessary in cement stucco applied over bales.

he learned from the old-time plasterers to go back over the cracks in the scratch coat with a vinyl patch material (different brands available in different regions) before applying the brown coat. At least in the warm Texas climate, this technique seems to do a fine job of controlling the initial round of cracking. It would not, presumably, be effective at controlling cracks that develop at stress points, through the service life of the building.

Control Joints

According to the experts at the Portland Cement Association, proper cement stucco application in cold climates requires control joints. These are gasketed seams between panels of stucco, which serve as official, controlled cracks. In the ideal configuration, control joints would be placed such that the stucco panels are limited to a maximum of 150 square feet, and made as close to square as possible. At this size, cracking due to curing shrinkage and temperature change is not supposed to occur, as any movement can be telescoped out to the perimeter of the panel.

Control joints in straw bale construction pose three problems. First, the straight lines of the joint material make a very unpleasant contrast with the soft irregularity of the plastered bale wall. The joints look completely out of place, like an invasion of a 1960s municipal facade upon your timeless bale wall. The second, more technical, problem is that a crack typically opens up right at the point where the stucco material meets the metal profile of the control joint. In conventional construction, where the entire stucco layer is backed by a drainage plane of building paper, any water that leaks through such a crack will be diverted down the outer face of the paper, to

For cold climates, gasketed control joints are commonly used in conventional stucco work, but their value in straw bale construction is debatable.

the base of the wall. In straw bale construction, lacking such a drainage plane, this type of leak is unacceptable.

The third problem is that the uneven thickness of stucco application on a bale building (often varying between ¾ inch and 2+ inches over a few feet of wall) makes it difficult to predict exactly where the tension in the stucco will be at its maximum, and thus where the cracking will occur. Considering all of these factors, control joints do not emerge as a practical component of a cement stucco system over bale walls. We believe they are best avoided, except in very predictable situations, such as to break up a long, windowless span of wall. If a control joint is used in this case, it is probably a good idea to back it with an 8- or 12-inch-wide strip of building paper.

Maintenance

We must emphasize strongly that cement stucco is not a maintenance-free finish material. Walls that are exposed to the weather should be checked each spring for any new cracks that may have developed, and these cracks should be patched. On an unpainted building, the patch is usually made of stucco. The area to be repaired should be cleaned with a wire brush and thoroughly wetted before any new material is applied. A higher-than-normal proportion of lime in the mix (as much as 1:1 with cement) will make a more flexible patch material, reducing the odds of a new crack forming in the same location. Unfortunately, it will be impossible to exactly match the color of the surrounding material. A periodic application of a spray—or brush-on color material (see "Coloring," below) is desirable, to even out the hue of the wall.

On a painted wall, a good-quality latex or polyurethane caulk can be used to fill cracks, and the caulk painted over. This will surely create headaches for someone fifty years in the future, but then so will the paint itself. The situation is no different from paint and caulk on wood siding; every fifty years or so some poor soul inherits the job of removing years of accumulated finishes, and starting fresh. To painters, this is just a part of their process.

Building Paper behind Stucco

In conventional construction, as mentioned above, a layer of 15-pound asphalt felt building paper is typically used over sheathing, behind self-furring stucco netting and cement stucco. This felt serves two purposes. It protects the stucco from the stress created when the sheathing changes shape as the moisture level and temperature change. It also acts as a drainage plane—a continuous shedding layer that protects the framing from any rainwater that makes its way through the stucco. The drainage plane is gen-erally considered to be necessary in areas that experience 20 inches (50 cm) or more of annual precipitation.

The fact that a drainage plane is a required part of a conventional assembly in wetter climates is an acknowledgment that cement stucco does not form a perfectly watertight coating. Some water is always admitted, through cracks and through seams where it meets dissimilar materials. So, why not employ a drainage plane of asphalt felt behind the stucco on a bale building?

A continuous layer of asphalt felt between bales and stucco isn't generally advisable, but covering wood with felt is a good idea, as the wood is sure to change shape with fluctuations in temperature and moisture levels, stressing the stucco.

There are three good reasons for the absence of this drainage plane. The first applies primarily to Nebraska-style construction—such a layer destroys the bond between reinforced stucco and straw, and this is the bond we are counting on, if the straw and its stucco skins are to act integrally, as a structural unit. Second, recent tests by the California Energy Commission and at Oak Ridge National Laboratory show that any voids left in the straw-and-plaster wall assembly significantly degrade the overall R-value of the wall. If the plaster cannot key into the highly uneven surface of the wall, many voids of varying sizes are inevitable. Third, the inclusion of a felt layer significantly reduces the drying options available to the bale wall. Because asphalt felt blocks the passage of water in its liquid state, any vapor that condenses into water on the back side of the felt will have to return to a vapor form before it can dry to the outside. If the felt is omitted, on the other hand, this water can be wicked as liquid into the stucco, from which it can evaporate directly into the air.

A felt drainage plane may be an acceptable idea in one situation: on windy sites in wetter climates (20+ inches per year). Regardless of the length of roof overhangs, the windward walls may take in water faster than they can dry it off. While the felt will certainly reduce the drying potential of the wall's interior, it will also protect the straw from excessive wetting from the exterior. It is crucial, in this case, that a continuous air barrier be maintained at the layer of the interior finishes, and that the walls and ceiling be painted with a vapor-retardant paint. If the drying potential of the wall is to be reduced by the felt, the amount of vapor that is allowed to enter the wall must be reduced, as well. Mechanical ventilation is even more important than usual,

here, to maintain the quality of the interior air, and to keep winter relative humidity levels down around 50 percent.

The best choice for this wet and windy situation is probably to avoid cement stucco entirely. Lime plaster makes more sense here, because it offers a greater drying potential, combined with less cracking. Siding of some sort would be an even better choice. In some cases, the building can be sited such that landscape features protect the wall from the brunt of the wind. If the building is kept down to one story, a broad porch roof can cut the velocity of the wind and protect the wall. Plantings can also do wonders to shelter a building, remedial measures need to be taken until the plants mature. A stack of firewood or a trellis, held a foot or more away from the wall, can protect it quite nicely. These work on the same principle as a rainscreen. (see "Siding," in chapter 9).

Some bale houses have used a housewrap layer, in place of asphalt paper, behind cement stucco. This might not be a good idea, as there is some evidence that housewrap products lose their water repellence when in direct contact with cement stucco. This is certainly the case if soap is added to the mix, as an air-entraining agent (discussed later in this chapter). The surfactants in the soap break the surface tension of the water, allowing it to pass through the housewrap material.

Coloring

Cement stucco can be colored in two different ways: integral colors, and paint. Integral colors are mineral pigments that are mixed into the finish coat. They tend to be subtle and earthy, though brighter colors are available from some manufacturers. Integral colors have the advantage of permanence. They have two drawbacks. In wetter climates, they tend, over time, to be overcome by a dingy grayness. It is also impossible to match a color perfectly when patching cracks; the patches, therefore, are quite visible. It is usually best to specify white cement for the finish coat if an integral color is to be used. Though it is more expensive than its gray cousin, it allows the color to come through much more clearly. Considering the thinness of the finish coat, the extra expense is usually not extreme. White cement can also be used with a light-colored sand, and no pigment, to achieve a fairly bright white finish.

La Habra stucco products offers an interesting material called Fog Coat, which is available throughout the western half of the United States. Similar products may be available in other regions. Fog Coat is a proprietary mix of lime, cement, and some other compounds, which is mixed with mineral pigments and sprayed or brushed onto the wall. Fog Coat is intended for the rejuvenation of tired-looking stucco surfaces, but it seems to work quite well in place of the conventional thin color coat. If the brown coat is well troweled, the Fog Coat finish is indistinguishable from a traditional color coat. According to Ted Butchart (who suggested this use for the material) and the manufacturer, Fog Coat is compatible with stucco pigments produced by any manufacturer. This is a lucky thing, because La Habra's pigments are a set of variations on mauve, apparently designed to give any building that unforgettable Southern California shopping-mall look.

Paint for stucco is available in a tremendous range of colors. Indeed, if you want a brightly colored house, painted stucco is probably the way to go.

Joe Lstiburek of Building Science Corporation (a preeminent building science wizard) advocates paint over cement stucco in climates receiving more than 20 inches of rain per year. That means a water-resistant but vapor-permeable latex paint, something with a perm rating at least as high as the 3.2 that is typical of cement stucco. In our experience, fewer than half of paint suppliers or contractors have ever even heard of perm ratings. Don't let their ignorance rub off on you— bale buildings are inherently different from anything they are likely to have experience with, which means that their usual assumptions don't apply. Most paint companies can supply perm ratings for their exterior paints; call around until you find a supplier or contractor who is willing to take the time to contact their manufacturers.

Paint over stucco makes sense for walls that will not be protected by a combination of siting, overhangs, or structures—specifically, it makes sense for two-story walls on wet and windy sites. The role of the paint is to prevent the stucco from acting as a sponge. This it will do, though it will not prevent water from entering through any cracks or poor flashing details.

Other Applied Waterproofing Materials

Many waterproofing products are available on the market, for use over cementitious materials such as concrete block or stucco. These are generally sprayed or brushed on. The better ones, which are usually based on silanes or siloxanes, maintain the vapor permeability of the original material, while largely stopping bulk water migration by capillary action. In short, they make a Gore-tex suit for your stucco.

Whether this is a benefit depends on how dry the walls are at the outset, and on whether keeping water out or maximum drying is a higher priority, over the life of the building. John Straube, another highly respected building scientist, puts it this way: "Take a shower, then wrap yourself in Gore-tex and run outside. Do you think you'll dry faster in the jacket, or naked?" The issue here is the same as with building paper or vapor-permeable paint; while these products (Gore-tex included) are vapor permeable, they block liquid water (a large bunch of water molecules) from passing through in either direction. Liquid water in the bale can no longer wick through the stucco to the surface and then dry by evaporation; it must change to the vapor state before it can pass through the wall.

Clark Sanders used a brush-on cementitious sealer as an extra layer of moisture protection on his hermitage in East Meredith, New York.

Mixes, Application, and Curing

The standard cement stucco mix is 3 or 3½ parts sand to one part cement, with enough water added to achieve the desired consistency. Experimentation will quickly yield the appropriate mix. A small amount of bagged, hydrated lime—typically no more than ½ part, is usually added to this mix, to increase workability. The lime makes the stucco mix softer and stickier, so that it is easier to trowel and adheres better to the wall.

It is a fairly common practice to use this rich mix (3 parts sand to 1 part cement), for the scratch coat, and then to use a leaner mix of somewhere between 4 and 6 to 1 for the brown and finish coats. The richer scratch coat will be quite hard and rigid, while the leaner coats will be a bit softer and slightly more flexible; this will reduce cracking to some extent.

Sand

Though we are usually inclined to think of the binder as the most important element of the plaster, it is really the aggregate, the sand, that is doing most of the work. When compacted by a trowel, the bits of aggregate lock together to form a stable matrix. The binder's job is to act as a glue, holding the pieces of sand together, and thus stabilizing the structure.

Quality of sand matters tremendously when it comes to plaster work. Sand should be angular, rather than rounded, so that the particles can lock together. We like to use sand with a maximum particle size of ¼ or ³⁄₁₆ of an inch for base coats, and finer material for the finish. The key is that the sand must contain a well-graded proportion of aggregates. What does this mean? Bob Shuldes, consulting engineer to the Portland

Cement Association, puts it this way:

Picture a dump truck full of basketballs. The truck can hold quite a few, but there is a substantial amount of empty space in the voids between the balls. Now, mix in some volleyballs. There is less space, but still quite a bit. Now mix in some softballs, then some tennis balls, golf balls, marbles, and keep going right on down to a microscopic level, so that the smaller particles keep on filling the remaining gaps, until there are no gaps left. This is what a perfectly graded aggregate would look like.

(Except, of course, for the fact that the perfect aggregate would not be made of round balls. . . .) In the theoretical perfect plaster mix, there would be just enough cement to put a thin coating over all of these particles. This ideal mix would contain no voids between bits of aggregate, because voids are inevitably filled with a cement and water solution. As the cement in this solution cures, it shrinks; this leaves voids in the stucco that become capillary channels, and can suck up water. Additionally, the small nuggets of cement that are formed within these pockets are much weaker than the aggregate that would, ideally, have been there.

Water and Curing Time

Water is a necessary ingredient in the curing of cement stucco. The cement reacts chemically with the water to produce the hardened plaster. In order to achieve maximum strength, therefore, the plaster must be kept moist throughout the curing process. On the other hand, too much water in the initial mix will weaken the finished product, because as these water molecules are taken up by the cement or lost to evaporation, gaps are left behind in their place. These gaps form capillary channels for the adsorption of rainwater; if this water then freezes and thaws, it causes tremendous stress to the stucco. This is the very process by which stone is turned into soil; because stucco is basically a poor quality of conglomerate rock, it is no less likely to happen in your wall than in nature.

According to the Portland Cement Association, cement stucco should be kept moist for three days from the time of application. If you think about the ratio of volume to surface area in stucco compared with any other cementitious product (concrete walls, beams, or even slabs), the accelerated rate of moisture loss due to evaporation quickly becomes clear. In cooler, moister conditions, lightly spraying the wall once or twice a day for three days ought to be sufficient. (Soaking the plaster deeply is not a good idea, as too much moisture can end up being absorbed by the straw behind it!) In hot, dry, or windy conditions, it is probably worth the investment to wrap the building in some sort of fabric—burlap, old bed sheets—which can be consistently moistened, to create a damp microclimate around the building.

There is some evidence that the straw substrate helps retain moisture, for a better cure. Chris Stafford noticed, on a project where the bottom of the wall was draped in asphalt felt, that the areas where the stucco was applied directly over the straw did not dry out as quickly as the areas where it was applied over felt. This led him to believe that the straw was initially absorbing some water out of the stucco, and then giving it back, as the curing process progressed.

Air-entraining Agents

Air-entraining agents are chemical admixtures that improve cement stucco in several ways. First off, they make the mix more plastic, so that somewhat less water is needed in the initial mix. Second, they slow the rate of evaporation, which means that the material sitting on the mortar table, waiting to be applied, does not stiffen up so quickly. This reduces the need to add extra water to keep the mix workable. Both of these features strengthen the plaster, by reducing the amount of water that is ultimately added to the mix.

The third benefit applies specifically to cold climates. Air-entraining agents are named as such because they create tiny air bubbles within the finished stucco mix. Unlike the open-cell air gaps that are created by a poorly graded aggregate or an excess of water in the mix, however, the bubbles created by air-entraining agents are of a closed-cell nature, which means they will not absorb water. In fact, they have exactly the opposite effect: Rather than stressing the plaster by holding water that can then freeze, the bubbles form tiny shock absorbers, creating space for expansion and contraction during freeze/thaw cycles. The Portland Cement Association (and other experts) highly recommends air-entraining agents for cold-climate cement stucco applications.

Commercially produced air-entraining admixtures can be purchased at any masonry supply yard. A cheaper solution is Ivory Snow; pure soap. A stucco containing soap should not be used over housewrap materials; the surfactants in the soap definitely undo the water repellence of the housewrap.

We do not see any good reason for using cement stucco over bale buildings, especially in wet climates, unless it is needed for structural strength. In these cases, it is best to keep it to the interior whenever possible, while finishing the exterior with a more vapor-permeable and more easily maintained material. When cement stucco is used for the exterior, the designer who is thinking in the long term will make optimum use of site and construction features to shelter the walls from direct rainwater contact, while providing enough air flow to allow for drying. In fifty years, we'll probably have a very clear idea of which climates, sites, and building configurations are appropriate for the use of cement stucco over bales; until then, we must proceed with caution and accept the inevitability of maintenance.

CHAPTER 11

LIME
PLASTER

BUILDING-QUALITY LIME predates Portland cement by several thousand years. The first historically reported use of a lime render (exterior plaster) on a wall was on the site of Çatal Höyük in Turkey. Its estimated date is 4000 B.C. Lime was used widely in ancient Greece and Egypt, and was refined by the Romans, the Mayans, and the Aztecs. Many of the great Roman remains are built of stones mortared with a lime and sand mix, or of monolithic lime concrete behind stone facing.[1] The Romans made great advances in the use of additives that speed the set of the lime and increase the compressive strength of the finished product; these are still known as pozzolans, after Pozzuoli in Italy, where they were first mined.[2] The Romans also made extensive use of lime plasters and renders. Based on the existing evidence, we can safely say that lime, when expertly prepared and installed, can be of service for two thousand years.

Lime has been in continuous use in continental Europe and Great Britain since Roman times (it also has an extensive history in Asia and Africa), though many of the more sophisticated techniques were forgotten during the Middle Ages. The Industrial Revolution brought

1. For this fact and many others in this chapter, the authors are indebted to: Stafford Holmes and Michael Wingate, *Building with Lime: A Practical Introduction* (London: Intermediate Technology Publications, 1997).

2. Jane Schofield, *Lime in Building: A Practical Guide* (Crediton, Great Britain: Black Dog Press, 1994), p.10.

a new demand for large-scale public works, leading to a rediscovery of some of the Roman technologies. The invention of Portland cement in 1824, followed by its extensive use for concrete preparation after 1850, pretty well halted research into lime mixes for large-scale construction. By that time, however, both materials and methods for the use of lime for wall finishes were highly developed. Though the skills required to properly work with lime have slipped from mainstream trade knowledge over the past half century, informed practitioners can still be found. Excellent books on the subject are now available, as well.

The Lime Cycle

Building-quality lime is produced by burning limestone in kilns, at a temperature of roughly 1,650°F (900°C). This intense heat creates a chemical change in the material. Water and carbon dioxide are driven off, and the material changes from calcium carbonate to calcium oxide. Calcium oxide is also known as quicklime.

When water is added to quicklime, a tremendous amount of heat is given off, hydrogen is taken on by the calcium oxide, and calcium hydroxide is formed. This is commonly known as "lime putty"; it is the timeless ingredient in lime-sand plaster and mortar mixes from around the world. In Europe, lime putty is either made and stored by construction companies, or is purchased as a ready-made mix. Lime putty must be aged at least two months before use, though several years is better. The process of making lime putty (known as slaking) is not difficult, but it is quite dangerous, because of the heat released in the process. It can severely burn the eyes, mouth, or skin. Anyone who is interested in making lime putty should first read the books

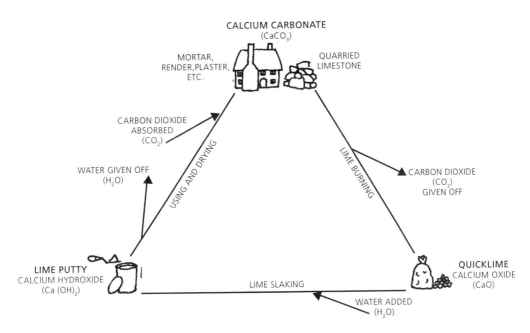

The lime cycle. Reprinted with permission from Lime in Building *by Jane Schofield (1997).*

listed in the Resources list, and should be sure to wear full protective gear.

In North America, lime is commonly available in hydrated form, in a bag. This material has been preslaked in a factory with a controlled volume of water; the heat from the process is used to dry the material down to a powder. It is known as hydrated lime because the change from calcium oxide to calcium hydroxide has already taken place.

Lime putty (hydrated lime and water) is mixed with sand and fiber, and applied to the wall as a plaster. At this point, the lime begins to react with carbon dioxide, and to return to its original form, calcium carbonate. That is, it returns to limestone, on the wall!

Advantages of Lime

Lime-based renders work very well in cold climates. Except in dry regions, we believe that lime is a superior material to cement, for use over bales. First of all, lime render is more vapor permeable than cement stucco. It is also less prone to cracking, and has some ability to heal its own cracks. Lime is much easier to work than cement, and is also easier to repair. Its manufacture is less energy intensive. And, because it is very alkaline, lime plaster is quite hygienic. Finally, lime also forms a beautiful finish.

Vapor Permeability

In Britain and northern Europe after World War II, the lime exterior skins of thousands of buildings were coated or replaced with cement stucco, in an attempt to reduce the maintenance required. One could say that these stucco skins achieved their objective—many of them remained on the walls for decades, apparently requiring little or no maintenance. What took some time to notice, however, were the problems developing in the substrates behind these facades. The ability of the wall material to dry through the finish had been greatly reduced, resulting in a buildup of moisture from interior sources and the ground. The unmaintained cement stucco was also allowing water to enter through cracks large and small. All of this led to a degradation of the underlying cob, stone, clay, and wood substrates, elevated interior moisture levels, and mold problems.

In the majority of the cases where such problems have occurred, restoration of the lime render (together with repair of any physical damage to the substrate) has been sufficient to bring the buildings back into equilibrium. If the apparent vapor permeability makes lime a good choice of finish over these traditional materials, it seems reasonable to suppose that the same will prove true over bales.

Daubois Inc.'s tests of lime mortars and Clark Sanders's empirical test of plastered bales (see sidebars) back up this line of reasoning. Essen-

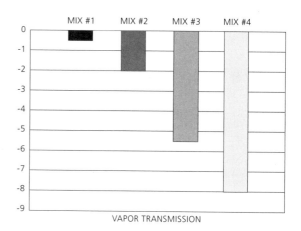

DAUBOIS TABLE OF MORTAR PERM RATINGS

MIX No.	PARTS PER VOLUME				PERM
	Portland cement	Masonry cement	Lime	Sand	
1	1	—	—	4	0.52
2	—	1	—	3	2.05
3	1	—	1	6	5.41
4	1	—	2	9	8.01

Notes

Tests were carried out under norm ASTM–E–96. Each mix used the same type of sand. The volume of water used for each mix gives a reading of 115 on spread table. Permeance is higher when lime is used.

Mortar Perm Ratings and Flow Rates of Water

Daubois Inc., a Montreal-based company and one of the major suppliers of pre-mixed mortars across Canada, has run tests to determine the perm ratings of their mixes. Because mortars are made with the same basic ingredients as plasters, these tests should give us a hint about the vapor permeability of our plasters. The table above shows that mortars with a higher percentage of lime are much more vapor permeable than the ones made only with Portland cement. We see that a 1:1 mix of cement / lime (mix no. 3) has a permeance ten times higher than a Portland-only mix (mix no. 1). By doubling the lime content (mix no. 4) the permeance is increased by another 50 percent, therefore becoming fifteen times more permeable. A masonry cement mix (no. 2) seems four times more permeable to vapor diffusion than the Portland mix but the 1:1 Portland cement / lime mix is still twice as permeable as the masonry cement one.

Among other tests carried out on the same mortars, one measured the rate of flow of liquid water through the mortar of a typical masonry wall. In other words, they were trying to determine how the mortar was taking on liquid water and at what rate that water was penetrating to the inside of the wall. The figures reveal that the 1:1 mix of Portland cement and lime was capable of adsorbing 0.1 liter of water per hour, while a masonry cement mix would adsorb as much as 8.4 liters per hour. Unfortunately, no figure is available on straight Portland cement mortars.

As Richard Gervais has said, "Although these last figures would make us expect lime mortars to be less water absorbant than cement mortars, tests [conducted] by John Straube of the Civil Engineering Department of the University of Waterloo seem to indicate the exact contrary. The only common conclusion of these two studies is that the drying potential of lime-based mortars is higher than cement ones."

Clark Sanders performed an interesting experiment in upstate New York. He dunked three bales under water for five minutes each, timed on a stopwatch. After the excess water ran out, each bale was plastered. One received a standard 3:1 cement/sand stucco, with just a bit of lime (½ part) added for plasticity; the second received a lime (3 lime:1 sand) plaster; and the third received a lime plaster with just enough cement to allow it to set up quickly (3 lime/1 sand/ ⅓ cement). The two lime plasters also included some chopped straw. The three bales were then placed in his furnace room, and poked periodically with a Delmhorst bale-moisture meter.

The lime-with-cement bale actually dried first, to 14 percent moisture content, in 127 days. Of those, 7 were spent outside under a tarp, and 120 in the furnace room. The cement bale, on the other hand, took 190 days, 7 outdoors and 183 indoors. The pure lime bale took 142 days, but only 105 of those were spent in the presence of the furnace. At the point when Clark brought in the first two bales, the pure lime bale had not yet set hard enough to be moved, and another month passed before he remembered to move it. So, we can safely assume that if all the bales had been given equal treatment, the pure lime bale would have dried at least as quickly as its slightly adulterated cousin. In every case, the straw was, in Clark's words, "good enough to put under my guinea pigs."

tially, vapor permeability serves as a safety valve for the bale walls. Because no construction is perfect, a higher drying potential translates into a greatly reduced probability of long-term moisture damage within the wall.

Higher vapor permeability in the exterior render also offers greater flexibility in the choice of interior finish materials; if more vapor can escape through the outside surface of the wall, more vapor can be allowed to enter at the interior surface. When lime is used for exterior work, there should be no problem with using clay or gypsum inside. (Of course, lime and sand makes an excellent interior plaster, as well.) Be-

cause it is somewhat chalky, interior gypsum plaster is almost always painted; the difference between a lime and a cement exterior is that with the lime, the gypsum need not receive a vapor-retardant paint. This opens the door to a much greater variety of paints, including traditional limewashes and milk-based paint mixtures.

Reduced Cracking/Easier Repair

Lime plaster is less prone to cracking than cement-based stucco, because it is less rigid. As the building moves over time (and with changes in temperature and moisture levels) the lime plaster can flex just a bit. This is a tremendous benefit on weather-exposed sites, where openings in the exterior skin can let in substantial quantities of water.

Lime also has some capacity to heal its own cracks. Stress-related cracks tend to form as a network of small filaments, rather than the individual crevices typical of cement stucco. Also, "because the lime is slowly carbonating, and carbonate molecules are bigger than hydroxide molecules, this process has the effect of compressing the render as well as filling any cracks."[3] Because the carbonation process takes years, the benefits of this expansion can accrue over the life of the structure.

Those cracks that are not healed by these autogenous processes can be fixed with the periodic application of limewash. One of the great benefits of maintenance is that it offers a chance to correct any faults in the render surface, before they have the opportunity to cause problems for the straw substrate.

3. Barbara Jones, "Working with Lime in England," *The Last Straw* (summer 1999): p. 24.

A lime-rendered barbecue pit, still in good condition after twelve years exposed to weather.

Works Easily

Lime plaster is more plastic, much stickier, and much slower to set than cement. This means it is easier to work with a trowel (especially for novices) and that it adheres better to bales. Indeed, a small percentage of lime is commonly added to cement stucco mixes to aid in plasticity. The slower set time means less pressure to get the material on the wall quickly, and to get the tools cleaned up. Lime is not so light and fluffy as gypsum, nor as sticky as a good earth mix, but it is a responsive material that adheres quite readily to straw. About the only drawback to working with lime is its alkalinity: it dries out the skin and eyes, so protective oil (petroleum jelly or Bag Balm) and goggles are a good idea.

Less Energy Intensive

While the lime production process is quite a bit more energy intensive than the clay production process, it is less so than that for cement. Lime is produced at a lower temperature than cement, so somewhat less fossil fuel is used in its manufacture.

One beauty of lime plasters is that they are completely recyclable. Lime-sand plasters and mortars can be reused as aggregate in fresh mixes, or, because the lime process is a cyclic one, they can be reburned, to produce fresh quicklime.

Beauty

This is why we are working with bales in the first place, right? Unlike cement stuccos, which begin to look dingy over time, lime renders take on a deeper beauty with each application of limewash. It is actually possible to build up a

A rendered wall that receives periodic applications of limewash catches the sun beautifully.

deep pastel effect, by applying successive coats of slightly varying colors. Or, if the building is consistently treated with uncolored limewash, it will always look fresh and clean.

Hygienic

It is safe to say that no normal biological activity can take place within the intensely alkaline environment of a lime plaster. It is really the only plaster (and we can include wood, sheetrock, ceiling tiles, carpet, and many other manufactured materials here, as well) that does not form a hospitable atmosphere for mold and mildew.

Paul once had a problem with mold growing in a wet clay plaster, on account, he believes, of a culture that started when the chopped straw that made up the bulk of the mix was allowed to sit around in a damp state. He tried spraying the wall with both hydrogen peroxide and a diluted bleach solution. Neither of these had any lasting effect, probably because they evaporated off the surface fairly quickly. A limewash brushed onto the sur-

face, on the other hand, seemed to do an effective job of killing the mold. Periodic applications of limewash have been similarly employed over earthen buildings in many cultures, both for hygienic reasons, and to brighten the interior spaces.

Disadvantages of Lime

The main disadvantages of lime plaster are that its structural capacities are currently unknown, that it requires periodic maintenance, that it has a fairly long set time, and that, at least in North America, the best materials and the skills required to prepare and install them are not widely available.

Structural Questions

It is generally assumed that lime plasters cannot be called upon to bear a portion of the live roof load, in Nebraska-style buildings, or a portion of the shear loads, in framed buildings. These assumptions are based upon the fact that lime-sand plaster does not have the compressive strength of cementitious materials, and that the absence of wire reinforcing also limits its tensile strength.

The extent to which these assumptions are correct remains to be proven. As mentioned earlier, lime concrete and mortar have a long record of excellent structural performance. Lime plaster makes quite a hard skin; it is possible that it possesses an appropriate combination of rigidity and flexibility, such that it can move just enough to avoid cracking when a major snow load is applied. Since in its historical applications lime plaster has not been called upon to bear significant compressive loads, we just don't yet know what its true capabilities are. A full round of structural testing on lime and bale walls would be very useful.

Similarly, it may be that a straw-lime composite panel is sufficiently strong to resist cracking (or sufficiently flexible to absorb the associated energy) in post-and-beam construction. This seems far more likely in buildings of one story than two, and also more likely on sites that do not experience heavy winds or earthquakes. (In most cases, we are currently not even assuming that cement stucco is capable of handling these shear loads.) Though evidence suggesting that it is not necessary is beginning to accumulate, framed bale buildings, regardless of their finish, are usually still diagonally braced.

Hydraulic lime, which is hydrated lime containing natural additives (fired clays) to speed the setting process and confer greater rigidity, might prove to be very useful for these structural situations. Hydraulic lime is less vapor permeable than standard lime putty or hydrated lime, however, and it is also not currently available in North America. Sufficiently strong plaster for Nebraska-style construction might also be achieved by the addition of pozzolans to the mix. The great Roman buildings, and many 18th- and 19th-century European bridges and other public works, make extensive use of these "artificial hydraulic" limes for increased compressive strength.

Maintenance

We are compelled to list maintenance as a drawback of lime plaster, because in North America, where everybody is so busy playing golf or surfing the Internet, building maintenance is considered an aggravation. Therefore, the fact that lime-sand renders usually receive a fresh coat of limewash every two to ten years (depending on exposure) is a strike against them. This attitude seems very odd, considering that people are willing to change the oil in their cars, clean their houses, water their house plants or gardens, and bring their kids to the doctor. Most things that matter seem to require some maintenance.

Vinyl siding, inspiring stuff that it is, has received its greatest boost from the fact that it doesn't need painting. This is understandable—while painting is not so unpleasant, scraping the paint from an entire clapboarded house is a horror if you do it yourself, and expensive if you hire a painter to do it. The benefit to painting (or staining, which doesn't require scraping) is that every seven or ten years, you have the option of changing the color of your house. What do you do if you want a new color of vinyl siding? You hire a dumpster, fill it with the old material, and start from scratch. A tremendous improvement! This is also when you find out how much damage the vapor-impermeable and (usually) shoddily installed vinyl has caused in the substrate.

Limewashing, and the occasional patching that accompanies it, is pleasant work. You mix up a batch of the stuff, and brush it on the dampened walls. If this is done consistently and with a proper mix, no scraping is required. In England, limewashing is traditionally done on the first of May; it's an extension of spring cleaning. It makes the house look fresh, and ritualizes a pattern of inspection. Whether or not it fits with the show of busyness that our culture has come to substi-

> If you want a house that has some life to it, then you had better be willing to accept some maintenance as a part of the package.

tute for useful work, paying attention is required of the owner of a natural building. If you want a maintenance-free house, then you should move into something built of solid steel or poured concrete. If you want a house that has some life to it, then you had better be willing to accept some maintenance as a part of the package.

Because lime plaster is softer and more permeable than cement, it will let you know if you have problems deeper within the wall. During the spring inspection of the exterior is when you will notice any odd staining or wet patches, which might indicate a problem with the straw behind the finish. With cement stucco, you will probably not receive such signs, because you are less likely to be looking closely at the building, and because the stucco creates a rigid shell that can hide problems beneath.

Long Set Time

The major drawback to using a pure lime plaster is that, depending on the type of lime used, it may take a long time to set. A traditional lime and sand plaster takes five to seven days to set to "green hard," the point at which a thumbnail can be pressed in but a knuckle cannot. A green hard set is generally required before a second coat or limewash can be applied, and before a render is considered to be safe from frost damage.

The long set time can be a major concern in cold-climate regions, where construction often does not begin until the late spring or early summer, and where, therefore, the building will not be closed in and ready for render until the late summer or early fall. If this work is to proceed through the autumn, the walls will probably need to be tented with polyethylene, and might even require supplementary heat. Unless an exoskeleton of scaffolding already encases the building, this tenting can be expensive and cumbersome. (The inflatable plastic bubble that would be so helpful in Nebraska-style construction would also be a great aid here.)

The two other options for dealing with lime's long set time are to wait, or to speed the set. Waiting is traditional to cob construction; the typical pattern was to build the walls and roof, finish the interior, and move in. The plasterers would commence the outside work in the late spring, after hard frosts but before the heat of summer. This was traditionally done because of timing, and also to allow the

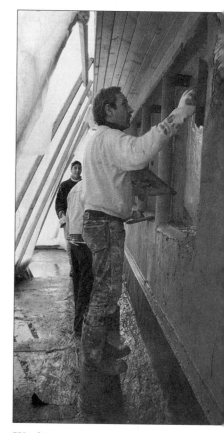

Working out the render under protection of a pitched tent is essential when it's cold outside. Pure lime plaster will not set at temperatures lower than 45°F (8°C).

Lime plaster can be applied over an earthen backing coat. This might be the best system for cold or wet climate bale construction.

cob walls an extra drying period. Whether this is practical on raw straw walls depends on the site: if horizontal rain is a serious concern the walls will want to be protected by tarps. Anyone who chooses this route must also expect to use extra heating fuel through this first winter; without the exterior skin to create a still air cavity, the bales will not insulate particularly well.

It is possible to create a situation that is quite like a cob wall. If the base coat over your bale walls is an earthen mix, it may be possible for volunteers to apply this material as the walls are built. The bales will then be protected over the winter. The elements should remove a layer of clay, hopefully exposing enough straw to create a good mechanical key for the lime render. (See chapter 12 for details on this clay/lime hybrid approach.) These calm approaches make obvious sense, though they don't always fit with the profit-centered "finish one project, get on to the next" mentality that seems to drive the North American construction industry. They can also create a problem with banks, which typically set a one year time limit on the period of a construction loan.

The second option is to speed up the set time of the lime, by including an additive. Several choices exist. The historically proven materials are grouped under the name of pozzolans, the most common of which today are pulverized brick and fly ash. Pulverized brick (or fired clay tiles and pots) is made by pounding or milling these materials. It is available in bagged form from pottery supply stores, where it is sometimes known as "grog." Fly ash is a waste product from the burning of coal for electricity production; it is often available from ready-mix concrete companies, where it is sometimes used as an additive in concrete (although fly ash may contain heavy metal residues). These materials actually combine with the lime to form various crystals whose structure is similar to calcium carbonate. The standard carbonization also continues, at the normal rate. Pozzolans do, allegedly, reduce the vapor permeability of the finished material.

It is also possible to speed the set by including some hydraulic lime in the mix. Hydraulic lime contains fired clays that act as integral pozzolans. Pascal Thepaut, an experienced lime plasterer and straw bale builder, uses a 50/50 mixture of hydraulic and hydrated lime for his first-coat mix, and straight hydrated lime for the second coat. This system allows the second coat to be applied much sooner than would be possible with a straight lime mix. The addition of hydraulic lime or pozzolans also improves the initial water resistance of the render.

Because cement is readily available, some builders also add this to their render. The cement sets quickly, conferring a degree of stability to the wall, and protecting it somewhat from frost by binding up much of the water in the mix. Cement also adds an initial weather resistance to the render. It still must be kept moist to cure properly. Michel has had good luck with this method in Quebec. He feels that when the volume of cement is kept to 20 percent or less of the volume of lime, neither permeability nor strength is greatly reduced, while the set time is reduced tremendously, to less than 24 hours. Paul has had

> The major drawback to using a pure lime plaster is that, depending on the type of lime used, it may take a long time to set.

equal success with a ratio of one shovel of cement per bag of hydrated lime, resulting in a set time of a day or so. These periods still offer sufficient time for surface corrections or modifications and for fine detailing and texturing. They also fit better with North American construction patterns. Many experienced European lime builders feel that even a small proportion of cement weakens the lime mix, because of the different chemical reactions involved in the setting of lime and cement. At this point, there is still no definitive answer to this question.

Infrastructure Unavailable in North America

Unlike in Europe, where lime putty is commercially available and tradespeople know how to properly slake their own, the North American lime industry is in an infant phase. Quicklime and lime putty are nearly unheard of, and the idea of using lime as a binder for exterior work (even if it's based on hydrated lime, with which they are familiar) drives most plasterers to distraction. Accustomed as they are to applying cement stucco over concrete or felt paper substrates, mainstreamers are rarely concerned with vapor permeability or the benefits of periodic maintenance. They are also not troubled by the tendency of cement stucco to crack, because it is always backed by a material that will not be damaged by water.

We must remember, however, that a supporting infrastructure for straw bale construction is only now beginning to grow up. There is no reason why lime technology cannot spread together with bale technology. Indeed, we believe that the long-term success of cold- and/or wet-climate straw bale construction will be based on the re-

discovery of lime (and clay) building techniques. This represents a business opportunity: plasterers who have experience with lime are already in demand, and that demand will only grow as bale construction moves closer to the mainstream.

Design and Application Details

Lime is not difficult to work with, but the quality of the finished plaster can vary greatly according to the techniques used in preparing and applying it. Following are the main issues to be concerned with, in working with lime.

Moisture and Curing

To properly carbonate, lime prefers warm, slightly damp conditions. Saturation, dryness, or severe heat retard the process; near-freezing temperatures halt it completely. Frost soon after application, before the material has set and while it still contains free water from the mix, can cause the render to blow apart, as the water expands.

Under normal circumstances, dampening the wall once per day during the plaster process and for a week or two after its completion should be sufficient to ensure a good set. In hot and dry or windy conditions, the curing material might need to be sprayed down two or three times per day, to prevent its drying out too quickly. Cold conditions may require tarping, and even supplementary heat (see above). Tarping can also be useful in dry or windy conditions.

Making Lime Putty

Though we may irk you, good reader, by doing so, we are going to restrict our coverage of slaking to two points. First, if you get so far into this

Lime plaster being applied by novices in a workshop.

allow it to work with fairly dry material, and also to crush brick or tile into pozzolanic additives. In North America, quite satisfactory plaster is produced in a mortar mixer, whose horizontal-axis, rotating paddles evenly mix the ingredients. In a pinch, it is possible to employ a rotating-drum concrete mixer. This device is less ideal, as the material will tend to stick around the perimeter of the drum, and must be periodically scraped off. Mortar and concrete mixers are usually available at rental yards; it is worth calling around for an electric model, as the noise and smell of the ubiquitous gas variety make it quite unpleasant to work around. Lime plaster can, of course, be mixed by hand, in a mortar trough or wheelbarrow, with a hoe or shovel. It would be hard to recommend this method, however.

We add the putty and sand by halves, the putty going in first. Water can be added as necessary, though it is safest to not add too much too quickly. After a minute or so in the machine these materials will be roughly combined; at this point hair or chopped straw is added. Straw will dry out the mix, so extra water will probably be required. Alternatively, the straw can be mixed with the putty in advance; this allows it to absorb lime water and soften, reducing the mixing time and making the finished mix less likely to dry out, as it sits waiting to be used and the straw absorbs moisture. Mixing time is usually ten minutes or so, until the material feels homogeneous and plastic.

that you really want to do it, you need to get hold of a book that covers lime in greater depth than is possible here (see the Resources list for suggestions). Ideally, you will also find someone who has some experience with the process. Preservation organizations are a good place to start. Slaking lime is not difficult, just dangerous. This leads to the second point: Be careful!

Plaster Proportions and Mixing

The standard mix for lime-sand plasters is 1 part lime putty to 3 parts sand. It is very important that the sand particles be sharp, and that their size be well graded (see "Sand," in chapter 10). The largest grains in a base coat mix can be up to 1/4 of an inch; a finish coat will want to be screened to 1/8 inch or less. The finer particle size makes a smooth finish easier to attain.

Where they are available (that is, in the British Isles and on the European continent), power-driven mortar mills are used for mixing. This machine employs heavy rollers for mixing, which

Reworking a lime plaster mix that has waited several weeks in a tightly covered bucket. Deprived of air, lime will not set.

Mixing Plaster from Hydrated Lime

There is debate in the lime building world over whether hydrated lime is as good a product as lime putty. The primary concern is that if the material has been stored in moist conditions, some of the carbonation (setting up) may have happened in the bag. This destroys the bonding qualities of the lime. It is always best, therefore, to obtain hydrated limes that are as fresh as possible, and which have been stored indoors.

Hydrated lime comes in two types, Type N and Type S. Type S is more common, and is considered to be superior, because, through an autoclaving process, the magnesium components in the lime are slaked, as well as the calcium components. The workability of either of these limes

is improved if they are mixed with water to form a stiff putty, and left to sit, with a covering of water, for at least 24 hours. Some people consider this step to be necessary with Type N lime. This sitting time allows any lime that was not slaked in the factory process to become slaked on-site. It also makes the lime stickier and more plastic, and therefore easier to work with. As with true lime putty, the longer this material can sit before it is used, the better the quality of the final plaster will be.

Putty is most efficiently produced in large quantities in a mortar mixer. One person can easily process a pallet of lime in a day, so the added cost is minimal. Paul has had good luck storing it in boxes made of plywood and 2-by-4s, lined with plastic. These boxes measure 4 feet x 4 feet x whatever height the mixer is capable of dumping into. With enough storage capacity, putty can be stored for several weeks before use; this yields a superior end product.

Putty can also be produced on a smaller scale in any available wide shallow container. The material can be mixed either with a drill mixer (commonly used for drywall joint compound) or a hand tool similar to a giant potato masher, to break down any clumps of lime into a nice thick putty. For storage, the material should be covered with a skim of water, and a layer of poly sheeting.

It is convenient to be able to dump bags of hydrated lime straight into the mixer, add sand, water, and fiber, and quickly produce a plaster. How well a material thus prepared will work depends on the quality of the lime. Characteristics of stickiness and plasticity definitely vary among brands of hydrated lime, presumably as a result of differences in both raw ingredients and processing methods. We find that this technique seems to result in a material that is more prone to cracking, and which is also less plastic and sticky than its presoaked cousin. We definitely recommend taking the small amount of extra time required to produce a putty.

Reinforcing Fibers

Hair has traditionally been added to interior lime plasters, and also to exterior base coats, to add tensile strength to the material. The hair functions in exactly the same manner as wire or fibers in cement stucco, or as straw in earth plasters. Horse hair is the most well known, though cow, goat, and pig hair are also suitable. Coarser human hair (not to be confused with hair from coarser humans) will also work. Hair is thoroughly teased before mixing, in order to avoid clumping. The resulting loose material is used in a proportion of ½ volume per volume of lime. To make finish troweling easier, reinforcing fibers of all varieties are omitted in the finishing coat. On exterior work, this also prevents the fibers from absorbing water, which can cause freeze/thaw problems.

It is a common practice in a wide range of industrial applications to use synthetic fibers in concrete mixes, as reinforcement and as a wire mesh replacement. Polypropylene fibers (interestingly called "hair" by concrete plant workers), which are the most common synthetic material used in cement stucco and concrete slabs, might also work well for lime.

Straw fibers have been used around the world as reinforcement for clay plasters, on interior and exterior work. We have also used them in lime and cement mixes, with excellent results. As with hair, volume is about half that of the binder content. The historic preservation community has also come to recognize the value of milled straw as reinforcement in lime plaster. Many restoration plasterers now believe that hair was the traditional choice primarily because it was plentiful, whereas finely milled straw was difficult to come by, in the days before power machinery. Encased in lime, the straw appears to calcify, which is to say that the empty spaces within its cell walls fill with calcium carbonate crystals. This makes it quite durable.

Render into Flashing and over Wood

The details of applying lime plaster into flashing and over wood are identical to those for cement stucco. Flashings receive expanded metal

On this project, jute fabric was used over wood and bales as a plaster support. Ile-Saint-Ignace, Quebec.

During the first winter, the lime plaster underwent minimal cracking over the clay-straw-backed sections, while many small cracks appeared at the paper- and lath-covered corners, band joists, and gable ends. The Gould/Crevier house, Leverett, Massachusetts.

lath or the equivalent (plastic netting or open-weave burlap are options) as a substrate and anchor for the lime. Wood is covered with 15-pound asphalt felt, and lathed as above. Self-furring metal lath, which has dimples stamped in it to hold the sheet away from the wall, allows a better key for the plaster. Wood lath, which should also be furred out from the wall to allow a key, is an option here as well.

We have both noticed a problem with increased cracking of lime-sand renders where they are applied over metal lath. This might be because of temperature-related expansion and contraction in the metal. The problem was particularly noticeable on the Gould/Crevier house where, over the first winter, many small cracks appeared in the paper-and-lath-backed sections, while almost none showed up in the clay-straw-backed areas.

It is possible that the alternative reinforcing materials mentioned above will provide a solu-tion to this cracking problem. We know that burlap is compatible with lime, as it has been used in interior work for centuries. What is not entirely clear is how it will perform, over the long run, on exteriors. Burlap also has the disadvantages of being floppy and absorbent; to compensate for this problem, it would be prewetted with lime water and worked into the surface of the freshly applied first coat. Plastic netting is quite rigid and seems durable; we would guess that it could be treated exactly as metal lath. Its compatibility with lime is unknown, however.

Coloring and Limewashes

Coloring can be achieved in lime plasters in two different ways: by adding dry pigments, or by applying colored limewashes over the finished plaster. Dry pigments are only used for exteriors in mixes that contain some proportion of cement. In a pure lime render system, limewash is an integral, protective element.

The dry pigments are added to the finish coat, and are the same as those used to color cementitious materials. In any given mix, these should total no more than 3 percent of the weight of the lime. Higher percentages can interfere with setting efficiency. It is important to mix the dry elements (pigment and hydrate) very well before adding water, otherwise the uniformity of the color can be compromised. If lime putty is to be used, the pigment might be mixed with the sand. We have never used this method, but it is reasonable to suppose that a longer mixing time would be required to achieve a uniform mix. A safer option might be to mix the pigment into hot water, then combine this solution with the putty. Tempera paints are also a coloring option, added to the putty. As with the powders, thorough mixing is required.

Limewashes—a mix of lime putty, water, and color—allow deeper hues than dry pigments. It is also possible to build up a fresco effect with limewashes, by layering shades one over the other. They are also somewhat capable of masking cold joints in the finish coat.

Limewashes form a lime render's first line of defense against the elements. They fill and waterproof hairline cracks, shed rain, and generally protect the main body of the render from weathering. They function similarly to paint over wood, except that, if they are maintained, they should never need to be scraped.

Limewashes really should be slaked from quicklime, or made from lime putty. Even in North America, where lime putty is expensive and only available by mail order from preservation supply houses, it is worth the investment, because so little is needed to produce limewash on the scale of a house. Paul has had good luck with an excellent hydrated lime that has been aged for six weeks as a putty before being diluted into limewash. The investment of time or money in starting with the correct materials will pay for itself in durability.

Limewash is really just watered-down lime putty, so regardless of whether the starting material is freshly slaked quicklime or aged putty, the process is basically the same: add water until it gets about as thin as skim milk (though it will be less white). Dry pigments are first mixed with hot water, then stirred in. Tempera paints can be added directly. The viscosity should be such that it just runs when brushed on the wall; the dripping material can then be brushed in. Though this will seem too thin in comparison to modern paints, it is crucial that the wash be built up in layers; if applied too thickly it will crack and flake off the wall. Limewash is always applied to a predampened wall, otherwise the plaster will absorb too much water, causing it to dry

Application of a limewash on interior bale walls.

before it has a chance to set. The best approach is to moisten the wall the day before application and then spray the surface again before the limewash is brushed on. Two or three hours before application is ideal, according to Bernard Gazonnet, a French expert.

An uncolored limewash should be nearly transparent when first applied, but will turn white as it carbonates. Colored washes will similarly lighten as they set; for this reason it is necessary to make test patches in advance of the actual work. Because it is applied so thinly, the limewash initially looks streaky. Four coats are usually enough to achieve a consistent coverage. These can be applied on successive days, with a damping-down of the wall before each application. Do not attempt to layer on coats in quick succession; it is very important that each be allowed to carbonate before the next is applied.

On exterior work, sand (1/16 inch and finer) is sometimes added to the first coat of limewash, to roughen the surface texture. This breaks up the flow of water down the wall, decreasing its velocity and, therefore, its erosive power. This is a good choice for walls that are expected to take a lot of weather, especially if they are in areas that will be difficult to access for maintenance. Tim Meek, Scottish lime expert extraordinaire, has used this method on castles, followed by as many as six coats of wash. His purpose is to increase the interval between maintenance rounds. (Once you've rigged a turret so that you can clamber around on its face, you may as well add a few extra coats of limewash.) It's not a bad idea to follow this pattern for the most exposed walls of bale buildings.

Oil is also sometimes added to the final coat of limewash, to increase the initial water resistance of the material. The oil will biodegrade over the first year or so, but this period will allow the lime to carbonate more fully. The trick here is that the oil component also slows the passage of necessary carbon dioxide into the wall, and makes it less vapor permeable. If oil is used, therefore, the rule of thumb is that in good weather it should be applied no less than six weeks after the final coat of render. It is also important that the render be basically dry, and that interior moisture production (for example from fresh plaster) be avoided. For projects on the scale of a house, you are probably best off sticking with the standard materials, and avoiding additives, which can throw complications into the mix.

Applying Lime Plaster

When it comes to application, lime plaster is not very different from other materials. It is stickier than cement, but less so than clay or gypsum. It dries the skin quite thoroughly, so Bag Balm or rubber gloves are a good idea.

The bales require no special preparation. Irregularities in their surface can actually create a better bond with the plaster. Except for a rough cleaning by hand to remove loose fibers, trimming is unnecessary, even when a very flat finished surface is desired. Our experience has been that the only way to create an even wall is by building up layers of plaster.

Whether the first coat is best applied by hand or trowel depends on the nature of the bales. On dense, uniform bales, where individual straws cannot act like catapults, trowels work well. On fluffier, more compressible, or less regular bales, the material is better applied by hand, at a consistency similar to a thick soup. This allows it to be forced into the bale and around individual straws and clumps of straw. Michel has had success applying this soupy mix with a 9-inch-thick brush; a rigid fiber broom would probably do a good job, too. The extra water in this first coat will increase cracking, but this can be corrected by properly working the second coat. On very hairy bales, the best bet is to first apply a thin parge coat by hand in the manner described above, with the goal of covering and anchoring to most, but not necessarily all, of the bale surface. This can be immediately followed by a troweled-on coat of thicker mix.

This first coat, which should total no more than $5/16$ of an inch, is scratched, and allowed to set for as long as two weeks, depending on the lime, additives, and weather. It should be kept moist, but not wet, through this period, and should be protected from freezing. A longer wait is fine. Deep holes in the wall should be built up in successive coats; adding too much material at once can cause slumping, while also reducing access to carbon dioxide, thus impairing the set. Unless pozzolaric additives are included in the mix, the material should never be applied thicker than $5/16$ of an inch. (Preparatory filling-out with a clay mix or, better yet, the application of a base coat of clay plaster over the entire wall, preempts this step; see chapter 12, "Earth Plaster.")

A scratch coat of lime render.

The second coat is applied in a similar thickness to the first. When it sets to the point that it is stable but still green (where a thumbnail, but not a knuckle, can be pressed in), it should be retroweled, to close any cracks that may be developing, and to thoroughly compress the material. After this hard troweling, the surface should be worked in a circular motion with a sponge, sponge float, or burlap sack. This roughens the surface, forming a key for the finish coat.

The finish coat is very thin, usually no more than $1/8$ of an inch. It, too, is retroweled, to achieve maximum compaction and water resistance. Color can be added to this coat. It is also the base for limewash.

Lime has been, is, and will continue to be an excellent finish for biodegradable wall materials, in cold or wet climates. Its combination of vapor permeability and weather resistance make it ideal for the job. What it lacks, especially in North America, is a network of experienced craftspeople who appreciate its strengths, and know how to work within its limitations. We believe that the long-term success of cold-climate bale construction will be dependent on the growth of such a network. The time is prime for lime!

CHAPTER 12

EARTH PLASTER

A N EARTH PLASTER IS ANY MIX in which clay is used as the binder. The clay is combined with variable proportions of sand and chopped straw, and occasionally with a smaller percentage of other materials, to impart particular properties. We call this an "earth plaster" because the clay and sand, which usually make up the great bulk of the mix, traditionally come directly out of the ground—often from the building site. On some lucky sites, the native subsoil is a mix of these materials, already combined in the proper proportions! Throughout this chapter, the terms "clay plaster," "earth plaster," and "mud plaster" will be used interchangeably.

Advantages of Earth Plaster

When used on a building's exterior in wet climates, earthen plasters must be substantially protected by site and building features. When attention is paid to these details, and for any interior work, clay-based plasters hold many advantages for cold-climate bale builders. First and most important, they have history on their side; this history teaches us that earth plasters are quite vapor permeable, that they help regulate the interior moisture level of a building, and that they seem to protect straw from moisture damage. Earth plasters are relatively easy to work with, and cleanup is simple. They form a beautiful plaster on their own, are compatible with lime, and dampen sound better than any other plaster. The materials possess a low embodied energy. They are nontoxic and reusable, and are usually quite inexpensive.

History on Its Side

Our long-term experience with cold-climate straw bale construction is limited to less than fifty buildings. These are found mostly in the relatively dry Sand Hills and plains regions of west-ern Nebraska, with scattered examples sprinkled throughout similar areas of North America. So, looking at the technique from a historical point of view, we cannot conclusively determine that straw bale construction is appropriate to wetter climates.

Straw combined with clay, on the other hand, has centuries of history behind it. The wall panels of many of the famous German half-timbered buildings are composed of light clay, which is a straw-clay mix. The cob buildings of Britain and northern Europe, many of which also date back hundreds of years, are composed of a mixture of earth and straw. A third historical technique hails from Denmark. The old-time Danes, needing insulation in their walls but lacking balers, wrapped straw around hazel sticks; these were then set into grooves in the frame, forming a substrate on which to apply clay and lime plasters.

Except in situations where the recent addition of cement stucco has caused a deterioration of the underlying material, the straw component of these walls can typically be found to be in fine shape. (See chapter 15, "Beyond the Bale.")

PROTECTION OF STRAW

While bale walls are quite different from these traditional walls, one thing they can have in common is the use of clay to keep the straw dry. Clay possesses several properties that allow it to act as a preservative for straw, wood, and other biodegradable materials. The first, and possibly the most important, is that regardless of relative humidity levels, the moisture content of clay will be lower than that of the straw around it (see graph).[1] If you look at the graph, you can see how

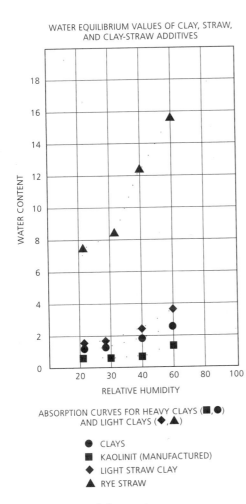

WATER EQUILIBRIUM VALUES OF CLAY, STRAW, AND CLAY-STRAW ADDITIVES

ABSORPTION CURVES FOR HEAVY CLAYS (■,●) AND LIGHT CLAYS (◆,▲)

● CLAYS
■ KAOLINIT (MANUFACTURED)
◆ LIGHT STRAW CLAY
▲ RYE STRAW

Moisture content of clay and straw.

1. Excerpted from Franz Volhard, *Leichtlehmbau: alter Baustoff— nueu Technik* (Light straw-clay construction: old material—new technique) 5th ed., C.F. Muller (1995).

the moisture content of plain rye straw increases dramatically with an increase in relative humidity, while the moisture content of both pure clays and straw light-clays rise only slightly. This makes a clear case for the ability of clay to protect straw with which it is thoroughly mixed (as in light-clay walls), but it also implies that clay plaster, since it will always be drier than the bale that it covers, will constantly be sucking moisture out of the straw. Later in this chapter, we will also talk a bit about ways of moving bale construction closer to these historical models. (See "Making Bale Buildings More Like Traditional Buildings," later in this chapter.)

The Steens' earth- and lime-covered test wall. When it was dismantled, the straw under the earthen section was found to be drier than the straw under the lime section.

VAPOR PERMEABILITY AND MOISTURE REGULATION

Though permeability varies somewhat between clays, as a group they are quite open to the passage of vapor. According to Volhard,[2] clay plasters are even somewhat more vapor permeable than lime plasters. This trait would seem to be borne out by an experiment carried out by the Steens, on an unroofed landscape wall. Half of the top of this wall was finished in 5 to 6 inches of clay-straw plaster, the other half in 2 to 3 inches of clay with 2 to 3 inches of lime-sand over it. When they dismantled the wall in September following a wet summer (18 inches of rain in three months), the straw below the clay-covered section was clearly much drier than that below the

2. Ibid. p. 51.

lime-covered section. The same pattern was observed in the straw on the faces of the wall. Also, the plaster on the clay-covered half of the wall was drier than that on the lime-covered half. It seems likely that two factors combined to create this situation: The clay cap must have let in less water than the lime cap, and it must also have allowed whatever moisture did get in to dry out more quickly. Bill adds that over the course of the summer, the clay section always seemed to dry between rains, while the lime cap pretty well remained wet. It makes sense that if the lime was saturated, or even damp, it would not be capable of drawing much moisture out from the straw. If the clay section consistently dried, on the other hand, it would then draw moisture from the bales, and pass it on to the exterior.

Many European earth builders also claim that clay has the ability to moderate interior moisture levels, by taking on vapor when production is high (such as when a family showers and cooks breakfast in the morning) and releasing it when the level drops (such as when everyone leaves for the day). Franz Volhard agrees, adding that while the high vapor permeability and low equilibrium moisture content of clay are important, the main factor is the speed with which clay gives up moisture. According to German tests, it releases water vapor much more quickly than other building materials.[3] This means that a clay interior plaster should work in concert with a house's ventilation system to smooth out the peaks and valleys of internal relative humidity, contributing to good indoor air quality.

COMPATIBILITY WITH LIME

All of this prattling on about clay being more vapor permeable than lime should not be read as a case against lime plaster. In the historical record, clay and lime stand side by side; examples abound of lime-rendered earthen buildings, and of limewashes over clay plasters. The Steens' example is an extreme one, as neither clay nor lime (nor cement, for that matter!) should be used in a horizontal position in a cold or wet climate.

3. Ibid, p. 54

Under normal conditions, the two materials work very well together. Lime plasters and renders are clearly permeable *enough* to prevent problems behind them on a wall, whether applied directly on the straw or over a clay substrate. Indeed, a base coat of clay plaster, followed by two or three coats of lime plaster, may turn out to be the best system for cold-climate bale buildings. (See "Making Bale Buildings More Like Traditional Buildings," later in this chapter.)

Workability

Clay is not caustic, like cement or lime; neither does it push your work pace, by constantly threatening to set up. People just seem to gravitate toward clay plaster. It is the ultimate in elemental materials, and more than any other kind of construction work, building with clay feels like being a kid at play. Because the material is minimally processed, it takes a good deal of skill to achieve a fine, hard finish. Just getting the stuff

---

Clay Walls and Mummified Straw

Some people assume that the straw in an earthen wall will rot away over time. Our research shows the contrary. After its initial drying period (which may take months), and assuming no unintended moisture sources (from the ground or a leaking roof), a cob wall maintains a fairly constant and low moisture level, even in very rainy places such as Britain. Kept below 24 percent moisture content, and encased in the oxygen-poor environment of the cob wall, the straw will not become a hospitable home for the microorganisms that cause rot. Essentially, the straw is mummified inside the wall. We have broken into cob walls 150 years old in New Zealand and found the straw still yellow and apparently as strong as when the wall was built."[4]

4. Michael G. Smith, *The Cobber's Companion,* 1998 (Cottage Grove, Ore: Cob Cottage Co.). p. 23.

on the wall, however, is easy, and inviting. Once you've put your hands in that mud mix you don't feel like doing any other type of plaster.

Carving potential and ease of remodeling are additional positive qualities of earth plasters. Because it is not chemically set, clay is relatively easy to remove when a section of wall is to be modified. Hardened earth plaster can be rewetted, and chiseled away with the claw of a framing hammer. The simplest technique is to chew out the plaster at the perimeter of the area to be removed; the remaining bale-and-plaster panel can then be cut out as a unit, and recycled as mulch. No waste!

Easy Cleanup

Immaculate (or timely) cleaning of tools is much less crucial with clay than with cement, gypsum, or lime work. The mix also need not be used up as soon as it is made. In fact, with an earth plaster, you want to let the material sit around for a half day or more before you use it. This time allows the clay and straw to fully soften, which makes them more plastic. It also increases the binding capability of the clay; as it rests in a moistened state, the particles separate more thoroughly, which means that they can do a better job of locking around the sand grains and straw fibers.

Building Up and Filling In

In addition to the above-mentioned advantages of using clay-based plasters to actually cover the walls, clay is also a great binder in mixes with high straw content, for semistructural applications. Clay-based plaster can be used to build up shelves or sculptures in walls. It can also serve as a good filler for larger gaps in walls, regardless

Demonstration of the carving potential with earth plaster, from a workshop at Athena and Bill Steen's Canelo Project in Arizona.

Once you've put your hands in that mud mix, you won't feel like using any other type of plaster.

of which plaster is to follow. When packed into the hollows that some-times form where the corners of bales meet, clay becomes a strong support for plaster that otherwise would need to be applied on some sort of netting. This type of solid filling forms a much firmer plaster substrate than loose straw, even if the straw is covered by netting.

Beauty

We think earthen walls are very beautiful. Many colors (and not only earth tones!) are possible, thanks to the many colored clays available at pottery supply houses. It is also possible to rub pigments into the finish, to create a mottled effect. If the finish surface is worked prop-erly, it takes on a leathery look that is very soft and inviting. Beeswax can also be rubbed in, to create a deep luster. The sand component of the plaster will often contain flecks of mica, which lend a sparkle to the wall. The bits of milled straw that appear on the surface also shine slightly. An earthen plaster is definitely the most alive of all available finishes.

Kalla Bucholz's shelf, built up of an earth-straw mix.

Quiet

Because it doesn't finish as hard as cement or lime, a clay-plastered room will not sound so bright as these other options. This is especially helpful in music rooms, TV rooms, or any space with a poured con-crete floor.

Environmentally Friendly

While cement is produced at a temperature of 1,200°F (650°C), and lime at 1,650°F (900°C), clay is used in an unrefined state, direct from the ground. It is sometimes dried in the sun and powdered in a hammermill, but this is the only processing required. So, unless the materials have been hauled a tremendous distance, a clay-based plas-ter can be produced with relatively little energy input.

Clay is nontoxic. Unlike most building materials, it is actually good for the skin! Excess clay, sand, and straw can be added to the local soil in a field or garden. At the end of the useful service life of the build-ing, an earth plaster can be rewetted and used on another project, or it can accompany the bales to the compost pile.

Straw fibers shining in the surface of an earth plaster.

Inexpensive

Clay is an inexpensive material, typically selling for $5 to $15 per yard. Trucking can get pricey, of course, so it is worth the trouble to find a good local source. As it is a common material, in many areas it is possible to dig it straight out of the ground, on or near the site. While it will often be difficult to find a pure clay, a clay-rich subsoil, which is quite suitable for plaster, might be readily available.

Shelves and bench of straw-clay mix, built by local people in Ciudad Obregon, Mexico, in collaboration with the Canelo Project.

Disadvantages of Earth Plaster

Far and away the greatest limitation to using clay plaster in wet climates is the fact that it is not well suited to serious weather exposure. Second is the general lack of experienced tradespeople. Identifying clay can be a tricky matter as well, and different clays will have different binding qualities. Processing the raw clay can be labor intensive. Because clay plasters are not as hard as others, they cannot take quite the same level of abuse. Finally, mold during drying is sometimes an issue in wet conditions.

Weather Exposure/Maintenance

Clay does not undergo any kind of chemical setting process; the bond between particles in an earth plaster is a mechanical one. This means that clay plaster has a limited ability to shed really serious weather. As the surface of the plaster adsorbs water, clay particles can come loose from the plaster matrix, and be carried away by water running down the wall. When enough clay has been washed off, sand particles can begin to dislodge as well, and a general erosion can begin. This is a slow process, taking a number of years if the plaster has been applied well. (Well, in this case, means such that its surface is compacted and closed, so that water cannot easily soak in.)

Traditionally, there have been three answers to the problem of clay plaster's vulnerability to the elements. Number one, of course, is maintenance. In the pueblos of the American Southwest, women traditionally applied a fresh coat of mud to their walls every year. This approach worked impeccably, for centuries. Second, in some wetter and colder climates, clay plasters have been treated with limewash, as a protective

Straw Daubs: How Fiber Cuts Erosion in Mud Plasters[5]

The greatest threat to an unprotected mud-plastered wall is erosion by water. Storms may unleash violent torrents that are intense mechanisms of destruction. Water flowing down a vertical surface, unless it is deflected from a straight downward path, will rapidly cut a channel out of mud plaster and threaten to expose straw bales underneath. One method of countering the flow of water erosion is to break the velocity of the downward flow of water. This may be done by redirecting water rivulets so that, instead of flowing straight down, they are forced to follow a random labyrinthine path to the wall base. Straw, properly mixed and applied in a mud render, is an effective device to retard erosion.

"While watching the women of Taos Pueblo remud a wall, I noticed that the mud was thrown onto the surface and then, using the heel of the hand, worked upward in a low arching motion away from the body. The print was that of a half-rainbow. The straw in the mix was no more than 2 inches long and most of the pieces, as a result of the hand motion, were embedded either horizontally or only a few degrees off the horizontal. When I looked at a wall that had not been remudded for several years I saw the efficacy of the technology. A rivulet beginning at parapet height encountered a barrier across its path and was diverted to one side. A few inches below, it was again diverted, and in some cases divided by the straw in the plaster. The downward velocity of water was broken, and erosion reduced.

"The same result can be achieved by using a hawk and trowel to apply the mud rendering. By 'cutting' the mud on the hawk away from the body using the edge of a trowel, the straw fibers are aligned perpendicular to the plane of the trowel. By cutting three or four times, most of the straw is aligned similarly. Then, by turning the hawk 90 degrees so that the alignment is parallel to the body, and 'cutting and lifting' the mud onto the trowel and applying it in vertical paths, the straw is embedded generally parallel to the ground. Again, the length of the straw is critical to the success of the render: long fibers won't align. One and a half to two inches is optimum length."

(Note: While straw daubing is an exciting technique for dry or warm climates, it is not a good idea in cold and wet climates. During spring and fall, and even on some winter days, the straw will be able to absorb water from daytime rains and then freeze at night, causing the plaster to blow off the wall.)

5. Ed Crocker, "Staw Daubs: How Fiber Cuts Erosion in Mud Plaster" *The Last Straw,* no. 9 (spring 1995) : p. 11.

paint, or covered with a lime-sand plaster. Third, in dry climates, including a high proportion of straw in the finish coat also helps: the straw reinforces the plaster against erosion, slows the progress of water down the wall (thereby reducing its erosive power), and acts like many tiny dripsills, diverting a portion of the water away from the wall, into the air. This approach really only works in dry or warm climates, however; in wet and cold climates, the straw will absorb water and then freeze, blowing bits of plaster off the wall. (See the "Straw Daubs" sidebar.)

Lack of Experienced People

In North America, there is very little tradition of earth plaster in cold-climate regions. It was somewhat common in early New England, but even there it was generally used as a backing coat for lime, or as a temporary plaster, until the owner could save enough money to afford lime. Even in northern Europe, where the material has a long history, experienced practitioners are not common, today. While getting the mud on the wall is easy, working the finish so that it is good and hard requires some experience. This is an important feature of weather resistance on exterior work, and crucial to the plaster's ability to take normal abuse, on interior work. Hopefully, this infrastructure will develop and spread, as bale construction gains in popularity.

Difficulties in Clay Identification

Clay is not always useful clay, and clay is definitely not silt. In the field, it can be difficult to tell the difference between clay and silt. If you ask any road crewman in Paul's section of New England about clay, he will tell you the stuff is everywhere, as often as not running in bands along the margins of each town road. In reality, the nearest clay deposits of any significance are at least two hours away. These road workers are plagued by silt. What silt and clay share is a certain imperviousness to water; for a person whose job is to get water off of roads and into the ground, the difference between silt and clay is of little significance. For plaster work, on the other hand, the difference is of primary importance, as silt is basically useless. Differentiation between the two is very important, but it can be difficult. (See "Clay vs. Silt," later in this chapter.)

Compounding this problem is the fact that not all clays are alike. Some bind better than others, some are more expansive than others. Often they come mixed with sand and silt and stones as a subsoil; this needs to be screened before samples can be made. In Germany and some parts of the American Southwest, milled clay, and even ready-made plaster mixes, are available by bag and bulk, delivered to the building site. The development of such an infrastructure across the rest of North America would make clay plasters much more accessible to people who are not already experienced with them. Somehow, it doesn't seem as if the demand for such products exists quite yet. . . .

Processing Raw Material

Processing clay is sometimes easy, and sometimes hard. Most clays, if used green from the ground, can be reduced to slip in a mortar mixer or bucket without too much trouble. They can also be soaked in water, in a pit, and slowly softened. Unfortunately, using clay green out of the ground is not usually practical; as it sits at the site or around the excavation yard, it dries into very hard balls. These cannot be soaked effectively, because the outer layers swell as they take on water, blocking water entry to the interior.

In many cases, therefore, the material must either be pounded into small pieces and sifted through a fairly fine screen, or run through a hammermill. Both of these processes are rather labor intensive; the milling also requires an investment in equipment. For this reason again, affordable bagged clay would be a great boon. (See "Commercial Clay Sources," later in this chapter.)

Abuse

Earth plaster is much more solid than most people would assume. For instance, it would be harder to put your foot through a properly mudded bale wall than through a stick-and-sheetrock wall. At the same time, however, earth plaster is not always as tough as more processed materials. For instance, it may gouge a bit if struck firmly with a sharp object, such as a chair back. Patching is easy, though on a wall of homogeneous color,

Sifting clay through a screen.

the patch will probably show. On the whole, properly applied clay plasters seem capable of withstanding normal wear and tear. For that subset of the population who are agents of entropy, however, another plaster might be a better choice.

Mold

In climates that are particularly moist during the building season, mold growth can be a problem in wet earth plaster. Mold occurs when a period of rainy weather prevents the plaster from drying. Paul has a hunch that the mold may actually enter the mix in the straw. In the few projects where he has seen any degree of mold, it has always seemed to be centered in the straw component. It may be, therefore, that by keeping the straw completely dry, mold can be prevented. "Completely dry" does not mean on the ground, covered by a tarp. It means indoors, or, if outdoors, on top of a sheet of plastic, with at least one layer of poly and one tarp over the top.

Paul did have one experience with a very intense growth of mold in a clay plaster. Plaster work on this particular project commenced toward the end of a summer that had seen no rain for two months. Mold spores of all sorts were dormant, and waiting for moisture to begin their growth. Rain came like crazy, beginning the very weekend that plastering began. Much of the straw pile was soaked through the tarp, and the pile sat upon bare ground. Though we tried to avoid using obviously wet straw in the mix, we had a multicolored bloom of mold all over the walls of the building. Straws that were exposed on the surface supported the strongest growth. As no mold appeared in any pure clay, or in any of the slips that were in various stages of drying in buckets and on the ground all around the site, it seems reasonable to conclude that the damp straw was the culprit.

Mold is less of an issue in a clay plaster that is stabilized with lime, as the alkalinity of the lime creates an atmosphere that is not conducive to biological activity. A light bloom on an unstabilized wall can usually be killed by spraying hydrogen peroxide onto the walls; a dilute bleach solution is also effective. Paul has also used limewash for this purpose. It may be that by soaking the straw in a borate solution before adding it to the mix, that mold may be prevented entirely. Before trying this, however, make samples to determine if the borate will affect the quality of the finished plaster.

Design Issues with Clay

Clay plasters can work exceptionally well on interiors in cold climates, if the materials are chosen and applied well. They can also work well on exteriors, under some circumstances. Before discussing the matters that affect both sides of the wall, let's have a look at the main exterior issue: protecting the wall from the erosive effects of water.

Protective Architectural and Site Features

In reality, those features that are required to reduce the maintenance on an exterior clay plaster are the same features that will protect any exterior. Erosion of the plaster is mainly prevented by building sufficient overhangs and other ar-

The wooded site and wrap-around porch roof protect the clay-plastered exterior walls of the Kirk/Starbuck house.

chitectural features, and by choosing a site that offers some protection. For one-story structures this is quite simple, but creative details must be applied for two or more stories. Porches and lean-to utility structures have been a popular response to that problem. On Pat Kirk and Dick Starbuck's retreat house, the second story is completely under the roof. A wrap-around verandah protects the first-story walls, and the gable ends are finished in wood. Combine these features with a wooded site, and it is safe to say that the clay-plastered walls of this building will not need attention for many years.

Another interesting design feature, found particularly on old European buildings, would be to recess the lower-story walls to give additional protection against wind-driven rain. This also has the advantage of breaking up the facade of the wall, bringing it down to a more human scale. These design features, though they seem limiting, often result in interesting and unusual buildings. Such an approach ensures bale walls that are very safe from moisture damage, as little rain will be hitting them, and they will have ample opportunity to dry, through the very permeable clay plaster.

Compatibility with Exterior Render

By this point in this book, it should be obvious that if clay plaster is used on the interior of a building, something at least as permeable (clay, lime, or wood siding) should be used on the exterior. Avoiding trapping moisture in the walls should be a main preoccupation of the straw bale designer; whether this appears as liquid water from the exterior or water vapor from the interior, it is crucial that it be allowed to escape.

Clay vs. Silt

Because clay and silt are both very small particles, they both feel slippery when wetted and rubbed between the fingers, and they both, if deposited thickly and purely enough, form a surface through which water will not readily pass. This is where the similarities end. Clay particles are flat, and when put into solution and then dried, they have a tendency to curl. This is why spilled clay slip always forms little curved flakes as it dries; it is also why clay makes a good binder. When water is added to clay, the particles separate from each other. When sand and/or chopped straw is added, the clay particles spread out, covering the grains of sand and the straws. The material is applied to the wall and begins to dry; as it does so, the clay particles start to stick back to each other, but they also curl around microscopic rough points on the surfaces of the sand and straw, binding the material together.

According to William Bryant Logan, "clay is plastic because it is made of infinitesimal plates that slide one across the other, held loosely in place by intervening layers of chemically combined water. It is very hard to pull the plates apart, but comparatively easy to slide them one across the other—as anyone who has tried to walk in the sticky gumbo-till clays that sometimes cover the face of the Earth can tell you. It can be almost impossible to lift your foot out of the suckling mass of the clay, while when you try to slide it forward, you may find it shoots ahead, leaving you sitting on your rump."[6]

Silt particles, on the other hand, are round. This allows them to feel slippery between the fingers, but obviously means that they are of little use in binding materials together. Though not as fine as clay, silt is fine enough that if a mix includes too much of it, it will interfere with the bond between clay and sand or straw. Silt also does not have nearly the ability to move moisture that clay does, so the most vapor-permeable earthen plasters will be those in which the lowest percentage of silt has snuck into the mix.

Different Clays, Different Qualities

Clays come under many names: illite, montmorillonite, kaolin, imogolite, bentonite; the list goes on. Each has a different chemistry and physical structure. Indeed, under an electron microscope, a Georgia kaolin will look different from an Iowa kaolin, and the many kaolins from China will each have their own distinct characteristics. Not surprisingly, these microscopic differences in shape and chemistry lead to noticeable differences in the three main working properties of clay: stickiness, plasticity, and expansiveness. The best clays for plaster are very plastic and very sticky, and minimally expansive. The fact that bentonite

6. William Bryant Logan, *Dirt: The Ecstatic Skin of the Earth.* (New York: Riverhead Books, 1995), pp. 130–131.

expands to nineteen times its dry volume when fully hydrated makes it very useful for below-grade waterproofing, but pretty useless for plaster. One could store a small fortune in jellybeans in the cracks of a bentonite plaster.

Because clays are so variable, finding clay does not mean that you have found a good clay for plaster. Most will work—extreme examples such as bentonite are rare—but the proportions of the mix and the hardness of the finished product will definitely vary, from material to material. This is part of the fun in working with preindustrial materials; in each new location, you must figure out how best to proceed, with what you have on hand.

Commercial Clay Sources

Far and away the easiest, most trouble-free method of procuring clay suitable for plaster work is to buy it from someone who knows what they are talking about. Clay can be purchased in bags from pottery suppliers. This is typically the most expensive way to buy clay, but since this dry, milled material is very easy to work with, it can save substantially on processing time, and therefore on labor costs. Suppliers who know their product well should be able to give you some idea of the stickiness and expansiveness of various clays. Your best bet is to ask which three or four clays might best suit your project; you can then bring home a bag of each, and begin making samples. Even if you use native clay for the bulk of the plaster, there is a good chance you will find yourself at the potter's supply when it comes time for finish work. This is the place to find clay in a multitude of colors, including white.

If your project is located in a clay-rich area, there is a good chance that somebody has capitalized on selling something that is just lying around, and is mining it for a commercial purpose. Pottery clay must come from somewhere, as must bricks. These materials are often very pure clays, so if you can find a factory that produces either one, you probably need look no farther. It may even be possible to purchase milled material in bulk through one of these sources, which will be substantially less expensive than buying it in bags. (It will also be less energy intensive, thanks to the shorter transportation distance.)

Clay is also used commercially in the construction of tennis courts, for lining ponds and other water-retention facilities, and for capping landfills. These applications do not require as pure a clay as pottery or bricks, however, so the material may possess a higher silt content. In all of the above cases (including the pottery and brick suppliers!), it is imperative that you test the material for clay content *before* having any delivered to the site. If you can't make it out to the yard, offer to pay for the shipping if they will mail you a coffee can full of material. Coffee cans seem to accumulate wherever heavy equipment is operated, so this shouldn't be a problem.

The key thing to remember is that, in this chapter and on the plaster site that it hopes to accurately represent, the distinction between clay and silt matters tremendously. In the world of the excavation contractor or sand and gravel yard, clay and silt are basically the same thing. So, when he tells you he's got clay, he means some undefined combination of clay and silt, maybe with some sand and gravel mixed in. When he tells you he's got pure clay, he means there isn't much sand in it. If you take delivery of a load that turns out not to be clay, it's pretty much your own fault, as your definition is a departure from the industry standard. This is why you need to check out the material, well in ad-

The primary ingredients in most earth plasters are clay, sand, and chopped straw. Wheat paste and manure are two common additives.

vance of the time when it needs to be delivered to the site.

Of course, it's not always feasible to purchase material from one of these sources. Even when it is, who wouldn't be attracted by the idea of reusing the excavated soil from the house site? It may be that every bit of soil that comes out of the cellar hole can be reused. As everyone knows, a soil is constituted of successive strata of different materials. The upper portion is the topsoil; on good land (maybe not the best place for a house, eh?) it may go as much as 2 feet deep. Because topsoil often contains a high percentage of decomposed organic matter, it is not suitable for plaster work. The best use for this soil will be for building up the garden, or for the growing medium in a living roof.

The ideal soil for earth plasters may be found underneath the topsoil, if it contains enough clay and not too much silt. Since the components of soil vary considerably from site to site and some-

times between locations on the same site, there is no other way of determining if a soil is appropriate for construction purposes than by testing it for its clay content. You can conduct various tests and it is advisable to do as many of them as necessary, until you have a pretty clear idea of the soil makeup. Samples will then reveal the working properties of the material.

Finding and Evaluating Soils for Mud Plasters

Virgin clay can be found in two forms: in relatively pure deposits (where it might be mixed with silt, and maybe a small percentage of sand or gravel), or as a component of a subsoil mix. Pure deposits are generally found in marine areas or past or present river bottoms (in Massachusetts this means that unless you are a corporation of some size, you risk a heavy fine for even thinking about mining them). Clay-rich subsoils are found in former seabeds, or occasionally in areas whose native geology was augmented by the munificence of passing glaciers.

Testing Pure Deposits

If you believe you have found a pure deposit, either on the site, in the wild, or among the mountains and monsters at the excavation yard, you can perform three simple tests to get an initial sense of whether it is suitable material.

LEG TEST
The leg test is the most obvious test in the world, which came to Paul in the shower, at the end of a long day of mixing plaster: Wet a small amount of the material in question, and rub it on your leg. Once it dries, try to rub it off. If it possesses

a high percentage of a good-quality clay, it will only powder off slowly, and only upon very vigorous rubbing. In fact, it should be easier to remove the material by peeling than rubbing, and if your legs are of the hairy sort, this will be quite painful. If the material is silty, rubbing will turn it painlessly to powder.

This test works best when you can compare the material in question to a clay of known quality, which can be rubbed onto your other leg as a control. If you can get someone to send you an envelope of clay that has been used successfully for plaster work, then you can compare the sample in question to that material. Otherwise, your best bet may be to get a bit of material from a local potter.

Worm Test

Take a small handful of the material and roll it between your hands until it is the size of a nightcrawler, about 4 inches long by the thickness of a pencil. Bend it into a U shape. If it can make the bend without cracking, it probably has a high clay content. If it cracks at all, it's probably too high in silt for plaster purposes.

Drop Test

Frank Andreson of Pro-clay, Brownfield, Maine, recommends dropping a thoroughly dried ball of the material in question from a height of 6 meters (20 feet.) If it shatters into many small fragments upon impact, it's too silty. If it breaks into only a few pieces, it's probably a suitable clay.

Potter Test

Take your sample to a potter, and ask them what they think of it. Potters are generally quite decent people, and most of them are really into clay. It shouldn't be hard to find one who will take some interest in your project, especially if your satchel of earth is accompanied by one of cookies. In clay-rich areas, it should be easy to find some potters who have at least experimented with digging their own material. Ask around among the potters in the phone book, they'll tell you where to find these kindred spirits. These people can be the most experienced at clay identification, and they might also be willing to tell you where to dig to find the best material.

Testing Clay-Rich Subsoil

Subsoils that contain clay, silt, sand, and gravel in various proportions are much more common than true clay deposits. If you are hoping to use the soil from the site, this is what you are most likely to find. Because the relative proportion of these components will influence the properties of the plaster, we must begin our testing by establishing the percentage of each material in the sample. The ideal proportions of a traditional clay and sand earthen plaster are from 15 to 35 percent clay, 55 to 75 percent sand (some gravel may be tolerated depending on the type of plaster), a maximum of 10 percent silt and a maximum of 3 percent organic matter. What you need to do is find out whether this soil contains a high enough percentage of clay, versus sand or silt.

The Jar Test

Paul likes to do the jar test two ways, the first giving an idea of the percentage of clay and silt in the entire soil, and the second giving a closer sense of the ratio of silt to clay. Each test requires two cups or so of raw, relatively dry material. For the first test, pick out all grains of sand or gravel larger than about 3/16 of an inch. Crush any balls of clay with a piece of wood. (Instead of

Further
Soil
Tests

Because the properties of soil components are highly variable, the initial tests described above do not always result in a clear determination. Here is a further round of tests taken from the books *Handbook for Building Homes of Earth* and *The Rammed Earth House* that will help to classify your soil.

Visual Tests

The appearance of a soil can tell you some important things about it. First spread the dried soil out in a thin layer on a flat surface. Then roughly separate the sand and gravel sizes by hand.

Do this by putting all of the particles, from the largest down to the smallest that you can see with the unaided eye, in one pile. This will be the sands and gravels. What is left (normally this will be very fine powderlike materials) will be the silts and clay.

If the sand and gravel piles together are bigger, you have a sand or a gravel soil. Decide which it is by putting all of the particles larger than ¼-inch (gravels) in one pile and all of the smaller particles (sands) in another pile. The soil is gravelly if the gravel pile is biggest and sandy if the sand pile is biggest. Remember which it is.

Here is what you do if you have a sandy or gravelly soil:

Take a small handful of the entire sample (not just the sand and gravel), get it moist but not soupy, squeeze it into a ball, and let it dry in the sun. If it falls apart as it dries, call it "clean." Clean sands and gravels are not suitable for earth houses unless they are mixed with other materials.

Here is what you do if you have a silt-clay soil or a sand or gravel that is not clean:

Take the entire sample and collect all of the soil that is smaller than medium sand (1/64 inch) by sifting it through a very fine screen or a piece of coarse cloth. The tests described below should be made with this fine material.

Wet Shaking Test

Take enough of the soil to form a ball the size of a small hen's egg and moisten it with water. The ball should have just enough water in it so that it will hold together but not stick to your fingers. Flatten the ball slightly in your palm and shake the ball vigorously. This is done by jarring the hand against some firm object or against the other hand until the shaking brings water to the surface of the sample. The soil may have a smooth, shiny, or "livery" appearance when this happens. (What you are looking for is to see how fast the water comes to the surface and gives the livery appearance.) Then squeeze the sample between your thumb and forefinger to see whether or not the water disappears.

The following are terms used in describing the speed of the above reaction:

1. *Rapid Reaction.* When it takes only five to ten taps to bring water to the surface, this is called a rapid reaction. Squeezing the sample should cause the water to disappear immediately so the surface looks dull. Opening the hand quickly should accomplish the same result. Continued pressure causes the sample to crack and finally crumble. This type of reaction is typical of very fine sands and coarse silts. Even a little bit of clay will keep the reaction from being rapid.
2. *Sluggish (or slow) Reaction.* When it takes twenty to thirty taps to bring the water to the surface, you have a sluggish reaction. Squeezing the sample after it has been shaken will not cause it to crack and crumble. Instead, it will flatten out like a ball of putty. This shows that the soil has some clay in it.
3. *Very Slow or No Reaction.* Some soils will not show any reaction to the shaking test, no matter how long you shake them. The longer it takes to show a reaction, the more clay the soil contains. These soils will require the other tests described below before you can proceed.

Bite Test

This a quick and useful way of identifying sand, silt, or clay. Take a small pinch of the soil and grind it lightly between your teeth. Identify the soils as follows:

1. *Sandy Soils.* The sharp, hard particles of sand will grate between your teeth and create an objectionable feeling. Even very fine sands will do this.
2. *Silty Soils.* Silt grains are much smaller than sand particles and, although they will still grate between the teeth, they are not particularly objectionable. They feel a lot smoother than sands.
3. *Clayey soils.* The clay grains are not gritty at all. Instead, they feel smooth and powdery like flour between the teeth. You will find that a dry pat of soil with a lot of clay in it will tend to stick when lightly touched to your tongue.

Shine Test

Take a pat of either dry or moist soil and rub it with your fingernail or the flat side of a knife blade. If the soil contains silt or sand—even with the remainder being clay—the surface will remain dull. A soil that has a lot of clay in it will become quite shiny.

Hand-Washing Test

You can tell a lot about a soil in the way it washes off your hands. Wet clayey soils feel soapy or slick, and they are hard to wash off. Silty soils feel powdery like flour, but they are not too difficult to wash off. Sandy soils rinse off easily.

Odor Test

Organic soils have a musty odor, especially when freshly dug. You get the same odor for dry organic soils by wetting and then heating them. Don't use these soils for earth walls.

Simple Touch Test

By just touching a sample of soil it is possible to evaluate its basic composition.

Take a soil sample and remove by hand the grains bigger than $1/16$ inch (5 mm), then crumble the sample between fingers and palm to determine the rough dimensions of the components:

1. *Silt.* The dry silt particles will also give a rough feeling but smoother and moist silt has some plasticity.

2. *Sand.* The dry sand particles give a rough feeling.

3. *Clay.* Dry clay comes in lumps or coarse grains and are hard to crush. Moist clay is plastic and sticks to the fingers. Silty and sandy soils make an audible crispy sound when rubbed together near the ear between thumb and index finger.

Unaided Eye Tests

By a simple glance at a sample of soil it is possible to determine roughly the relative proportions and sizes of the bigger particles and, by deduction, of the finest. However, the finest visible particles are $1/64$ inch (0.80 mm), and clay and silt particles are invisible.

Color is important in classifying soils. Olive green and light brown to black colors mean organic soils. Red and dark brown colors may come from iron in the soil. Soils with a lot of coral, limerock, gypsum, and caliche may be white or some shade of gray.

picking grains, you can run the material through a $1/8$- or $3/16$-inch screen, after crushing the clay.) Place a cup of the resulting material in a quart jar, add a tablespoon of sea salt, fill three-quarters of the way with water, and shake vigorously for a minute or two, until the particles are all separated.

For the second test, crush any clay balls, and run the material through a piece of old window screening. This will remove all but the finest sand. Add a cup to a quart jar, and proceed as above. After an hour, the sand in both jars should have settled to the bottom, and the silt will be deposited on top of it. (This is domesticated geology.) The clay will still be in suspension. Carefully mark the outside of the second jar at the top of the silt layer, as this line will often be difficult to discern once the clay has settled. After eight to twelve hours, the clay will have come out of suspension, and the water should be clear. The thickness of each layer should correspond to the proportion of each material.

The goal of this test is to determine whether the soil, once the unsuitably large particles are removed, will contain enough clay to work as a plaster. Too much clay is no problem, as sand is ubiquitous and cheap, and can always be added. The key is to consider the relationship between the two jars. Look at number two, first. Ignoring the sand in this jar, what is the ratio of clay to silt? This material should be at least 80 percent clay; any less and it will probably not make a strong plaster. Now look at jar number one. The required ratio of clay/silt to sand will vary, according to the ratio of clay to silt. If very little silt is present, a mixture as low as 15 to 20 percent clay/silt to sand might work. If the percentage of silt is higher, as much as 40 percent may be required to make a strong plaster.

Leg, Worm, and Potter Tests

If the results of the jar test look promising, then pass some more material through the window screen, and try some of the tests described above. If these look good, it's time to move on to making samples!

Preparing Earth Plasters

Earth is the most common wall material on the planet, and there are as many mixes for mud plaster as there are earth-building cultures. We can safely say, therefore, that no recipe is set in stone. We will concentrate our attention on the two types of clay plaster that have been used successfully over straw bale walls. These are clay-sand and clay-straw plasters.

Clay and Sand Plaster

In most traditional recipes from Europe and North America, an earthen plaster is composed of a ratio of 1 part clay to 2 to 4 parts sand, the percentage varying between coats and with the specific qualities of the clay. One or so parts of chopped or milled straw is usually added to the mix, to give it some tensile strength. The sand forms the main structure of the plaster, grains

This bench was built during a workshop with Michel Bergeron. It looked good after completion, but over the following winter the plaster started to crumble, and we realized that the binder in our mix was silt, rather than clay as we had presumed.

ranging in size from ⅛ or ¼ inches and down for the backing coats, to 1/16 inch or less for the finish. It is crucial that the sand be sharp, and that particle size be well graded (see "Sand," in chapter 10, for a more detailed explanation).

The ratio of sand to clay depends upon the stickiness and expansiveness of the clay, and also on the percentage of silt in the mix. When the "clay" portion of the mix is actually a combination of clay and silt, more will have to be used, as the silt does not help with binding. What happens when the percentages of the various components are off?

Too much clay: The plaster will have a tendency to crack severely, taking on the look of a dry lake bed. The base coat can have a greater proportion of clay to help it stick firmly to the bale substrate; excess cracking in this coat is acceptable, as it will not usually telegraph out through the succeeding layers.

Too much sand: The clay binder will not hold all the sand particles together and as a result the plaster will be very brittle when dry. Finish coats will tend to have a maximum sand content, to prevent cracking.

Too much silt or organic matter: This makes a crumbly, powdery, unstable mix that will not be able to take even the normal amount of abuse, will be especially vulnerable to water, and will decay with time. Some silt in the base coats would be acceptable, but it should be avoided completely in finish work. If your local material is silty, buy some bagged clay for the finish coat. It won't cost much.

Clay and Straw Plaster

In their work with the "Casas que Cantan" owner-built housing initiative in Ciudad Obregon, Mexico, Bill and Athena Steen (and their local collaborators) came up with a plaster recipe that seems to work particularly well over straw bale walls. This plaster is based on a clay slip about the consistency of a milkshake, one part of which is mixed with 4 or so parts of chopped straw, and, optionally, 1 or 2 parts of sand. The resulting plaster has an incredible tensile strength, and works extremely well as a fill coat, applied in a thickness of ½ to 2 inches over the entire wall. Paul has used this mix as the base coat on several projects (see "Making Bale Buildings More Like Traditional Buildings," later in this chapter) and has found it to work extremely well.

The main advantages of straw plaster, over a more traditional sand plaster, are that it can easily be applied with bare hands (this is especially true of the no-sand version), that it can be built out to substantial depths without slumping, and that it is very sticky and malleable, and therefore easily worked into the face of the bale. Because the straw resists perfect smoothing, this plaster

Bill Steen tosses handfuls of straw-clay plaster at a bale wall.

With its excellent surface for sculpting, straw-clay plaster receives an international vote of approval.

forms a rough surface, leaving an excellent key for succeeding coats, be they of clay or lime. This is an ideal material for building sculptural features into the face of the wall. The drawback to this method is that mold can be a serious issue in humid climate.

Making Clay Slip

If you are working with a relatively pure clay, it is often best to mix it into a thick slip, and then mix this material with the sand and/or straw. By making the slip in advance, the clay is allowed maximum time for the adsorption of water, resulting in a stickier, more plastic material that requires less mixing time.

With some clays, it is possible to break up chunks with a shovel or sledgehammer (depending on dryness), add water, and after a very short time begin mixing. Mixing can be done by hand in a tub or bucket, with a joint compound paddle on a drill (in a bucket), or in a mortar mixer. The drill method is typically the most effective of these, especially if the clay is allowed to soak for a half hour or more, in the bucket, before drilling begins. This process requires a heavy duty drill and someone to operate it, resources that are not available on every site. Some clays that retain dry pebbles through this process will respond to being soaked for several days; this can take place in buckets, or on a larger scale in a pit built of bales and lined with polyethylene. The most stubborn of clays, in which the outer particles in any given ball will expand upon contact with water, sealing access to the interior, will either need to be milled to a powder before water is added, or mixed in a mortar mixer, with some sand.

Sand is effective at grinding down pebbles of clay, exposing successive layers to water. It is a slow process, and therefore often not practical on a site with only one mortar mixer, which needs to remain constantly engaged in producing plaster. (This is a second benefit of the drill method; while the mixer is churning up a batch of plaster, the mix master can be producing slip for the next batch.) For soils that already contain a high percentage of sand, it is really the only mixing option. Luckily, sand-clay soils (as opposed to purer clay deposits) usually tend not to chunk up as badly as the purer clay. Where they do, soaking may be an option. If neither direct mixing nor soaking works with a clay soil, you're probably out of luck. When none of these techniques will work smoothly with a pure clay, you can always use a hammermill.

The Hammermill

After the mortar mixer, this is the clay plasterer's most useful piece of equipment. A hammermill is one of several varieties of chipper/shredder. It has a horizontal shaft with lots of steel bars hung from it. When the shaft rotates, the bars swing around and utterly destroy anything that you might put down the throat of the machine, except for wet clay. It makes sand out of rocks (you should not think we are advocating making your own sand), but wet clay sticks to the side walls and eventually causes the whole thing to gum up. A good hammermill has interchangeable exit screens; the size of the openings determines the fineness of the grind. Milling clay requires a screen of about 3/16 inch.

From conversations with local farm equipment rehabilitators, Paul is fairly sure that such

Grinding clay in a hammermill. This machine mills straw, as well.

The "bale chopper" ate forty bales in an hour and a half.

a machine is available on a larger scale, which would run by power take-off from a tractor. The ideal mill would grind dry clay as quickly as a person could shovel it in; this would substantially reduce the labor time involved in making usable material of stubborn clays.

Chopping Straw

Straw can be chopped in many ways: manually with an axe, a machete or any similar hand tool on a chopping block; with a chain saw; with a weed whacker in a bucket; or with a lawnmower, inside a plywood trough. These methods typically reduce the straw to a length of two to three inches, and partially demolish the tubular shape. This straw is suitable for the base coats of sand plasters, and for clay and straw plaster. For finish work, it should be sifted through ¼- or even ⅛-inch screens.

A hammermill makes the best straw, especially for finish work. Using a ¾-inch screen, it consistently mills to a length of 1½ inches or so, and completely breaks down the tubular structure, resulting in strips of fiber that are each less than ⅛ inch wide. Paul has also come across a machine specifically designed for this job, known, of course, as the "bale chopper." This baby chews up whole bales and spits out chopped straw. It is probably designed to make bedding for animal stalls, but we found it in the possession of a local landscape company that uses it for mulching. It processed forty bales in an hour and a half! The finished product was not so fine, 2 to 3 inches long and maybe half of the tubes broken up, but this worked fine for a straw-clay plaster. Where we needed smaller fibers, the hammermill was able to process this chopped material much faster than long straw.

Additives

Over the millennia, many different compounds have been added to earth plaster to induce various properties. We recommend that you begin with the basics, and add these materials only if they turn out to be necessary. Samples are the best way to determine whether your plaster will need such bolstering.

WHEAT PASTE

Wheat paste is a protein-based glue, which helps bind plaster, and can also make it harder. It is most conveniently (and rather inexpensively) purchased as wallpaper paste. We have had success with it at a ratio of one-half of a 6-ounce bag per two 5-gallon buckets of very stiff clay slip. This material wants to be mixed with water in advance, a gallon or two for a half bag of paste. It should be mixed thoroughly (with a joint-compound mixer or large whisk) and allowed to sit for a half-hour or more before it is incorporated into the mix. This allows time for the paste to fully hydrate.

Wheat paste can also be made from white flour, or better yet, from high-gluten flour. Remember, it's the protein that we want here, so carbohydrates, bran, and the like, do nothing but provide food for unwelcome guests. Flour is even less expensive than wallpaper paste, but it must be boiled for twenty to thirty minutes, with constant stirring to prevent sticking, before it is ready to use. The flour should first be whisked into some cold water (this prevents clumping), then mixed into the boiling water. It's ready when it turns thick and gelatinous.

MANURE

Manure (usually from cows or horses) has been a plaster ingredient for longer than anyone can remember. In some exterior plaster recipes, it makes up more than half the total volume. Compounds in the manure add weather-shedding and binding qualities, and the fine fibers act in a manner similar to straw, providing tensile strength to the plaster. Fresh manure can be added directly to the mix, while dry material must be soaked in water first. Fresh material is believed to be better at imparting waterproof-

ing qualities. We have had good luck substituting manure for as much as half the straw in a mix, and others have used it to entirely replace the straw.

LIME STABILIZATION

Lime stabilization of clay plaster is a very exciting field, which has been underexplored by straw bale and other natural builders. The lime actually combines chemically with the clay particles, ultimately forming a harder plaster with improved water resistance. The addition of lime also creates an environment that is less hospitable to mold growth. Here's how Stafford Holmes and Michael Wingate describe the process:

> *Lime will react with the clay minerals—mainly kaolinte, montmorillonite, and illite—in two ways. The first and most important reaction is for the calcium in the lime to substitute for the exchangeable alkali elements such as sodium and potassium that exist, together with water molecules, between the thin sheets of the alumino-silicate crystal structure of the clay minerals. . . . The clay particles will no longer remain in their original dispersed state, but will flocculate to form coarser agglomerates of clay. The soil therefore becomes less plastic, will absorb less moisture, and compacts more readily to give an increased compressive strength.*
>
> *With time, another and more important reaction occurs in which the calcium combines chemically with the silica and alumina in the clay mineral. This follows dissolution of the clay minerals and their recombination to form complex aluminum and calcium silicates. It is a low grade of pozzolanic reaction, for which moisture must be present, and which can be accelerated by a higher temperature. The product is a bind-*

ing material, comprising insoluble calcium silicate and silica gel. This binding material is also the main mineral produced when water is added to Portland cement. In addition, and in conjunction with the above reactions, carbonation occurs. The lime reacts with carbon dioxide from the air to form carbonated elements. [See chapter 11, "Lime Plaster."]

There is an optimum quantity of lime for each soil. Generally it ranges between 3 and 10 percent, tending to be at the middle of this scale for soils containing an optimum clay fraction.[7]

Clearly, experimentation must be carried out on any given site, in order to determine the appropriate ratio of lime to other ingredients. Paul has had good luck using lime to stabilize materials whose silt content would otherwise have been too high to make a suitable plaster. In the two cases where he has used this technique, samples (between 3:1 and 4:1 clay/silt:lime) yielded a binder that, when mixed with sand and milled straw, produced a very hard plaster.

Mixing Clay and Sand Plaster

If slip has already been produced, this is added to the mixer, first. If you are beginning with a dry clay, allow it to soak in water at the bottom of the mixer for a few minutes (or as long as an hour, depending on the clay), before starting the motor. If you crank up the machine before adsorption begins in earnest, some clays will ball up on the paddles, and refuse to go into suspension. If you are working with a sand-clay soil, it is also best to allow this to soak for a while, be-

fore disturbing it. Once the machine is going, put the sand in. If the slip is very stiff (such that it is almost a solid), you will probably need to add water, to combine the clay with the sand without overworking the mixer. Still, you will want to keep the mix fairly dry at first, so the sand can help grind up any unsoftened pebbles of clay. Wheat paste, manure, lime, or any other additives should be added next. As the clay, sand, and any additives combine, straw can be added by handfuls, and water as needed. It's a good idea to soak the straw for a half-hour or more before adding it to the mix; this reduces the amount of water it will take on later, making the moisture level of the finished plaster more stable. Limewater is a good soaking medium, as it will inhibit any mold spores that might be on the straw.

Once the materials look like they are becoming homogeneous and the water level is about right, the mixer can be left alone for fifteen or twenty minutes, to thoroughly combine the various ingredients into a sweet-smelling mud pie! All of this can also be done in a wheelbarrow or mason's mixing boat, of course. This is honest

A mortar mixer makes short work of combining plaster ingredients.

7. Stafford Holmes and Michael Wingate, *Building with Lime: A Practical Introduction* (London: Intermediate Technology Publications, 1997), p. 153.

work, but a lot of it. If having a mixer on site through the entire project is not an option, renting one at the beginning of each week and stockpiling material might just be the best bet.

Mixing Clay and Straw Plaster

Mixing straw plaster is very easy. Clay is made into a slip as above, though it is much thinner, about the consistency of a milkshake. Chopped straw is added to this material at a rate of four or five parts per part of clay. A part or two of sand can also be included, though it is optional. The ideal ratio will yield a product that is sticky and holds together well, but does not have a lot of extra slip globbing out of it. A few samples will make the desired consistency quite clear.

This material can be mixed very quickly in a mortar mixer. Mixing by hand, in a mortar tray, is also quite practical. During a work party, large volumes of plaster can be cranked out by people in bare feet. The technique is to alternately stomp and lift the material, adding clay or straw as necessary to achieve a properly sticky mix.

Samples

The ideal plaster mix will vary from site to site, so the only way to really get a sense of your local materials is to begin working with them. If the project is on a tight schedule, it is best to begin making samples several weeks before the plaster phase will begin in earnest. This will allow time to be sure that the materials at hand will work suitably, and to refine mixes over several generations of experimentation.

With any given soil, the most efficient sampling method is to make four or six initial patches, using varying ratios of sand to clay.

Mixing straw plaster the old-fashioned way, by foot! Volunteers of all ages enjoy this, and can rapidly produce large volumes of plaster.

Clay content has a major effect on cracking. The mix used on the upper half of this wall was too rich; the bottom half is about right.

These can be put on at a half-inch of thickness or so, and evaluated for cracking and hardness, as they dry. The ideal mix will strike a balance between stickiness (imparted by the clay) and excessive cracking (caused by too much clay). What you are looking for is the leanest mix that will still bond well to the bales, and still hold together.

Once the proper ratio of sand to clay has been determined, it may be worth trying one or more of the additives described above, to determine whether they make any noticeable improvement in the plaster. We'll say it again: If the basic ingredients do the job, then don't mess with them. Additives are only necessary if the fully dried samples show the basic mix to be too powdery, or not hard enough.

Application

Preparing different mixes for different coats is a common practice in earth plaster work. The base will probably want to be a bit richer in clay (or be clay-straw) in order to achieve a better bond to the bales. It will probably also be looser than the succeeding coats, which makes it easier to work into the straw. Both of these factors will cause cracking, but that's acceptable, as the surface is usually scored anyway to create a better key for the second coat. The only real rules for the first coat are that the plaster wants to be worked into the straw, and that it doesn't want to be crumbly, when dried. Finer details can wait until later coats.

It is usually best to apply the first coat by hand, to a thickness of ¼ to ½ inch over the entire wall. The fingers are used to work the material between chunks of bale, while the heel of the hand is used to create pressure, forcing the plaster into the wall. Trowels also work on very uniform

Burlap can be used to reinforce clay plaster where it spans over wood.

bales; on hairier bales the many protruding straws tend to fling the material back in your face, or to get between the plaster and the wall, preventing a good bond. One great benefit of using the clay-straw plaster for the first coat is that it is much easier on the hands. Rubber gloves are also an option, though they reduce dexterity a bit. Depending on the mix, it may be possible to fill deep hollows with this coat, though it is often easier to spread a thin layer over the entire wall, and then come back with a fill coat of dryer material, to bring up the low spots. Clay-straw plaster is superb for this filling job. Once it has stiffened, the first coat, and any subsequent filling, is scored or scratched.

The best working consistency for the second coat is described by Michael Smith in *The Cobber's Companion.* "When you grab a handful [of the mix], it should stick more to itself than to your hands, but when you throw it against a cob wall [or the first coat on a straw bale wall] from a distance of several yards, most of it should stick. If it doesn't behave this way, adjust the mix by adding more water (if it doesn't level itself in the wheelbarrow), more sand (if it sticks to your hands), more clay (if it doesn't stick to the wall), or more chopped straw (if it is too loose)."[8] This coat can be applied by hand or trowel. Those who are skilled with it will find the trowel faster at this point. When this coat has stiffened, it is rubbed down with a sponge, creating a somewhat coarse texture for the finish to adhere to.

The finish usually receives a finer sand than the backing coats. Sifting through window screening works well. The finish coat is applied, usually by trowel, in a layer of 1/8 inch or less. Any straw included in this mix should be finely milled. As the material dries, the surface should be remoistened and retroweled, as many times as is necessary to prevent cracking. The finest, most closed surface is produced by polishing with 3- or 4-inch-diameter plastic circles, cut from yogurt containers. Careful polishing brings clay to the surface, creating a leathery look. Colored clays and mica can also be added to this coat. The combination of mica, straw, and the supple clay finish make for a very beautiful wall.

LINSEED OIL

Linseed oil can be painted onto a finished exterior surface, to increase its weather resistance to some extent. Presumably, it also reduces the vapor permeability. Justin Idoine did this on a less-protected portion of the Kirk/Starbuck house, and it seems to have worked well.

LIMEWASH

Limewash can be applied to a clay plaster in much the same way as it is applied to a lime plaster. Successive coats may be required to achieve a uniform shade. (See "Limewash," in chapter 11.)

8. Michael G. Smith, *The Cobber's Companion* (Cottage Grove, Ore.: Cob Cottage Company 1998), p. 115.

The finish coat can be worked with a sponge to remove a layer of clay and bring out the golden flecks of chopped straw.

ALIS

An *alis* is an interior clay paint, made of wheat paste, colored clay, and sometimes masonry pigments. As in a finish plaster, milled straw or mica can also be added, for relief. "Fill a clean, 5-gallon bucket 1/5 full with flour paste and add water until it is about 3/5 full. Add about 3 quarts of powdered clay, 1 quart of fine sand, and 1 or 2 quarts of mica powder. According to Carole (Crews, of Gourmet Adobe, Taos, N.M., who made up this recipe), 'These proportions may be varied depending on the wall surface and the clay used. Use more sand if the clay cracks, less if a finer alis is preferred.' Keep adding and stirring until the mix is the consistency of medium cream."[9]

9. Ibid, p. 120.

The *alis* is then painted onto the wall. When it is nearly dry, it can be rubbed with a soft sponge to polish the surface and expose the straw and mica.

Making Bale Buildings More Like Traditional Buildings

Early in this chapter we mentioned cob, light clay, and an old Danish technique of wrapping straw around hazel sticks. All of these techniques have three things in common. First, the straw is kept in intimate contact with clay, which seems to modify swings in moisture levels and assist in the passage of vapor. Second, exterior coatings were typically of lime, wood, or clay, all of which are quite vapor permeable. Third, deterioration began on a large scale only with the introduction of modern, supposedly maintenance-free finishing materials, such as cement stucco.

The major difference between bale walls and these other walls is that in the latter, the straw is everywhere in contact with clay. Since clay seems to act as a preservative to straw, this may turn out to be a very significant difference. Thus, the big question is, is there any way to get some clay into the bales? Eric Thompson and Naoto Inoe at the Foundation for Biodynamic Shelter in Skyler, Virginia, have made some efforts in this direction. They have dunked bales of straw into a tank of slip, while sucking the air out of the bales through a tube attached to a powerful fan. They found that they could control the depth to which the clay was drawn into the bales, and generally aimed for 4 to 6 inches of penetration. Since all surfaces of the bale are coated in this method, bales so prepared would have to be dried before being stacked into the wall, to prevent mold from forming deep inside the wall, along

the wet joints. They could be bonded together with a thin bead of clay mortar along each edge. A fringe benefit of this technique is that the bale surface becomes much more rigid. This makes plastering easier, and reduces the thickness of plaster required to form a solid wall.

Another variation on this idea comes from Tom Rijven, who is originally from the Netherlands, but now works in France. Tom dunks the inner and outer faces of his bales in a clay slip before laying them into the wall. This practice

Justin Idoine dunks each face of a bale in a trough of wood and plastic, then trowels off the extra slip.

Installing slip-covered bales can be a muddy job.

A contemporary approach modeled on historical techniques. Bales were dunked in clay slip, then plastered first with clay-straw and secondly with lime plaster, subsequently to be limewashed. Note the structural stud, and the flashing and wire lath around the spigot's mounting block.

slippery and somewhat dangerous. A better method may be to allow the bales to dry, then glue them together with slip.

The next layer is the base coat of plaster ½ to 1 inch thick. We tend to work with a clay-straw plaster when the application will be by volunteer hands, and with a clay-sand-straw plaster when the material will be pumped on by a machine. At this point, the bale wall has been made somewhat like a light-clay or cob wall. It is very stiff, as the thick earthen plaster dries quite hard. It is now ready for its protective coating. We have generally used ½ to ¾ inches of lime-sand plaster (applied in 2 or 3 coats) followed by limewash, inside and out. The interior could easily be finished in clay, as could the exterior, on the right site.

provides four benefits. First of all, it allows clay to work into the outer inch or two of the bale surface, where it can protect the straw from moisture damage, and increase the bale's resistance to airflow. Second, because some clay laps 2 or 3 inches around the corners of the bales, it glues the bales together, forming a very solid wall. Third, it creates a surface to which the first coat of plaster can easily bond. Fourth, it protects the bales from any weather that might blow in before the wall is plastered.

In our latest projects, GreenSpace has been working toward a wall system modeled on historical straw building techniques. The first step, borrowed from Tom Rijven, is dipping the bales. They can be left to dry before they are installed, or they can be placed in the wall while still wet. Immediate placement allows the bales to be glued together, and small gaps filled, by the slip; the drawback to this method is that it is very messy, eventually resulting in a floor that is rather

"Tanks" made of bales and plastic sheeting contain slips of two different consistencies—a thin one for dipping bales and a thick one for plaster—and also delineate an area for mixing the plaster.

This system is quite vapor permeable. It also possesses a tremendous potential for drying any water that might appear by condensation at the back side of the exterior plaster. The highly absorptive clay and lime plasters will readily draw in this water, and then give it off by evaporation to the outside air. This method also maximizes the value of volunteer labor; if the group is large enough, the base coat plaster can go on as the bales go in. People of all sizes, ages, and skill levels find jobs suited to them; nobody is standing around trying to figure out where they fit in, and everybody feels useful and has a great time. The bales are immediately protected from weather and fire. When the professional plasterers show up to trowel on the lime, they find a solid base that accepts plaster quickly, and which doesn't spring it back in their faces. They are very happy to leave their goggles at home.

Of course, this being bale construction, we certainly have some questions about this system. It's messy. It's labor intensive, though less so than the traditional systems on which it is modeled. As Rob Tom has pointed out, from a structural point of view, it is not clear that putting the harder lime over the softer clay is a good idea. It is a general rule in construction that as layers move outward from the load-bearing structure, rigidity should decrease, and flexibility increase. (This is exactly the problem with cement stucco;

it is more stiff and brittle than most substrates, so as they move, it cracks.) There is no way to know, in advance, whether this arrangement will cause problems. If so, whether they manifest themselves in five years, fifty years, or five hundred years depends on maintenance, the site, whether some jerk comes and nails vinyl siding over the whole thing, and who knows what else. We also don't really know whether dipping or dunking the bales introduces enough clay to replicate the characteristics of traditional walls. It would seem that the areas nearest the wall surfaces will experience the most moisture activity, but we do not yet have enough testing data to know for sure. Maybe the bales should be filled to their center with clay. This would require a lot of material, and would significantly reduce the R-value of the wall. It might also be difficult to dry bales that were so thoroughly saturated, not to mention the difficulty of moving them around.

Clay has a long history in cold-climate construction. Those who can separate quality from grandeur will recognize it as a glorious history. More than any other two materials, clay and straw just go together. Clay binds and preserves straw, while straw gives clay structure and tensile strength. Where good materials can be found, earth plaster can be a tremendous complement to straw bale walls.

Anne Thrune's Massage Studio

WHIDBEY ISLAND, WASHINGTON

by Ted Butchart, GreenFire Institute

Architectural design is always a matter of juggling a great number of competing and even conflicting imperatives. Rare is the project that allows a designer to give flight to all his or her sculptural and tactile longings, because the more subtle aspects of a design often must give way to more prosaic, but far more practical, considerations. Anne Thrune's project was that rare exception for me.

Anne came to me with a simple request. She wanted a small building to house her massage and healing practice, and to function as a short-stay retreat for a person wanting some concentrated introspection time. Functionally, the list of requirements for this project was much shorter than that of a typical house design. It only had to provide a small arrival space for a waiting client, a changing room with toilet and shower, and a main room for massage and other healing work. Certainly less demanding than a house, with its stipulations for eating, cooking, entertaining, noisy areas, quiet areas, and so on, the relative simplicity of this program allowed us to go quite deeply into the subtle needs of the space.

I have had two principal threads of fascination through my life—architecture and medicine—and all my divergent interests weave back into those primary plaits. I approach my design work as medicine, be it houses or healing spaces; and I often ponder what it is that makes a space conducive to therapies. Foremost is the ideal of a safe and sheltering space that will support a patient's healing work. I believe that as designers we must grapple with the more subtle aspects of health, and in building design our work should reflect the shift toward empowering the patient and toward the emotional and spiritual content of the space. Although my "medicine" is oriented toward built space, it springs from Chinese and Tibetan medical thinking, and the overlap with Anne's medical models gave us a common vocabulary. The trust that quickly formed between us was an important key to the success of the final product.

My approach to the building was guided by the experience of a person receiving a massage. I wanted that experience to flow from a feeling of complete safety and security. To fully relax, physically and emotionally, we have to know that we are safe and this building had to communicate on many levels that "here was sanctuary." Straw bale walls are ideal for that; their thickness makes the person inside feel invulnerable, the walls are highly soundproof, the reflected sound is soft, not harsh, and the stucco exterior adds yet more to the feeling of complete safety.

Another important part of the experience is what the client sees and feels while lying on the massage table. Assuming we don't immediately fall asleep, the visual field can be important. A boxy room with a flat white ceiling and sharp corners can actually interfere with drifting into deeper states of relaxation. The eye is constantly stopped, or pulled repeatedly to some bland view. This is emotionally neutral at best, if not annoying, and the only option is to close one's eyes. I wanted a space that was somehow mysterious, that pulled the eye toward unusual patterns and engaged the right brain more than the left. I believe that where we enter into psychotherapies, somatic therapies, or any emotional and spiritual healing, the space should be visually complex, but never jarring. Smooth curves and complex ceiling planes allow the logical mind to wander, giving the other aspects of consciousness a chance to come to the fore.

I rolled these ideas around in the back of my mind for some time as I played with various designs for the building. One day Anne traded me a massage session against some design time. She is a multitalented practitioner, and as I lay on the table slowly melting into a pool of limpness and relief, I focused on the tendons and verte-brae of my neck that she was delineating. Suddenly I had the answer, or at least a vision that I could attempt to replicate in the new building. I wanted to have the building reflect the work she did: cleaning up the interplay between the bones and the tendons, or in my case, the posts and the beams. The net of tendons became a complex ray of beams, and the spinal column became a steel-ring-bound cluster of thin cedar poles making up the center support post. The brief image there on the massage table also showed a wonderful quality of light filtering down through the "tendons" of the roof. As I chased this idea it evolved into a multilayered roof with thin windows filling the space between the layers. This would allow light to enter at the top of the space and directly illuminate the wood of the ceiling, drawing the eye upward.

The problem of daylighting the space was only partly solved by the roof windows. A more critical problem was placing windows so that

Anne Thrune's massage studio, designed by Ted Butchart of Greenfire Institute.

daylight would enter, but privacy would be preserved. Anne's property is forested, and it is large enough that the chance of anyone peeping in through the windows is fairly slight. But when it comes to the experience of feeling secure, the perception of safety is far more relevant than the reality. For the space to work on all the levels that we desired, we needed windows that would allow us to connect to the natural world outside, yet would not require curtains to prevent any imaginary peeping Toms from peering in. The answer came while juggling yet another subtle need: the desire to have the building quietly acknowledge the presence and the importance of the client.

This may sound odd at first reading. How can a building acknowledge a person? It can, and builders have been using perceptual tricks to do just that since classical times. It is a subtle conversation based on how we perceive space. If a building swells out toward you with a convex surface it is subtly indicating that you are not important. Something on the other side of it seems to be "pushing it outward," and your tiny presence has no counter "push." However, when a wall falls away from you in a concave form, just the opposite is being stated in its form—your side of the wall is "pushing" it away to create space and the building is respectfully backing away. If you have seen a picture of St. Peter's Basilica in Rome, or happily had the chance to experience it in person, perhaps you remember the grand out-curving colonnade that surrounds the plaza in front of the cathedral. The great curves seem to have been placed to surround and envelop a great crowd of people and their presence in that plaza is important and articulated even when the crowd is absent. The colonnade is being pressed back by an unseen force.

The windows on the Thrune massage studio are oriented to provide privacy for the people inside.

Generally only important civic spaces engage in that sort of interplay. But on a rural, forested lot, what is to prevent us from acknowledging these subtleties? The activity inside Anne's studio is critically important to the participants as they struggle with healing physical and emotional wounds, or delve into the hidden vistas of their spiritual landscapes. The individual has a "personal space bubble" around them, and the social act between healer and patient creates a virtual space bubble that is a great deal larger. We can acknowledge that social space, and very subtly support the act, by allowing the walls to flex outward and mark the edges of the space. The presence and innate worth of the client is visually marked.

I realized that this concept of acknowledgment offered an elegant solution to my problem with the windows. Even a straight bale wall is much more sensual than a boring old wallboard wall, but a curved bale wall is a wonder of sensuality and texture. And the best way to light such a wall is with a glancing light across its face to highlight the subtle variations on the surface. If we were to step the curved walls out and insert a tall thin window in the step-out, we would get exactly the right sort of light and a high degree of privacy, too. In this design, the windows are set on the radius of the building, always at right angles to, and invisible from, the massage table. As the sun progresses through the day there is a constantly changing play of light and shadow on the wall.

Externally, the building is composed of two different materials: stucco on the bale walls and cedar on the standard stud walls that make up the entrance and changing rooms. The cedar walls reflect the forested setting and harken back to the older cultural history of the area. From one vantage point, if you know where to look, the public face of the building makes a visual allusion to the traditional Long Houses of the coastal Indians, an attempt at respecting the history of the place without overtly mimicking another culture's forms.

For the technically inclined, I offer a brief description of the structural system. Although I have designed straw bale buildings with every imaginable structure, my personal preference is for a system that allows the straw bales to be used as flexibly as possible. I often set structural piers outside the bale wall so that the bales can be set both more rapidly and in any curved form I desire. In the case of this studio I did not want the outer posts exposed, I did not want to use concrete or cantilevered posts to take the lateral

forces, and we did not then have the engineering test results to justify using the stucco skin as the lateral bracing system. What we came up with were basically box columns, sufficiently stiff and sufficiently anchored to the concrete foundation to resist movement in the plane of the supported beam. These box columns formed the end of each curved segment of wall (18 inches), included the thin window between the segments (12 inches), and formed the start of the next segment (another 18 inches). So each was approximately 4 feet wide. These boxes-columns, arrayed around the north side of the building, combine with the standard plywood-braced

Central load-bearing column, where the main rafters converge.

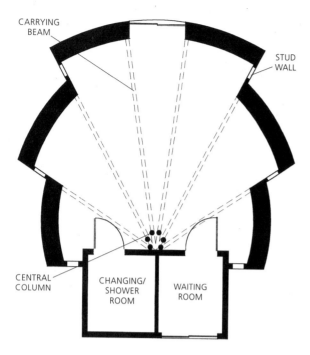

CARRYING BEAM

STUD WALL

CENTRAL COLUMN

CHANGING/ SHOWER ROOM

WAITING ROOM

Floor plan.

walls on the south side to sufficiently stabilize the building in this high-seismic zone. The great strength of the stucco walls, as is often the case with straw buildings, simply offers a very high level of backup.

The interior of the building was finished as naturally as was possible. The floor was intended to be a troweled-on earthen floor, but a lack of suitable material on Whidbey, a glacier debris island, eventually caused us to switch to a concrete slab floor. The radiant heat in the floor works perfectly with the high insulation level of the straw walls, and the brownish acid-wash coloring on the concrete gives a remarkably

"earthen" look to the floor. Where Anne must stand to work around the table she has a circular carpet to soften the concrete. The walls are covered in a pure white clay plaster, which further softens the straw walls acoustically. The exposed beams and wood decking of the ceiling were flamed and brushed to seal the surfaces and highlight the grain without the use of chemical sealers. Excellent local craftsmen created fine detailed doors covered with split bamboo to bring the scale of the studio down to the very small where people would approach it most closely.

The final space is meditative and exudes what I would have to call a welcoming quiet. It simply feels good to be inside that space. That Anne and her husband, Crispin, were actively involved in the construction undoubtedly contributes to that sense. When I teach courses on home building I like to take the participants onto the unbroken ground of the building site and have them sit quietly and just "feel" the space in its natural state. When the building is complete and they are surrounded by walls and roof, I tell them, it should still feel that good to sit there. The use of straw bale and other natural materials can intensify the feeling of connection to the site instead of arbitrarily cutting it off at the wall. The rediscovery of straw provides the ideal building material for eliciting the subtle possibilities of a project, and gives us yet another way to create buildings that are supportive of the people that use them.

PART 4

Straw
Matters

CHAPTER 13

ALTERNATIVES for INTERIOR WALLS and FLOORS

AMONG THE WIDE VARIETY of finishing options we have picked a few unusual techniques and considerations that might be appropriate for you to evaluate in case none of the others seem to suit your needs satisfactorily. They are related to very specific situations, so you should remember that some special care may be required to work them out successfully. The focus here is on interior partitions, floors, and gypsum plaster as an interior wall finish.

Partition Wall Options

Once most of the building energy has been concentrated and spent on finishing the exterior shell, many people feel exhausted and let their old biases take the lead when figuring out how to build partition walls and connect them to the bale walls.

It is understandable that to spend a minimum of effort in this phase of construction is usually a well-deserved relief from the pressure built up during the previous construction phases. But the experience of visiting new houses with beautifully plastered bale walls and creative fine detailing, only to find the space divided up by impersonal drywall partitions, is very jarring.

Of course, there are many technical reasons that drywall partitions are so popular; they are very cheap, are erected quickly, and do divide spaces effectively. At that point in a project, when there is generally not much time left, little energy, and certainly no more money, we tend to go for the easiest and the cheapest route, unfortunately. . . . But as a contrasting statement in a plastered straw bale environment, drywall partitions get the gold medal.

Even if aesthetics are not a concern, the active and sometimes hyperactive family life we live these days makes sound-insulated partitions a necessity. Considering that a typical modern house is occupied by family members with their own individual sets of electronic equipment, not to mention the communal rooms containing all kinds of noisy appliances, it makes sense to plan for rooms that are acoustically insulated from each other. However, it is difficult and expensive to build good soundproof walls with industrial materials. That should be incentive enough to look for alternative wall systems that would simultaneously provide good sound insulation and visual harmony with the interior finishes on the bales.

The techniques described here are experimental. Because they are not standardized and are labor intensive, they would probably be quite expensive if done by professionals; thus, they are more appropriate for owner-builders. Most are well-suited for family work, as they don't require the operation of fancy power tools, and are easy to learn. Some of these systems can be worked into a frame previously built by carpenters; others can simply be prepared ahead of time when energy and motivation are still at their peak. All of them can make good interior partition walls in some circumstances. In chapter 15, "Beyond the Bale," you will find more details about some of these and other techniques applied to exterior walls.

Mini-Bales[1]

The Shelter Resources Institute of Darby, Montana, U.S., has been experimenting with applications of mini-bales. They used a stationary baler and even designed small pedal-powered and photovoltaically powered balers to make their mini-bales at one-half, one-third, or one-quarter the size of full three-string bales. Their small straw blocks are designed for load-bearing or non-load-bearing walls, and intended mainly for use where limited floor space is a concern. The most common size, at 6 inches by 8 inches by 16 inches, can be infilled between uprights, or laid up like masonry blocks with adobe mortar. Pinning and/or horizontal stabilizers are used to achieve out-of-plane rigidity when necessary.

1. Rod Miner, "Building with Mini-Bales," *The Last Straw*, no.13 (winter 1996): p. 17.

The mini-bales created by Montana's Shelter Resources Institute can be made with pedal power or solar energy, and offer interesting possibilities for interior partition walls.

Samples of straw-clay poured between uprights and finished in different ways. The Canelo Project, Arizona.

Long straw and clay wrapped around sticks to form a ceiling plaster substrate. This traditional German technique was demonstrated by Frank Andreson at Athena and Bill Steen's place in Arizona.

In non-load-bearing applications, minibales can make nice curving walls, and they can be plastered exactly like the main bale wall surfaces.

Leichtlehmbau (Light clay-straw)

Light straw-clay mixes (*Leichtlehmbau* in German) are made of loose straw lightly coated with a clay slip. The straw-clay can either be left exposed or coated with a finish, depending on the desired texture. The finishing options are similar to those for bale walls, with earth plaster being especially attractive.

Light straw-clay is a good alternative to soundproofed drywall because it uses the same type of framing and is an interesting way of recycling all the loose straw left from bale manipulation during the construction of the walls (see chapter 15, "Beyond the Bale").

Straw Wattles[2]

Straw wattles are manufactured from rice straw wrapped in an 8- to 9-inch-diameter tubular plastic netting, which is available in a variety of lengths; 25 feet is the standard length. Once filled with straw, a 25-foot wattle weighs about 35 pounds.

John and Sherryn Haynes of Northern California developed straw wattles as a method of erosion and sediment control, revegetation of slopes and stream banks, and rehabilitation of areas damaged by forest fires. But they also have used the wattles stacked, pinned, and plastered like bale walls in utility buildings. While they are obviously not suitable in load-bearing applications, the cost of wattle walls is comparable to

2. Kat Morrow, "Straw Wattles," *The Last Straw,* no. 17 (winter 1997): p. 7.

bale walls, and they are more versatile because the material is lighter and thus more easily manipulated and curved. Plastering, an appropriate finish, highlights the natural shape of the tubes, preserving the originality of the basic component.

Cob Walls

If compared to *Leichtlehmbau,* cob could be described as a heavy straw-clay mix. The total earth content of cob is greater, so that it looks more like mud reinforced with loose straw.

The main advantage of cob is that it has an almost unlimited sculptural potential and can be styled in many ways without the use of any formwork. Because of its high mud content, cob takes a long time to dry and has a low insulating capacity. On the other hand, because of its weight, cob absorbs sound well and functions very effectively as thermal mass. It is extensively used in making permanent furniture such as benches inside or under porches, carved shelves, ovens of all shapes and sizes, and chimneys. However, before building interior walls out of cob it would be advisable to carefully estimate the load-bearing capacities of the floors on which it will bear (see chapter 15, "Beyond the Bale").

Wood Chips and Other Light Clay Mixtures, Adobe and Straw-Clay Blocks, Paper Blocks

The list that heads this section illustrates the range of other alternative systems that could be used for partition walls when different materials are mixed with the same basic binder: clay. In fact, the preceding discussions all share a common idea: creating one's own mixture with any natural waste product, as long as the binder is

The cob technique meshes very nicely with straw bales, as in this window under construction at the Canelo Project in Arizona.

An interior cob wall at Sun Ray Kelley's yoga studio. Sedro Wooley, Washington.

available and its basic working requirements are known and respected. Making blocks, or formed or carved structures, simply means using different proportions of the basic ingredients and sometimes an anchoring structure for the final work.

Any kind of block has an advantage over formed-in-place alternatives because blocks can be prefabricated ahead of time, before the pressures of meeting a construction schedule have intensified. They can even be produced in a remote location before the final construction site has been selected. Mixed with a clay slip, almost any kind of loose recycled material can be poured into rough forms (also potentially made of recycled materials) and left to dry over time. These blocks are then stacked in masonry fashion and mortared with a straw-clay mortar. This technique can be a very interesting way of getting acquainted

Blocks of sawdust, wood chips, straw, and clay. The Schenstrom/Tordo house, Brownfield, Maine.

Mud-mortared straw-clay blocks serve as interior partitions for this office building built under the Steens' supervision. The blocks were fabricated in a local park by kids, who were paid per unit. Ciudad Obregon, Mexico.

with the basics of methods and materials to be used for the larger project (see chapter 15, "Beyond the Bale").

Cordwood Masonry

Cordwood or stackwood masonry is, as its name describes, a mortared piling of firewood-size logs laid transversely to the wall thickness. This may be a rather intricate technique to master when building exterior walls, because air tightness is tricky to achieve and requires careful detailing. But for those who are attracted to their rustic look, cordwood masonry partition walls can be advantageous in many ways. For one thing, cordwood masonry could be an ideal application for recycling any type of log leftovers, which can

Cordwood masonry walls made with recycled logs. Note the living roof as well.

easily be mixed with recycled jugs and bottles to create interesting translucent lighting effects. Cordwood experts have created beautiful designs just by alternating the shapes and sizes of the logs used. For indoor placement, no rule says that a cordwood wall couldn't be mortared with a strong straw-clay mortar, as long as it doesn't have a load-bearing function. Rather labor intensive, cordwood walls can also be fun and very cheap to build.

One-String Bales

For the Kirk/Starbuck retreat house, Paul needed to come up with a way of fitting a finished bale wall into an existing 12-inch-deep cavity. The answer? Cut the bales in half, lengthwise, and make them into one-string bales. These do require some care in handling—we probably had a 20 percent explosion rate—but they did the job quite nicely. These one-stringers are about 9 inches wide, before plaster. Stacked between studs, they would form beautiful interior partitions with excellent soundproofing qualities.

Though we cut the bales in half with a chain saw, a portable band saw mill would probably do a better job. It would make a straighter cut, with less hassle.

Floor Finishes

Floor finish options are even more numerous than partition wall options. But to maintain some sort of harmony in the building, the choice may come down to a short list of materials and techniques that are especially compatible with the bale wall environment. Floor finishes should also be evaluated with regard to their expected performance in different locations in the building.

Stacked in columns between studs, one-string bales make fine interior partitions with good sound insulation.

Different flooring materials should be matched to the different activities that take place in specific rooms. An appropriate surface finish for an entrance hall, for example, would have to combine very low maintenance needs in high-traffic conditions, a capacity to resist mud, water, and snow, durability, and a warm visual feel. After careful consideration, the list of possibilities will probably be reduced to ceramic tiles, slate, linoleum, and concrete slab. A wooden floor would probably not be an ideal choice based on these criteria. Cost will probably eliminate other options. Other factors to consider include acoustic properties, heat storage capacity (in the case of passive solar design or radiant floor heating), coloring capacity (will it change color over the years?), light absorptivity (versus reflection), and resilience (for high-traffic areas such as a kitchen). The type of framing under the floor may also make some alternatives more attractive than others. Slabs on grade and wood frames can support any type of floor finish, but some combinations work better than others, in terms

of cost or practicality. As more criteria are introduced, the most appropriate flooring choice will usually make itself evident.

Conventional Flooring

If you choose a conventional flooring material that is usually installed and finished at the very last stage of construction, special planning may be required ahead of time to effectively match it with the base of the undulating bale walls. However, if any flooring is installed before the plaster work is over (often the most practical choice), be aware that the resulting messy environment can have disastrous effects on the finish. Floors must be carefully covered to keep them in their best condition.

Concrete Slabs

If your design is oriented toward simplicity and harmony, you might want to marry the floor finishes with the wall finishes. If you have chosen plasters for the walls, you might appreciate the continuity created by beautifully finished concrete slabs. Originally used for heavy-duty commercial floors in storage buildings, garages, and unfinished basements, exposed concrete slabs are gaining increased popularity because creative approaches to finish can make them quite beautiful. Although they can be covered with almost any other kind of floor finish, they offer an interesting low-cost alternative if left exposed. Slabs can be colored, stained, painted, and sealed in different ways. Patterns can be stamped on to make them look like slates, bricks, or flagstones. They can be polished and waxed to a very shiny finish. Slabs are almost maintenance-free and will last forever if they are properly built. They are also very popular in combination with hydronic radiant heating; when well insulated underneath, a concrete slab has a high heat-storage capacity that makes it work as a very efficient heating system. In a passive solar house design, a slab creates important thermal mass in combination with the plastered walls.

Staining Concrete Floors

Don Wenig and his wife had already finished their house with concrete floors when they realized that they didn't like the dull gray look of the concrete. Looking for inexpensive solutions, they started to make tests with colors. Here is how Don describes his experience: "My wife called upon her art background in oil painting and began mixing colors from her painting tubes. We chose a spot that was to be covered with cabinets and tried several earth colors diluted with turpentine to varying degrees, colors such as burnt and raw umbers and siennas. When we finally arrived at a shade we could agree upon, we mixed up a goodly amount and started spreading it on the unfinished concrete floor with a rag. (It is important that the concrete be unfinished for color penetration.) Of course, we ran out of mix in the middle of the operation and had to mix some more. It almost matched. Much to our surprise and delight the two shades didn't really matter. Different areas of the floor accepted different amounts of the color. It all blended into a pleasing tint of umbers and siennas, and the slight roughness in the slab finish tended to disappear. We didn't want to make a bold statement, just to take the raw edge from the cement color. The pigment penetrated sufficiently to accept later minor scratches without showing."[3]

3. Don Wenig, "Staining your Concrete Floors," *The Last Straw,* no.3 (spring 1993): p. 9.

Dry Shake Slab Coloring

The best way to get a durable slab color is by mixing dry pigments into the mass of the concrete before pouring. The technique is well known as a way to achieve a uniform color, but the choice of colors offered is limited and the cost can be astronomically high for large surfaces. When Michel was looking for a more economical solution for the Sivananda project and for an easy way to get the variegated color of the existing cliff (see the Sivananda profile at the end of chapter 8), he came across the dry shake method, in which dry pigments are sprinkled on top of the concrete surface while it is being floated. Usually, the coloring is done by adding a large amount of pigment. This yields a uniform color, but can still be expensive.

At Sivananda, the decision was to use just very small amounts of two different pigments and mix them during the floating process in order to obtain the desired marbling. It was done this way: After the slab had been bullfloated (a bullfloat is a 4-foot-wide, trowel-like blade with a long handle) and excess moisture had evaporated from the surface, the surface was power-floated once (a power float is a machine used for bringing a high gloss to concrete slabs). Then the two (iron oxide) pigments, a Brazil red and a yellow, were sprinkled sparsely on the surface, at a ratio of approximately two cups of each for a 10-square-foot area. As soon as the pigment had darkened by absorption of the concrete's moisture, the surface was hand-troweled to incorporate the pigments. In order to achieve a smooth and hard surface, the slab was floated twice more; once by hand and trowel, once by a power float. The delays between these finishing phases are crucial. These operations should be carried out by experienced workers who know how to evaluate the variable humidity and temperature conditions that may have considerable influence on the drying process.

If conditions are too dry, a very light water mist should be sprayed over the entire surface just after the troweling is completed; then the slab should be covered immediately with plastic sheets and left to cure for at least seven days.

This floor has to be sealed after it is fully cured. A linseed oil base, dissolved and applied in two successive coats, makes a good natural sealant. A hard protective finish can be obtained with a variety of waxes, including natural ones with carnauba as the main ingredient.

Earthen Floors

Using local dirt is certainly the oldest method of flooring a house. The concept has recently evolved into making fancy-looking surfaces suitable for almost any type of environment. If you're looking for a very inexpensive floor combined with enviable aesthetics, relative softness, high thermal mass, low technology, and reasonably low maintenance, earth might represent the ultimate solution for your ground floors and maybe even for your elevated floors.

An earthen floor is made with the same basic ingredients as a mud plaster, essentially a mix of clay, sand, and finely chopped straw. Your local soil can be tested for this use in the same way as for plasters (see "Finding and Evaluating Soils for Mud Plasters," in chapter 12). Because it is very heavy like a concrete slab, an earthen floor has to be built on a strong support, whether it sits on the ground or on an elevated structure. On the ground it has to be situated on a well-drained and well-compacted soil, preferably inorganic. In cold climates, of course, placing in-

This natural earth floor, which covers radiant-heating tubes, is stamped in a tile fashion, with joints made of hardwood strips. Lauzon, Quebec.

sulation underneath the earthen floor is highly recommended. As with a concrete slab, radiant tubing installed in the base layer of an earth floor makes a very efficient heating system in combination with its substantial thermal mass.

The finished earth floor is usually sealed with natural oil such as linseed, tung, cottonseed, or even hemp oil. For a glossy and more resistant finish it can be waxed with a natural hardening compound once the sealant has dried. For those who prefer more conventional or hard finishes, an earthen floor can serve well as a base for tiles, linoleum, or even carpets. Earthen floors can also be imprinted with many different patterns according to personal taste.

THE STEENS' EARTHEN FLOORS

"One of the most beautiful things about earthen floors is that there is no exact formula for constructing one. Formulas vary according to available materials, cultural traditions, climatic conditions, and individual preferences. Depending on the clay mixture used, the thickness, and the experience of the installer, some floors can be more susceptible to damage and require more repair and upkeep than others. By understanding the principles common to all earthen floors and the characteristics of the material used, it is possible to create a beautiful, natural floor that will be long-lasting and require little maintenance."[4]

This excerpt gives an idea of the type of information that can be found in the Steens' booklet (see the Resources list), which we recommend to anyone who wants to build an earthen floor.

BOB MUNK'S FLAGSTONE-STYLE ADOBE FLOOR

"In Bob Munk's house, on the outskirts of Santa Fe, the floors are adobe mud, mixed with a traditional combination of dried ox blood and manure. They were topped with a mixture of mud, structolite (a lightweight interior plaster mix containing expanded mica), and blue corn meal. After the mud dried, the cracks were grouted with a lighter colored mud, which, when fully dried, creates a pattern similar to flagstone flooring. As a finish, the floors were sealed with linseed oil."[5]

Elevated Floors

Elevated floors are floors supported on a frame. They can be a first-story floor (usually over a basement or crawlspace) or an upper-story floor. Unless it is a monolithic reinforced structural slab, the frame will be in the form of parallel joists spanning between structural walls or beams. Elevated floors can be finished in the same way as ground floors, but they present an additional concern: sound transmission. If they separate rooms that have different functions, as is almost always the case with bedrooms located either above or below a kitchen, living room, or other noisy rooms, blocking sound transmission to preserve intimacy becomes a major issue in the modern family environment.

People living in straw bale houses often describe the beneficial bubble effect of bale walls dampening exterior sound pollution caused by traffic and normal social activities. On windy locations too, bale walls may have a very calming and comforting effect. But the interior of a bale house can sometimes become as noisy as the exterior environment as a result of the type of finishes used on walls and floors. Hard, glossy plastered walls and concrete floors can keep those sounds bouncing back and forth in the house, and thus may require some special detailing.

There are two types of sound in buildings, the control of which requires different treatments. Ambient sounds—talking, music, the dreaded television, a whistling tea kettle—are sourced in the air. These can be reflected, absorbed, or conducted by building materials, depending on the characteristics of the material. Furniture, rugs, shaggy dogs, and even softwoods and the softer plasters mitigate the effects of these sounds.

Impact sounds, on the other hand, originate in the building materials, and are projected from the fabric of the building into the air. In a house, the most common example of an impact sound comes from people walking on an elevated floor. The vibrations associated with impact sounds are blocked only by absorbing materials. If a solid

---

4. Athena and Bill Steen, excerpt from: *Earthen Floors* (a Canelo Project Booklet).
5. David Eisenberg, "The Land of Enchantment, Fertile Ground for the Straw Bale Revival," *The Last Straw,* no.7 (summer, 1994): p. 6.

structure such as a concrete floor is laid directly on a frame, impact sounds will be transmitted horizontally throughout the slab and vertically to the frame and then to the air below. The only way to prevent that effect is by placing absorbent materials between the slab and the frame members. In the Sivananda Lodge project (see profile, following chapter 8), all three sound sources were blocked successfully by one system: Straw bales were inserted between floor joists and topped with a concrete slab.

Gypsum Plaster

Gypsum has a long history in construction. It has been used for centuries both on its own and as a setting agent for interior lime plasters. As the main ingredient in drywall, it is the most common wall material in contemporary new construction. Gypsum plaster is available as a ready-mix under a number of trade names, and has been used successfully in straw bale houses. Let's have a look at its strong and weak points.

Advantages

The main advantage of gypsum plaster is that it's available at lumberyards in a ready-to-use form. It is very light, doesn't require much skill to apply, and doesn't crack badly. It is also vapor permeable, though in the vast majority of cases it is painted with commercial paint.

READY MIX

If you say the word "plaster" to a mainstream builder, he will assume you are talking about gypsum plaster. This is because the material is available at every lumberyard in a just-add-water formulation that makes it easy to use. It can be mixed in a bucket, with a drywall mixer. Gypsum plasters are available under a variety of trade names, some national or international, some more local. Some are intended to be used on their own, over metal or wooden lath; others are meant for skim coat application over old plaster or drywall.

EASY TO APPLY

Some gypsum plasters contain no aggregate at all, others use vermiculite or perlite. Compared to a traditional sand plaster, applying gypsum plaster is about as much work as frosting a cake. Because the material is mixed directly out of the bag and goes on easily, the application of com-

Jean-Guy Savoie, a plasterer with fifty years of experience, demonstrating the fine art of hand-forming gypsum moldings, a tradition almost lost today. Here, he is gently pushing a profiled jig loaded with fresh plaster. The work gets its final texture from a few passes with a smooth, moistened brush. A skilled plasterer will leave a surface that requires no further finishing before paint is applied.

mercial gypsum plaster requires little skill. Gypsum expands as it sets; this tendency naturally minimizes cracking. Some brands (Paul has worked with Imperial) can be laid on quite thickly, without substantial cracking. This is useful for rounding out corners where partition walls meet bale walls, or to give some texture to drywall partitions and ceilings. Gypsum sets fairly hard, and quite quickly.

Vapor Permeable Unless Painted

Gypsum is quite vapor permeable, and it can be integrally colored, with mineral pigments or paints. Almost always, however, it is surface painted with commercial interior paint. Most builders who will choose cement stucco for the exterior will choose gypsum for the interior; as the two most common plaster products, they seem to go together. In this case, paint seems like a wise choice. Gypsum is probably the simplest option for anyone who wants a conventionally painted interior finish or drywall-type look.

Disadvantages of Gypsum

Gypsum does have some substantial disadvantages, including that it is not weather resistant.

Expensive

A bag of ready-mix gypsum plaster is two or three times the price of an equivalent volume of lime or cement, and the gypsum is not usually stretched by the addition of cheap sand (though it is possible to add some sand to add texture to the finish coat, as discussed in a moment). This extra expense is mitigated somewhat by the fact that the material is very predictable, and quite easy to apply. It is still the most expensive plaster option, however.

Chemical Setting Agents

Few things in this world are free; the price for the quick, relatively hard set of commercial gypsum plasters is chemical setting agents, which continue to offgas for some time. If you are sensitive to such chemicals, avoid this material.

Work Pressure

Because gypsum plaster sets fast, it, not the plasterer, is in control of the process. This creates pressure to time the work to keep up with the hardening mud. Tool cleanup is also a concern.

Watch Out for Flat Walls!

The biggest danger with gypsum plaster, in our opinion, is that it is so light and smooth that it takes some doing to not smooth all of the character out of the bale walls. If you want a drywall-type look, gypsum plaster is the material for you.

Gypsum as a Skim-Coat Material

Paul has had good luck with both gypsum plaster and drywall joint compound as a skim-coat material, over wallboard or over an interior cement stucco. They also accept both sand and finely milled straw nicely. Because these materials are water soluble, their surface can be sponged after it has set, to reveal flecks of golden straw. This technique is very useful on drywall ceilings, bringing them into a more harmonious relationship to bale walls. It is also possible to mix a fairly large amount of chopped or milled straw with joint compound or gypsum, to create a fill mix for rounding out angular drywall corners. Paul has built out ceiling joints to a depth of more than an inch with a joint compound–straw mix, with no cracking or other adverse effects.

CHAPTER 14

MOISTURE STUDIES and SENSORS

THROUGHOUT THIS BOOK, we have talked about the need for a more detailed understanding of how moisture actually moves in straw bale walls. We have also talked about moisture sensors as the straw bale homeowner's insurance against moisture problems. Presumably, sensors will indicate a problem developing in a wall at an early enough stage that the source can be detected and eliminated, before any major decomposition begins. Thus, moisture sensors serve two functions in bale walls: they are an early warning system for the health of the walls, and an agent of pure science. Clearly, every cold-climate straw bale home should have at least a few. In order to think about the best places to install moisture sensors, we will first look at the studies that have supplied us with some basic information.

Moisture Studies of Bale Buildings

The following sections summarize the moisture tests that have been conducted to date. They have taught some valuable lessons about how to detail walls, and have suggested the best patterns in which probes might be installed.

Clark Sanders's Tests

The earliest studies of moisture levels in bale walls were carried out by Clark Sanders, on three buildings in East Meredith, New York. The first of these, a meditation hermitage that Clark built in 1989, is a concrete (gunite) building, with the bales as insulation and formwork for the steel-reinforced concrete shell. The building is heated intermittently in winter, though since it is sited and built for solar gain, the interior rarely or never freezes. It contains an internal courtyard, so some walls are completely unheated. Five years after its completion, in the fall of 1994, and again in the spring of 1998, Clark drilled holes in the walls of this building and investigated their moisture content with the probe of his Delmhorst bale-moisture meter.

Two patterns emerged. First, in heated areas where the moisture content was above 15 percent or so, moisture tended to migrate such that the levels were higher toward the bottom and (to a lesser degree) toward the outside, and lower toward the top and inside. In unheated walls, striation was from top to bottom; inside to outside did not seem to matter. In areas where the level was generally less than 15 percent, no significant striation occurred. This figure of 15 percent should be taken as an indication of a trend, not as gospel. This is Clark's supposition, based on a limited number of readings, and the number itself is based on a meter whose margin of error is at least 3 per-

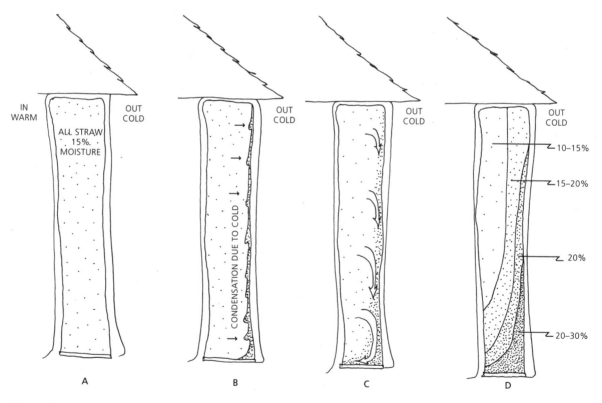

Observed pattern of moisture stratification in a wall over time. Note that moisture gravitates toward the bottom of walls. Diagram by Clark Sanders, first published in The Last Straw, *no.8 (Fall 1994): p. 14.*

Clark drilled holes in the walls of the hermitage, and investigated their moisture content with the probe of his Delmhorst bale moisture meter.

cent. (Clark's control bales were stacked in a barn, and these varied from 11 to 14 percent moisture content (MC), depending on their density.)

In the first round of tests, two-thirds of the lower section of this building was above 20 percent moisture content; 20 to 22 percent is generally considered to be the threshold at which biodegradation begins. Below 20 percent, straw (like wood) can safely store moisture, and damage is not a concern. In nearly all cases, the middle and upper sections of the wall were below 20 percent, and most were between 12 and 16 percent, only a tad damper than the control group. Clark believes there is a good chance that most of this moisture entered the walls during the gunite process, and that it was able to exit only very slowly, because of a waterproofing compound that was sprayed onto the walls about six months after the gunite.

The second pattern was a general drying trend, from the 1994 to the 1998 tests. By the spring of 1998, 14 of 21 bottom positions had dropped below 20 percent MC, a 100 percent improvement. Middle and upper positions tended lower as well, by 1 to 4 percentage points, a rate that would seem statistically insignificant, if it were not so consistent. It is reasonable to assume that, over this intervening period, the exterior waterproofing agent would have begun to break down, allowing greater drying. This trend strengthens Clark's theory that the bulk of the moisture in the walls entered during construction.

A few readings stayed high, or actually increased.

Ricky Baruc

Clark Sanders's hermitage, built in 1989.

One situation has an obvious cause: An unroofed section of wall, with cracked gunite, stayed at 30 percent MC (the top of the scale) through both tests. This allows us to say conclusively that bale walls want a roof in wet climates, but we probably knew that already. A section of roofed wall just around the corner from this area, which was pretty wet in 1994, actually increased to more than 30 percent across the board in 1998. It's a good bet that water is migrating around the corner, from the unroofed section.

Two other areas are anomalous, however. The bottom center of the tall east wall had risen by 10 points, from 15 or 16 percent to 22 to 29 percent MC. Clark could find no cracks that would obviously have been admitting water. A bottom reading on the north wall had also climbed, from 22 to 26 percent to 30 percent. It is possible that whatever is causing this problem was present from the outset (maybe a small roof leak?), and the problem became worse over time. We have no good answers to these questions.

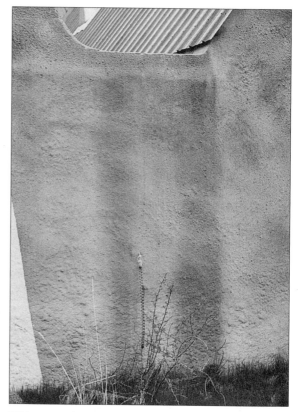

This unroofed section of wall showed consistently high moisture readings. Note water staining.

This bale cabin with poly behind the interior plaster and felt paper behind the exterior stucco seems to be doing fine.

In 1992, Clark built a cabin at the hermitage site, a post-and-beam with bale infill. Polyethylene was hung behind the interior plaster, and tar paper behind the exterior stucco, the idea being to detail the building as conventionally as possible. The building is heated through the winter, but not continuously occupied. Also, as it is a retreat center, it is safe to assume that interior moisture production is less than what it would be in a fully occupied house experiencing the normal round of daily activities. In the 1994 tests, the cabin walls were quite dry, with readings ranging from 8 to 15 percent. This seems to back up Clark's idea that much of the moisture in the hermitage entered during the gunite process. By 1998, the average level had actually risen a bit, with values ranging from 10 to 17 percent. As this is still comfortably below the threshold for decomposition, Clark did not pursue any further tests. That fact that the moisture level increased slightly from the fall of 1994 to the spring of 1997 is good evidence that the general drop in values in the hermitage was part of a real drying trend, rather than some sort of seasonal variation. Several Canadian tests underscore this logic, as well (see discussion below).

Never one to call it a day and go home early, in 1995 Clark built a sauna. Exterior walls were variously plastered with lime or earth, while three of the four interior walls were paneled in wood. It was a dry sauna, but used infrequently, so it should be considered as a mostly unheated building. In the initial test, in 1996, 8 of 14 readings showed a moisture level of 20 percent or more, somewhere within their profile. As in the hermitage, the higher readings tended to be found toward the bottom, but less consistently so. Inside to outside seemed to make little difference.

By the spring of 1998, the moisture content of all but one of the locations had dropped well within the safe zone. One bottom position had remained at 21 (exterior) and 17 (center), and another bottom percent (center and inner) read 18. All other readings ranged from 9 to 16 percent MC, with most at the lower end of the scale. The clay and lime plasters, coupled with the unsealed interior faces (no backplaster was used behind the wood), had apparently allowed excellent drying. Another interesting fact about this second test is that it was conducted on a rainy day. Though the earthen plaster that covered the east wall was noticeably damp on the exterior, the straw behind was quite dry, ranging from 11 to 13 percent moisture content.

One cold morning in January of 2000, Clark awoke to a faint burning smell. He figured it was just his woodstove, until he looked out the

Clark Sanders's sauna, with clay and lime exterior plasters.

window, and saw a column of smoke rising straight up from the direction of the sauna. Clark's son and some friends had fired it the night before, and Clark figures the cheap stove must have opened at a seam, allowing a pile of embers to ignite the wood deck. By the time Clark got to it, the floor, roof, and interior boards were pretty well burned up, and the interior surface of the bales was burning nicely. The bale walls possessed no firestop at the top or bottom to separate them from the building's wooden elements. The wall that was plastered on both sides did last longer than the others, but eventually everything burned out around it, and it fell into the center of the fire. The lesson: Use a decent stove in a sauna! And while you're at it, be sure to backplaster any wood siding or paneling, and install a firebreak (plaster works fine) between bale walls and wooden roof framing.

Ship Harbour Project Test

At about the same time that Clark Sanders was poking probes into his various buildings, Kim Thompson, in Ship Harbour, Nova Scotia, engaged the Technical University of Nova Scotia (TUNS) in a project to consistently monitor the relative humidity level of the walls of her new house. Probes were permanently embedded in the north and west walls, at a height of 3 feet above the floor, and midway through the thickness of the wall. Hooked to a computer, these probes gave hourly readings of temperature and relative humidity.

In the spring of 1996, after eighteen months of testing, Kim reported that "RH (relative humidity) peaked at 72 percent for two weeks in early August of the first year, dropping to 42% through the fall and winter. The second year RH peaked at 66 percent and dropped to 30 percent through the winter."[1] Presumably, the general drying trend from the first to the second year is a result of walls giving off moisture introduced during plastering. The house was also framed with green lumber, adding a significant moisture load over the first year, and less in the second.

It is generally assumed that biodegradation can begin in straw at a relative humidity above 70 percent. (The threshold may actually be 75 or 80 percent, or higher, depending on temperature. It's the moisture content of the straw itself, rather than the RH of the air around it, that really counts.) Assuming 70 as the danger number, the

1. Kim Thompson, "Research and Development in Canada," *The Last Straw,* no.14, (spring 1996): p. 12.

Kim and Caigeann Thompson at the Ship Harbour Project.

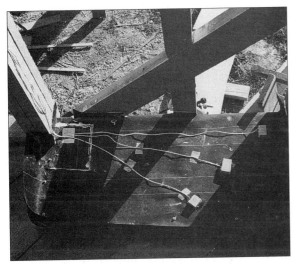

Sensors were arranged in sets of three, and at three heights in the wall.

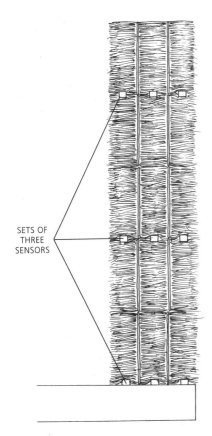

SETS OF
THREE
SENSORS

Positioning of moisture sensors at the Willson house.

Ship Harbour house rose above it for only two weeks in the summer of its first year, at the positions tested.

Brian Willson House

In the fall of 1996, Paul wired Brian Willson's house in Massachusetts, which was then under construction, with a series of moisture probes, in an effort to test Clark Sanders's findings of striation patterns within the wall. These probes, designed by wood scientist Paul Lipke, are a block of wood embedded into the wall and connected to the surface by wires. The assumption is that at any given time, the moisture level will be about the same in the wooden block and the straw around it. Readings are taken with a wood moisture meter. (See "Building Remote Sensors," later in this chapter, for construction details.)

The probes were placed nine to a wall, at three heights and three depths, with the intention of mapping, over time, any seasonal patterns of moisture striation in the wall. Unfortunately, readings have not been taken on a consistent basis, as Brian's life is quite full with other commitments and interests, and as he is away for a large portion of each year. We did learn one very interesting thing from this house, however. Because some sensor pins were also set in the building's structural frame, it is possible, from the readings taken early on, to guess at a relationship between the moisture content of the wooden structure, and that of the bales.

The bales were stacked in the fall of 1996, around a frame of green hemlock. The first readings were taken on December 19 of that year, after the exterior siding and all insulation had been installed, and after the bales had been in place for about two months. By this time, the bales had come up to the moisture level of the green lumber, 19 to 22 percent MC everywhere in the building, straw and wood. The next test was not made until sixteen months later, the 29th of April, 1998. Interior plaster had been applied during the intervening summer, and the building left minimally heated through the next winter. Moisture levels had dropped to 6 to 12 percent throughout the frame and walls, with the straw always very close to the moisture level of nearby wooden members. This indicates that the same details employed to keep wood dry might also work well to protect bales.

Portland Community College Study

During the second half of 1995, students, staff, and volunteers at Portland Community College in Portland, Oregon built a 10-foot x 12-foot unoccupied, unheated building, the north and south walls of which were outfitted with moisture sensors. The sensors are a more official version of those in the Willson house, supplied by Delmhorst. Each is a small rectangular piece of wood (like a heavy matchstick) with conductive paint on opposite sides, and wires running to the wall surface. They were checked with a Delm-

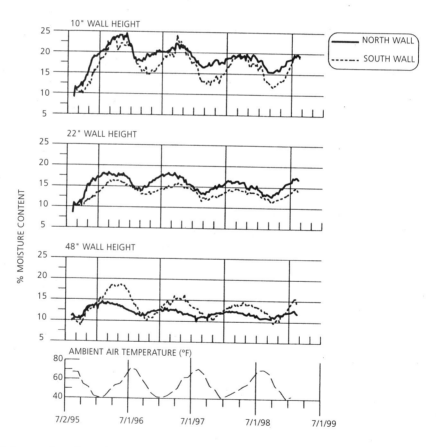

A comparison of the north and south walls of the Portland Community College test building over three years reveals a tendency for the south wall to remain drier than the north wall during times of high precipitation and also a general drying trend from the first to the third summer.

horst wood-moisture meter. Probes were placed at 10, 24, and 48 inches above the floor, and at the center and exterior (2 inches into the straw bale) of the wall. Walls received a poly air/vapor barrier on the interior and a Tyvek air/water barrier on the exterior, so as to most closely parallel mainstream construction. Additionally, the bottom bale was wrapped in 15-pound asphalt felt. The floor slab was separated from the earth by poly and rigid foam.

The patterns in this building are more or less as to be expected, though with a bit of a wrinkle on account of the wet winters and dry summers typical of the Pacific Northwest. We quote from a report of February 25, 1999, by Joanna Karl, who runs the moisture-testing portion of the project:

On both walls, the changes in moisture content (%MC) correlate with rainfall (see graphs). In the wet winter the %MC steadily increases, and in the late spring and summer it falls off.

"As one might expect, the highest moisture levels are found at the exterior base of the north wall. It is not clear whether these higher levels are due to rain hitting the wall, the stucco wicking moisture up the wall, or both. In either case, moisture at the base of the wall must make its way through the stucco, the air barrier (Tyvek), and two layers of 15-lb. felt paper [because the felt is folded all around the bottom course of bales, it is doubled toward the outside], all of which are relatively vapor permeable.

During the first year, the moisture content of the north wall remained high enough in the warm summer temperatures to be of some concern. It dropped lower the second year (summer 1997), and has dropped even lower in the summer of 1998. . . . This is despite precipitation in the first two years being greater than normal by approximately 30 percent and 50 percent, respectively.

The south wall is clearly affected by the warmth of the sun, as can be seen by the significant moisture drop in the spring/summer. The south wall never seemed to be in danger of maintaining high summer moisture levels that could lead to problems.

The three-year trend over time has been toward lower moisture content. A likely explanation for this is that building materials, such as stucco, contributed significant moisture loads in the first year. (Since only bales with 13 percent moisture content were used during construction, it seems reasonable to assume that the straw was not the moisture source.) This decreasing trend does not seem attributable to rain, especially in the first two years when rainfall increased.

While moisture measurements for the center of the walls generally follow the same trends seen in the exterior of the walls, they lag by a few months and are more attenuated. Since the ambient moisture moves from the exterior to the center of the wall [there are no interior moisture loads in this building], this would be expected. In the late spring and summer with ambient temperatures increasing and minimal rainfall, the moisture movement is reversed and begins drying—long before a significant amount of moisture from the exterior wall has penetrated to the center of the wall.[2]

This study shows that bales kept out of contact with liquid water will stay dry, even under the very damp conditions that prevail in the Pa-

2. Joanna Karl, Lis Perlman, and Bill Kownacki, "Portland Community College Straw Bale Construction Research Project," February 25, 1999.

cific Northwest. Because the building is unoccupied, its relationship to a real-world situation is somewhat limited, though it does speak well for the prospect of using straw bales for accessory buildings. The administrators of the study have since installed heating and humidification equipment, and hope, in the future, to collect data that more closely resembles the patterns of an inhabited dwelling.

CMHC Studies of Straw Bale Structures

More than any other governmental organization in the world, the Canada Mortgage and Housing Corporation has recognized the potential inherent in straw bale construction. Canada has straw and Canada has a need for warm houses, and the CMHC has been in the forefront of straw bale research and testing. CMHC has funded some structural testing of bale wall systems—of Louis Gagné's mortar system in the 1980s and Fibrehouse Ltd.'s Prestressed Nebraska system in the 1990s—and they have also taken an interest in moisture issues. Under the authority of Don Fugler, three studies have been commissioned of moisture in straw bale walls, and one of moisture in straw bale slabs.

Bob Platt's Study of Moisture Control in Stuccoed Straw Bale Walls

In early 1997, CMHC commissioned engineer Bob Platts to test three existing bale buildings in the Outaouais region of Quebec, just north of Ottawa. This was designed as a "worst case" study—areas chosen for investigation were specifically those where some problem was suspected.

The first test case, of two freestanding walls with concrete drip caps, showed the importance of a proper drip edge. Quoting from the study: "The east-facing wall—most exposed to driving rain—is sound and dry under its concrete cap with proper drip edge; while the south-facing wall . . . mostly under an amply wide drip cap but the reverse of drip edged, is badly eroded. . . . The latter wall has just been knocked down for inspection, exposing the bottom of its straw bale core . . . where it had rested on soil-cement mortar on the ground. The straw is super-saturated and rotting, fibres very weak. Moisture from below as well as above clearly exceeds the drying regime despite the generous water vapour 'breathability' of the deeply eroded soil-cement skins."[3]

The second test case was a six-year-old straw-insulated foundation wall, built with Gagné-style mortar joints, and surfaced with 1½ inches of a straw-soil-cement slurry, then finished with an approximately equal thickness of formed in-place, cementitious mortar. This assembly was built atop a thin footing of shredded straw-soil-cement mortar 6 inches below finished grade, which, in turn, sat above a rubble trench, drained to daylight. The footing was built directly atop the rubble trench, with no intervening poly or other dampproof material. According to the report, "what we have is an upside-down concrete bottle with its open mouth a few inches above water or vapor at 100 percent RH—a humidifier that's warmer than the outer zone of the bottle's interior much of the winter. And it's filled with straw." The "upside-down concrete bottle,"

---

3. Bob Platts, "Pilot Study of Moisture Control in Stuccoed Bale Walls," Report to Canada Housing and Mortgage Corporation, June 1997, p. 7.

in this case, is the foundation wall, faced and capped with relatively vapor-impermeable concrete. The "humidifier" is the trench; whether at any moment it contains liquid water or simply air that is moistened by its contact with native soil, the trench is capable of continuously supplying water vapor to the straw filling in the bottle, through the vapor-permeable soil-cement footing. In winter, the foundation wall, or at least the outer zones of the foundation wall, will be cold, on account of contact with ambient air. This means that water vapor that migrates into the foundation materials from the trench below will have ample opportunity to condense.

Here are two excerpts: "Sampling at 3 ft. above grade, into a bale which is separated from the 100 percent RH trench by at least two layers of cement-rich mortar between the bales.... Cement-rich outer finish broke away from inner slurry, so no sample obtained with straw bonded into slurry. Straw is moist and deteriorating, and is weak in tension. Moisture meter reading 37 to 42 through the bale, 38 to 43 percent MC corrected for temperature. Saturated. Smells just slightly musty."[4]

"Sampling just above grade, below the first spot. Lacy white mould indicates advanced rotting; straw very weak. MMR off scale, straw super-saturated."[5] Interestingly, in this location they managed to get a section of the shredded straw-soil-cement material off in one piece, and it contained some "bright, sound straw." Apparently, where it was in intimate contact with the soil-cement mix, the straw remained in good condition, even under these very damp circumstances. This counters a common concern about alkaline finish materials degrading straw; it also makes an interesting case for saturating the surfaces of bales with clay or some similar material.

The third case was a two-story house, also built in the Gagne style, with bales laid in a lime-rich mortar and finished with a lime-rich exterior render. The straw was found to be in fine condition at all but two locations, the first under the corner of a windowsill laid flush with the stucco surface (no dripsill) and about 1½ feet above the slab. Readings at this point were between 25 and 35 percent MC. The second trouble spot was also near the slab, in a bottom bale. In this case, a sample taken one bale higher, and above a mortar joint, was in fine condition at 15 to 17 percent MC. The study surmises that the high moisture levels in these locations results from a "slab effect" or "rising damp," that is, moisture moving by capillary action or vapor diffusion through a slab that is not isolated from the ground, and passing up into the bales. Extruded polystyrene insulation or poly sheeting below the slab (or a moisture barrier layer between bales and slab) would likely have prevented this problem.

Moisture in Straw Bale Housing, Nova Scotia[6]

This study, conducted in 1997 and 1998 by Shawna Henderson and submitted to CMHC in November 1998, aimed to test both the air tightness and wall moisture levels of four houses in Nova Scotia. Air-tightness tests were done with the Minneapolis Blower Door, and moisture tests were conducted with homemade probe-type sensors of the type described below, retrofitted into the walls.

4. Ibid., p. 9.
5. Ibid.

6. Shawna Henderson, "Moisture in Straw Bale Housing." Report to the Canada Mortgage and Housing Corporation, November, 1998.

The blower door test on these buildings indicated that, as in conventional construction, rates of air leakage depend very little on the field of the wall, and vary tremendously according to how much attention is paid to sealing seams between components and holes that pass from conditioned to unconditioned spaces. As we have assumed, plastered bale walls are quite airtight. Shawna found a substantial variation in levels of sealing at the usual locations: at the intersection of window units with rough openings; within the windows themselves; at electrical and plumbing penetrations between heated and unheated spaces; around the attic hatch; around and through ductwork, through wooden ceilings and

the intersections between ceilings and walls. The lesson here is simple: Bale-and-plaster walls are no panacea for reducing heating-energy use in a house. Attention to air sealing (and insulation levels of nonbale areas) is as important as in any building.

MOISTURE TESTS

Each house was fitted with twelve sensors, three on each of the four main walls. Positions were in the top and bottom bales in the wall, and at the midheight; all at a depth of about halfway through the thickness of the wall. To install the probes, holes were drilled in the stucco surface, and a pointed dowel was used to jab an opening into the bale. The sensor housing was then in-

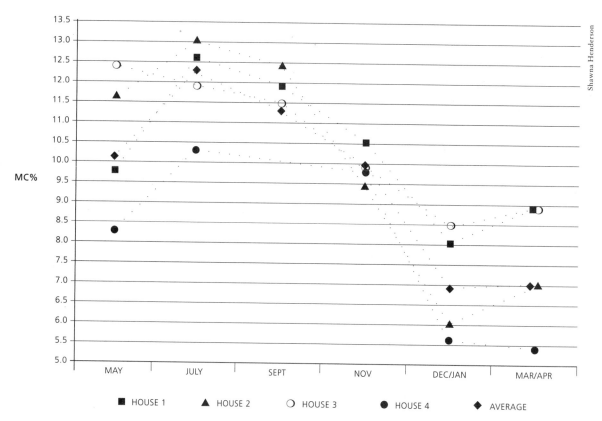

Moisture content of straw in the walls of four Nova Scotia houses.

serted into the wall, the wood block/wire sensor placed inside, and the lid snapped on. This entire assembly rested within the bale portion of the wall. The hole was then replastered, such that the ends of the wires were left exposed on the surface. Readings were taken with an Electrophysics wood moisture meter, calibrated for Eastern White Pine. At the outset, all sensors showed a moisture content of 12 percent.

Readings were taken bimonthly, for a total of six per sensor, from May 1997 through April 1998. The general trend was the same as in Kim Thompson's house. (Indeed, Kim's house was one of those studied.) Moisture levels reached their peak around July, with average readings per house ranging from 10.5 to 13 percent MC. Moisture levels then dropped through the fall, to a low of 5.5 to 8.5 percent, in December/January. In late winter and through the spring, levels would begin to rise again. At no point during the study did the midbale moisture content rise near the 20 percent level that is considered to be the threshold for biological activity (see graph). This is a strong indication that plastered bale walls can be counted on to remain dry enough to avoid rotting and maintain their high insulation value, in the damp Nova Scotia climate. As Shawna mentions in the summary, however, this study does not give any indication of what might be going on in the outer regions of the bale, where wetting from both rain and condensation are most likely to be a concern. Luckily, another CMHC study does investigate that issue.

Rob Jolly's Straw Bale Moisture Monitoring Report

Submitted to Don Fugler of CMHC in February of 2000, Rob Jolly's report includes data gathered from nine houses, between July 1997 and January 2000. This is the most extensive study to date. Eight of the houses were in the relatively dry climate of Alberta, and receive somewhat less than 20 inches of precipitation per year, on average. One house was in coastal Washington, in an area of nearly 40 inches per year. All houses are coated on their exteriors with cement stucco, some with a Tyvek moisture barrier behind the stucco, some without. Most readings were of relative humidity, some of percentage of moisture content. Interestingly, when the relative humidity levels were plotted to theoretical moisture content on a sorption graph, the resulting numbers often did not agree with the direct moisture content readings. This makes interesting fodder for a future study.

The results of the study are not surprising, but they do hold some interesting lessons. First is the fact that site and architectural features have a much greater effect on the moisture level of the walls than whether the stucco is backed by a

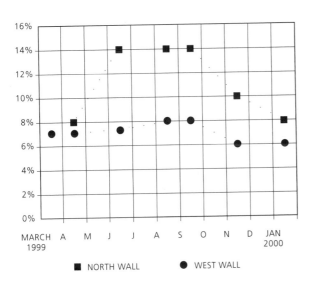

Comparison between north wall and west wall moisture content. Rob Jolly, February 2000.

moisture barrier layer. The building in the study that consistently maintained the lowest moisture levels is one in which the site is "Subject to Chinook/drying trends through winter. House is located in a slight depression and surrounded by trees. This exposure allows for significant protection from the weather."[6] At no time of the year did the relative humidity at any sensor point in this house rise above 60 percent, or moisture content above 8 percent. Additionally, differences between mid-bale and exterior bale readings were slight, usually far less than 10 percent RH.

On exposed building facades, on the other hand, sensors installed near the exterior stucco tended to show spikes after a rain, as the stucco would take on water and transmit it, in the vapor or liquid state, to the straw. In the short term, these spikes seemed to be lessened by the presence of Tyvek behind the stucco, but this did not seem to carry over into a generally reduced level of moisture near the exterior of the walls. Presumably, whatever got in could get out, with or without Tyvek. Midbale readings on exposed facades seemed to be quite a bit less volatile than exterior readings, indicating that, under normal conditions of no leaks or large cracks, rainwater was not migrating deep into the bale. Some cracks in exterior stucco on exposed walls showed signs of dark staining, however, and this appeared to be the result of water infiltrating at the crack. This tendency to crack is certainly a major drawback to cement stucco. While Rob Jolly never found anything beyond minor decomposition at the very exterior of the bale wall under these circumstances, his observations certainly reinforce concerns about cement stucco on exposed sites and facades in wetter climates.

The importance of protective architectural features was pointed out very dramatically by a house with exterior moisture content sensors in two very different walls. The first was on a north wall that has "no overhang and bathroom is not vented. Snow accumulation on exterior often higher than monitor placement. Minimal to moderate seasonal wetting of wall due to rain." This location was quite dry in winter, between 8 percent and 10 percent MC from November to April, but during the summer, even with only "minimal to moderate wetting," levels rose to 14 to 17 percent. On the adjacent west wall, which is "entirely protected by a 1.5m [5 foot] verandah," moisture content never topped 8 percent, and stayed at 6 percent for most of the year.[7]

The Jolly report also found consistently lower moisture levels on the south sides of buildings, especially during the summer months, which in all cases was the time of peak relative humidity and moisture content. "Walls with southern exposures were generally much drier than other exposures and were able to handle significantly more exterior wetting."[8]

The one wet-climate building in this study was on the coast of Washington State, in an area of nearly 40 inches of precipitation per year. This site was also significantly warmer than any of the Alberta sites, and as the interior had not yet been plastered, substantial amounts of moist interior air may have been passing through the insulation layer, and causing some condensation in winter months near the outer edge of the wall. The north side of this building is protected by a large roof overhang and has woods within 12 feet; while the south side is much less protected from precipitation, but receives far more sun-

6. Rob Jolly, "Straw Bale Moisture Monitoring Report." Canada Mortage and Housing Corporation, February, 2000, p. 35.

7. Ibid. p. 18, 22.
8. Ibid. p. 58.

light and air circulation, which presumably facilitates drying. The readings in the north wall were 14 to 17 percent MC in midsummer, dropping to 8 percent in October, and then rising again in December, presumably due both to the intimate contact between the bale wall and the interior air, and the generally wet conditions in winter in the Pacific Northwest. (See Portland Community College study, earlier in chapter.) The south wall, on the other hand, remained substantially drier through the summer, never rising above 11 percent. It only rose to 14 percent on the first of January, the last reading of the study.

One interesting case was a building that was sheathed on its exterior with plywood, with stucco applied over a layer of asphalt felt. In all locations but one, the bales, which were to the interior of the plywood, remained at a moisture content between 6 and 8 percent, throughout the year. The only wetter location was 6 inches from the ground on a wall abutted by a flower bed, which was watered consistently. Even in this case, the RH (unfortunately, a %MC meter was not installed at this location) climbed to 82 percent in mid-June, but by January had dropped back to the low 40s.

Another interesting observation was in a house where radiant heating in the slab floor extended under the bale wall. Through the heating season, a sensor installed near the floor consistently showed lower RH values than one three feet higher in the wall, a reverse of the usual pattern. Once the heat was turned off for the summer, this difference disappeared. Apparently, the added heat keeps the bottom of the walls dry, in this house.

The Jolly report demonstrates that cement stucco, in the relatively dry Alberta climate, generally seems to work with or without a backing layer, so long as reasonable attention is paid to protective site and architectural features and to details around windows, and so long as the stucco is not irrigated or allowed to run all the way to the ground. (High readings were found in the location of leaks, and also on a wall where the stucco ran to grade, and could continuously soak up water from the topsoil.) We look forward to a similarly thorough test in a wetter climate, and which covers a range of plaster finishes. In the meantime, the full text of this report is available from CMHC.

Archibio's Straw Bale Insulated Slabs

One of the details that Michel has popularized in many of the straw bale homes he has designed during the past sixteen years is the "Straw Bale Sandwich Insulated Slab," also called the "Waffle Slab" by some people (which he thinks is a misnomer because it is not exactly made in a waffle pattern); for a detailed description of the technique see "The Archibio Sandwich Slab" in chapter 5.

THE RESEARCH

In May 1999, while the Bourke house in Montreal was under construction, Michel had the opportunity to meet Don Fugler of the CMHC research division. Don has managed research projects for CMHC for fifteen years. Many are related to moisture and mold; many have dealt with the moisture problems of conventional basements and the health implications of mold growth there. Don suggested that basement or slab floors were the wrong places for straw, given the tendency for any slab in soil to face leakage and migrating moisture. Michel considered his slabs well protected by good drainage. The scene was set for a research confrontation. Meet at noon in the village square with drawn moisture monitors.

The research project, funded by CMHC, was simple: Michel was to visit several of the earlier structures, cut a hole in the floor slab, extract a sample of straw for laboratory analysis, fill the hole with new straw, and leave a moisture monitor in the cavity for long-term observations. Michel would have a tradesperson restore the floor to its previous condition, so as not to inconvenience the homeowner. The structures that he decided to visit were those examples that would most challenge the straw, in part because the newer, well-drained slabs would have been too expensive to restore and because most of those hid radiant tubes, which stood a good chance of being ruptured by drilling.

Because Michel was busy during the construction season, he deliberately chose the late fall for the tests because summer had been hot and humid and a very rainy autumn had followed. He expected that if moisture had ever had a chance to penetrate those slabs, this was the appropriate time to check. In the end, four Montreal-area sites were investigated in November 1999:

Retrieval of core samples from floor, and preparation for installing moisture monitors.

1. The 1984 swimming pool in Chateauguay.
2. A 1992 solarium in Mandeville.
3. A house built in Saint-Damien-de-Brandon in 1994, but never occupied.
4. An occupied, 1995 house in Saint-Bernard-de-Lacolle.

The Results

Of the ten samples taken, two in the occupied house were in the range of 20 to 30 percent moisture content (MC). All the others exceeded 45 percent; a 1-inch rotting bottom layer where water was found tested 275 percent, with the top part at 55 percent. The driest sample, in which virtually all of the straw was in perfect condition despite the 26 percent reading, had a ¼-bottom layer turning black and testing at 365 percent MC. Unfortunately, we did not make separate readings for the bottom and top parts of the preceding samples as we did for these two last ones. The actual readings, which range between 47 and 68 percent, would probably have shown similar differences between top and bottom, as photos and touch tests were demonstrating.

MOISTURE CONTENT OF CORE SAMPLES

PROJECT	SAMPLE NO.	DATE	% MC
The swimming pool	#1	11-02-99	46.7
	#2	11-02-99	61.4
The de Guise solarium	#1	11-02-99	49.8
	#2	11-02-99	60.0
The Saint-Damien house	#1	11-02-99	67.7
	#2	11-02-99	49.4
	#3	11-02-99	49.9
The Lacolle house	#1	11-04-99	27.7
	#2 (top)	11-04-99	54.4
	#2 (bottom)	11-04-99	275.3
	#3 (top)	11-04-99	26.4
	#3 (bottom)	11-04-99	365.3

Six of the cored samples showed the presence of puddles upon the bottom slab, a clear indication that either drainage or waterproofing of the concrete perimeter was faulty. In fact, further investigation of the sites revealed obvious signs of the faulty drainage.

All of the samples had at least some discoloration at the base of the concrete cavity; the straw was rotting from the bottom up in those where water was found. The longer the straw had been wet, the more developed was the rot. Several bales had lost volume and subsided within the concrete cavity. In the worst case, the old pool, there was nothing but a pile of black compost in the base of the cavity with a layer of darkening straw left on top. Due to the high moisture content in the pool,

The straw bale swimming pool, built in 1984.

no long-term monitoring was conducted there. In the other samples where drainage had been or was going to be corrected, and in the remaining six, new straw was put in and sensors installed. Readings will be taken periodically to monitor seasonal and long term moisture fluctuations.

On the positive side, the "plunger pile" structure still seemed solid, despite the fact that the straw often receded from the top floor. The straw bales, while in a damp environment, frequently did not show any sign of decay except at the very bottom, where it was most wet. No strong odors were encountered when the concrete floors were pierced for sampling, nor was any sign of mold developing observed (probably due to the lack of oxygen).

These results do not mean that all straw-insulated floors will rot. It is likely that a house with excellent drainage and diligent maintenance will keep straw at or below grade in a sufficiently dry state to avoid rot. However, the consistency of these field results indicate that any flaws in drainage will lead to straw rot (although this may take years), and in such case the insulating function of the straw in the floor will be degraded or lost.

The current advice on prevention of straw rot recommends that straw be kept under 20 percent MC. Rot begins typically at 20 to 22 percent MC in a normal building environment. Further monitoring will tell if this rule also applies for an oxygen-deprived space such as the sandwich slab.

In conclusion, we have a few certitudes:

1. If water gets inside the slab it will definitely damage some part of the straw. How much damage might be related to frequency of infiltration, but if water stays the process will

A residence built in 1995 in Saint-Bernard-de-Lacolle.

The de Guise solarium, built in 1992.

The Saint-Damien house, built in 1994 but never occupied.

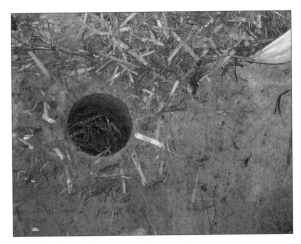

Sample from the swimming pool.

Sample from the Saint-Damien house.

Samples from the Lacolle house.

likely continue until there is no more straw, though this will probably take many years. Therefore, drainage below a straw bale slab must be impeccable, and the safest course may be for the entire thickness of the slab to lie above finished grade.

2. Deprivation of oxygen where the straw is located seems to considerably slow down the decomposition process, as demonstrated by the high moisture levels where the straw is unaltered and normally should—according to theory—be all rotting.

3. The structural capacity of the slabs (the "plunger pile system") as designed and built is never altered by any type of straw decomposition underneath.

4. In almost all cases, even with some composted matter at the bottom, the insulation value of the straw may still be sufficient, although we should conduct tests to determine the insulation value of the straw versus its moisture content.

5. At the worst, after the straw has all composted, the foundation becomes a crawlspace under a concrete slab.

A few questions:

1. Are there noticeable variations in the moisture content along with exterior and climatic changes, like in rainy seasons, frost conditions, and heating of the building? Further monitoring may give us some clues.

2. Would it solve part of the problem if a layer of draining material were to be put on the bottom slab before laying the bales? That would prevent the straw from ever being in contact with water, in which case it may well never decompose, even in infiltration conditions.

The Bourke House

Since the CMHC Straw Bale Slab Study was carried out, we have collected some readings for the Bourke slab, (see profile, following chapter 3) and will continue to monitor it until we can get a clear view of what's happening. Sensors will have to be installed in other slabs as well, if we want to have readings to compare with the Bourke project. The Bourke sensors were installed at four locations in the slab, on two different levels, one at a couple of inches from the bottom slab and one near the top of the bales. Nine months after its completion, we have three sets of readings from before the start of the heating season. At two locations, each along the perimeter walls, the moisture content at the lower level was stable at its original reading of 14 percent, while it rose to 18 percent at the top levels. The two other sensor locations, which are in the middle of the house, had risen to 18 percent at the lower levels and at one upper level, while the second at the top level had gone up to 22 percent.

We also have one set of readings taken after three months of heating, which is provided by radiant tubes buried in the top slab. Because the slab was intentionally left as permeable to vapor diffusion as possible (by finishing it with linseed oil and wax), Michel was expecting the heat to draw some of the moisture from the straw. As expected, the readings taken on February 24th show a decrease in moisture content of the straw at every sensor location. They all show a drop of 4 percent MC, to 12 percent, 14 percent, and 18 percent, respectively. It will be interesting to follow the MC fluctuations over the next twelve months.

Monitoring Your Walls

Because we don't yet really know how moisture moves within each different version of a straw bale wall, and also because code bodies need data if they are to accept bales as a standard construction material for wetter climates, it is a very good idea to plan on some level of moisture testing of all new straw bale buildings. Such monitoring will also serve as insurance against moisture damage; well-placed sensors should give evidence of any systemic problems, before they get out of control.

Probably the most important question regarding sensors is, "Are the people who will be living in the house truly interested in testing?" This will determine whether it is worth installing a full package of sensors, which have a chance at generating some real data, or whether it is best to install just a few, in potential trouble areas. Paul has found that people have a tendency not to check the sensors in their houses very often (if at all). This rather undermines their usefulness. Let's have a look at the different types of sensors.

> Well-placed sensors should give evidence of any systemic problems, before they get out of control.

Building Sensors

In do-it-yourself-scale moisture testing in bale houses, it is simplest to work with percent moisture content, rather than relative humidity. This

Wood-block remote sensor used at the Willson house.

is because RH means nothing in and of itself, but must be charted to moisture content in order to have meaning. As pointed out in Rob Jolly's report, the fact that RH is inherently a measure of the air in a bale can be deceiving; low RH at low temperatures can mean water has condensed out of the air, onto the straw. Also, at high RH levels (which indicate a theoretical problem in the straw), straw was often found to be in fine condition. So, our best bet for simple, inexpensive, relatively accurate sensors are the wood block-type of %MC sensor, read with a wood-moisture meter.

Wood-block sensors come in two types, remote and probe. A remote sensor is a small block of wood with wires attached to it. The block is buried in the wall during construction, and the wires run to a convenient location on the wall surface. This is the best type of probe to use for a house that will have multiple sensors. A probe sensor is built on the same principle, but with a

shaft that comes straight to the wall surface, at the sensor location. This is a good choice if only a few sensors are to be installed, or as a retrofit.

REMOTE SENSORS

Back in the fall of 1996, Paul presented his friend Paul Lipke, a wood science consultant, with the question of designing a simple moisture monitoring system for bale walls. Lipke explained how long-term remote sensors are set up in the wood science world: two stainless steel pins are driven into the piece to be sampled, and wires are run from those pins to a place where they can be conveniently accessed by a hand-held wood-moisture meter. In short order we were able to adapt this design to create a cheap and simple remote probe for bale walls.

The basic sensing unit is a small block of wood, cut out of ¾-inch stock and something like 1-inch square. We have used white pine because, as the most common timber tree in Massachusetts, it is abundantly available in small pieces under the workbench on every site. Moisture meters tend to be calibrated for Douglas fir, but good-quality ones come with correction charts for all of the common woods, so choice of species is not a big issue.

Each wood block is first drilled and counterbored to receive two stainless steel pan head screws, roughly a ½-inch apart. The exact distance is not significant. As the screws are turned down, the stripped end of a wire is twisted around the head of each. Telephone wire works well here, because it's cheap and comes with two or three pairs of conductors, perfect for a set of two or three probes (see below). Wire lengths vary according to where the sensor will eventually rest in the wall. As with all such work, it is best to leave extra length. Once the screws are countersunk, a dab of silicone caulk over each prevents any possible short-circuit across the face of the block. It is important that the screws be of stainless steel, otherwise the connection with the copper wire will corrode, over time.

Some concern exists about inaccuracy in the readings, on account of variations in voltage drop across different lengths of wire. While this certainly does happen to some degree, it does not seem to be statistically significant. Paul has tested sensors newly made from the same wood stock and with wires ranging in length from 10 to 70 feet; they all tested within 1 percent of each other. This seems like an acceptable margin of error.

PLACING REMOTE SENSORS

If you are using remote sensors, you are probably interested in using more than one of them. The arrangement that is likely to yield the most interesting data, in terms of actually mapping out any patterns of moisture stratification in the wall, is to follow the pattern in the Willson house, above. Taking the full height of the wall, regardless of stories, sensors are inserted below the first bale, at the midheight, and below the top bale. True fanatics might place them atop the first course of bales, as well. Sensors would be placed in triplets, near the interior, at the center, and near the exterior of the wall. Alternately, an "economy model" regime would omit the inner sensor, as this seems to be the least active location. Sensors can also be installed in the frame, periodically, if the wire contains an extra pair of conductors for this purpose.

In the ideal case, a set of these multiple sensors would be installed in each wall of the house. Further sets of three can be installed under a window or two, and at any position in the house where there is some concern about water infiltration. All of the wires can then be run to one or two junction boxes. It is crucial that all wire ends be carefully labeled! At the box, these can be fitted to strips of paired poles, available from electrical supply houses. Don't worry if the poles are too close together or too far apart for the pins of the meter, as these can be bent to accommodate your needs, without affecting the reading. It is technically possible to take readings off the ends of the wires, but this is time consuming and frustrating. It is best to hook up the poles as early as possible in the process, because until they are there, readings tend not to happen, and readings taken during plaster application can be useful for later comparisons, as the building dries.

PROBE-TYPE SENSORS

At the same time that Paul was messing around with remote sensors, the Canada Mortgage and Housing Corporation looked into how they might establish a simple, standard sensor configuration for use in homes across Canada. Don Fugler of CMHC contracted with Dr. George Vandrish of Instuscience, Inc., Ottawa, to come up with an inexpensive sensor. This design, also based on a wooden block, was printed in issue 22 of *The Last Straw,* in the spring of 1998; presumably, by now, it has been installed in quite a number of homes.

For her 1998 moisture study,[10] Shawna Henderson simplified this design somewhat. Shawna's probe is suited to retrofit situations, (this is how she used it) as well as to new construction. The probe begins with an outer housing, of 1-inch-diameter ABS pipe. This pipe is cut to a length appropriate for the probe, anywhere from 9 to

10. Shawna Henderson, "Moisture in Straw Bale Housing," 1998, Section II, p. 7.

17 inches, depending on the desired depth in the wall. A bunch of holes are drilled in the last four inches of the pipe. The first ¾ inch of the opposite end of the pipe is then jammed into a film canister, whose bottom has been removed. The joint between canister and pipe is sealed with red contractor's tape.

A small wafer of white pine (Shawna used a piece 1½ x 1 x ⅛) is then drilled with two small holes ¾ to 1 inch apart. These receive short stainless steel machine screws, and nuts. The end of a copper wire (offcuts of Romex cable work well) of appropriate length is twisted around each screw, and the nuts tightened down. Wire length is chosen such that the wood will lie just short of the drilled holes, 5 inches or so up from the end of the pipe. This keeps the wood (or more appropriately, the sensor screws) out of direct contact with the straw. It is thus not necessary to caulk over these screw connections. The opposite end of each wire is passed through a tiny hole predrilled in the cap of the film canister. It's a good idea to leave 1½ inches or so of the wires sticking out, so they will not be completely covered up by the plaster. The soft plastic of the cap should seal around the wire. The cap, wire, and block assembly is then slid into the canister and ABS pipe housing, and the cap snapped in place. The probe is now ready for laying into the wall. For retrofit situations, a hole can be drilled, the housing pushed in, and the wire and block apparatus inserted within the housing.

Michel, recognizing that the plastic housing is really not necessary in the case of new construction, came up with a variation on this idea for the Bourke house. He used a film canister with holes drilled in it to house the wood block, and simply ran the electrical cable to the surface of the wall, where the leads were stripped and allowed to pro-

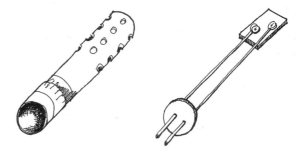

Shawna Henderson sensors.

trude from the plaster. It would be simple enough to do the same with the remote sensors described above; they could be built with electrical cable instead of the lighter-duty phone wire. It would still be necessary to countersink and caulk the connections, in this case. The idea here, whether a plastic housing or film canister or countersinking and caulk is used to do it, is to protect the sensor screws from contact with the straw. Remember, we are trying to read across the block, as wood is what the meters are calibrated for.

PLACING PROBES

Because in the case of probes there will probably be only five or ten throughout the entire building, they must be placed judiciously. It is always a good idea to monitor different parts of walls exposed to distinctive conditions. Below windows is an obvious place for probes; every house should have at least one in this location. Exterior bathroom walls make sense. The base of exterior walls is of prime importance, but so are upwind and downwind walls where patterns of wetting and drying due to wind-driven rain can vary tremendously. These locations might also show different reactions in condensation situations. Direct sun exposure on a wet wall should normally show a faster drying process, especially in combination with wind. South and north walls are exposed to such differentials in weather exposure and variation that they might eventually show very interesting readings. If problems occur, comparisons between readings can be much more useful than plain guessing, at revealing solutions.

Reading the Sensors

Wood-block moisture sensors are read, of course, with wood-moisture meters, which exist in great profusion. We have had good luck with the low-end Protimeter and the low-end Delmhorst, each of which retails for about $120 U.S. The Protimeter is especially user-friendly, as the readout is given in 1 percent intervals with light-up LEDs, at the touch of a button. These are both simple meters, which require only one hand to operate. This can be convenient in the period before the system is fully rigged out, when it may be necessary for the meter to find the ends of lots of little wires, floating in space. It helps tremendously to have two hands available for this job. The Timber Check wood-moisture meter also works well, and at $50 U.S., is much less expensive. (Available through Lee Valley Tools, 800-267-8767.) The Timber Check has two drawbacks. The first is that two hands are required to operate it. The second is that the gradations are not as fine as on the other meters. It reads by increments of 1 percent from 6 to 11, then jumps to 12 to 14, 14 to 17, and 18 to 22. This degree of accuracy is fine for casual testing, but if you are really into collecting this data, it is worth the extra expense for a more precise meter.

Obviously, the more often the sensors can be read, the better. Every hour would be nice, every five minutes better yet. Getting more realistic, if you really want to track what is going on in the walls over the year, every week would be a useful interval. Once a month, if it were done consistently, might still yield some useful data, though the numbers would be more likely to be thrown off by individual rain events. It's pretty obvious that the main determining factor will be the temperament of the person taking the readings. This will be influenced tremendously, however, by the relative ease or difficulty of the process. If the leads all go to one central box, and this is placed such that it is easy to access but the cover doesn't need to be screwed back on every time a reading is taken (inside a pantry or walk-in closet, for instance), it is possible to take a full set of thirty or forty readings in five minutes. At this rate, an interested person might take a reading daily for the first two years, eventually cutting down to weekly, once the moisture level in the building has stabilized. If, on the other hand, the testing area is a mess of coded wires, or if individual probes stick out of the wall in places that turn out to be inconvenient, such as behind the sofa, it might be hard to get excited about ever taking readings. The system should be sized to the temperament of the person who will be checking it, but regardless of size, it must be laid out so that checking is easy. Even if it's easy, many well-intentioned people won't get around to it, without the prodding of the neighborhood straw bale gadfly.

We believe all new bale houses in cold climates should have at least a few moisture sensors in the walls. Even if we could rely on the governments and universities to do the big-picture testing for us (which we can't), these agencies still could not be expected to monitor every house. For peace of mind, then, and to offer evidence as to causes, if something does go wrong, some cheap wood-block sensors should now be considered standard equipment in straw bale houses.

CHAPTER 15

BEYOND THE BALE
Traditional and Experimental Exterior Walls

AS ANYONE WHO HAS READ this far in this book must realize, straw bales have tremendous potential as a cold-climate construction material. They insulate well, they provide beautiful, thick, nontoxic walls, and they can be great fun to build with. They are not appropriate to every site, design, or temperament, however; and some people would argue that they don't have a long enough track record in wet climates, or that they don't make the most efficient use of the straw resource.

In the introduction, we mentioned Bruce Millard's prediction that "we will soon realize that straw is very valuable—it'll start going into particleboard and panelized materials; it might be mixed with wood fiber for paper production." This chapter will look at several straw-board products. Use of straw in its unbaled state need not be a technologically advanced process, however. Walls built of combinations of straw and earth predate baling and panel-making equipment by thousands of years. Any question about whether these techniques are relevant today should be answered by the fact that earth is still the most common building material on the planet, and much of this earthwork is reinforced by fiber, in the form of straw. We will explore several techniques relevant to cold-climate construction.

Light Clay

"Light clay" is an imperfect translation of the German *Leichtlehm,* or "light loam." It is a mixture of straw and clay, that is packed between forms to fill wall cavities. Though it is often known in North America by the more descriptive name of "straw-clay," "light clay" conveys a sense of the place of the material in the loam-building tradition of northern Europe.

"Loam," as defined in the German construction tradition, is a mixture of clay and sand, in any of various proportions. Wall panels of timber-framed buildings were apparently infilled with straight loam for some years before anyone came up with the idea of lightening the mix by including straw; thus the term, "light loam."

Unfortunately, "loam" does not translate well into the English, where it implies a fertile, humusy soil. Witness *Webster's*:

1. a rich soil composed of clay, sand, and some organic matter.
2. a mixture of clay, sand, and straw used in making foundry molds, plastering, etc.
3. popularly, any rich, dark soil.

Though the second definition gets across the right idea, there is no question that the common usage of the word implies a soil mix that is high in organic matter. As this partially decomposed organic material is definitely not a desirable component in a construction-grade loam mix, the tendency in North America has been to translate "loam" as "clay." This has served well enough. Most masonry techniques include a sand or stone aggregate component; what differentiates between them is the choice of binder. The unique qualities of the clay binder (as compared to lime, gypsum, or cement) are what make of loam an interesting building material.

Light clay, then, is a mixture of clay and straw. No sand is used in the mix, unless a small percentage happens to exist as an impurity in the clay. It is traditionally and typically infilled, at an 8 to 12-inch depth, as wall panels between the columns and beams of a timber-framed, joined structure. It would work equally well with any post-and-beam system, or even between the studs of a stick-framed building. Double studding, of 2-by-4s and 2-by-3s, would be appropriate in such situations. The light clay could also be made to wrap continuously around a frame, with some or all of the depth of the framing members exposed to the interior.

Mixing

The first step in the light clay process is preparation of the straw and clay mix. This is made of two components: loose straw and a clay slip. The straw is easily prepared: a bale is opened, and the flakes shaken until the material lies loose in a pile. This is typically done atop a sheet of plywood or some similar material, to conserve the clay slip. Any straw is suitable, though oat is thought to be the least ideal, as it resists the eventual compression into the wall.

The slip is prepared by mixing as for a plaster, either in a mortar mixer, or with a joint compound mixer, in a five-gallon bucket. A proper slip for this application will have the consistency of a runny pancake batter; a finger dipped into this solution will come out with its print completely coated with the slip.

The slip is then poured over the pile of straw. Two or three people work their way around the pile with pitchforks, teasing the flakes loose and

Making light clay is like dressing a salad for a small army; the goal is to get the straw minimally but completely coated with clay slip.

by-2 or 2-by-3 stock, on 2-foot centers. Each pair of verticals is framed as a Larsen Truss: the uprights held at a fixed distance apart by an occasional web of plywood or 1-by stock. The outside edges of this truss define the eventual plane of the finished wall surface. A hole is drilled in the center of each web; these holes will receive horizontal reinforcing sticks, which are laid into the wall as it goes up.

Form boards are next screwed to the outside surfaces of the trusses, and also to the main framing members, if appropriate. Form boards are either 1-by stock, or 2-foot-wide strips of ¾-inch plywood. The frame is now ready to be filled.

Filling the Walls

Straw-clay material is placed into the formwork by the large handful, and tamped into place with a blunt stick. Care must be taken to properly fill the corners and edges of the cavity; it is easy to get going too quickly, and end up leaving voids in the work. The material should be tamped only such that it is fixed firmly into position; smashing the straw down to the point where it becomes a solid mass will degrade the insulation value of the finished wall. As the height of each web is reached (every 2 feet or so) a stick is placed horizontally in the wall, with its ends stuck through the holes in the webs. These horizontal members help to rigidify the wall, and to control settling. The light-clay work then continues upward, entombing the stick in the wall.

Forms are raised in leapfrog fashion, which is to say that once two form heights have been filled, the bottom form is moved to a position above the top form. Work can proceed consistently in this manner, because the material, if properly tamped, forms an immediate set.

adding more slip as needed. The idea is to get each straw completely but minimally coated with slip. Presumably, the higher the percentage of straw in the final mix, the higher the R-value of the finished wall. This is fun work which does not require tremendous skill, just a willingness to pay attention to the proportions of the ingredients.

The finished material is typically stockpiled, for use the next day. This resting period gives the straw time to absorb some water from the slip, softening it somewhat, and making it easier to tamp into place. The partial drying of the slip also makes the material a bit less messy to work with, though this is not a technique for those who are afraid to get their hands dirty.

Preparing the Frame

The areas between structural framing members are typically furred with pairs of lightweight 2-

The light clay mix is tamped between forms with a stick.

Drying

Drying is the key to the success of any wet-fill wall system. The material must be allowed to dry completely before the onset of freezing weather. According to Frank Andreson of Proclay, Brownfield, Maine, who has many years of experience with light clay in his native Germany, a 12-inch-thick wall can be expected to take roughly twelve weeks to dry, in midsummer. This number is based on Frank's experience in Germany and New England; it is reasonable to assume that in less humid climates, drying would proceed more rapidly. A person who plans to use this system for their exterior walls, therefore, should begin framing as early in the construction season as possible, as the light clay work should be completed by sometime in June or July.

Only four lifts left to go on this wall section.

Alternately, the frame and roof might be left to overwinter, with the light clay infill proceeding the next summer.

On account of the limitations of the drying season in New England, Frank and his cohorts in Maine have embarked on some very interesting experiments in block making. The idea is that the blocks can be produced in the summer, or even in winter in a heated building, ahead of time, and then stacked into the walls during any season of the year (see below).

Insulation Value

No specific figures exist for the R-value of light clay walls. It is reasonable to assume, however, that the insulation value will be less than for bale walls of comparable thickness, on account of both the greater compaction of the straw in the light clay wall, and the addition of the clay. (Clay, in comparison to straw, is relatively conductive of heat.)

The clay does add mass to the wall, which might improve its "effective" R-value. This phenomenon is more relevant to warm climates than cold ones, but even in cold climates, it seems to help. A common parallel is found in log construction. A log wall, at an R-value of about 1 per inch, would not meet energy codes in most cold-climate jurisdictions, and would, presumably, insulate rather poorly. In tests of actual energy use, however, log walls perform far better than their R-value would indicate. What is going on here is that a thermal flywheel effect is set up within the mass of the wall, and this combines with the insulation value to hold the temperature at a steady state. The same, presumably, would happen within a light clay wall.

Finishing

One great advantage of light clay walls is that they are very easy to finish. Interiors usually receive a clay-based plaster; this can be as thin as a ¼-inch skim coat, followed by a ¹⁄₁₆-inch finish coat. Because the wall and the plaster are of the same materials, bonding is excellent. Also, because the wall is quite solid, the plaster need not be applied thick enough to form a rigid skin which can resist damage, as is the case with plaster over a more pliable bale wall. In Germany, the clay plaster is usually finished with a limewash.

A beautiful light clay wall finished with a pure clay plaster sealed with linseed oil.

1) This conventional frame is being prepared to be filled with a light clay mix. Donald Thériault's house, Lauzon, Quebec.

2) Preparing a mix of straw, clay, and water by adding the ingredients alternately in a large box.

3) Before being used the mix is stored for twenty-four hours under plastic sheeting or a tarp, allowing the straw to soften.

4) The thick mixture is packed between the studs, held in place with moveable forms. If the mix has been well-prepared, green sprouts will appear on its surface.

5) Base coats are sometimes applied with layers of jute fabric sandwiched between. The finish coat goes directly onto the previous coat of earth plaster.

In Europe, exteriors are finished with either lime render or wood siding. In this case, the trusses that formed the nailers for the slip forms are lucky enough to enjoy a permanent purpose, as nailers for the siding. The air tightness of this system is uncertain, as small gaps do tend to form in the wall as it dries. A plaster layer on each side would provide more complete air sealing than could be achieved by plastering one side only. A thin clay skim coat over the exterior would not be a bad idea before the siding is applied; if this coat were rich in milled straw, it should be possible to nail right through it.

> Straw that is coated with clay is protected from fire, insects, rodents, and all moisture sources other than standing water.

Inspired by light clay methods, Cyril Gallant of Notre-Dame-des-Anges, Quebec, renovated this house using lime and prepared hemp fibers in a pre-mixed product ordered from France. He only needed to add water before placing this mixture inside the building's original frame, which he left exposed in the European manner.

Durability

Light clay buildings that are five hundred years old are not uncommon in Germany. You've probably seen photos of them—half-timbered structures infilled with plastered wall panels. It is also possible, according to Frank Andreson, to stockpile the material during remodeling projects, so that it can be rewetted and placed back in the walls! If durability is the standard by which we judge building materials, light clay seems second only to stone.

The secret to the longevity of this material is the clay component. A straw that is coated with clay is protected from fire, insects, rodents, and all moisture sources other than standing water. Straw and clay seem to naturally reinforce each other's best qualities. Straw dramatically increases clay's tensile strength and insulation value, while clay protects straw from the armies of microbes that are forever on the prowl for their lunch.

Wood Chips and Clay

The main drawback to light clay construction is the time required to mix the material and tamp it into the walls. Though some clever folks have come up with mechanized mixing systems, the process is not one that can be adapted to work with commonly available machinery. In response to this, German clay builders have developed an interesting new system, which replaces the straw component of the mix with wood chips. Chips, the byproduct of milling operations, are very

A cage of wooden lath contains the wood chip–clay mix. Note also the light clay ceiling blocks.

After only a few minutes of mixing, Frank Andreson unloads a batch of wood chips and clay.

This doorway is flanked by light clay to the left, and wood chip–clay to the right.

available in the Maine woods and in other forested regions.[1]

The beauty of this system is that the process can be highly mechanized, while remaining at a human scale. Clay slip is produced as above; the chips are then added, by the bucketful, to the mortar mixer. After a few minutes of mixing, the material is ready to be added to the wall.

Because this wood chip and clay mix is more crumbly than the straw and clay mix, the walls are prepped in a different manner. The frame is enclosed in a cage of wooden lath (which can be attached quickly with a pneumatic stapler) and the chip-clay mix is poured in by the wheelbarrowful. Each pour is minimally tamped, just enough to settle and lock the chips into place.

This method certainly provides less insulation than a similar wall built of a straw and clay mix, but it offers the advantages of faster construction and use of a material that is ubiquitous—and therefore inexpensive—in timbered regions. If you live far from sources of straw, wood chips might be an excellent choice.

Clay and Fiber Blocks

The major limiting factor in wet-fill clay-and-fiber systems is the long drying time. In cold climates, this can translate into a significant amount of pressure to get the wall built and dried between the first and last hard-frost dates. Because

1. Most of the information in this section is gleaned from two articles by Frank Andreson: "Oh Muddy Clay, O Clayish Loam," *Joiners Quarterly,* no. 34 (spring 1997); and "Building with Wood Chip and Light Clay Infill Systems," *Joiners Quarterly,* no. 35 (fall 1997).

construction work often does not begin until late spring, an owner-builder or small crew is likely to find that by the time they have completed the foundation, framing, and roofing stages of a project, the calendar has been flipped almost to the end of summer, and not enough weeks remain for the full process of installing and drying these clay-and-fiber materials.

The simple solution to this problem is to form the material into blocks ahead of time. Blocks can be produced and dried during summer, and stacked into the walls, with a thin bead of clay mortar, at any time of the year.

German builders have long been using blocks of light clay reinforced with sticks as infill between ceiling joists or rafters. These are formed with an integral notch that allows them to hang on furring strips nailed to the side of the ceiling framing members. The blocks provide both insulation and a substrate on which to spread plaster.

Sawdust, Straw, and Wood-chip Blocks

A very promising new clay-and-fiber block has been developed by Frank Andreson and others at the Fox Maple School of Traditional Building in Brownfield, Maine. The block is composed of 4 parts coarse sawdust (the sort that is produced by a circular sawmill), 2 parts wood chips, 1 part chopped straw (4-inch lengths), and 2 parts stiff clay slip (pea-soup consistency).

The materials are combined in a mortar mixer and then packed, typically by poking with a stick, into wooden forms. The size of the finished blocks can vary: the 8 x 8 x 16 module of a concrete block is a good choice; Paul has experimented with some as small as 6 x 12 x 4. These blocks dry very quickly (two to three weeks in the humid New England climate) if protected from the nighttime dew. In a production system, the blocks could be dried under a tunnel greenhouse with its ends removed and its axis turned to catch the prevailing winds. This would speed drying time, while reducing the labor required to cover and uncover the blocks daily.

Properly made, these blocks contain a substantial volume of air, in pockets of various sizes. The three fiber elements act in a manner somewhere between an aggregate and an insulation material—their different sizes allow them to lock to-

In timbered areas, sawdust and wood chips can often be had for little more than the cost of the trucking.

The sawdust, wood chip, straw, and clay mix are stuffed into a form, and the finished block pops free!

gether into a strong block, while the unevenness of their shapes creates small voids throughout. The clay acts as both binder and sealant, filling out the walls of the individual voids such that air should not move between them.

In GreenSpace's experiments, we added a small amount of Portland cement, maybe 2 percent of the volume of the mix, to one batch of blocks. This had the expected effect of quickly stiffening the mix, so much so that we had to hurry to get all of the blocks formed before the material became too stiff to work with. However, the cement component actually slowed the rate at which the blocks ultimately dried, relative to the clay-only model. This effect was especially pronounced under the side of the tarp that leaked during a severe rainstorm; the clay-only blocks recovered within two or three days, while those with a cement component were set back nearly a week, relative to their protected neighbors.

The cement-component blocks did finish harder, which opens the possibility of a block that would work in a structural capacity. For infill blocks, however, the clay-only variety are clearly superior, and not only because of their quicker drying time. They have a pleasingly clean mineral smell, and their clay surface is smooth against the skin. If it were possible to include a scratch-and-sniff panel in this book, you would understand immediately; as it is, you will have to make a batch for yourself.

A second beauty of these clay-and-fiber blocks is that, in a timbered region with clay soils, the component materials are nearly free. The straw, oddly enough, will probably turn out to be the most expensive component. It must be included, however, if the block is not to crumble to pieces. As in earth plaster, straw provides the tensile strength in these blocks.

The real expense with these techniques is in the labor. Owner-builders with a network of friends and family who don't mind getting covered with clay slip might do well with these blocks. Also, because the skills involved are not difficult to learn, it should be possible to hire a temporary crew whose pay scale is lower than that expected by professional tradespeople.

What this technique is really waiting for, however, is a lever-arm press, which could efficiently pop out blocks. The trick here is that the large size of the wood-chip aggregate means that a block that is pressed all in one pass is likely to have voids at the corners. Also, the block does not want to be pressed too firmly; because it is expected to act as an insulation material, small voids throughout are desirable.

Papercrete Blocks

Another experimental block, which is being developed in the American Southwest but is relevant to cold-climate construction, is composed of repulped newspaper, a small amount of sand,

Cutting the partially dry papercrete slurry into blocks.

and a cement binder. This is basically the same stuff as cellulose insulation, made into block form so that it can be stacked and then plastered.

The New Mexico pioneers of the genre, Mike McCain and Sean Sands, pulp newspapers in a drum, 55 gallons or larger, outfitted with a lawn-mower blade at the bottom, like a giant blender. The paper is tossed in whole, with enough water to cover it, and blended until the fibers separate into a gelatinous mass. This rig is typically powered off the drive axle of a truck. We have found that a mortar mixer also does a passable job of pulping the paper, though the paper must first be torn into strips, which slows the process.

A surprisingly small amount of cement seems quite sufficient to stabilize these blocks. To a 6-cubic-foot mixer full of paper pulp, we added 1½ shovels of sand and roughly ½ a shovel of cement; this did the job quite adequately. We also experimented with adding a clay component to the blocks. This caused them to dry more quickly and into a harder block, but also added substantially to their weight; it seems safe to assume that the clay makes the blocks stronger, but reduces their R-value to some extent.

The two main drawbacks to papercrete blocks both involve water. In our humid climate, they took quite some time to dry. As with the sawdust/ wood chips/straw blocks mentioned above, a hoophouse with the ends removed would make the perfect drying shed. Papercrete blocks absorb water like a dry sponge; this we learned from the leaky areas of our tarps, during a rainstorm. Of course, bales do not fare very well under a leaky tarp, either, so it seems reasonable to assume that if the same precautions that are applied to a straw bale wall are applied to a wall of papercrete blocks, the blocks ought to last indefinitely.

Papercrete material can also be formed into walls, and applied to a wall surface, as an interior plaster. (In extremely dry climates, it might be possible to use it on an exterior.) Its many reinforcing fibers make for a strong plaster. Globs of papercrete, possibly mixed with coarsely chopped straw, should also make a strong, insulative fill for the hollows formed where bales butt together, in the wall.

We believe that we have barely begun to scratch the surface of what is possible with these various forms of cellulose blocks. All of the materials mentioned above—straw, wood chips, sawdust, newspapers, clay, and cement, and others such as planer shavings and lime—can be combined and recombined into blocks and poured walls, to serve any number of specific needs in buildings. All of them, if kept dry, should provide years of service.

Cob

Cob is a mixture of clay, sand, and straw, which is hand-formed into lumps (cobs), and the lumps stacked and tamped to form a wall. While variations on this technique can be found in traditional architectures from around the world, the method that has begun to come into circulation in North America (thanks largely to the work of the Cob Cottage Company of Cottage Grove, Oregon) hails across the centuries, from Great Britain.

> We believe that we have barely begun to scratch the surface of what is possible with these various forms of cellulose blocks.

If you hold in your mind an image of the archetypal English or Welsh cottage—rounded corners, thatched or slate roof, small windows, lime plasters—there is a good chance that you are imagining a building whose walls are built of cob.

The material is typically mixed by human feet (though "tractor cob" is gaining in popularity), in very rough proportions of 20 percent clay, 20 percent loose straw, and 60 percent aggregate. The aggregate should be well graded, from fine sand through small stones. The cob mix is then formed into small loaves, and laid into the wall. Each cob is stamped into place, bonding it to its neighbors. Walls vary between 1 and 3 feet of thickness, depending primarily on their height, and therefore on the weight above to be supported. Walls are built up in increments of 1 to 2 feet, which are allowed to stiffen for a week or two before further courses are added.

Cob might be the most flexible of building materials. Because it is laid up without formwork of any sort, there are few limits on the range of possible curves. The walls of most of the recent North American cob buildings are purposely constructed in convex curves, to increase their resistance to earthquakes. Such curved walls do not topple as easily as straight ones, and if they do fail, are very unlikely to fall inward.

Mixing cob with feet and a tarp.

Because it is laid up without formwork, cob offers the option of nearly unlimited curves, as at the office of the Permaculture Institute of Northern California.

Properly maintained cob is very durable. Five hundred-year-old examples exist in Britain and other parts of northern Europe. Three buildings dating from the 1830s have survived quite well in the harsher climate of upstate New York. All successful cob buildings have three things in common: wide overhangs, to protect the walls from rain; a solid (typically dry-laid stone) foundation, to elevate the walls above ground sources of moisture; and a history of owners who were consistently engaged in patient maintenance of the exterior wall surfaces. The parallels with bale construction are obvious.

Unplastered cob can make a very beautiful wall, as at this house built by Clark Sanders in East Meredith, New York.

The cob construction season is rather limited, in cold climates. All work must take place between the two hard-frost dates, and the walls will, ideally, have performed a high percentage of their drying before the first hard frost of fall. Walls must also be protected somewhat from weather during construction. Unlike with bale walls, tarps are usually sufficient for this purpose.

The major drawback to cob construction, in cold climates, is that cob has very little insulation value. In climates such as the southern British Isles or the coastal areas of Oregon, Washington, and British Columbia, where the difference between interior and exterior temperatures is not so great, it is not difficult to keep the interior surface of these massive walls at a reasonable temperature. In colder climates, however, the flow of heat through the walls to the outdoors would be substantial.

The antidote to high heating bills in cold-climate cob buildings is the fact that they are usually quite small. Cob might be the ultimate material for those who believe in quality of space over quantity, and one of the side benefits of such an approach is that small spaces, regardless of their thermal properties, simply do not require much energy input to keep warm. Even among conventional buildings, size has a greater effect than insulation levels on total energy consumption, according to *Environmental Building News.*[2]

Cob makes a superior material for interior partitions in houses whose exterior walls are of bales. Walls can be extensively curved, or they can be built in generally straight lines, and their uneven surface texture left to match that of the bale walls. Massive cob walls serve as an excellent thermal storage mechanism, and their high clay content should help to some extent in moder-

2. Alex Wilson, "Small is Beautiful: House Size, Resource Use, and the Environment," *Environmental Building News,* Vol. 8, No. 1, (January 1999): pp. 7–8.

ating moisture levels within the building. Unfortunately, they also take up a significant amount of floor space.

Traditionally, cob walls are either left unplastered, are limewashed, or are finished with a two-coat lime render. This choice is made by a combination of site and aesthetic preference: On a protected site, render or limewash is not necessary, but is often applied to achieve a cleaner look. On an exposed site, the application of a lime render (which is more water resistant than the cob itself) reduces the amount of maintenance required.

The Pailloblock System

Yvon Saucier of Lac Simon, Quebec, was inspired by the idea of stacking bales in a masonry-like pattern to build structural walls. Well aware of the multiple drawbacks of a Nebraska-style bale-wall system in a short construction season, as in his cold-climate country, he decided to upgrade regular bales into load-bearing bale blocks.

Saucier's system is simple: Bales custom-made at 14 inches thick, 16 inches long, and 18 inches wide are placed individually into a form system and a thick mortar mix made of cement, lime, and sand is poured as a coating on the lateral faces of the bale, making a 1-inch-thick mini stressed-skin panel on each side of the bale.

The 20-inch-wide finished blocks are stacked like regular concrete blocks, bonded with a layer of mortar between the skin panels. The skins are intentionally poured a little smaller in their overall plane than the cross section of the bale, which enables a perfect tight joint between the butted straw surfaces of adjacent blocks while allowing a sufficient gap for mortaring. A variety of shapes are also made, with angles for corners

In the Pailloblock system, the plastered sections of bale-blocks are mortared as in a masonry wall.

Quebec homes built with the Pailloblock system.

and sides of openings, and special features such as precast holes in the skins to accommodate electrical outlets, and predrilled holes through bale cores as forms for eventual poured-in concrete columns.

Combining the load-bearing capacities of the bales and of the stressed-skin panels in one operation makes this system very versatile compared to the usual Nebraska-style assemblies and other types of stressed-skin systems. The main advantage is the ability to prefabricate the blocks inside a heated structure, during the winter. The load-bearing walls (and roof) can then be raised very quickly, thus reducing considerably the period when bales are exposed to the weather.

Once the walls are raised, they can be skim-coated for a nicer uniform finish, but they also can be left untouched for a long period of time because no straw is visible. And for those who like the Middle Ages revival look, the walls have a castle-like appearance when they are left untreated; special textures and colors could also be made at the pouring phase.

Though Pailloblocs are currently custom-made on a small scale, with some testing and standardization their production could easily be transformed into a very refined industrialized system (see photos).

The Baleblock System

Architect Erem Birkani and engineer Robert West of Celestial Construction of Santa Fe, New Mexico, have developed their own approach to non-load-bearing wall assemblies. In the Baleblock system, holes are drilled through bale cores at predetermined distances; the bales are then stacked with these holes aligned vertically, creating form-work for concrete columns inside the bales. Pinning rods and the need for attachment devices between bales and frame are thus eliminated. Some of these inner voids can also be used for electrical wiring or as conduits for plumbing. The main drawback to this system, of course, is that the bales still need to be stacked before the roof can go on.

Bioblock

Research on baling equipment has led Fibrehouse to work with a very interesting group that can produce better building blocks

Yvon Saucier

Pailloblock walls ready for roof assembly. Note bond beam and opening jambs with thermal breaks.

from organic fibers.[3] They use a specially designed hydraulic-ram baler that can compact any kind of fiber into a supertight building block. These blocks are called Bioblock and the company producing them, not en masse as of yet, is called Internatural Incorporated. They are based in Wakefield, Quebec. So far, blocks have been produced from straw and shredded bark wood wastes. These blocks do not need further compressing and are dry stacked in the same way as straw bales. However, they are far more sturdy and dimensionally stable than straw bales. They require no doweling and only the corners require bracing during construction.

3. Description provided by Linda Chapman, Fibrehouse Ltd.

Bioblock demonstration home, without final stucco coating or windows. Near Wakefield, Quebec.

Bioblock baler with a typical Bioblock in front.

The Bioblocks are encased in plastic mesh and need no additional meshing before stucco application. They are stacked and mortared along their edges only, not through the wall, as they are laid up into place. Bioblocks can be created from any dry cellulose fiber. They are currently being produced as 12 x 12 x 24-inch blocks. These 12-inch walls require less lumber in the door and window bucks and use the same slim top plate Linda Chapman and her associates developed for the Prestressed Nebraska wall system. So far, one demonstration house has been built with the blocks, and work continues on, refining the block maker to handle mass production.

Bioblocks have been structurally tested and are exceedingly strong. The wall system behaves like a stressed-skin structure, wherein the stucco skins end up taking all the final loads. The wood waste block has been analyzed (but not lab tested) for thermal values and is estimated to be in the R-20 range. This system has the promise of yet another good alternative construction material made from "waste" products, entailing no pollution in its manufacture and placing lower burdens on our resource systems.

The Nova Scotia Load-Bearing Style

The Nova Scotia system designed and used by David Cameron and Nancy Sherwood for their house is a hybrid of the Nebraska and the Louis Gagné systems. It achieves the structural strength of the Gagné system with less labor intensity. While the Gagné system is a latticework of horizontal concrete beams and vertical concrete columns poured between rows and stacks of bales, in the Cameron system bales are dry stacked vertically without mortared joints but still with 3-inch-thick concrete columns tamped between the stacks. Double horizontal runs of rebar are laid at each layer of bales to tie all the concrete verticals together. The steel rods provide horizontal shear resistance while the vertical concrete columns become load-bearing members. Cameron claims a time savings over the Gagné system of one-third to one-half, and a substantial reduction in the amount of concrete required.

Composite Cellulose-Fiber and Expansive Clay

Lance Durand of International Resource Institute in Fairfield, Iowa, has been experimenting with composite natural materials since 1992.[4] One of the primary design goals of the Institute is taking a biomimetic approach to improving the performance of straw bale wall and roof systems by incorporating the superior performance characteristics of nature's architecture. (Biomim-

The Cameron/Sherwood house, built with 3-inch-thick concrete columns tamped between stacks of bales, with horizontal runs of rebar for lateral strength.

etics is the science of emulating nature.) Thus their designs are based on old techniques, revisited.

Their first reported attempt was the creation of structural wall coatings of fiber-impregnated clay, made from locally derived soils and macroscopic and microscopic cellulose fibers. Like the builders of the Middle and Far East have been doing for centuries, they added cow dung in their clay mix to improve workability, tensional strength, water resistance, softness, and sound absorption. Unlike the old builders who used to let the cow dung-and-clay mix ferment for about a week, they did not let the fermentation take place. According to Lance, plastering their vegetal-pole (made of either bamboo, kenaf, or willow) reinforced straw bale walls with 2 to 4 inches of these coatings makes a strong, durable, structural composite "sandwich" wall of all-natural building materials.

The institute has also used the same set of materials for foundations, which are waterproofed by a base layer of gravel, perimeter French drains, and coatings of beeswax, waterglass, and bentonite clay.

4. This section is a composite of excerpts from the following sources: Lance Durand, "Fibre-Impregnated Clay Plaster," *The Last Straw,* no.9 (spring 1995):7; and Durand, "Composite Cellulose-Fiber and Expansive Clay," *The Last Straw,* no.17 (winter 1997): pp. 6–7.

Based on these early experiments, they pursued their research to develop a composite material made exclusively of cellulose fiber and expansive clays such as bentonite and hectorite. Tests run on extruded samples of their composite mix approximated the same modulus of rupture as construction lumber.

Those tests led them to use the composite for virtually every part of a building: from the foundation to structural wall components, structural skins, millwork, and cabinetry. For foundations they start with a cellulose-clay composite mix and add sand and aggregate to form a pourable "concretelike" footing material. Currently, for the walls and roof they use a thick pastelike mixture of the cellulose-clay material to literally glue straw bales together to form a catenary dome.

The wall finish is a high-performance structural skin applied as a three-coat composite in the following fashion: The first coat is of the thick paste-like mix that was used to glue the straw bales together. It is applied to both the inside and outside of the exterior walls. While it is still wet they apply a long-straw fill mix made of the same cellulose-clay composite material cut about six times with water and with a relatively high percentage of long straw fibers mixed in. That is used to fill and level any unevenness and to provide good cross-bale surface bonding. Once this coat dries they apply a mixture of the same cellulose-clay composite cut about three times with water and with short, 1- to 3-inch straw mixed in. This is used as exterior and interior putty coats to provide a smooth, tight finish.

They have also experimented with variations of the three-coat process to build cabinets, shelves, and flooring, all with success.

Some disadvantages have still to be worked on before the system is considered failure-proof.

These are mostly related to moisture problems. Like any other clay-based plaster, their walls need to be well protected from rain and from ground moisture sources. They have been working on linseed oil–chalk permanent waterproof coatings with highly promising results, and have also experimented with gypsum added to their mix to make the plaster dry faster for cold- and damp-climate applications.

Manufactured Straw Boards

At the opposite end of the simplicity spectrum from straw-clay composites, we find a range of panelized, straw-board products. Straw is now being reconstituted as particleboard, as freestanding panels for interior partition walls, and, in combination with oriented strand board, as structural, stressed-skin panels.

Though straw boards are only beginning to catch on in North America, they do have a history in Europe. In the late 1920s in France and Switzerland, a pressed-straw board, held together by wires, was sold under the name of "Solomite." It was typically affixed over a load-bearing structure, as an exterior insulation material and plaster substrate. The "Stramit" brand of interior partition wall has been in use for nearly fifty years in Britain; it forms the interior partitions of 300,000 homes.

Easiboard/Easiwall

Easiboard/Easiwall is a Stramit-type straw board, used primarily for interior partition walls and ceilings. The North American producer, Pierce International, should be in production in Colfax, Washington, by the time this book is published. Other production sites are planned for the near future.

The Stramit process creates a pressed-straw panel that contains no glue, except that which is used to adhere the paper facing. The boards are bound by compounds exuded from the straw under heat and pressure.

Easiwall partitions and ceilings offer better fire protection and substantially better sound insulation than stud-and-drywall systems. Because the straw boards are solid, artwork and interior decorations can be hung from any point on the wall. Installed costs should be competitive with conventional stud-and-drywall systems; the material cost is somewhat higher, but the manufacturer claims a labor savings of 50 percent to create finished partition walls.

Easiwall panels also have something of an R-value, which makes them an interesting option as an interior sheathing to a stud frame. Framing cavities can be filled with additional insulation, as in conventional construction. The manufacturer claims an R-value of 12 for a standard 2¼-inch panel, which is difficult to believe, considering the documented R-value of Agriboard, whose core is a similar straw board (see below). Even an R-value of only 5 or 6, however, would add substantially to the performance of a 2-by-4 or 2-by-6 framed and insulated wall.

The office at the Fox Maple School of Traditional Building is insulated with Stramit-type panels (although they were not produced by Pierce, nor sold under the Easiwall/Easiboard trade name). The walls were furred out such that a secondary layer of insulation could be blown in behind the panels, if necessary. Through two winters, the staff at Fox Maple reports a comfortable building at a moderate level of fuel usage, without the supplementary insulation.

At first glance, Easiwall panels, like the others mentioned here, would seem a logical interior partition system for buildings whose exterior walls are made of straw bales. The problem is that the two materials possess such different surface qualities that they really don't seem to be compatible at all. It's like the intersection between a bale wall and a sheetrock wall: The contrast between the wavy and straight can be quite stark and unpleasant. Since Easiwall partitions are even straighter than drywall partitions, this problem is magnified with the Easiwall panels. If only these folks would be less careful in their production process, we might have a perfect match! Those adventurous souls who do wish to try their hand at meshing these two very different materials might try lathing out the resulting interior corners. A coat of plaster can then be skimmed over the Easiwall and into the bale wall, to create something of a uniform appearance.

Agriboard Structural Panels[5]

The Agriboard panel is an interesting hybrid of straw and wood fibers. It consists of a Stramit-like straw core faced on both sides with oriented strand board, the whole of which forms a stressed-skin panel. Like their foam-core cousins, Agriboard panels are engineered to bear substantial compressive loads and to span impressive distances, in both the vertical and horizontal planes.

Agriboard offers whole-house kits, whose walls, roof, and floors are composed of panels, augmented by occasional structural elements, such as carrying beams and collar ties. Panels have been used in the roofing system of bale-walled houses; they have also been hung from

5. As of this printing, Agriboard Industries has ceased operations, citing lack of operating capital. It is reasonable to assume, however, that this product will be back, under some name, before long. We have thus chosen to include this description.

steel frames, sheathing commercial buildings of up to three stories.

Panels are factory-cut to the specifications of each individual project. According to the company literature, they are available in sizes up to 9 feet high and 24 feet wide, and in thicknesses from 4⅜ inches to 7⅞ inches. The panels are very heavy; a crane is required for their installation. A complete shell is assembled on site in one or two days, depending on size and complexity of the building.

A 7⅞-inch panel, which has seven inches of compressed straw as its core, has a rated R-value of 17.79, according to tests at Oak Ridge National Laboratory. The fact that the wall has very few thermal breaks means that it should perform at least as well as a standard 2-by-6 framed wall with R-19 cavity-fill insulation. In hot climates, the great mass of the panel boosts the effective R-value as high as 25.44; this mass effect would be less in cold climates, but it would still contribute somewhat to the ability of an Agriboard building to hold in heat. Needless to say, an insulation level of 18 or so is not sufficient for a roof, in cold-climate construction, and would need to be boosted with something else to get at least to R-30.

A visit to an Agriboard house under construction in Fairfield, Iowa, revealed impressively solid walls. Their incredible flatness made the place feel like a drywall contractor's dream house. Agriboard claims that their product can save 2 to 4 percent in construction costs, over an equivalent stick-built house. The material also has received a fire rating of 1.5 and 2 hours (depending on thickness) and has effective sound-deadening qualities.

Straw-Based Particleboard

Two types of straw-based particleboard are currently available.

ISOBORD

Isobord is a direct replacement for wood-based particleboard. It is made of wheat straw and MDI resin, which contains no formaldehyde. Isobord is price competitive with similar grades of wood-based particleboard, all of which are produced with urea-formaldehyde resins. The manufacturer claims added benefits of lighter weight, greater moisture resistance, and superior machining qualities. According to a Massachusetts wholesaler, customers have been very happy with the product. Isobord is manufactured in Manitoba, Canada. In the summer of 1999, Isobord panels were available in 4-foot by 8-foot size and thicknesses of either ⅝ inches, ¹¹/₁₆ inches, or ¾ inches.

PRIMEBOARD

PrimeBoard is very similar to Isobord. It is available in three grades and a variety of thicknesses, from ⅜ to ¾ of an inch in standard 4-by-8-foot to 4-by-10-foot sizes. Thicknesses to 1¼ inches are available in custom sizes as large as 4-by-18 feet. PrimeBoard is produced in North Dakota, and is currently available in the western half of the United States, where it is cost competitive with similar wood-based particleboards.

Clearly, straw has a future in construction, and in forms other than bales. These various techniques and materials open many options to the skilled designer, options that make ecological sense!

The Kirk/Starbuck Retrofit

NEW HAMPSHIRE

by Paul Lacinski

Pat Kirk and Dick Starbuck's retreat house is an unlikely building. Comfortable in its site but very far from its roots, its seems to hover, pleasantly, somewhere between upland New Hampshire and rural Japan. The site is 100 percent Granite State: boulders, sand, moss, white pine and red maple, mountain laurel. The building also begins locally, with its granite footstones and pine-decked porches. The protruding porch roof rests on New Hampshire pine posts, protecting the clay-plastered walls from the ornery Yankee weather. Even the main roof, the huge and eminently Japanese cedar roof, is supported on a structure of solid New Hampshire pine, much of it cut from the site or remilled from the timbers of an older barn. Once you step inside, however, the rhythm of structure and squarish wall panels, softened by an occasional round log and ceilings of hand-planed yellow cedar, transports you around the globe and across any number of centuries, into a space that could never have grown from the rocky New England soil. The bales in the walls are an afterthought.

Pat Kirk met Yann Giguere at a natural building workshop taught by Robert LaPorte in Fairfield, Iowa, in the summer of 1995. Between pitching and pounding forkfuls of light clay, they discovered a mutual interest in the traditional architecture of rural Japan. This was a fortuitous meeting. Pat and Dick Starbuck were considering what to build on their land in the Lakes Region of New Hampshire, while Yann is a furniture maker, skilled in the use of traditional Japanese tools and joinery, who had begun to turn his attention to buildings. The eventual design was something of a hybrid. It called for a very traditional Japanese structure, with the wood to be milled on site and hand planed. The wall panels, rather than the 3 to 4 inches of solid clay that is typical of these houses in Japan, would be 12 inches of light clay. This wall system would fit within the structural constraints of the Japanese timber framing-tradition, while providing quite a bit more insulation than the original.

Yann assembled a team of carpenter/cabinetmakers, consisting primarily of himself, Attila Gardo, and David Sibos. Over the next two years, they (and many other friends who worked on specific components of the project) worked up the rough lumber and logs into the most impeccably joined frame that I have ever seen. A person wielding a credit card would become intimate with most of the structure before finding a joint where they could lodge it. A person wielding a trowel (this part I know from personal experience) would be under strict instructions to limit the effusiveness with which they deliver their mud, lest it miss its mark and stain the silky finish of the hand-planed wood.

Products of an imperfect species, all buildings have their difficulties. In this case, the house demonstrates the conflict between its parentage

Before the retrofit work began, in some places mushrooms were growing out of the silt and straw walls, staining the woodwork.

and its circumstances, an issue that the owners and builders grappled with all through the process. They wanted to faithfully re-create the Japanese archetype, yet they meant to do it halfway around the world, on a site whose climate and geology were very different from those that had shaped the original. This was also not to be a museum piece. Though their patterns of living vary a bit from those of a Japanese peasant family from a century ago, Pat and Dick fully intended to use the building.

This conflict shows up in some major features of the house, where it was usually solved with grace. Take the roof, for instance. In the great majority of traditional cases, the roof on such a building would be made of thatch. Considering the skills and materials available, however, thatch was not a practical option, so the builders borrowed a Japanese shingling technique, which seems aptly suited to the New Hampshire climate. The roof is clad with five layers of cedar shingles—scaled down from the traditional seven—and nailed off with somewhere upward of 10,000 nails. (These are nearly all the nails in the building.) When rain hits this roof, it swells and locks together, forming a surface that will probably still be keeping the water off the heads of Pat and Dick's great-grandchildren.

There is also the matter of the chimney. The traditional buildings did not have them; smoke would make its way from the open hearth up through the structure and the thatch, acting as a natural insecticide. As this secondary function of the fire is neither necessary nor desirable in this case, the building was equipped with a masonry oven, with a cooktop and a chimney. While he clearly recognizes its practicality, Yann is visibly pained by the sight of the chimney, even topped, as it is, by his beautifully carved granite capstone.

The windows embody a more difficult compromise. They are double-pane, low-e glass in wooden sliders on wooden tracks, fitted about as well as is humanly possible. Yann glows faintly as he slides them back and forth, expressing his craftsman's love for a purely wooden joint. Glass was not a part of the traditional Japanese materials kit, but rice paper would obviously not have been the best choice for the New Hampshire climate. Neither would it provide enough light or connection to the outdoors to suit 20th-century American sensibilities. Gas-

Plaster drying on the interior gable.

kets were not a part of the tradition either, and the line of deviation was drawn between them and the rice paper. They are very beautiful windows, which leak air like an old New Hampshire double-hung.

And the walls? The thin but high-mass, zero-R-value walls typical of the traditional Japanese construction were clearly not suited to the New Hampshire climate, especially for a building that would be mostly used on weekends. By the time the walls began to come up to temperature, it would be time to go home. Light clay was chosen for its similarity to the original system; also for its higher insulation value and strong historical track record. This relatively massive system may not have been the very best choice for this situation, but installed correctly, it would have been serviceable enough. Unfortunately, it was not installed correctly.

There is a danger in borrowing building systems from around the world and applying them in places where the relevant expertise is not lo-

cally available. (This is a hazard for straw bale construction, as the techniques for working with the best plaster materials are not widely known.) Materials that are not manufactured for use in the building industry can be highly variable, and to select and apply them well, a practitioner must be familiar with their various properties. These very talented builders learned this the hard way. Concerned as they were with finding a local source for the wall materials, they allowed themselves to believe that the Granite State would yield a suitable clay; when it did not, they settled for some available silt, assuming, since it is like clay, that it would be good enough to do the job.

Silt has two properties that separate it from clay (see "Clay vs. Silt," in chapter 12). First, the particles are round, instead of flat, which means that they do not bind well. Second, silt does not dry nearly as quickly as clay, which is to say that its tendency to hold on to moisture is much greater. So, as the builders packed the silt-straw mixture into the wall forms, they found that they had to use more of the material then they had expected, to achieve proper cohesion. Because the binder is applied as a slip, this also meant more water. The slow drying rate of the silt, combined with the fact that the work was done in December (it shortly froze solid), made for a less than ideal set of conditions.

When Frank Andreson (a German clay builder who knows his materials quite well) came to apply the plaster the following spring, he had no choice but to deliver some very bad news—the walls were basically standing compost. While the straw was not wholly degraded, the decomposition process had certainly begun. The fibrous structure was breaking down, and mushrooms were growing out of the walls in places and staining the woodwork.

When I got a call asking whether it might be possible to insert 18-inch-wide bales within a 12-inch-thick wall designed for a wet-fill system, I was not at all sure that it sounded like a good idea. Obviously the bales would need to be modified substantially, which contradicted all of my assumptions about how to use them well. Because the framing was clearly detailed for a loose-fill wall system, it was possible that the walls should be redone in light clay, only properly this time. Yann, however, was not willing to subject the wooden frame to another large moisture load. The plan we evolved for retrofitting the walls enlarged my sense of what is possible with bales.

Each bale was sawn in half, lengthwise, yielding two 9-inch-thick, one-string bales. Yann called them "suitcases," because this is just what they looked like. We used a chain saw, though if one had been available to come to the site, a band saw wood mill would have been a better choice. Additionally, most bales required further notching, so that they could fit between the multiple horizontal braces that take the place of diagonal braces in Japanese timber frames. Although no problem in the original loose-fill design, these braces kept the chain saw busy during the bale retrofit. They also served as an attachment point for the otherwise wobbly 9-inch-thick by 14-inch-high bales, a great benefit. The bales were variously sewed and pinned into place; ultimately forming a solid wall. All

told, the process actually took less time than I had anticipated, a bit under two weeks for three people.

The clay plaster adhered very nicely to the cut faces of the bales, though there were places where it was built out as much as 3 inches, in order to bring each wall panel to the desired plane. (The Steens' clay-straw plaster would have been tremendously useful, here; see "Clay and Straw Plaster," chapter 12.) Thanks to the wooded site and wrap-around verandah, the exterior clay plaster required no limewash or other protective coating, except on the one bump-out, where Justin Idoine, who led the plaster work, painted on several coats of linseed oil; this has worked very well.

As Pat and Dick's gardens grow up around it, the building seems to be settling deeper into its site. The finished walls are indistinguishable from their light-clay counterparts, and the bales are comfortably protected behind the plaster finish. That bales can be used effectively in a building that was so obviously not designed for them is a testament to their versatility, and also to the wide range of possibilities inherent in the combination of clay and straw.

The finished exterior.

RESOURCES

Organizations

Archibio
6282 de Saint-Vallier
Montreal, Quebec H2S 2P5
Canada
(514) 271-8684/fax (514) 271-3242
www.archibio.qc.ca

Canada Mortgage and Housing Corporation
National Office
700 Montreal Road
Ottawa, Ontario K1A 0P7
Canada
www.cmhc-schl.gc.ca/cmhc.html

The Canelo Project
Bill and Athena Steen
HC1, Box 324
Elgin, AZ 85611
(520) 455-5548 / fax (520) 455-9360
e-mail: absteen@dakotacom.net
www.caneloproject.com

Chelsea Green Publishing Company
205 Gates-Briggs Building
Post Office Box 428
White River Junction, VT 05001
(800) 639-4099
www.chelseagreen.com

CREST's Straw-bale Listserv
To subscribe, send a message with *subscribe strawbale* in the subject line to:
majordomo@crest.org
For archives of past discussions, see:
http://solstice.crest.org/efficiency/strawbale-list-archive/index.html

Development Center for Appropriate Technology (DCAT)
Post Office Box 27513
Tucson, AZ 85726-7513
(520) 624-6628 / fax (520) 798-3701
e-mail: info@dcat.com
www.dcat.com

GreenSpace Collaborative
PO Box 107
Ashfield, MA 01330
(413) 628-3800

The Last Straw Journal
HC 66, Box 119
Hillsboro, NM 88042
www.strawhomes.com

Out On Bale, (un)Ltd.
Matts Myhrman and Judy Knox
1039 E. Linden Street
Tucson, AZ 85719

Recommended Reading

Alexander, Christopher, et al. *A Pattern Language: Towns, Buildings, Construction.* New York: Oxford University Press, 1977.

Baggs, Sydney and Joan Baggs. *The Healthy House: Creating a Safe, Healthy and Environmentally Friendly Home.* London: Thames and Hudson, 1996.

Benson, Tedd, with James Gruber. *Building the Timber Frame House: The Revival of a Forgotten Craft.* New York: Charles Scribner's Sons, 1980.

Bergeron, Michel, with Clôde de Guise. *Maisons Originales Autoconstruites du Québec: Principes et Techniques d'Autoconstruction Écologique.* Mandeville, Québec: Édition l'Oiseau Moqueur, 1989.

Clark, Peter, with Judy Landfield. *Natural Energy Workbook # 2.* Berkeley, Calif.: Visual Purple, 1976.

Clark, Sam. *The Real Goods Independent Builder.* White River Junction, Vt.: Chelsea Green, 1996.

CRATerre, with P. Doat, A. Hays, H. Houben, S. Matuk, and F. Vitoux. *Construire en Terre.* Paris: Éditions Alternative et Parallèles / Collection AnArchitecture, 1979.

CRATerre, with Hugo Houben and Hubert Guillaud. *Traité de Construction en Terre.* Marseille: Éditions Parenthèses, 1989.

Day, Christopher. *Places of the Soul: Architecture and Environmental Design as a Healing Art.* Northamptonshire, England: The Aquarian Press, 1990.

de Guise, Clôde. *Vers un Habitat Écologique: Ce qu'il faut savoir avant d'entreprendre la construction de sa maison.* Boucherville, Québec: Éditions de Mortagne, 1992.

Easton, David. *The Rammed Earth House.* White River Junction, Vt: Chelsea Green, 1996.

École d'Avignon. *Techniques et Pratiques de la Chaux.* Paris: Éditions Eyrolles, 1995.

Elliott, Stewart, and Eugene Wallas. *The Timber Framing Book.* Kittery Point, Mass.: Housesmiths Press, 1977.

Greenfield, Steven J., and C. K. Shen. *Foundations in Problem Soils: a Guide to Lightly Loaded Foundation Construction for Challenging Soil and Site Conditions.* Englewood Cliffs, NJ: Prentice Hall, 1992.

Holmes, Stafford, and Michael Wingate. *Building with Lime: A Practical Introduction.* London: Intermediate Technology Publications, 1997.

Jeannet, Jacky, Gérard Pollet, and Pascal Scarato. *Le Pisé: Patrimoine, Restauration, Technique d'avenir.* Les Cahiers de construction traditionnelle — Volume A. Nonette, France: Éditions CRÉER, 1985.

Kahn, Lloyd. *Habitats: Constructions traditionnelles et marginales.* Paris: Éditions Alternative et Parallèles, 1973.

Kern, Barbara, Ken Kern, Jane Mullan, and Otis Mullan. *The Earth Sheltered Owner-Built Home.* North Fork, Calif.: Mullein Press/Owner-Builder Publications, 1982.

Kern, Ken. *The Owner-Built Home: A How-to-do-it Book.* New York: Charles Scribner's Sons, 1972.

King, Bruce. *Buildings of Earth and Straw: Structural Design for Rammed Earth and Straw-Bale Architecture.* Sausalito, Calif.: Ecological Design Press, 1996.

Leclair, Kim, and David Rousseau. *Environmental by Design: A Sourcebook of Environmentally Aware Choices.* Vancouver, B.C.: Hartley & Marks, Ltd., 1992.

Lemieux, Germain. *La Vie Paysanne, 1860–1900.* Sudbury, Ontario: Éditions Prise de Paroles, 1982.

Lstiburek, Joseph and John Carmody. *Moisture Control Handbook: Principles and Practices for Residential and Small Commercial Buildings.* New York: John Wiley & Sons, 1996.

Lyle, David. *The Book of Masonry Stoves: Rediscovering an Old Way of Warming.* White River Junction, Vt.: Chelsea Green, 1998.

Mason Hunter, Linda. *The Healthy Home: An Attic-to-Basement Guide to Toxin-Free Living.* New York: Pocket Books, 1989.

Morse, Edward S. *Japanese Homes and their Surroundings.* New York: Dover Publications, 1961.

Myrhman, Matts, and S.O. MacDonald. *Build it with Bales: A Step-by-Step Guide to Straw-Bale Construction.* Tucson, Ariz.: Out On Bale, 1997.

Ramsey, Charles George. *Architectural Graphic Standards*, Ninth Edition. John Ray Hoke, editor in chief. New York: John Wiley & Sons, 1998.

Roberts, Wayne and Susan Brandum. *Get A Life! How To Make A Good Buck, Dance Around The Dinosaurs And Save The World While You're At It.* Toronto: Get A Life Publishing, 1995.

Rural Development Commission. *The Thatcher's Craft.* London: Rural Development Commission, 1960.

Schofield, Jane. *Lime in Building*: A Practical Guide. Crediton, Devon: Black Dog Press, 1994.

Smith, Michael G. *The Cobber's Companion: How to Build your Own Earthen Home.* Cottage Grove, Oreg.: The Cob Cottage Company, 1998.

Steen, Athena Swentzell, Bill Steen, and David Bainbridge, with David Eisenberg. *The Straw Bale House.* White River Junction, Vt.: Chelsea Green, 1994.

Steen, Bill, and Athena Swentzell Steen. *Earthen Floors: A Canelo Project Booklet.* Elgin, Ariz.: The Canelo Project. n.d.

Tanguay, François. *Petit Manuel de l'Habitat Bioclimatique.* Boucherville, Québec: Le Mont Vert, Les Éditions de Mortagne, 1988.

Van Lengen, Johan. *Manual del Arquitecto Descalzo: Como construir casas y otros edificios.* Mexico: Editorial Concepto, 1980.

Watson, Donald and Roger Camous. *L'Habitat Bioclimatique: De la conception à la construction.* Montreal: L'Étincelle, 1983.

INDEX

118–20, 154–55
preparing, 280–89
processing raw material for, 270–71
professionals, use of, 270
samples, 286–87
semistructural application of, 266–68
silt compared, 270, 273, 357
site, effect of, 217, 272–73
straw daubs to control erosion,
  269–70
tests for pure and subsoil sources of,
  275–80
types of clay, 273–74
virgin clay, sources and testing of,
  275–80
weather exposure, effect of, 268–70,
  272–73
earthquakes. *See* seismic loads
Easiboard/Easiwall, 352–53
Echelson, Duncan, 236–37
economy of bale use. *See* costs
Edminster, Ann, 22
Eisenberg, David, 60, 120
electrical installations, 68
  in Baleblock system, 349
  in basement, 88
  conduits, channels for, 108
  fire risks during construction, 207
  outlets, niches for, 229
  wiring chases, 102–103
elevated floors, 308–109
elevation of bales from ground, 47, 50–
  51, 102–103. *See also* toe-ups
  basements, use of, 86–88
  pole framing, 112
energy, embodied
  cement stucco, 235
  clay, 235, 267
  concrete, 100, 127
  lime, 235, 249
  straw and cellulose, 22
Energysmiths
energy use, reduction of, ix
engineers. *See* professionals
environmental benefits, 4, 9–10, 23
Environmental Building News, 100
exterior finishes, 42–44, 72. *See also*
  finishes

inner finish, relationship with, 44,
  217–18, 248, 273
maintenance of, 48–49
vapor diffusion capacity, 43
exterior pinning of bales, 133–34

F
fans, 30–32, 36–37
farmers, bales purchased from, 76–79
Faswall blocks, 94, 102
Fibrehouse Ltd., 116–17, 142, 231, 349
fill coat, 222–23
Fine Homebuilding, 16
finish coat, 241
finishes, ix, 213–30. *See also* floor finishes; paints; plaster
  aesthetic concerns, 216
  cellulose-fiber and expansive clay
    composite, 352
  colors, 230
  light clay construction, 340–41
  oil-based, 72
  relationship between inner and
    outer finish, 44, 217–18, 248,
    273
  samples, 208, 229–30, 286–87
  site concerns, 217
  structural concerns, 216–17
finish work
  costs, 65, 229
  owners/volunteers, completion by,
    68
fire resistance, 13, 170, 206
fire risks
  during construction, 185, 206–207
  thatch roofs, 194–95
Fisk, Pliny, III, 10, 23
flashing, ix, 47, 51–52, 140–42
  intersecting roofs, 50
  lime plaster into, 257–58
flax, 77
floating frame structure, 178–79
floor finishes, 304–307
  Archibio sandwich slab, 104
  concrete slabs, 305–307
  conventional flooring, 305
  dry shake slab coloring, 306–307
  stains, concrete floors, 306

floors
  bales, elevation of, 88
  basement, 92–93
  cantilevered, 159
  color of, 202
  dead loads on, 159
  earthen, 307–308
  elevated, 308–309
  framed structures, 158
  piers, buildings on, 110, 159
foam
  rigid, 46
  in toe-ups, 101–102
foam-core, stressed-skin panels, 170
foam-formed walls, 91, 93–96
Fog Coat, 240
foundation drains, 89–91, 100–101
Foundation for Biodynamic Shelter,
  289
foundations, 85–114. *See also* basements; concrete slabs
  bale infill framed structures, 176–78
  bale wrap framed structures, 158–59
  cellulose-fiber and expansive clay
    composite, 351–52
  contractors, built by, 68
  crawlspaces, 95
  functions of, 87
  piers, 109–11
  pole framing, 111–12
  rubble trench and grade beam,
    112–13
  stone and earthbags, 113–14
  walls, 93–98
Fox Maple School of Traditional
  Building, 343, 353
framed structures, 150–89
  bales above windows, support of,
    163–65
  bale wrap, 158–69
  balloon frame with straw bale infill,
    71–72, 156
  construction phase, 151–54
  costs, 156–57
  floating frame, 158, 178–79
  infill, 158, 169–79
  light clay construction, 337
  loads, handling of, 154–55

Internet, information on, 18
invasive exotic species, 10, 23
Investigation of Environmental Impacts of Straw Bale Construction, 22
Isobord panels, 72, 354

J
joint compound skim coats, 234, 310
Jolly, Rob, 323–25

K
Kern, Ken, 105
Khalili, Nader, 113
King, Bruce, 119, 121
Kirk/Starbuck house, 272, 288, 304, 355–58

L
labor, 19–22, 66, 344. *See also* professionals, use of; volunteers; work parties
La Habra stucco products, 240
Lambert, Tim, 123
leakage, 218
  Archibio sandwich slab, 104
  into basements, 89–91
length of bale, 8, 77–78
liability, 66, 67
light clay blocks, 302–4
light clay (clay-straw) construction, 263, 301, 302, 336–41, 357
  drying, 338–39
  durability, 341
  filling walls, 337
  finishing, 340–41
  frame preparation, 337
  insulation value, 339
  mixing process, 336–37
lime plaster, 44, 45, 214, 239, 244–61
  additives, 253–54
  advantages of, 246–50
  aesthetics of, 249–50
  application, 260–61
  availability of, 232, 254
  backplaster layer, rainscreen system, 226
  clay, use with. *See* earth plaster
  cob construction, 348

coloring, 258–60
cracks, 248–49
disadvantages of, 250–54
ease of use, 249
energy consumption, 235, 249
exterior use, interior finishes and, 248
to fill notches, 184
into flashing, 257–58
history of, 244–45
hydrating of lime, 74
hydraulic lime, use of, 251, 253, 256–57
hygiene of, 250
interior/exterior finishes, 217
lime cycle, 245–46
loads on, 217
maintenance, 249, 251–52
mixing and proportions, 255–57
moisture and curing, 254
on Nebraska-style bale walls, 119–20, 122–23, 154–55
over wood, 257–58
professionals, use of, 254
reinforcing fibers, 257
set time, length of, 252–54
site, effect of, 217, 239
structural issues, 250–51
vapor permeability, 246–48
lime putty, 259
  availability of, 254
  making, 254–56
  for mortar joints, 135
  to stabilize bales, 132
limewashes, 202, 221, 234, 259–60
  cob construction, use on, 348
  to kill molds, 250, 272
  light clay construction, use on, 340
  over clay plasters, 265, 268–70, 288
limitations, bale construction, 18–24
linseed oil, 288, 340
lintels, 129, 136, 138
  framed structures, 164–65
  steel, 165
Lipke, Paul, 331
live organisms, on bales, 80
Living Design Systems, 206
loads. *See also* roof loads; seismic loads;

snow loads
bales and plaster, dead load on floor of, 159
on bale walls, 4. *See also* Nebraska-style bale walls
on cement stucco, 216
on earth plaster, 217
load-bearing window boxes, 138–40
Nova Scotia load-bearing style, 351
window framing as load-bearing columns, 156, 171–77
low-income housing, 21–22
Lstiburek, Joe, 167, 240

M
MacDonald, Steve and Nena, 16–17
machine accuracy, 78
maintenance
  bale structure, 47–49
  cement stucco, 233–34, 237–38
  earth plaster, 268–72
  green roofs, 197
  lime plaster, 249, 251–52
manure, 284
Mar, David, 15, 121
McCain, Mike, 345
mechanical rooms, 111
mechanical ventilation. *See* ventilation
Meek, Tim, 260
metal foils and films
  vapor diffusion capacity, 43
metal lath, 236, 257–58
milk paints, 72, 202
Millard, Bruce, 4
mini-bales, 300–301
moisture, monitoring, ix, 218, 330–34. *See also* sensors, building
moisture control, viii–ix, 28, 36–52
  Archibio sandwich slab, 104
  cellulose-fiber and expansive clay composite, 352
  during construction, 23, 37, 46–47, 123–25, 151–53, 204–205
  exterior moisture sources, 47–52
  floor slab, 100–101
  Nebraska-style construction, 122–23
  plaster used for, 218–22, 263–65, 290–91

CHELSEA GREEN

Sustainable living has many facets. Chelsea Green's celebration of the sustainable arts has led us to publish trend-setting books about organic gardening, solar electricity and renewable energy, innovative building techniques, regenerative forestry, local and bioregional democracy, and whole foods. The company's published works, while intensely practical, are also entertaining and inspirational, demonstrating that an ecological approach to life is consistent with producing beautiful, eloquent, and useful books, videos, and audio cassettes.

For more information about Chelsea Green, or to request a free catalog, call toll-free (800) 639–4099, or write to us at P.O. Box 428, White River Junction, Vermont 05001. Visit our Web site at www.chelseagreen.com.

Chelsea Green's titles include:

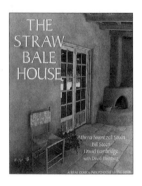

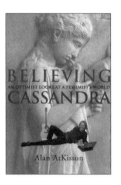

The Straw Bale House
The New Independent Home
Independent Builder
The Natural House
The Beauty of
  Straw Bale Homes
The Resourceful Renovator
The Rammed Earth House
The Passive Solar House
The Earth-Sheltered House
Wind Power for Home &
  Business
Wind Energy Basics
The Solar Living Sourcebook
A Shelter Sketchbook
Mortgage-Free!
Hammer. Nail. Wood.
Toil: Building Yourself
Grassroots Marketing

Four-Season Harvest
The Apple Grower
The Neighborhood Forager
Breed Your Own
  Vegetable Varieties
The Bread Builder
Keeping Food Fresh
Simple Food for the Good Life
The Flower Farmer
Passport to Gardening
The New Organic Grower
Solar Gardening
Straight-Ahead Organic
The Soul of Soil
Good Spirits
The Contrary Farmer
The Co-op Cookbook
Whole Foods Companion

Believing Cassandra
Gaviotas: A Village to Reinvent
  the World
The Man Who Planted Trees
Beyond the Limits
Who Owns the Sun?
Global Spin: The Corporate
  Assault on Environmentalism
Seeing Nature
Hemp Horizons
The Northern Forest
Genetic Engineering, Food and
  Our Environment
Scott Nearing: The Making
  of a Homesteader
Loving and Leaving the
  Good Life
Wise Words for the Good Life
The Maple Sugar Book